D7

Poet

CW01277067

YEATS ANNUAL No. 4

In the same series

YEATS ANNUALS Nos 1, 2
Edited by Richard J. Finneran

YEATS ANNUAL No. 3
Edited by Warwick Gould

THOMAS HARDY ANNUALS Nos 1, 2, 3
Edited by Norman Page

O'CASEY ANNUALS Nos 1, 2, 3, 4
Edited by Robert G. Lowery

Further titles in preparation

Series Standing Order

If you would like to receive future titles in this series as they
are published, you can make use of our standing order facility.
To place a standing order please contact your bookseller or, in
case of difficulty, write to us at the address below with your
name and address and the name of the series. Please state with
which title you wish to begin your standing order. (If you live
outside the U.K. we may not have the rights for your area, in
which case we will forward your order to the publisher
concerned.)

Standing Order Service, Macmillan Distribution Ltd,
Houndmills, Basingstoke, Hants, RG21 2XS, England.

Olivia Shakespear (from a photograph by H. S. Mendelssohn), reproduced in *The Literary Yearbook* (1897).

YEATS ANNUAL No. 4

Edited by Warwick Gould

M

First published 1986

Published by
THE MACMILLAN PRESS LTD
Houndmills, Basingstoke, Hampshire RG21 2XS
and London
Companies and representatives
throughout the world

Typeset by
Wessex Typesetters
Frome, Somerset

Printed in Hong Kong

British Library Cataloguing in Publication Data
Yeats annual.
1. Yeats, W. B.—Societies, periodicals, etc.
821'.8'19   PR5907
ISBN 0–333–35332–3

Contents

SHORTER NOTES

"MASTERING WHAT IS MOST ABSTRACT": A FORUM ON *A VISION*

REVIEWS

Drama and Theatre

Letters and Critical Studies

BIBLIOGRAPHICAL AND RESEARCH MATERIALS

List of Abbreviations

The works listed below are cited in the texts by abbreviation and page number. Some individual essays use additional abbreviations, as explained in the appropriate notes.

Au   *Autobiographies* (London: Macmillan, 1955).

AV[A]   *A Critical Edition of Yeats's* A Vision (1925), (eds) George Mills Harper and Walter Kelly Hood (London: Macmillan, 1978).

AV[B]   *A Vision* (London: Macmillan, 1962).

E&I   *Essays and Introductions* (London and New York: Macmillan, 1961).

Ex   *Explorations*, sel. Mrs W. B. Yeats (London: Macmillan, 1962; New York: Macmillan, 1963).

L   *The Letters of W. B. Yeats* (ed.) Allan Wade (London: Rupert Hart-Davis, 1954; New York: Macmillan, 1955).

LDW   *Letters on Poetry from W. B. Yeats to Dorothy Wellesley*, intro. Kathleen Raine (London and New York: Oxford University Press, 1964).

LMR   *Ah, Sweet Dancer: W. B. Yeats Margot Ruddock, A Correspondence* (ed.) Roger McHugh (London and New York: Macmillan, 1970).

LNI   *Letters to the New Island* (ed.) Horace Reynolds (Cambridge, Mass.: Harvard University Press, 1934).

LRB   *The Correspondence of Robert Bridges and W. B. Yeats* (ed.) Richard J. Finneran (London: Macmillan, 1977; Toronto: Macmillan of Canada, 1978).

LTSM   *W. B. Yeats and T. Sturge Moore: Their Correspondence, 1901–1937* (ed.) Ursula Bridge (London: Routledge & Kegan Paul; New York: Oxford University Press, 1953).

LTWBY *Letters to W. B. Yeats* (eds) Richard J. Finneran, George Mills Harper and William M. Murphy (London: Macmillan; New York: Columbia University Press, 1977).

Mem   *Memoirs* (ed.) Denis Donoghue (London: Macmillan, 1972; New York: Macmillan, 1973).

Myth   *Mythologies* (London and New York: Macmillan, 1959).

OBMV	*The Oxford Book of Modern Verse, 1892–1935.* Chosen by W. B. Yeats (Oxford: Clarendon, 1936).
SB	*The Speckled Bird, With Variant Versions* (ed.) William H. O'Donnell (Toronto: McClelland and Stewart, 1976).
SS	*The Senate Speeches of W. B. Yeats* (ed.) Donald R. Pearce (London: Faber & Faber, 1961).
UP1	*Uncollected Prose by W. B. Yeats*, vol. 1 (ed.) John P. Frayne (London: Macmillan; New York: Columbia University Press, 1970).
UP2	*Uncollected Prose by W. B. Yeats*, vol. 2 (eds) John P. Frayne and Colton Johnson (London: Macmillan, 1975; New York: Columbia University Press, 1976).
VP	*The Variorum Edition of the Poems of W. B. Yeats* (eds) Peter Allt and Russell K. Alspach (New York and London: Macmillan, 1957).
VPl	*The Variorum Edition of the Plays of W. B. Yeats* (ed.) Russell K. Alspach (London and New York: Macmillan, 1966).
VSR	*The Secret Rose: Stories by W. B. Yeats; A Variorum Edition* (eds) Phillip L. Marcus, Warwick Gould & Michael J. Sidnell (Ithaca: Cornell University Press, 1981).
Wade	Allan Wade, *A Bibliography of the Writings of W. B. Yeats*, 3rd edn, rev. Russell K. Alspach (London: Rupert Hart-Davis, 1968).
YA	*Yeats Annual* (to be followed by number and date)
YAACTS	*Yeats: an Annual of Critical and Textual Studies* (to be followed by number and date).
YO	*Yeats and The Occult* (ed.) George Mills Harper (Toronto: Macmillan of Canada, 1975; London: Macmillan, 1975).
YT	*Yeats and The Theatre* (eds) Robert O'Driscoll and Lorna Reynolds (Toronto: Macmillan of Canada, 1975; London: Macmillan, 1975).

Editorial Board

Notes on the Contributors

James Lovic Allen is Professor of English at the University of Hawaii at Hilo, where he has taught since 1963. He is the author of *Yeats's Epitaph: a Key to Symbolic Unity in his Life and Work* as well as many articles upon Yeats. His most recent work is a study of "The Second Coming" and *A Vision*.

Pamela M. Baker is Senior Assistant Librarian at the University of London Library.

Genevieve Brennan is working on the folklore revival and on W. B. Yeats's early interest in folklore.

Richard Burton works in publishing. He has recently completed a doctoral thesis at The Royal Holloway College, University of London, on the accommodation of science in the development of W. B. Yeats.

Richard Allen Cave is Reader in Drama in the University of London and currently teaches in the Department of Drama and Theatre Studies, The Royal Holloway College, University of London. He is the editor of *Hail and Farewell* and *The Lake*, and author of *A Study of the Novels of George Moore*. He is the general editor of the series, *Theatre in Focus*, and the author of *Terence Gray and the Cambridge Festival Theatre*. His British Academy Chatterton Lecture on Yeats's late plays is noticed in this volume.

Yoko Chiba was educated at Tsuda College, Tokyo, U.C.D., and the University of Toronto. She is currently completing a Ph.D. there at the Graduate Centre for the Study of Drama.

David R. Clark is retiring as Professor of English, University of Massachusetts, Amherst. He is co-editor of *Druid Craft: the Writing of "The Shadowy Waters"* and of *Yeats and King Oedipus*. He is the author of

Yeats at Songs and Choruses and of *Visible Array: Yeats's Theatre of Dream and Reality* (forthcoming). He is now editing *The Plays* for the new Macmillan *Collected Edition of the Works of W. B. Yeats*.

Elizabeth Cullingford is Assistant Professor of English at the University of Texas at Austin. She is the author of *Yeats, Ireland and Fascism*, and has edited the Casebook, *Yeats: Poems 1919–1935*.

J. G. P. Delaney is working on a biography of Charles Ricketts and Charles Shannon. He is the editor of Ricketts's *"Michael Field"*, *Pages from a diary in Greece*, and *Letters from Charles Ricketts and Charles Shannon to "Michael Field"*. He has compiled a catalogue, *The Lithographs of Charles Shannon* and is the author of articles in *The Connoisseur* and *The Nineteenth Century*.

Karen Dorn is the author of *Players and Painted Stage: the Theatre of W. B. Yeats*. Her study of D. M. Thomas will shortly be published, and she is working on a study of Yeats's radio broadcasts.

John Harwood is Senior Lecturer in English at The Flinders University of South Australia. He is currently at work on a study of Olivia Shakespear.

A. D. Hope, the distinguished poet and critic, is Professor Emeritus of the Australian National University. His most recent volume of poems is *The Age of Reason*, 1984.

K. P. S. Jochum is Professor of English Literature at the Universität Bamberg. He is currently working on a revised and enlarged edition of his bibliography of Yeats criticism.

Frank Kinahan is Associate Professor of English at The University of Chicago, where he is also Director of University Theatre. He is the author of articles upon Yeats and his *Early Yeats in Context: Folklore, Occultism, and the Early Work and Thought* is forthcoming from Allen & Unwin. He is currently working on a book on contemporary Ulster poetry.

James Longenbach is Assistant Professor of English at the University of Rochester, New York, and has published essays upon T. S. Eliot, Ford Madox Ford, Pound, and Yeats.

Colin McDowell wrote his thesis at Monash University on *"A Vision*: a Study of its Meaning". He is a public servant in the Australian Bureau of Census and Statistics and associate editor of *Scripsi*. He is the author of several articles for *Eire–Ireland* and *Paideuma*.

Thomas Sturge Moore (1870–1944), English artist, poet and dramatist.

Nancy Rutkowski Nash is a postgraduate student at Emory University.

Ruth Nevo is Renée Lang Professor of Humanities and Chairman of the English Department, Hebrew University of Jerusalem. She is the author of *The Dial of Virtue*, *Tragic Forms in Shakespeare* and *Comic Transformations in Shakespeare*. She is currently working on a theory of tragicomedy, and a series of essays on central figures in the literary world of W. B. Yeats.

Edward O'Shea is Professor of English at the State University of New York at Oswego. He is the author of *Yeats as Editor*, and his *A Descriptive Catalog of W. B. Yeats's Library* is noticed in this volume.

Donald R. Pearce is Professor of English at the State University of California at Santa Barbara. He has written numerous articles upon classical and modern poets, and is editor of *The Senate Speeches of W. B. Yeats*, co-editor (with Robert Essick) of *Blake in his Time* and (with H. N. Schneidau) of a collection of Ezra Pound's correspondence with John Theobald.

James Pethica was educated at Merton College, Oxford. The holder of a Junior Research Fellowship at Wolfson College, he is editing Lady Gregory's diaries, 1892–1902.

Jo Russell is currently working on a Ph.D. on Stevie Smith at The Royal Holloway College, University of London.

Olympia Sitwell is engaged in newspaper research in London.

David C. Sutton has done research on W. B. Yeats and the Irish Ballad tradition. He has worked as a librarian at Trinity College, Dublin, the Polytechnic of Central London, and at the University of Reading.

Deirdre Toomey is assistant editor (with David Bindman) of *The Graphic Works of William Blake*.

Donald T. Torchiana is Professor of English at Northwestern University. He is the author of *W. B. Yeats and Georgian Ireland* and his *Backgrounds for Joyce's Dubliners* is in the press. He is working on W. B. Yeats and the western philosophical tradition.

Peter G. W. van de Kamp took his *doctoraal* at Rijksuniversiteit Leiden, and taught in the English Department there before completing a Ph.D.

at U.C.D., where he currently teaches. The author of articles in Dutch and English on modern literature, he is working on a concordance to Yeats's prose and a biography of Katharine Tynan.

Katharine Worth is Professor of Drama and Theatre Studies in the University of London, and is the Head of the Department of Drama and Theatre Studies, The Royal Holloway College, University of London. Her books include *The Irish Drama of Europe from Yeats to Beckett* and a recent study of the plays of Oscar Wilde.

Helen M. Young is Assistant Librarian at the University of London Library.

List of Plates

Frontispiece: *Olivia Shakespear* (from a photograph by H. S. Mendelssohn), reproduced in *The Literary Yearbook* (1897).

List of Figures

Editor's Note

This fourth number of the *Yeats Annual* contains a new and wider provision of information upon current postgraduate research in Europe and North America, including the reprinting of dissertation abstracts held over from No. 3 for lack of space. Bibliographers resident in Japan, Australia and France have contributed to our current bibliography, and in *Yeats Annual* No. 5 a wider net will be thrown to catch current writing upon W. B. Yeats in many countries outside the English-speaking areas.

Our new features – shorter notes, a forum upon *A Vision*, surveys of research collections of interest to the Yeats scholar, the Location Register of Twentieth-Century English Literary MSS Yeats listings, have proved popular with readers and will also continue. In No. 5 a fully revised and updated list of Yeats manuscripts from the Location Register will be printed, as will a revised and updated checklist of portraits of W. B. Yeats. Readers who know the location of books dispersed from W. B. Yeats's library may care to send such information as they have to the editor for the compilation of a checklist of such titles and their annotation to be printed in No. 6. Readers are also encouraged to contribute fugitive bibliographical details to Colin Smythe (P.O. Box 6, Gerrards Cross, Bucks SL9 8EF, UK) for his revision of the Wade/Alspach *Bibliography*, and to K. P. S. Jochum (Lehrstuhl für Englische Literaturwissenschaft, Universität Bamberg, Postfach 1549, D-8600 Bamberg, West Germany) for his revision of his *Classified Bibliography of Criticism*.

I am most indebted to the contributors and potential contributors, who continue to overwhelm me with material, as well as to the team of distinguished editorial advisers listed above. Others who have assisted me include Francis John Byrne, Richard Allen Cave, Martin Dodsworth, R. A. Gilbert, George Mills Harper, John Harwood, Graham Hough, A. Walton Litz, Phillip L. Marcus, Roger Nyle Parisious, Richard Taylor and Deirdre Toomey, who has had a shaping role at every stage of the production of this volume and whose judgment and assistance have been those of a collaborator.

The *Yeats Annual* aims to publish the best work in the field from around the world. Contributions to No. 6 (1987) should reach me, in the first instance, by 31 March 1986, at

English Department
The Royal Holloway College (University of London)
Egham Hill
Egham
Surrey TW20 0EX
UK

to which address offprints, review copies and other bibliographical information should also be sent.

WARWICK GOULD

Acknowledgements

I am indebted to Miss Anne and Mr Michael B. Yeats for permission to use both published and unpublished materials by W. B. Yeats included in this volume; to Colin Smythe Ltd, on behalf of Anne de Winton and Catherine Kennedy for permission to use unpublished material by Lady Gregory; to Dr Roger Lancelyn Green for permission to use unpublished material by Gordon Bottomley; to Mr Alan Clodd for permission to use quotations from the unpublished diaries of his grandfather, Edward Clodd, and to the Ezra Pound Literary Property Trust and New Directions Publishing Corporation for permission to use unpublished materials by Ezra Pound and Ernest Fenollosa.

The jacket design, adapted from Thomas Sturge Moore's designs for H. P. R. Finberg's translation of *Axel*, unpublished designs by Thomas Sturge Moore, and Moore's 'Do We, or Do We Not, Know It?' are published with the permission of Miss Riette Sturge Moore and other trustees of the Thomas Sturge Moore Estate, to whom an especial debt of thanks is due. Miss Sturge Moore has also authorized quotation of unpublished materials by Charles Ricketts and Charles Shannon, and 'Michael Field' (i.e. Katherine Bradley and Edith Cooper).

Dissertations Abstracts International and *ASLIB Index to Theses* kindly authorized the reprinting of thesis abstracts, and I am also grateful to Mr Richard Coleman and Mr Geoffrey Paterson for their kindness in this matter. I am grateful to Mrs Anne Amosu and Phaidon Press for permission to reproduce photographic material, and to the Witt Collection, Courtauld Institute, University of London; Sotheby's, the University of London Library Photographic Services, Mr David Ross of The Royal Holloway College, Dr Ian Fletcher and Gabinetto Fotografico Soprintendenza beni artistici e storici di Firenze for photographs.

Plates in the volume are reproduced also by permission of The British Library, The Uffizi Gallery, The Victoria and Albert Museum, the National Gallery of Canada, Ottawa, Mr Omar Pound and Dr Ian Fletcher.

Imogen Taylor and Linda Shaughnessy of A. P. Watt & Co., Julia

Steward and Frances Arnold of The Macmillan Press, and Kim Scott-Walwyn of Oxford University Press were particularly helpful during the preparation of this volume.

Unpublished materials in the possession of the Beinecke Library; the John Quinn Collection, New York Public Library (Astor, Lenox and Tilden Foundations); the Humanities Research Centre, University of Texas; the British Library and the University of London Library are published with the permissions of those institutions. I am grateful to Miss Angela Carter and Mr Roger Davidge of The Royal Holloway College Library, Miss Pamela M. Baker and Miss Helen M. Young of the University of London Library, the staff of the British Library, Reference Division and Newspaper Library, Colindale, and to Miss Anne Yeats and Mr Roger Nyle Parisious for assistance when working in W. B. Yeats's own library.

For bibliographical assistance I am indebted to a number of scholars who are thanked elsewhere, but all of the contributors to this volume have also been of such assistance. My colleagues at The Royal Holloway College, and Valerie Murr and Christina Pyke have also been of much assistance to me.

WARWICK GOULD

ARTICLES

Yeats and Croce

Donald T. Torchiana

I

In pursuing Yeats's reading of Croce, his agreement and occasional disagreement with the philosopher, we also touch a part of his revived devotion to philosophy after completing *A Vision* in 1925. In fact, the volumes in his library by or about Croce are but a few of his books on Mussolini's Italy, and but a handful of those that helped him attack British positivism, Marxist materialism, and historic liberalism, or what Yeats called Whiggery. Since the English-speaking world had only recently become familiar with Croce, we might ask what an Irish writer from Co. Dublin, that includes a Vico Road overlooking a strand and sea like the Bay of Naples, might have in common with a native Neapolitan writer who took as his philosophic forebear Giambattista Vico. Yet the Irishman and Italian had, and would have, much in common. They were born, for instance, within a year of each other. Both hailed from distinguished families; both gave themselves to reviewing and journalism as young men. Neither became an academic, doubtless a surprising fact for our times. Both occasionally enraged the Catholic and Marxist churches. Neither understood music. History, especially that of their countries, absorbed both men. Both reacted against Fascism, Croce fairly early, Yeats later on. Both became senators yet expressed strong criticisms of their governments. At one time or another, each lived as a virtual exile in his own country. Croce was for a while Italian minister for education; Yeats served on a government committee to look into the condition of Irish schools after the Civil War. Both gave over the better part of their lives to the pursuit of the Spirit, Yeats in *A Vision*, Croce in his massive *Philosophy of the Spirit*. Yet both devoted almost equal time to the contemplation of intuition, art, imagination, aesthetics, and, generally speaking, lyricism. No less, each was determined to unify his thoughts about the good, the true, the beautiful, and the useful in this world and the world of the spirit. For them life moved as a wheel or a circle might; it did not progress to a pinnacle. If we may daringly denominate cultural Ireland from 1900 to the Emergency as Yeats's Ireland, we may even more easily name the Italy that will be remembered from 1900 to 1950 as Croce's. Yet neither man had completed his system in the end; both came closer to embodying certain truths than to espousing them with any real finality.

What remains to be said of their intellectual affinities? Perhaps I should sketch at least three main points: first an account of Yeats's study of Croce and a listing of the pertinent volumes in Yeats's library; then a look at what Croce meant to Yeats and how their philosophies differed; and finally a glance at a few of Yeats's poems in an effort to discover the possible presence of Croce's thought itself. I should add here the briefest summary of Croce's philosophical position. It represents one of the more succinct attempts to corral some of the more repetitious, windy, and Italianate lucubrations of the Neopolitan master. Here is Croce in brief by his famous English editor, Douglas Ainslie:

> The Spirit is Reality, it is the whole of Reality, and it has two forms: the theoretic and the practical activities. Beyond or outside these *there are no other forms of any kind.* The theoretic activity has two forms, the intuitive and individual, and the intellectual or knowledge of the universal: the first of these produces images and is known as *Aesthetic*, the second concepts and is known as *Logic.* The first of these activities is altogether independent, self-sufficient, autonomous: the second, on the other hand, has need of the first, ere it can exist. Their relation is therefore that of double degree. The practical activity is the *will*, which is thought in activity, and this also has two forms, the economic or utilitarian, and the ethical or moral, the first autonomous and individual, the second universal, and this latter depends upon the first for its existence, in a manner analogous to *Logic* and to *Aesthetic.*
>
> With the theoretic activity, man understands the universe, with the practical, he changes it. There are no grades or degrees of the Spirit beyond these. All other forms are either without activity, or they are verbal variants of the above, or they are a mixture of these four in different proportions.
>
> Thus the Philosophy of the Spirit is divided into *Aesthetic*, *Logic*, *and Philosophy of the Practical* (Economic and Ethic). In these it is complete, and embraces the whole of human activity.[1]

It follows that the intuitive is the basis of the beautiful; the pure concept that of truth; individual striving aims at the useful; and the ethical promotes the good. Reality is immanent mind or Spirit, and each of the four concepts is comprised of opposites which are not negations. So the ugly, the erroneous, worthless, and evil are nevertheless included in the beautiful, true, useful, and good.

II

Joseph Hone and Virginia Moore, perhaps more familiar with Western philosophy than Yeats's other critics, give Yeats's study of Croce the most attention. Yeats's own correspondence tends to bear out their claims. For instance, Hone relates that Yeats had heard Ainslie lecture on Croce's *Aesthetic* in London; Moore gives the date as 1923. Hone goes on to say that Yeats "read and annotated Croce's *Philosophy of Vico*" in 1924. In 1926 he applied the same treatment to Croce's *Philosophy of the Practical* and his *Hegel*.[2] Yeats's letters tend to agree. In March 1926, he recounts to T. Sturge Moore his initial reading in Berkeley, Croce, and Gentile after a sustained immersion in Plato and Plotinus. In May, he distinguishes Croce's idealism from the realism of Sturge Moore's brother, G. E. Moore. In September 1927, he informs his poet friend that he is "deep in Croce. I have finished his *Philosophy of the Practical*, all of his *Aesthetics* [sic] except the historical chapters, which I shall return to, and am half through the *Logic*". Yeats then emits a statement repeated many a time in these years but nevertheless worth restating here: "I find this kind of study helps my poetry which I have believe been at its best these last few months." In February 1928, he advises Moore, "You say again that philosophy is dependent upon science. . . . Read Croce on the subject in *Aesthetics*."[3] To Mario Rossi, Yeats admits in 1931 that Vico was known to him through Croce's volume.[4] Then how touching – or astounding? – to note in Lady Gregory's unpublished journals that she too was reading Croce's *Philosophy of the Practical* around 11 May 1926: "I have been reading the introduction to Croce's philosophy that Willie is studying, to try to get some sort of idea of it. I liked a sentence in Ainslie's: 'Thought is democratic in being open to all, aristocratic in being attained only by the few, and that is the only true aristocracy: to be on the same level as the best.' "

A glance at Yeats's own library more than supports these glimpses from his reading, especially since the bulk of his books by and about Croce amounts to almost the same volumes as those by and about Plato and Berkeley. *The Philosophy of Vico* (London, 1913), a gift from George Yeats, is dated August 1924 on the flyleaf. The first 14 chapters contain marginal strokes, underscorings, and a few brief notes. The *Logic* (London, 1917) presents a great deal of marking and marginalia, usually in the terminology of the recently completed *A Vision*. Yet he also had his new reading in mind, for at the bottom of page 42, Yeats writes in a startlingly legible hand: "What he [Croce] calls definition of group Berkeley calls a name—much of this book is Berkeley clarified." *The Philosophy of the Practical* (London, 1913) is dated April 1926 on the flyleaf and is also heavily marked and annotated. Amazingly enough, the inside cover holds a list of plays, dramatic references, and symbols (like the moon) – for what possible reason I know not. I suspect, however, some relevance to *Wheels and Butterflies*. The *Aesthetic* (London, 1922; 2nd edn), has fewer markings than its two companion volumes. I speculate that Yeats never *did* return to its historical part. H. Wildon Carr's *The Philosophy of Benedetto Croce* (London, 1917) announces in Yeats's hand on the short-title page, "Read in 1926", and displays markings from pages 50 to 66. Most of the comments again are in the patois of *A Vision*. What then remains? A few more volumes, largely unmarked: Croce's *Hegel* (London, 1915); his *Poetry of Dante* (New York, 1922); the *Autobiography* (Oxford, 1927) with Yeats's bookplate; Croce's *Ariosto, Shakespeare and Corneille* (London, 1920); and *Historical Materialism and the Economics of Karl Marx* (London, 1922), with many unopened pages after page 121. Yeats's copy of Angelo Crespi's *Contemporary Thought of Italy* (London, 1926) contains an essay in part critical of Croce that was not marked.

III

What then do Yeats's correspondence, prose references to Croce, and marginalia suggest? First of all, needless to say, Yeats, in *A Vision* (1937), acknowledged Croce's system as frequently close to his, with some important exceptions. Joseph Hone discovered among the Yeats papers some of the equivalents Yeats made between what would become the later *A Vision* with its Four Principles (rarefied Faculties) and some of Croce's key terms: Croce's General Will becomes Yeats's *Celestial Body*. "His own *Spirit* was all forms of abstract thought, not only the Pure Concept of Croce. . . . His own *Passionate Body* was reflected in the Imagination or Pure Intuition of Croce. . . ".[5] Virginia Moore claims that Yeats celebrated Croce's

> . . . statement that man with his theoretic activity understands the cosmos, with his practical activity transforms it; and applauded also Croce's insistence that the will, as thought in action, is and must be free, as well as his idea that the theoretic and the practical are not opposite but analogous or corresponding, not a parallelism but a circle. For of course Croce's "theoretic" was to Yeats his own "subjective"; Croce's "practical," his own "objective"; and Croce's circle, his own Great Wheel.[6]

Referring to his Four Faculties in *A Vision* of 1937, Yeats acknowledges that his "*Will* is very much the Will described by Croce" (*AV[B]* 82),[7] and then adds in a footnote, "The *Four Faculties* somewhat resemble the four moments to which Croce has dedicated four books; that the resemblance is not closer is because Croce makes little use of antithesis and antinomy" (*AV[B]* 82 n.i). On that score, ten pages earlier, Yeats had already pointed out that "Croce in his study of Hegel identifies error with negation" (*AV[B]* 72 n.1). "Croce and his like," he once exclaimed, he read so that he could make his idea of the Daimon clear – "Croce because it is the opposite of his thought in many ways" (*L* 719). Then again, on the subject of philosophical realism, Yeats had written Sturge Moore in May 1926 that "Croce describes matter as created by 'intellect' from the mental images by its imposing upon those images the abstract conception of the external" (*LTSM* 92). Yet, so typical of Yeats in pursuing support for his thought in the most professional, sometimes the most daunting of thinkers, he does an about-face and offers a delightful impertinence at the expense of his "authority" or "sage", in this case his Italian ally. This quip takes the form of a postscript: "What's wrong with Croce is that he knows how the bird gets out of the egg but has no notion how it got in" (*LTSM* 113). I take it that Yeats here fixes on one of the more singular omissions in Croce's thought that balances his rather astounding admission of the useful – namely, Croce's relegation of religion to mythology and his refusal to consider spiritism or any other prenatal origins of the individual spirit.

Still, Croce's *Vico* had also made a solid impact on Yeats's theory of history, though he had yet to write "Dove or Swan". In *A Vision* (1937), however, he was later to complain: ". . . half the revolutionary thoughts of Europe are a perversion of Vico's philosophy. Marx and Sorel have taken from Vico's cycle, writes Croce, his 'idea of the struggle of classes and the regeneration of society by a return to a primitive state of mind and a new barbarism' " (*AV[B]* 261). That complaint has its more positive expression in Yeats's Introduction to *The Words Upon the Window Pane*:

> Both Sorel and Marx, their eyes more Swift's than Vico's, have preached a return to a primeval state, a beating of all down into a single class that a new civilization may arise with its Few, its Many, and its One. Students of contemporary Italy, where Vico's thought is current through its influence upon Croce and Gentile, think it created, or in part created, the present government of one man surrounded by just such able assistants . . . (*Ex* 354).

IV

A reader may well then ask, what, pray tell, do Yeats's annotations add to these prose sentiments on the philosophy of the Spirit? I might answer, much of the above, to be sure, yet also something more, sometimes in trivial queries, sometimes in a stubborn hewing to the line of *A Vision*, sometimes by a sudden insight, sometimes by a near-cussedness that looks to Blake, Shelley, or Boehme to ventilate Croce. Again, I must at least try to be brief, but the gist of my answer lies in those two heavily

marked volumes, the *Logic* and the *Philosophy of the Practical*. In the
former, Yeats scores passages where Croce insists that concepts must be
concrete (pp. 43–4). Likewise, Yeats is quick to catch at any passage that
hints his own wish for Unity of Being. He wrote that phrase, for instance,
in the margin after Croce made the ringing statement that "man is man,
in so far as he affirms all his activities and his entire humanity, and yet
cannot do this, save by specializing as a scientific man, a politician, a
poet, and so on" (p. 81). Croce's argument for matter as at best an
empirical – and thus an impossible – concept gets this pat on the head
from Yeats in the margin: "Berkeley's non-existence of matter" (p. 344).
The importance of opposites in the true concept itself, moreover, draws
this demurrer from Yeats: "Blake distinguishes opposites and negations" (p. 97). Equally on the hunt for arguments to rejoin Realism,
Yeats concurs in Croce's refusal to accept being as external to the human
spirit with a notation in the margin: "sense-data realism" (p. 172). Most
heavily underscored by Yeats is Croce's usual paradox at the expense of
his opponents – all philosophies *are* ideal: determinism makes an idea of
cause, materialism an idea of matter, and naturalism an idea of nature
(p. 266). Or as Yeats scrawls at the bottom of page 305, "Yes, we never
affirm anything as real; all that comes is or nothing."

Croce's *Philosophy of the Practical* may have been even more convincing
or, better, amenable to Yeats. For example, he ponders closely Croce's
intricate theory of the force of will before judgment by offering a slash
here and there in the margin and then agreeing at the top of page 45,
"Will comes before judgement." His touchstone of Unity of Being again
graces the margin of Croce's words asserting "the intrinsic law of the
Spirit, which consists in always preserving or in continually attaining to
full possession of itself" (p. 86). In the same way, the pages treating the
identity of pleasure and pain with good and evil get a flurry of
underlinings and much terminology from *A Vision*. The chapter titled
"Activity in Special Forms" gets Yeats's benediction at the end in these
words: "Morality implicit in Will / Philosophy implicit in aesthetic"
(p. 347). The closing of the ring joining the useful and the ethical elicits
from Yeats a recognition in these parallels: "economic=volition of
individual (*Will*) / ethic=volition of universal (*B.F.*)" (p. 443). Croce, of
course, was not immune to the horrors of our nonphilosophic everyday
world. As a matter of fact, he sometimes took a logical glee in defending
them, as he does elsewhere in praising the Inquisition. Hence, in this
volume, after acknowledging the power of force over abstract morality in
the world of nations and politics, Croce writes, " 'Disarmed prophets'
will be efficacious in poetry, but ridiculous in practical reality." In this
case, Yeats, another unarmed prophet, efficacious in poetry, has simply
appended in the margin "Modern Italy" (p. 540). In Croce's *Vico*, Yeats
had made a number of like markings, but the words over the beginning of
chapter IX treating Vico's three types of society are provocative, if not

chilling, in the light of his growing heroic pessimism on historical development:

    State of nature = savage
    Practical certitude = heroic or barbaric
    Practical truth = civilized

Yeats noted all too well Vico's – and Croce's – explanation of the law of reflux, the aftermath of civilization and its barbarism of reflection, then the subsequent fall into a new savagery of violence and sensation (p. 122).

V

At last then, how do Yeats's determined markings of Croce in his library, how do his prose statements, correspondence, and sustained enthusiasm for this Italian man of letters affect Yeats's poetry? The answer may lie in the fact that Croce lends Yeats a certain attractive support in refining his beliefs that are bolstered by many another idealist, immaterialist, and conservative thinker. How many times does one look up from some of the great poems to sense the combined presence (at Yeats's elbow) of Plato, Plotinus, Berkeley, Blake, or Nietzsche. But one occasionally reads a poem that a page or idea from Croce alone may suddenly light up, by parallel or influence – who can say? There is a passage, for instance in Croce's *Logic* where he claims that our ecstasy in reading a poem or in playing music does not alter either one. But, with a philosophic proposition, we possess it only to change it. We devise new arguments, solve new problems, and remain unsatisfied with our initial reading. At the bottom of pages 316–17, Yeats queries this thought in language clearly derived from "Sailing to Byzantium": " 'experience' which 'consumes itself away' not being anti-thetical. The representative ephemeral in event is immortal being a wish. It confers its immortality on what enters it. Revelation because it meets desire is not consumed away – desire of life not of proof". Thus a roundabout defence of poetry over philosophy in terms of one of Yeats's greatest poems.

In the same volume of Croce, part of the living memory of "The Tower" is caught in the idea that "all perceptive judgements are . . . commemorative and historical, because the present, in the very act by which we hold it before our spirit, becomes a past, that is to say an object of memory and of history" (p. 156). Yeats marked that page. A shorter, less important yet rather enigmatic poem like "Statistics" may become clearer if we reread Yeats's heavily annotated pages 304–5 in the *Logic* where Croce sternly inveighs against any reduction of history to a science, mere classification, or statistic rather than to a concern with concrete individuals and events. The diagram in the poem – showing more women born than men – hardly explains the cursed Platonist's claim that God's fire is on the wane. Then, in the poem "In Memory of Eva Gore-Booth and Con Markiewicz", the poet had wished to "mix / Pictures of the mind", certainly very close to Croce's *Aesthetic* where one moves from intuition to image and the universal. On the other hand, the use of force in life, tragically actual life, is defined by blood and power, the "property of the living" in "Blood and the Moon", a poem written by an "efficacious prophet" for a dead politician that nevertheless celebrates the glory of the imagination even if wisdom is the property of the dead.

The poem "Death" also commemorates the assassination of Kevin O'Higgins and concludes with the terse assertion, "Man has created death". The heroic nature of that statement may well go back to Carr's book on Croce, owned by Yeats, where the author devotes two pages to showing how Croce's theory of opposites is demonstrated in the conjoining of life and death – opposite terms that cannot be thought of without each other. Taken separately, each is an abstraction, death a fearful one created by man.[8] O'Higgin's triumph was to know the greater truth in his fearlessly confronting murderous men. In "A Dialogue of Self and Soul", Soul would urge the Self to rid itself of the Four Faculties, or Croce's Four Moments, the *"Is"*, the *"Ought"*, the *"Knower"*, and the *"Known"*. The Self will have none of that, but in a circle of repetition would continue in the realm of the immanent spirit, if need be in the very slough of ditch water, proud women, remorse, and youthful ignominy, for even they may be the necessary complementary part of joy, the Spirit on this earth. Finally, then, when listening to Crazy Jane harangue the bishop, we certainly catch the echo from Macbeth in her cry that "Fair and foul are near of kin, / And fair needs foul". But when we continue to read that lowliness and pride go together as do love and excrement, then we recognize that the bishop would separate these opposites – sty or mansion – and turn them into lifeless abstractions. But not Croce or Yeats.

Let me then conclude with their separate statements; in *Logic*, page 97, Croce's text reads:

> The opposites are the concept itself, and therefore the concepts themselves, each one in itself, in so far as it is determination of the concept, and in so far as it is conceived in its true reality. Reality, of which logical thought elaborates the concept, means, not motionless being or pure being, but opposition: the forms of reality, which the concept thinks in order to think reality in its fullness, are opposed in themselves; otherwise, they would not be forms of reality, or would not be at all. *Fair is foul and foul is fair*: beauty is such, because it has within

it ugliness, the true is such because it has in it the false, the good is such becuase it has within it evil. If the negative term be removed, as is usually done in abstract thought, the positive also disappears; but precisely because, with the negative, the positive itself has been removed.

At the bottom of this page Yeats has written an affirming statement that may best sum up the surest likeness in the thoughts of both men:

P[hase] 17 affirms its "intensity" against the "dispersal" of p[hase] 3 which in its turn is physically radiant as against the concentration of p[hase] 17. Each affirms the other.

NOTES

1. Benedetto Croce, *The Philosophy of the Practical*, trans. Douglas Ainslie (London: Macmillan, 1913) pp. xvii–xviii.
2. Joseph Hone, *W. B. Yeats, 1865–1939*, 2nd edn (London: Macmillan, 1962) p. 368; Virginia Moore, *The Unicorn* (New York: Macmillan, 1954) p. 322.
3. *W. B. Yeats and T. Sturge Moore: Their Correspondence, 1901–1937*, ed. Ursula Bridge (New York: Oxford University Press, 1953) pp. 82, 93, 113, 123.
4. *The Letters of W. B. Yeats*, ed. Allan Wade (London: Rupert Hart-Davis, 1954) p. 784.
5. Hone, p. 375.
6. Moore, p. 324.
7. From hereon, where possible, I shall try to incorporate obvious footnotes in the text itself.
8. H. Wildon Carr, *The Philosophy of Benedetto Croce* (London: Macmillan, 1917) pp. 143–4.

Yeats's Passage to India

Ruth Nevo

The Herne's Egg, written two years before Yeats's death, is a very difficult play. Yeats wrote to Dorothy Wellesley that it was "wild": "as wild a play as *Player Queen*, as amusing but more tragedy and philosophic depth" (*L* 843). This is itself a paradoxical judgment. In letters to Ethel Mannin, he called it "the strangest wildest thing I have ever written" (*L* 845), "my very Rabelasian play" and added, "but do not ask me what it means" (*L* 904). Critics and interpreters, needless to say, have asked, and have come up with a variety of (mostly) unenthusiastic answers. Helen Vendler,[1] to whom it is an allegory of art as sublimation finds it "rather arid and contrived, with very little 'humanity' and less stage-craft", its "tragic-comic levity tiresome, its grotesquerie a fatal flaw" (1963, 160, 164ff). Bloom finds it "squalid", "unequivocally rancid", its "tone of the apocalyptic absurd", unsuccessful and unfunny. Since he takes the play's irony to be "indeliberate" he comes to the conclusion that it "is as bitter as it is confused, and every kind of a failure". "Yeats," he says, "meant to purge himself of some of his own obsessions by this play, but his poems written after it do not show that the purgation was effective" (1970, 422, 424, 426). Ure, one of the most sympathetic of Yeats's major critics, claims that while, "in *The Herne's Egg* all runs sweetly up to the pinnacle, which is firmly set" nevertheless "Yeats seems to have been betrayed into muddling his own design", chiefly, he feels through the theme of metempsychosis (1963, 156). Wilson (1958, 95–136), an ardent admirer of the play is helpful in alerting us to the importance of Indian philosophy but finds no convincing way to account for the play's strangenesses and mixtures, perhaps because his reading of the opposition between Congal and Attracta is reductively simplified. It is interesting to note that where he finds Attracta a puritan-saint, to Vendler she is at the opposite pole in Yeats's system – an avatar of art. Melchiori (1960, 164ff) decodes occult symbolism from Brahman and Hermetic sources and leave us enlightened as to parts but not perhaps entirely happy with a whole of which little seems left alive once it has been decoded. The play remains a criticial impasse.

13

It will be my thesis in the following pages that it is only by entertaining the dichotomies of this text that we can read it at all. It is otherwise unreadable. But its "unreadability" will finally yield meaning, on its own terms. Contemporary critical theory, dislodging the unities, has achieved a notable gain: it has given us the confidence to encounter splits, divisions, disunities, bifurcations in literary works without the imperious demand for the unequivocal cramping of our intellectual muscles. Relaxed, we can see, and see into, the contradictions and irresolutions in texts rather than attempting to bring them into conceptual line. All texts, we are told, contain their own contradictory *alter ego* with or without the sanction of an author's awareness, implied or explicit. How doubly legitimate then, in an author like Yeats, whose very mark and signature is bi-polarity, the irreconcilable conflict of contraries, the "whirling and . . . bitterness" (*AV*[*B*] 52) of the dialectical gyres, to embrace the postulate that it is the radical conflicts in his works which give them their life; and, rather than attempting to find or construct a factitious entity, or dismissing our failure to do so as his, to read the disjunctions.

Readers of the following attempt to explicate the play will no doubt welcome a brief reminder of its fable. A man commits sacrilege, steals a sacred object and is punished for his *hubris* by an implacable god. Congal, King of Connacht, in an interval between fighting Aedh, King of Tara, sends a retainer to steal the eggs of the Great Herne for a truce banquet to be held at Tara. The eggs of the god are of course, sacred objects and whoever touches them, let alone consumes them, is cursed: "He that a herne's egg dare steal / Shall be changed into a fool. . . . And to end his fool breath / At a fool's hand meet his death" (*VPl* 1018). The egg-stealing is the pivot of the plot and to its symbolism I shall presently return. The evangelist of this curse is Attracta, priestess and bride-to-be of the Herne. Congal, who derides the god and his taboos, and proposes to cure Attracta of her attachment to superstition by sexual intercourse with seven of his men, finds himself dishonoured by Attracta's substitution of a common hen's egg for his herne's egg at the banquet table. This insult precipitates renewed warfare with Aedh and Congal's determination, now at least partly in revenge, to carry out his re-education of the virginal Attracta. Inducing six rather reluctant followers to comply, he fulfills his missionary enterprise. Attracta, however, is convinced that she has lain with the god, who may come in "Whatever shape he choose" (*VPl* 1020), that not Congal's seven "held [her] in their arms last night," but that "[her] husband came to [her] in the night" and that she "lay beside him, his pure bride" (*VPl* 1031), so that the rape is merely the predestined fulfilment of divine will. Congal, called to the holy mountain to meet his fate, is in fact wounded by a vagrant Fool, and finally dies by his own hand, upon the Fool's sharpened spit. As he dies, he appeals to Attracta, who attempts to prevent his reincarnation in some lower form of life by procreation with her servant Corney, but Corney's donkey breaks free and it is his impregnation of another donkey which will provide the new vehicle for the transmigration of Congal's soul. The play ends with Corney's ribald laughter:

> All that trouble and nothing to show for it
> Nothing but just another donkey. (*VPl* 1040)

Clearly these incongruities conceal as much as they reveal. And one is as puzzled by just what is concealed or revealed as by the strange medley of comic characterization and tragic structure, farce and mythopoeia. These modalities make a weird mixture. The initial fighting between Congal and Aedh and their men is presented as a formal ritual – a sheer symmetry of conflict between doubles or mirror images of each other ("Where is the wound this time? / There, left shoulder-blade. / Here, right shoulder-blade") without issue or resolution – "*The men move rhythmically as if in a dance; when swords approach one another cymbals clash; when swords and shields approach drums boom*". . . "*but sword and sword, shield and sword, never meet*" (*VPl* 1012–13). This dance ritual beautifully enacts pattern in movement, movement in pattern: a prelapsarian resolution of dialectical opposites; yet the dialogue which follows, in which Aedh dreams of four fleas ("We hop like fleas, but war / Has taken all our riches") upon a "fat, square, lazy dog" who doesn't scratch, is burlesque.

The representation, moreover, plays fast and loose with the semiotics of the theatre, drawing attention, blatantly, to fracture in the means of theatrical signification itself. Corney's donkey is a life-size toy on wheels, and when the eggs are stolen, the donkey appears with a creel full of eggs *painted* on its side. No weapons ever touch each other in fighting; no real stones are thrown, but "real", i.e. audible, theatrical thunder is heard, and when the moon rises it is the "round smiling face" of "comic tradition" (*VPl* 1034). A cauldron lid becomes a shield, a pot a helmet, a kitchen spit a spear.[2] The placing of the spit between stones to keep it upright for Congal's suicide is overtly phallic (*VPl* 1038). One may recall the famous first performance of Jarry's antinomian farce, *Ubu Roi* in 1896, with its aggressive anti-illusionist decor, its grotesqueries, its cardboard horses and wicker figures, which impressed Yeats sufficiently to evoke his equally famous remark, "After us the Savage God" (*Au* 349). Whether it was the seed sown then which sprouts in *The Herne's Egg*, or rather Mary Bell's substitution of an imitation cuckoo's nest for the real cuckoo's nest which is sought by her cuckolded husband (who dies happy, though deluded) in the antic stories which preface *A Vision* (*AV*[*B*] 45–9), there is certainly no naiveté concerning theatrical representation here. What we have in *The Herne's Egg* is a parody of illusionist theatrical mimesis, in which signifiers both are, or are tied by

resemblance to, referents, and at the same time announce their symbolic
emancipation. This obtruded gap between signifier and signified serves
notice that we have to do with irony as well as with allegory – an ironic
enunciator and an allegorical enunciation – a co-presence which has
bewildered many readers.[3]

A similar bewilderment is induced by the play's mixture of comic and
tragic modes. The characterisation of that blunt "weather-stained,
war-battered / Old campaigner" (*VPl* 1016), Congal, hovers between
the burlesque and the heroic. He and his adversary Aedh, and his
companion-prompter, the laconic Mike, make stage-Irish comic pairs:
the retainers' reluctant prudery, one on the grounds of a promise to his
mother to keep from women, another who has a wife "that's jealous / If
[he] but look the moon in the face", and a third promised to "an
educated girl" (*VPl* 1028), and their later disavowals when in fear of the
thunder are *comic* consternations (*VPl* 1032). So is the *ingenue* perturba-
tion of the three timid but inquisitive girls who question Attracta about
her coming wedding night. But the latter modulates immediately into
the revelatory allegorical mode of "No bridal torch can burn / When his
black midnight is there" (*VPl* 1022), which retrospectively solemnizes
the girls' questions too. The allegorical sublime is throughout in
unresolved ironic dissonance with the comic discomfitures and the comic
dialogue. The egg-stealing is readable simultaneously and indeterminately as a fatal error in a tragic sequence of reversals and recognitions,
and as a comic device – a mock deception which will engineer a higher
truth – in a comic sequence of disguise, mistaken identities and
confusions, issuing in the resolution of a marriage. As comic sequence
Attracta's marriage to the Herne would be triumphantly validated, and
the whole would become a divine comedy of the transcendant Will. But
the absence of any indication, at the point of closure, of an equivalent to
"In thy Will is our Peace", and indeed the presence of a sardonic
rebuttal appears to put this possibility into question. The comic thrust
and the tragic thrust remain in perpetual strife, like the war-dance of
Aedh and Congal, neither dominating, absorbing or containing the
other.

In the tragic reading, Congal's worldly wisdom – he who will be
changed into a fool and die at a fool's hand – is the *hubris* which propels
him towards tragic downfall:

> Women thrown into despair
> By the winter of their virginity
> Take its abominable snow
> As boys take common snow, and make
> An image of god or bird or beast
> To feed their sensuality (*VPl* 1016)

he says, and insists, with all his rationalist scepticism, upon his whim:

> . . . Must old campaigners lack
> The one sole dish that takes their fancy . . .
> Because a woman thinks that she
> Is promised or married to a bird? (*VPl* 1015–16)

His first reaction to the curse following the theft of the eggs is splendidly nonchalant and in character for a sturdy old campaigner, robber of sheepfolds and cattle trucks: He has been, he says,

> So cursed from morning until midnight
> There is not a quarter of an inch
> To plaster a new curse upon (*VPl* 1018–19)

and his rationalist's confidence does not desert him:

> That I shall live and die a fool,
> And die upon some battlefield
> At some fool's hand, is but natural,
> And needs no curse to bring it. (*VPl* 1018)

But the killing of Aedh, the first consequence of the curse, unnerves him: "I would not have had him die that way / Or die at all. . . . Our fifty battles had made us friends" (*VPl* 1026) and it is in vengeful animus that he claims the power to make the Great Herne suffer through the violation of his bride. This is in itself a yielding of the naturalistic view to the transcendental, for he has up to this point denied the power, even the reality, of the Herne. In terms of tragic structure, his move represents the impossible choice or double-bind of the tragic situation. He has sworn to cure Attracta of her "abominable" virginity. And he has defied the god. Either he can renounce his stubborn human will and, granting the god his power, be forsworn, or, by violating the god's bride as well as his sacred emblems, compound his human *hubris*. What he does is properly tragic, and puts him at the mercy of his adversary. In wilful self-assertion, he and his six retainers commit the violation. The failure, however, of the rape to transform Attracta from devoted priestess and Herne's bride to "all woman, all sensible woman", (*VPl* 1031), together with the confirmatory thunder produces the creeping fear that Attracta's assertion:

> You were under the curse, in all
> You did, in all you seemed to do (*VPl* 1033)

is indeed true. Stubbornly set upon the course of heroic defiance, Congal, doom-eager – "*because* [he is] terrified" (*VPl* 1034) goes to the holy mountain to face his destiny. It would be his third bout he says, with the Herne, man against his fate. So far they have each won one: the Herne, the curse; he, the rape.

> Seven men lay with you in the night,
> Go home desiring and desirable,
> And look for a man (*VPl* 1031)

The third bout is a tissue of dramatic irony, of doubting, of alternating blindness and insight. The Fool he meets is clearly no match for him, so he concludes, with staggering impercipience, "There must be another Fool on the mountain" (*VPl* 1036). When the Fool wounds him ("It passed out of your mind for a moment/That we are friends," he says, "but that is natural" [*VPl* 1037]), his nonchalance gives way at last to fear.

> A scratch, a scratch, a mere nothing.
> But had it been a little deeper and higher
> It would have gone through the heart, and maybe
> That would have left me better off,
> For the Great Herne may beat me in the end (*VPl* 1037)

Still defiant, however, he will kill himself, die by his own will, not the Herne's; but the realization of what this means comes to him at once:

> Fool! Am I myself a Fool?
> For if I am a Fool, he wins the bout (*VPl* 1038)

Nevertheless, his grand final self-identification is a paradigmatically heroic affirmation:

> I am King Congal of Connacht and of Tara,
> That wise, victorious, voluble, unlucky,
> Blasphemous, famous, infamous man . . .
> What does it matter what they think?
> The Great Herne knows that I have won (*VPl* 1038)

But has he?

Congal is the wilful hero as supreme Iconoclast. His model is in *A Vision*, at Phase 10 of the Great Wheel (*AV*[B] 97). There we find "the image-breaker" and this is his description. Such a man's True Mask (or "object of desire or idea of the good") is Self-reliance. His False Mask (that "deformation which is imposed by circumstances too strong for the will") is Isolation. His True Creative Mind is "Dramatisation of Mask" – a dramatised heroic Self-reliance. His False Creative Mind (a fatal inversion) is "Self-desecration". And his Body of Fate ("the series of events forced upon him from without") is, as Yeats's oracular brevity puts it – "Humanity" (see *AV*[*B*] 83, 97).

In other words, less cryptic than Yeats's, a true iconoclast will always be afraid of the isolation, the Yeatsian solitude of separatist individualism which appears to motivate him; afraid to be the Fool on the Hill of Congal's vision of the fools who will plague him on Slieve Fuadh. If he is to realize himself, however, he must repress this fear, must cling to his own true Mask or anti-self or idea of self reliance, consciously playing the role which is in extreme tension with the hidden and contrary impulses of his natural self. If he does not destroy the Image he will destroy himself. It is the Image that is his enemy, Attracta's entranced preoccupation with the "abominable snow" of which women make "An image of god or bird or beast/ To feed their sensuality" (*VPl*1016) that threatens his will. Congal is wilful human self-assertion; Attracta self-abnegation. The scheme for Attracta can be found in Phase 24, not unexpectedly, since 10 and 24 are opposites on the Wheel.

> . . . the rage of Phase 10 to destroy all that trammels the being from without is now all self-surrender. There is great humility – "she died every day she lived" – and pride as great, pride in the code's acceptance, an impersonal pride, as though we were to sign "servant of servants" . . . the code must rule . . . for its subconscious purpose is to compel surrender of every personal ambition; and though it is obeyed in pain – can there be mercy in a rigid code? – the man is flooded with the joy of self-surrender; and flooded with mercy – what else can there be in self-surrender? – for those over whom the code can have no rights . . . (*AV*[*B*] 170)

Attracta must "complete . . . her task, her circle"; and so, moving puppet-like, a somnambulist, "in long loops like a dancer", she removes the Herne's egg from the banquet table leaving the hen's egg in its place. Profane "hen" is, it is worth noticing, contained in sacred "herne", and the insulting hen's egg, as has been observed, precipitates the tragic, or the divinely comic, sequence of events. There is neither comic nor tragic closure, however, and neither protagonist is validated by the play's outcome. Congal capitulates to the supernatural when he fears lest the Herne put him "into the shape of a brute beast", and Attracta deserts the Herne "code" when she attempts to determine the form his reincarnated soul will take, entering the human order to do so.

"There's a work" she says, / "That should be done", the work – astonishing palinode! but Phase 24, we recall, is "flooded with mercy . . . and forgiveness" (*AV*[*B*] 170) that needs –

No bird's beak nor claw, but a man,
The imperfection of a man (*VPl* 1040)

And yet in this too, she fails.

Questions proliferate concerning both these strange protagonists. First of all, is the god-defying Congal indeed hero or fool? If he is a hero of the human, the rational, then why is his exposure of a girl's delusive fantasies, undertaken to melt "out the virgin snow, / And that snow image, the Great Herne" and free her "from all obsession" to "live as every woman should" (*VPl* 1028) rewarded not only by death, but by reincarnation as an ass? Is he then a fool, for not understanding the reality and power of godhead, and his death simply the fulfilling of the curse, working itself out like a self-fulfilling prophecy? Is Congal's crude sensuality simply that of a natural materialist unredeemed by any theophany such as is available to Attracta? But then his winning of the sympathy, if not even the love, of the Herne's votaress must surely reassert his humanist domination, and Congal *has* won, Pyrrhic victory though it be.

For Attracta at the play's start, "There is no reality but the Great Herne" " . . . no happiness but the Great Herne" (*VPl* 1016). She is immoveable in her conviction that she lay, not with Congal and his retainers, but with the Herne, his pure bride. We can see why she would wish to have "one man among the gods" on Slieve Fuadh where Congal will die, since his death would be a trophy for her beloved; but why, when he is defeated, would she betray the god she has worshipped by attempting the redemption at least in the next life of the blasphemer Congal, transforming herself from visionary priestess "whose 'virginity renews itself like the moon' " (*AV*[B] 140) to mere vessel of procreation, and be defeated by sheer random animality in this aim? Was she self-deluded in her vision of the Herne? Has she now fallen in love with the old campaigner, with the "imperfection of a man" rather than with the perfection of the god she has imagined? Has flesh conquered spirit? Schopenhauerian Will overcome Idea, or Image? Whatever else it is, it is, indisputably a Fall. The allegory then is a Genesis myth, complete with curse for taboo, egg for apple, a fall, with Congal and Aedh as Cain and Abel.

Let us consider the language of the allegory.

Not in the flesh but in the mind;
Chosen out of all my kind
That I may lie in a blazing bed
And a bird take my maidenhead,
To the unbegotten I return,
All a womb and a funeral urn (*VPl* 1017)

This "chosen" is a phoenix: the "unbegotten", a sun-matrix of life and death, source of all generative life in its passage from egg to dust. Congal dissolves the revelation in the acid of his bawdy cynicism. Ovid, says Congal,

> . . . had a literal mind,
> And though he sang it neither knew
> What lonely lust dragged down the gold
> That crept on Danae's lap, nor knew
> What rose against the moony feathers
> When Leda lay upon the grass (*VPl* 1016)

The impasse of interpretation contaminates the revelatory language itself with naturalist "realism": the Heraclitean fire dissolves into the fantasy fires of "lonely lust".

Attracta's reply to Agnes's timid question, "When he comes – will he? . . . Do all that a man does?" (*VPl* 1020), is similarly Janus-faced and unreadable in its reversibility.

> Strong sinew and soft flesh
> Are foliage round the shaft
> Before the arrowsmith
> Has stripped it, and I pray
> That I, all foliage gone,
> May shoot into my joy (*VPl* 1020)

On the face of it this is ascetic, anti-sensual. The "foliage" of strong sinew and soft flesh are to be stripped[4] before the arrow can fly, and Attracta "shoot into her joy". But the ironic view transforms "stripped" into "disclosed", rather than "denuded" and ascesis into orgasm. The image of Attracta as justified saint of the transcendental is contradicted by the possibility of an Attracta saved, by Congal, for the winding path of sensuous experience and of unrepressed sexuality. The central bridal song, too, is deeply ambivalent.

> When I take a beast to my joyful breast,
> Though beak and claw I must endure,
> *Sang the bride of the Herne, and the Great Herne's bride,*
> No lesser life, man, bird or beast,
> Can make unblessed what a beast made blessed,
> Can make impure what a beast made pure.
>
> Where is he gone, where is that other,
> He that shall take my maidenhead?
> *Sang the bride of the Herne, and the Great Herne's bride,*

Out of the moon came my pale brother,
The blue-black midnight is my mother.
Who will turn down the sheets of the bed?

When beak and claw their work begin
Shall horror stir in the roots of my hair?
Sang the bride of the Herne, and the Great Herne's bride,
And who lie there in the cold dawn
When all that terror has come and gone?
Shall I be the woman lying there? (*VPl* 1029–30)

Attracta's fantasy is of a will-less surrender to the bird/beast from the panerotic world of Ovidian metamorphosis who will take her maidenhead and confirm her sanctity. But the second stanza introduces the moon, satellite to the unbegotten Sun. "Out of the moon came my pale brother" – is this brother then Congal, a man of the moon in his separateness, his solitude, his self-assertion as she, image-maker, is also a daughter of the lunar night? Who then indeed (the question is proleptic) will turn down the sheets of the bed? In the third stanza is inserted, explicitly, the question of human sexuality, and of human identity, the perplexing relation between violence, terror, desire and self-image. And the question whether this invasion of the inviolate human self is to be feared or desired is not answered. Nor is the question whether the invasion is within or beyond the realm of human will. It is the question of "Leda and the Swan" which also contains within its tightly compacted allegory and the controlled irony of its final question, indeterminately rhetorical or literal, the antithetical possibilities: brute indifference or divine transfiguration. It is indeed, for Yeats, the question of questions, and will lead me into the topic suggested by the title of this essay.

For Yeats, the question of questions, put at its bluntest, is simply this: Can individuality be reconciled with immortality, carnal nature with discarnate spirit in terms of any doctrine but the specifically Christian gospel to which he could no longer assent?[5] When he writes of his faith: "my Christ, a legitimate deduction from the Creed of St. Patrick as I think, is that Unity of Being Dante compared to a perfectly proportioned human body, Blake's 'Imagination,' what the Upanishads have named 'Self'; nor is this unity distant and therefore intellectually understandable, but imminent, differing from man to man and age to age, taking upon itself pain and ugliness, 'eye of newt, and toe of frog' " (*E&I* 518), he makes one of the most outrageously misleading statements he ever made. Its putative truth – his craving for unity – is unquestionable; but the attempt to annihilate antimony at one bold stroke is patently factitious. And, indeed, he at once goes on to speak (in connection with the conflict in him between an Irish and an English allegiance) of "still

... wag[ging] between extremes", of the "hatred that tortures [him] with love, [the] love with hate", "I am like the Tibetan monk", he says, "who dreams at his initiation that he is eaten by a wild beast and learns on waking that he himself is eater and eaten" (*E&I* 519). Neither the "Self that is in all selves" of the Upanishads nor the "imminent" [sic] "source of all energy", the Schopenhauerian Will to life (*E&I* 461) have any concern with the individual, only with the One, or with the species. It is " 'the third antinomy of Immanuel Kant, thesis: freedom; antithesis: necessity',", which he quotes in the preface to *A Vision*, that truly contains the kernel of his belief, characteristically restated: " 'Every action of man declares the soul's ultimate, particular freedom, and the soul's disappearance in God; declares that reality is a congeries of beings and a single being; nor is this antinomy an appearance imposed upon us by the form of thought but life itself which turns, now here, now there, a whirling and a bitterness' " (*AV[B]* 52).

But the Upanishadic Self of the credo quoted above provides a major clue for further explication of *The Herne's Egg*.

In 1935, Yeats was engaged in studying and translating the *Upanishads* under the tutelage of Shri Purohit Swami. In a letter to Dorothy Wellesley he tells her that the play was the Indian's "philosophy in a fable, or mine confirmed by him" (*L* 844). We do well to take him at his word, for we can gloss *The Herne's Egg*, and in particular, its moon symbolism, more fully with the aid of the Vedantic essays, "An Indian Monk", "The Holy Mountain" and "The Mandukya Upanishad" than with *A Vision* alone.

The moon was full, Agnes tells us, the last time Attracta went away (*VPl* 1021). Yet Agnes has heard that Attracta and the Herne couple "In the blazing heart of the sun (*VPl* 1022) Kate denies this. "you have heard it wrong!/ In the blue-black midnight they couple" (*VPl* 1022). Agnes insists on the sun, Kate on the blue-black midnight. Mary concludes with

All I know is that she
Shall lie there in his bed.
Nor shall it end until
She lies there full of his might,
His thunderbolts in her hand (*VPl* 1022)

Is this coupling then under the aegis of Sun or Moon, of the primary principle of objectivity or of the antithetical principle of the subjective? We cannot resolve the question by recourse to *A Vision's* "harsh geometry" (*E&I* 518). There it is always the "*conflict* of light and dark, heat and cold, that concerns me most" (*AV[B]* 246) [my italics].

It was the Indian mystic pursuit of Samādhi, the zero whole, union of Godhead and manhood, a "single, timeless act", "seedless" and

objectless, in which "all existence [is] brought into the words: 'I am' "
(*E&I* 462), which seemed to Yeats to resolve his own earlier conviction
of irremediable conflict between Sun and Moon. The four stages of
concentration in the meditative progress towards union with Self –
"consciousness bound to no object, bliss bound to no aim, *Turiyā*, pure
personality" (*E&I* 457) – is represented by the sacred syllables "*Aum*"
(*E&I* 457, 476). The first stage is merely the selection of an object of
meditation. The second is *Turiyā*, the gift of the "bright fortnight", or
"conscious *Samādhi*". This is the state of the "dreamer creating his
dream, the sculptor toiling to set free the imprisoned image" (*E&I* 477)
associated by Yeats with "full moon, mirror-like bright water"
(*E&I* 472). The third is the ascetic *Sushupti* – "moonless night, 'dazzling
darkness' " (*E&I* 472) "the dreamless sleep of the soul in God"
(*E&I* 465). This is the disappearance of "the sculptor in his statue, the
musician in his music" (*E&I* 462). The fourth, "expressed by our
articulation of the whole word", is "The Self, whereto man is now
united" (*E&I* 476).

Though stages two and three (u and m) seem to be but old Phase 15
and Phase I writ large – "Am I not justified in discovering there the
conflict between subjectivity and objectivity, between Self and Not-Self,
between waking life and dreamless sleep?" (*E&I* 470) – nevertheless the
difference in the new articulation is all important:

> The visionary must have seen in those cycles [the lunar and the solar]
> [a] conflict between Moon and Sun, or when Greek astronomy had
> reached India, between a Moon that has taken the Sun's light into
> itself, "I am yourself," and the Moon lost in the Sun's light, between
> Sun in Moon and Moon in Sun. The Eastern poet saw the Moon as the
> Sun's bride; now in solitude; now offered to her Bridegroom in a
> self-abandonment unknown to our poetry. A European would think
> perhaps of the moonlit and moonless nights alone, call the increasing
> moon man's personality, as it fills into the round and becomes perfect,
> overthrowing the black night of oblivion. (*E&I* 470)[6]

We begin to see how these Eastern circuits, as opposed to the Western
dialectic, gave him the model he needed to solve, and to maintain, the
part/whole antinomy which tormented him. But his problem has its
temporal as well as its spatial dimension. "In space things touch, in time
things part", says E. M. Forster's shocked Adela Quested encountering
in the traumatic void of the Marabar caves the "Boum".[7] Yeats could,
always, come closer to Godbole than Forster could. For Forster,
speaking through Cyril Fielding as he travels back to Europe, "The
Mediterranean is the human norm. When men leave that exquisite lake,
whether through the Bosphorus or the Pillars of Hercules, they approach
the monstrous and extraordinary; and the southern exit leads to the

strangest experience of all" (*F* 275) and his melancholy conclusion is unequivocally Western. But Yeats too was a man of the West. Attracta's troubling question, "Shall I be the woman lying there?" leaves unanswered not only the question of a woman's loss or finding of herself in sexual experience, but also the larger question whether unity of being, being in itself, is to be found in the loss or in the finding of individual personality, in its refulgence or in its eclipse, in Nature or in Spirit.

If, therefore, we can understand Attracta as a Vedic saint who can, to the Brahma's question "Who are you"? answer "Yourself" (*E&I* 469):

> I lay with the Great Herne, and he,
> Being all a spirit, but begot
> His image in the mirror of my spirit,
> Being all sufficient to himself
> Begot himself (*VPl* 1039–40)

how can we also understand the meaning of her Fall and the even more troubling meaning of the derisive foiling of her compassionate attempt?

The Hindu philosophy, Yeats tells us in "An Indian Monk", "seems to me something I have waited for since I was seventeen years old" (*E&I* 428); a philosophy which, with its ancient discipline, "satisfied the intellect", was "all I wanted" (*E&I* 429). What Yeats found in the East was not only an anti-dialectic but a symbolism finer, subtler, more delicate and sensuous than that of Europe. European mystics, he says, seem

> . . . indifferent to Nature, may perhaps dread it like Saint Bernard who passed the Swiss Lakes with averted eyes. The Indian, on the other hand, approaches God through vision, speaks continually of the beauty and terror of the great mountains, interrupts his prayer to listen to the song of birds . . . recalls after many years . . . the softness of a pillow, the gold embroidery upon a shoe . . . (*E&I* 431)

The antinomy of carnal nature and discarnate spirit, as of Being and Knowledge or Self and Not-Self seems resolved in the seamless continuity of a late poem such as "What Magic Drum" in which ascesis and sensuality, male and female, human and bestial, unite in the ecstatic moment.[8] But Yeats was irredeemably a man of the dialectical West. "Is it that whenever I have been tempted to go to Japan, China, or India for my philosophy, Balzac has brought me back, reminded me of my preoccupation with national, social, personal problems, convinced me that I cannot escape from our *comédie humaine*?" (*E&I* 448) "There is a continual conflict", he elsewhere imagines Balzac saying, "I too have my dialectic – the perfection of Nature is the decline of Spirit, the perfection of Spirit is the decline of Nature" (*E&I* 467). So the ending of *The Herne's*

Egg sets the gyres whirling yet again. Congal is foiled and Attracta is foiled, punished perhaps for their attempts to totalize what must be but partial, *or to humanize what must be transcendental*. "Fragment delights in fragment", he says in *Dove or Swan*, "and seeks possession, not service; whereas the Good Samaritan discovers himself in the likeness of another, covered with sores and abandoned by thieves upon the roadside, and in that other serves himself. The opposites are gone; he does not need his Lazarus; they do not each die the other's life, live the other's death (*AV*[*B*] 275).

In terms of the fable, the Herne has won. But then who, or what, is the Herne? Is it sheer carnal procreation in time that is the secret of the Herne's being, the "mystery that makes love-loneliness more sweet"? Yet we recall the donkey the stage has presented: the painted toy which invited us to understand that all our representations are mere image, and that without Mind and its images Nature is dead, *love-loneliness without sweetness*, the world excrement, as Yeats said in repudiation of Lockean empiricism. Is the Herne then a blind, brute life force, as implacable and indifferent as Schopenhauer's Will, or Idea, the consciousness of Will? It is Corney, ironic intruder into the fiction, who snorts, "All that trouble, and nothing to show for it / Nothing but just another donkey". And then we recall too, that Corney's donkey is itself a reincarnation of a "rapscallion Clare highwayman", slitter of purses and breaker of hearts.

The Herne's Egg elaborates upon "Leda and the Swan" and asks the same question. It is indeterminately a myth of origin, or the origin of a myth. But it is a "whirling and a bitterness" that it enacts, the impossibility of escape from a Great Wheel. It is always when he is most split, most torn, most at war with his own antithetical self that Yeats takes refuge in the dissimulations of an antic disposition, in the self-mockeries of farce which always masks deep anxieties. In the burlesque prolegomenon to *A Vision*, where he splinters himself into half a dozen personae, "Michael Robartes called the universe a great egg that turns inside-out perpetually without breaking its shell" and "a thing like that", observes the fictive narrator casually, "always sets Owen [Aherne] off" (*AV*[*B*] 33). Later Robartes produces "an egg the size of a swan's egg . . . Hyacinthine blue . . . bought . . . from an old man in a green turban in Arabia, or Persia, or India . . . the lost egg of Leda, its miraculous life still unquenched" (*AV*[*B*] 51). In Hindu mythology it is the Swan of Eternity that produces the World Egg;[9] in "The Holy Mountain" "white-winged, red-beaked, red-legged water birds" are Vedic emblems of the soul. An egg is an intact sphere, an enclosed space in which, in "Among School Children", "two natures [blend] . . . into the yolk and white of the one shell". It is also generation, the incipient future, the dynamic germ of change in time. It is the species, it is the individual; it is repetition, it is non-repetition. There can be no unitary reading of *The Herne's Egg* any more than there can be of its central symbol.

Yeats's *A Vision* is an immense endeavour to master the whirling polarities. His poetry records the living passing moments of stress, or of composure, or captures in splendid symbol the vicissitudes of the reflective life. His plays open on to the deeps of the mind, revealing the struggle of conflicting impulses through personae who are fragments of their author's psyche, set in ironic inversion of each other, at perpetual warfare without closure, without cessation, with at most

> . . . a kiss
> In the mid battle, and a difficult peace
> 'Twixt oil and water, candles and dark night,
> . . . the hot-footed sun,
> And the cold sliding slippery-footed moon,
> A brief forgiveness between opposites
>
> [*On Baile's Strand*, (*VPl* 478)]

NOTES

1. The following is a list of standard critical references to the play. Dates of editions used and page numbers cited are for convenience given in the text in my summary of critical responses. Bloom, Harold: *Yeats* (New York: OUP, 1970); Jeffares, A. Norman, & Knowland, A. S.: *A Commentary on the Collected Plays of W. B. Yeats* (London: Macmillan, 1975); Melchiori, Giorgio; *The Whole Mystery of Art etc.*, (London: Routledge & Kegan Paul, 1960); Ure, Peter,: *Yeats the Playwright*, (London, Routledge & Kegan Paul, 1963); Vendler, Helen,: *Yeats's Vision and the Later Plays*, (Cambridge, Mass., Harvard University Press, 1963); Wilson, F. A. C.: *W. B. Yeats and Tradition* (London: Gollancz, 1958).

2. The "Cauldron, and the Whetstone, and the Sword, and the Spear" and the "love" for them of "the Sidhe of Ireland" form part of the secret message given to the Magi by the dying woman in "The Adoration of the Magi" (*VSR* 170 v). These ancient sacred objects also had their place in the rites Yeats helped to devise for the Celtic Mystical Order: the farcical treatment of such materials in this play recalls perhaps the similar reversal of treatment of closely-held concerns in *The Player Queen*. See *VPL* 761.

3. See, however, Worth, Katharine J.: *The Irish Drama of Europe from Yeats to Beckett* (London: Athlone, 1978). 65–70; and Cave, Richard Allen: *Yeats's Late Plays: "A High Grave Dignity and Strangeness"* (Chatterton Lecture on an English Poet, British Academy 1982) published in *Proceedings of the British Academy*, LXVIII (1982) pp. 299–327.

4. Yeats translated a passage from the Katha-Upanishad thus: "Man should strip him of the body, as the arrow-maker strips the reed; that he may know Him as perpetual and pure; what can He be but perpetual and pure? (*The Ten Principal Upanishads*, put into English by Shree Purohit Swāmi and W. B. Yeats, (London: Faber, 1937) p. 38. See also Wilson, op. cit., 111.

5. There is possibly a buried or repressed figuration of the crucifixion in Attracta's account of the curse ". . . so ancient that no man / Can say who made it, or anything at all / But that it was nailed upon a post / Before a herne had stood on one leg" (*VPl* 1017–18). One notes (ironically) the names of Congal's retainers, saints and apostles to a man.

6. Joseph Campbell notes that "the 'meeting of Sun and Moon' is everywhere symbolic of the instant when the mind turns inward and realises an identity between the individual and the universe, and when all opposites (eternity and time, male and female, Artemis and Aphrodite) are brought together in one order of act" (*The Masks of God*, [New York: Viking Press, 1964] pp. 163–4).

7. E. M. Forster, *A Passage to India* (Harmondsworth: Penguin, 1961 etc.) p. 189. Subsequent reference to this volume is cited in the text, preceded by the symbol *F*.

8. I am indebted to Denis E. Smith and F. A. C. Wilson ("The Sources of Yeats's 'What Magic Drum' " [*Papers on Language and Literature*, Edwardsville, Ill., 9:2, Spring 1973, 197–20]) for their explication of the link between the poem and the Vedantic essays. Their article throws light upon my theme and upon the nodal character of Yeats's mystical beasts who recur whenever the complex encounters between "the spiritual and the atavistic" (in Smith's and Wilson's phrase) are at work in Yeats's mind.

9. C. Kerenyi describes an Orphic creation myth as follows: "In the beginning was Night— a bird with black wings. Ancient Night conceived of the Wind and laid her silver Egg in the gigantic lap of Darkness. From the Egg sprang the son of the rushing Wind, a god with golden wings. He is called Eros, the god of love . . . his name of Phanes explaines what he did when he was hatched from the Egg: he revealed and brought into the light everything that had previously laid hidden in the silver Egg . . . the whole world. Up above was a void, the Sky. Down below was the Rest . . . 'Chaos' which simply means that it 'yawns'." (*The Gods of the Greeks* [Harmondsworth: Penguin, 1958] pp. 14–15).

Yeats and Women: *Michael Robartes and the Dancer*

Elizabeth Cullingford

Michael Robartes and the Dancer (1921), is a volume with two central preoccupations: sexuality and politics.[1] It celebrates both the Easter Rising of 1916 and Yeats's marriage in October 1917 to Georgie Hyde-Lees. Yeats's initial contention is that sex and politics do not mix; that women should eschew political or intellectual conflict in order to cultivate the wisdom of the body. "Opinion", according to the male speaker in the first poem, is "not worth a rush", and in the culminating poem, "A Prayer for My Daughter", Anne Yeats is admonished to "think opinions are accursed", to shun "the opinionated mind" of her father's former love, Maud Gonne. Even the heroes of "Easter 1916", including Constance Markiewicz who spent "her nights in argument/ Until her voice grew shrill", have given themselves to a "passionate intensity" of political opinion that ultimately turns the heart to "stone".

Despite the fact that Constance Markiewicz was heavily outnumbered by male patriots, Yeats customarily saw women as more susceptible than men to the dehumanization of opinion. In a passage from his 1909 diary he wrote of Maud Gonne:

> I fear for her any renewed devotion to an opinion. Women, because the main event of their lives has been a giving of themselves, give themselves to an opinion as if [it] were some terrible stone doll. We [by which he means men] take up an opinion lightly and are easily false to it, and when faithful keep the habit of many interests ... opinion becomes so much a part of [women] that it is as though a part of their flesh becomes, as it were, stone, and much of their being passes out of life. (*Mem* 192)

Although Yeats can see that the difference between the sexes arises because men have "many interests" while for women "the main event of their life has been a giving of themselves", he accepts this disparity as if it were an unchangeable law. Freed from opinion, then, his ideal woman

29

becomes the guardian of "ceremony": "Rooted in one dear perpetual place", she is the custodian of all those values which depend both on leisure and on the sacrifice of individuality to the requirements of family and tradition. While "opinion" is a matter of abstract ratiocination, the determined choice of an individual, "ceremony" for Yeats is a matter of doing instinctively what has always been done. The personal will is both lost in, and blessed by, the customary rituals of a community: a community that, like Edmund Burke's nation, embraces the dead, the living, and those who are not yet born.[2] The first poem in *Michael Robartes and the Dancer* introduces the word "ceremony" with an important emphasis upon sacramental physicality:

> Paul Veronese
> And all his sacred company
> Imagined bodies all their days
> By the lagoon you love so much,
> For proud, soft, ceremonious proof
> That all must come to sight and touch . . . (*VP* 386)

"A Prayer for My Daughter," repeating the word three times in its closing stanza, emphasizes that "ceremony" is a necessary condition for the cultivation of spiritual as well as bodily loveliness:

> How but in custom and in ceremony
> Are innocence and beauty born? (*VP* 406)

In *Michael Robartes and the Dancer* the debate between "opinion" and "ceremony" takes place in a biographical context dominated by women. In 1916, after the execution of Maud Gonne's estranged husband, John MacBride, Yeats visited her in Normandy for a last proposal of marriage. On being, as usual, refused, he suggested matrimony to Maud Gonne's beautiful daughter Iseult, then twenty-two years old. Iseult Gonne, who at fifteen had proposed to Yeats and been herself refused, now wavered for a time. According to Richard Ellmann, "she had thought to keep Yeats about as her mother had done, but he became very decisive". In the autumn of 1917, they met at a teashop in London, to discuss the matter. "She tried to equivocate, but he said, 'Yes or no?' At this she could only say no."[3] Yeats's unusual decisiveness is accounted for by the fact that he had already made plans to visit Georgie Hyde-Lees and her mother. While Georgie Hyde-Lees had for some time been both a friend and a possible candidate for Yeats's hand, it is clear that Iseult Gonne, Lady Gregory's choice, had the first refusal. On being rejected, however, Yeats moved fast, and within a month was married to Georgie Hyde-Lees. His haste reflects the fact that his horoscope pointed to October 1917 as an unusually favourable time for matrimony,[4] but he was aware that his actions might appear heartless, and his letters reveal that he was suffering considerable emotional anguish about the strange situation between him and these three women. "Life is a good deal at white heat", he wrote, with some understatement (*L* 632). After his marriage he became severely depressed, believing that he had betrayed three people (*L* 633). His wife tried to lift his depression by attempting automatic writing, producing a reassuring message from the spirits which declared that his marriage was right for both herself and Iseult. To her surprise the writing continued, and her nuptial stratagem initiated the thousands of pages of automatic script upon which Yeats based his book of occult philosophy, *A Vision*. Yeats's excitement about these revelations was at its height while he was composing many of the poems in *Michael Robartes and the Dancer*. Because of recent events in his personal life, and also because the revelations came and continued to come through his wife, his occult and his sexual excitement were often indistinguishable. George Mills Harper writes:

> From one perspective VA [the first edition of *A Vision*] was stimulated by and based on the mystery of Yeats's relation with three women: his wife and Iseult and Maud Gonne. The AS [automatic script] was begun four days after his marriage, much of the early Script is concerned with Iseult's knots or complexes, and great numbers of questions (but fewer answers) are devoted directly or indirectly to Maud. (*AV*[*A*] xxiii)

Nowhere is the relation between sexuality and revelation clearer than when Yeats fits his friends and enemies into his system of psychological classification, assigning them to appropriate phases of the moon. Around the perfection of Phase Fifteen, the phase of complete subjective or antithetical beauty, he groups Iseult Gonne (Phase Fourteen), Maud Gonne (Phase Sixteen), himself (Phase Seventeen), and George Yeats (Phase Eighteen).[5] The passages from *A Vision* which describe these phases read more like spiritual autobiography than occult speculation, and part of their importance is that they helped Yeats to codify, and thus to control, his turbulent and bewildering feelings about women.

The appearance of the fictitious character Michael Robartes in the title poem of *Michael Robartes and the Dancer* further emphasizes the volume's connection with Yeats's system. According to the introduction of *A Vision* Robartes, a wandering philosopher who has escaped from the world of Yeats's early stories, discovers in Cracow an ancient text entitled *Speculum Angelorum et Homenorum* by Giraldus Cambrensis. On his return to London he communicates the secret of this text and all his occult papers to Yeats for arrangement and publication. Robartes is not, it must be emphasized, simply another name for Yeats: he has a distinct personality of his own. In *A Vision* we find him in the National Gallery standing "before the story of Griselda pictured in a number of episodes, the sort of thing he had admired thirty years ago" (*AV*[*A*] xv). It is not by chance that we find Robartes admiring a pictorial version of Chaucer's story about a submissive woman and her sadistic husband. Where women are concerned Michael Robartes has an iconic imagination: he likes them beautiful and he would prefer them frozen into silent images. At the opening of the poem he is escorting a young lady around a picture gallery, and naturally he focusses on a traditional image of male power and feminine helplessness, the stereotype of romantic dreams: St. George and the Dragon. He gives the old story a new twist, however: his St. George is fighting to save the lady from herself, not from some external monster. The lady, however, is obstinately ungrateful, and the poem offers the comic spectacle of a knight in shining armour confronting a damsel who refuses to recognize her own distress. There is an element of self-parody in the humorous exaggeration of Michael Robartes' position, but the issues are nevertheless serious.

Iseult Gonne, who inspired the poem, had no time for her mother's politics but was intent on becoming "learned like a man" (*Ellmann*, p. x). Michael Robartes, however, defends learning as a male preserve. He has a brutally economic metaphor for the proper relation between the sexes and woman's role in that relation: he bids the lady "bear in mind your lover's wage/ Is what your looking glass can show" (*VP* 385). The female body is seen as payment, presumably for the lover's feats as dragon-killer. Her mute image in the looking glass reveals a "beating breast" and a "vigorous thigh": the knowledge that Robartes would permit her is clearly carnal. She is urged to reject Athene, the virgin patroness of independent and learned women; and she is forbidden to attend college. She will not thereby escape "Adam's Curse", however, for in the poem of that name Yeats has already made one of his "beautiful mild women" say:

'. . . To be born woman is to know –
Although they do not talk of it at school –
That we must labour to be beautiful.' (*VP* 205)

What is this labour? If the Dancer does not go to college, how must she spend her time? In another poem written for Iseult Gonne, "To A Young Beauty", she is jocularly advised to "keep in trim": coming as it does immediately after "A Song", in which Yeats describes his attempts to prolong youth with "dumb-bell and foil" (*VP* 334), the phrase suggests that she must dedicate herself to physical beauty. In *A Vision* Yeats speaks with evident scorn of a hypothetical "woman of New York or Paris who has renounced her rouge pot to lose her figure and grow coarse of skin and dull of brain, feeding her calves and babies somewhere upon the edge of the wilderness" (*AV*[*A*] 213). "To A Young Beauty" equates the discipline of the rouge pot with the labour of the poet: Iseult Gonne is addressed as a "fellow-artist", and Yeats commiserates with her upon a footing of equality:

> I know what wages beauty gives,
> How hard a life her servant lives . . . (*VP* 336)

Michael Robartes, however, makes no such assumptions. He concludes the poem with a piece of outrageous sophistry that clearly reveals his double standards. He has argued that a beautiful woman must not become "learned like a man" because she alone can provide us with a vision of Unity of Being: mind as body, and body as mind, that Fifteenth Phase where "All thought becomes an image and the soul / Becomes a body" (*VP* 374). He supports his contention, however, with intellectual pedantry:

> I have principles to prove me right.
> It follows from this Latin text
> That blest souls are not composite . . .[6] (*VP* 386–7)

He now draws his proof from that very learning to which he would forbid his lady access – the "Latin text", which is presumably the *Speculum*. Is he perhaps afraid that, if she were "learned like a man", she might read his text differently?

Did Yeats know that he had created an amusing portrait of a male chauvinist sparring with an arch young New Woman, or did he approve of Robartes' sentiments? When Iseult Gonne got a job as assistant librarian and student of Bengali and Sanscrit at the school of Oriental Languages, Yeats was so happy that he burst into tears.[7] When Iseult Gonne and George Yeats later became friends he wrote approvingly that "both according to the new fashion for young girls are full of serious studies (both work at Sanscrit)" (*L* 634). If Michael Robartes had been away in the desert for twenty years, Yeats had not, and the comically urbane tone of "Michael Robartes and the Dancer," together with the deflating simplicity of the young girl's rejoinders ("You mean they argued") and her determination to have the last word ("They say such different things at school"), combine to suggest that we have here the portrait of an attitude rather than a portrait of the artist.

Yeats's feelings about female beauty, however, were certainly complex and deeply troubled. His early absorption in the Romantic and Decadent traditions, his admiration of Pater, Wilde, and Moreau, and his own unhappy personal experiences, combined to produce in Yeats an adherence to what Giorgio Melchiori calls the "decadent idea of the fusion of love and death, of beauty and destruction".[8] The image of "La Belle Dame Sans Merci", under the guises of Helen, Aphrodite, Salome, or Mary Hynes, is everywhere in his work.[9] As he wrote in *A Vision*, "Aphrodite rises from a stormy sea . . . Helen could not be Helen but for beleaguered Troy" (*AV*[*B*] 267–8). Beauty, moreover, destroys itself as well as others, for as an old Irish peasant once told Yeats, "beauty was thought to have come from the Sidhe, and to bring misfortune with it . . . beauty had never brought happiness to anybody" (*Myth* 30).

The beauty of three women, Iseult Gonne, Maud Gonne and Constance Markiewicz, pervades *Michael Robartes and the Dancer*. Maud Gonne is "the loveliest woman born / Out of the mouth of Plenty's horn," and in "On a Political Prisoner" Constance Markiewicz is remembered as "the beauty of her country-side". Iseult Gonne's beauty differs slightly in quality from that of the two older women, being essentially more passive. Her type, the type of Phase Fourteen, evokes

> the women of Burne-Jones, but not . . . Botticelli's women, who have too much curiosity, nor Rossetti's women, who have too much passion; and . . . we see before the mind's eye those pure faces gathered about the Sleep of Arthur, or crowded upon the Golden Stair. (*AV*[*A*] 68)

Yet this very passivity generates violence, for Helen of Troy, like Iseult Gonne, is a woman of Phase Fourteen:

> Is it not because she desires so little and gives so little that men will die and murder in her service? One thinks of THE ETERNAL IDOL of Rodin: that kneeling man with hands clasped behind his back in humble adoration, kissing a young girl a little below the breast, while she gazes down, without comprehending, under her half-closed eyelids. (*AV*[*A*] 68)

This image of Beauty as the uncomprehending cause of violence modulates easily into its opposite, and indeed Yeats notes that women of Iseult Gonne's phase, "are subject to violence . . . [which] seems accidental, unforeseen and cruel – and here are women carried off by robbers and ravished by clowns" (*AV*[*A*] 69). "Clown" probably refers to Iseult Gonne's husband Francis Stuart, whom she married shortly after refusing Yeats,[10] and who appears in "Why Should Not Old Men Be Mad" under the unflattering appellation "dunce".[11] Beauty "carried off by robbers" was depicted by Yeats in his earlier poem on Iseult Gonne's mother, "A Thought from Propertius".

In celebrating Maud Gonne's noble and statuesque loveliness, "A Thought from Propertius" shows her first as a companion to Pallas Athene, virgin goddess of war and wisdom, and then, in an abrupt shift, as a victim of rape, "fit spoil for a centaur / Drunk with the unmixed wine" (*VP* 355). This poetic paradox reflects the agonizing doubleness of

Yeats's actual relationship with Maud Gonne. On the one hand he knew her as the unattainable goddess, sexually frigid, pleading her "horror and terror of physical love" (*Mem* 134),[12] while on the other he saw her as mistress of Lucien Millevoye, mother of his two illegitimate children, beaten and emotionally brutalised by John MacBride. In "A Thought from Propertius" his evocation of the opposing female archetypes, the sexually pure and the sexually violated (which appear in slightly different configurations as the "harlot", "child" and "queen" of "Presences" and the "virgin", "harlot" and "child" of "Those Images"), is given iconic coherence through the type of beauty which Yeats is attempting to evoke for his readers: the heroic beauty of classical sculpture. Both as virgin and as victim Maud Gonne remains monumentally calm. Yeats once wrote that "her face, like the face of some Greek statue, showed little thought" (*Au* 364), and on the Olympia pediment depicting the wedding feast of Pirithous, during which the drunken centaur Eurythion abducted the bride, and to which Yeats undoubtedly alludes, the face of the female victim maintains a striking impassivity[13] (Plates 1 and 2).

In *Romantic Image* Frank Kermode connects Yeats's evocation of the expressionless face atop the sculpturally beautiful body with the Symbolist and Decadent traditions. Kermode concentrates particularly upon the image of the Dancer, an image that Yeats associated with Iseult Gonne rather than with the statuesque Maud Gonne. (Several of his poems about Iseult Gonne evoke the scene in which she dances on the shore: "To a Child Dancing in the Wind" and "Long-Legged Fly", for example.) Iseult Gonne is the "Dancer" of "Michael Robartes and the Dancer", linked by proximity to the dancing girl in the last poem of the previous collection, "The Double Vision of Michael Robartes". As a beautiful woman of Phase Fourteen Iseult Gonne moves in a "dance that so returns into itself" that she "seem[s] immortal" (*AV*[A] 67). The price of immortality, however, is death. At Phase Fifteen, depicted in "The Double Vision of Michael Robartes", the girl who has "outdanced thought" to arrive at bodily perfection is "dead yet flesh and bone" (*VP* 383–4). Kermode asserts that the image of the dancing girl with the dead face is "the central icon of Yeats, and of the whole tradition".[14]

There is undoubtedly something terrible about such a beauty. Yeats thought that Maud Gonne disliked her own looks, because "Beauty is from the antithetical self, and a woman can scarce but hate it, for not only does it demand a painful daily service, but it calls for the denial or the dissolution of the self" (*Au* 365). It calls, to be more exact, for the dissolution of many selves, for beauty is the culmination of a process. In "The Phases of the Moon" Yeats describes the progression of the soul through many incarnations towards the transcendent perfection of Phase Fifteen in overtly sado-masochistic language:

. . . those that we have loved got their long fingers
From death, and wounds, or on Sinai's top,
Or from some bloody whip in their own hands. (*VP* 375)

While both male and female spirits must undergo the same painful
transformation, Yeats visualizes it most frequently in feminine terms. In
The Only Jealousy of Emer, written at the same time as *Michael Robartes and
the Dancer*, he analyses the loveliness of Cuchulain's mistress Eithne
Inguba (modelled on Iseult Gonne):

A woman's beauty is like a white
Frail bird, like a white sea-bird alone . . .
A strange, unserviceable thing,
A fragile, exquisite, pale shell . . . (*VPl* 529, 531)

This unserviceable fragility, however, is born of terror and pain:

What death? what discipline?
What bonds no man could unbind, . . .
What pursuing or fleeing,
What wounds, what bloody press,
Dragged into being
This loveliness? (*VPl* 531)

What is meant, intellectually, is that Eithne Inguba is as near to physical
perfection as a living woman can be, having traversed many cradles and
lived many lives. What is suggested, verbally and imagistically, is
torture, murder, rape. Mario Praz has documented the connection
between beauty and pain fostered by the Romantics and the Decadents,
and it is clear that Yeats continued to work within those traditions. In his
early novella *John Sherman* he had asserted that love is "a battlefield
where shadows war beside the combatants".[15] He developed this idea in
his *Memoirs* when he wrote,

All our lives long, as da Vinci says, we long, thinking it is but the moon
we long [for], for our destruction, and how, when we meet [it] in
the shape of a most fair woman, can we do less than leave all others for
her? Do we not seek our dissolution upon her lips? (*Mem* 88)

In his last prose work, *On The Boiler*, he repeated his conviction that,

When a man loves a girl it should be because her face and character
offer what he lacks; the more profound his nature the more should he
realise his lack and the greater be the difference. It is as though he
wanted to take his own death into his arms and beget a stronger life
upon that death. (*Ex* 430)

In his preoccupation with the intermingling of Eros and Thanatos, Yeats reveals his romantic literary ancestry as much as the peculiarities of his own psyche: his longing for dissolution on the lips of a most fair woman was shared by numerous nineteenth-century writers, including Shelley, Swinburne, and Dante Gabriel Rossetti.

Yeats also encountered the union of love with death in the Irish political tradition. Nineteenth-century Irish patriots and poets frequently expressed their readiness to give their lives for Roisin Dubh, the Little Dark Rose – a beautiful captive woman. Yeats too equated the love of country with the love of woman, writing of John O'Leary that he "cared nothing for his country's glory, its individuality alone seemed important in his eyes; he was like some man who serves a woman all his life without asking whether she be good or bad, wise or foolish" (*Au* 215). When he praised his countrymen for being good lovers of women he added that they "had never served any abstract cause, except the one [Ireland], and that we personified by a woman, and I wondered if the service of woman could be so different from that of a Court" (*Au* 545). In his own life the intermingling of love and politics was ensured by his devotion to Maud Gonne, who played Cathleen ni Houlihan in the first performance of his play, and whom he thought of "as in a sense Ireland, a summing up in one mind of what is best in the romantic political Ireland of my youth" (*Mem* 247). Ireland, in fact, was Yeats's other Muse. In "September 1913" he explicitly links the "delirium" of Irish political martyrs with sexual passion, for could they return, he says,

> You'd cry, "Some woman's yellow hair
> Has maddened every mother's son":
> They weighed so lightly what they gave. (*VP* 290)

Only the love of a woman is a strong enough metaphor for the love of country: a love that leads, in both "September 1913" and "Easter 1916", to death.

After the Rising Yeats was forced to reevaluate his countrymen, and to admit that " 'Romantic Ireland's dead and gone' sounds old fashioned now" (*VP* 820). His reflections on the newly romanticized present led Yeats back to the great Romantic model of his youth, Shelley, whose poem *Alastor* did more than any other work to mould his developing literary consciousness. In *Alastor* a young poet sees in his sleep a dream-vision of ideal feminine perfection. Contemplating this image, "His strong heart sunk and sickened with excess / Of love".[16] This "excess of love" drives him on a desperate search for the dream-woman: a search that can only end in death:

> . . . Lost, lost, forever lost,
> In the wide pathless desert of dim sleep,

That beautiful shape! Does the dark gate of death
Conduct to thy mysterious paradise,
O Sleep? (*Shelley*, p. 19)

Worn out by his disappointment, the poet descends, as Shelley says in a
note, "to an untimely grave". Shelley acknowledges the destructiveness
of the poet's fatal passion, but he is much more contemptuous of those
who have never felt the power of the dream:

They . . . deluded by no generous error, instigated by no sacred thirst
of doubtful knowledge, duped by no illustrious superstition, loving
nothing on this earth . . . are morally dead. They are neither friends,
nor lovers, nor fathers, nor citizens of the world, nor benefactors of
their country. (*Shelley*, p. 15)

Yeats, in meditating on the dubious practical efficacy of the rebellion,
remembers Shelley's Poet: one whose heart "sickened with excess of
love", who was deluded by a generous error, who sought his vision first
in dreams and afterwards in death:

Was it needless death after all?
For England may keep faith
For all that is done and said.
We know their dream; enough
To know they dreamed and are dead;
And what if excess of love
Bewildered them till they died?

To that final question Yeats has no answer: he simply reaffirms their
transformation: the rebels,

Are changed, changed utterly:
A terrible beauty is born. (*VP* 394)

A "terrible beauty" born of "excess of love" is clearly a paradoxical
construct. Another poem by Shelley suggests the traditional romantic
provenance of that construct. In "On the Medusa of Leonardo da Vinci
in the Florentine Gallery", (Plate 3), Shelley emphasizes that the
severed death's head of the Medusa is both alluring and repellent.[17] He is
fascinated by

Loveliness like a shadow, from which shine,
Fiery and lurid, struggling underneath,
The agonies of anguish and of death. (*Shelley*, p. 582)

Yeats, disciple of both Shelley and Walter Pater, was certainly familiar with this lyric, and also with Pater's highly charged appreciation of the Medusa painting,[18] which originally contained a reference to Shelley's poem:[19]

> The subject has been treated in various ways; Leonardo alone cuts to its centre; he alone realises it as the head of a corpse, exercising its powers through all the circumstances of death. What may be called the fascination of corruption penetrates in every touch its exquisitely finished beauty.

Pater goes on to describe the forehead of the corpse as "a great calm stone against which the wave of serpents breaks" (*Pater*, p. 83), possibly providing a hint for the "stone" image of "Easter 1916". It is Shelley, however, who has the most powerful linguistic and conceptual influence upon Yeats's poem. He repeatedly juxtaposes terror and beauty:

> Its horror and its beauty are divine . . .
>
> 'Tis the tempestuous loveliness of terror . . .
>
> . . . all the beauty and the terror there—
> A woman's countenance, with serpent-locks,
> Gazing in death on Heaven from those wet rocks. (*Shelley*, p. 582–3)

Shelley's contention that "it is less the horror than the grace / Which turns the gazer's spirit into stone", helps to explain why in Yeats's poem the beauty of a generous love is balanced by the terrible consequences of single-minded devotion:

> Hearts with one purpose alone
> Through summer and winter seem
> Enchanted to a stone
> To trouble the living stream. (*VP* 393)

"Too long a sacrifice" has the same effect as the glance of the Medusa: it makes a stone of the heart. Yeats criticizes the rebels for their life-denying fixity of political purpose, but he includes himself in the condemnation. "Easter 1916" is about his own state of soul as well as about the rebels, for he too had served a political Medusa with desperate fervour. In youth he had "gathered from the Romantic poets an ideal of perfect love"; he might never marry in church, but he would "love one woman all [his] life" (*Mem* 32). When he wrote "Easter 1916" he was staying in the house of the woman he had idolized for twenty-seven years. A poem written at the same time, "Men Improve with the Years", suggests that he too has permitted his "dreams" to turn him into stone:

But I grow old among dreams,
A weather-worn, marble triton
Among the streams. (*VP* 329)

The waters of generation surround him but he cannot partake of them; enchanted to a stone by the terrible beauty, he cannot respond to "The Living Beauty"; he cannot "pay its tribute of wild tears".

Yeats was aware of the horror as well as the loveliness of his icons. His prayer for his daughter is carefully qualified:

May she be granted beauty and yet not
Beauty to make a stranger's eye distraught,
Or hers before a looking-glass . . . (*VP* 403)

For the Image, be she Muse or ungrateful Mistress, may inspire creativity in the male, but is not in herself creative. The children she begets are born of a man's mind, and not of her own lovely body. Her connection with the poet, indeed, is fruitful only in failure. The man of Phase Seventeen, Yeats's phase, "selects some object of desire . . . some woman perhaps, and the *Body of Fate* snatches away the object. Then the intellect (*Creative Mind*), which in the most *antithetical* phases were better described as imagination, must substitute some new image of desire" (*AV*[*A*] 76). Absence, it seems, is the precondition for poetic inspiration, because "The poet finds and makes his mask in disappointment, the hero in defeat. The desire that is satisfied is not a great desire" (*Myth* 337).

How, then, does a poet cope with marriage to a woman who is "not entirely beautiful"? Having declared that "we begin to live when we conceive life as tragedy", what can he make of the social comedy of matrimony, the banality of a satisfied desire, which by his own definition cannot be a "great" desire? *Michael Robartes and the Dancer* shows Yeats rising to the occasion. Both "An Image from a Past Life" and "Under Saturn" reassure his wife that she need fear no competition from ideal images or past lovers. In his long and esoteric note to "An Image from a Past Life", Yeats includes an anecdote that demonstrates his awareness that preoccupation with the ideal may destroy the possibility of real happiness. Once before he had allowed an image to obliterate a relationship: in 1897 thoughts of Maud Gonne had ended his affair with Olivia Shakespear:

She looked in my heart one day
And saw your image was there;
She has gone weeping away. (*VP* 152)

Now, ostensibly writing of the fictional Kusta-Ben-Luki, he shows that he has drawn some conclusions from that earlier experience. Ben Luki,

> saw occasionally during sleep a woman's face and later on found in a Persian painting a face resembling, though not identical with the dream-face, which was he considered that of a woman loved in another life. Presently he met & loved a beautiful woman whose face also resembled, without being identical, that of his dream. Later on he made a long journey to purchase the painting which was, he said, the better likeness, and found on his return that his mistress had left him in a fit of jealousy. (*VP* 821)

George Yeats told Richard Ellmann that she did consider leaving Yeats during the bout of gloomy abstraction and depression that preceded her automatic writing (*Ellmann*, p. xii). No woman wants to come second to a painted image, itself but a poor reflection of the Ideal Form. The "gift" of the automatic writing, however, helped Yeats to make a remarkably swift adjustment to life as a husband. In "Under Saturn" he wisely and gently reminds his young wife that he cannot forget his past, but asserts that it has lost its power to dominate him:

> Do not because this day I have grown saturnine
> Imagine that lost love, inseparable from my thought
> Because I have no other youth, can make me pine;
> For how should I forget the wisdom that you brought,
> The comfort that you made? . . . (*VP* 390–1)

He wrote to Lady Gregory, "my wife is a perfect wife, kind, wise, and unselfish" (*L* 634), and he placed George Yeats at Phase Eighteen, the phase where love begins to be possible (*AV*[*A*], Notes, p. 23). His description of Phase Eighteen, however, provides no real image of her: what we find instead is a description of Yeats-as-the-lover-of-George Yeats. His

> object of desire is no longer a single image of passion, for it must relate all to social life; the man seeks to become not a sage, but a wise king, no longer Ahasuerus, and seeks a woman who looks the wise mother of children. Perhaps now, and for the first time, the love of a living woman ('disillusionment' once accepted) . . . is an admitted aim . . . Goethe did not, as Beddoes said, marry his cook, but he certainly did not marry the woman he had desired, and his grief at her [his second choice's] death showed that . . . he could love what disillusionment gave. (*AV*[*A*] 80–1)

Yeats's emphasis on wisdom reflects his delight in George Yeats's role as oracle as well as housewife. Having exchanged the mask of the solitary and celibate Ahasuerus for that of a "wise king," he adopts the persona of Solomon. Many years earlier he had written, "It seems to me that true love is a discipline, and it needs so much wisdom that the love of Solomon and Sheba must have lasted, for all the silence of the Scriptures" (*Au* 464).

"On Woman," written before his marriage, also uses the character of Sheba, but she is very different from the Sheba of the post-nuptial "Solomon and the Witch". It is clear that the wisdom and sexual pleasure that she offers are dearly bought, for the speaker has been

> . . . driven mad,
> Sleep driven from my bed,
> By tenderness and care,
> Pity, an aching head,
> Gnashing of teeth, despair;
> And all because of some one
> Perverse creature of chance . . . (*VP* 346)

This earlier Sheba has led Solomon a "dance": she is thus distantly related to the inaccessible "fatal women" of Yeats's iconography,[20] although his insistence that he has "had" and "known" her "once" may also reflect the story that some time in 1908 Yeats and Maud Gonne briefly established a physical relationship.[21] The Sheba of "Solomon and the Witch", however, modelled on George Yeats rather than on Maud Gonne, is an entirely positive figure. The magical powers of the "witch" are not destructive, but serve only to increase the wisdom of her lover. If the Sheba of "On Woman" was a creature of "chance", in her later embodiment she represents the union of both "chance" and "choice", demonstrating Yeats's new-found confidence that marriage to the woman he had not initially loved had nevertheless turned out to be exactly what he wanted. The torture of courtship and unrequited love endured by the speaker in "On Woman" reaches homicidal proportions in "Solomon and the Witch", for

> . . . love has a spider's eye
> To find out some appropriate pain –
> Aye, though all passion's in the glance –
> For every nerve, and tests a lover
> With cruelties of Choice and Chance;
> And when at last that murder's over
> Maybe the bride-bed brings despair,
> For each an imagined image brings
> And finds a real image there . . . (*VP* 388)

This violent eroticism, however, is safely in the past, for Solomon and Sheba have found in the bride-bed not despair but a blessing, and the poet discovers that Woman is not generically Fatal.

The two Shebas share a frank sensuality: desire and pleasure in the earlier poem appertain to both male and female partners, and the later Sheba concludes her poem with a direct invitation to lovemaking. In both poems Yeats accepts and indeed celebrates female sexual desire, but only in "Solomon and the Witch" does the perfection of intercourse suggest a momentary absorption in the divine. Sheba's involuntary cry at the climax, the moment when the feminine "oil" and the masculine "wick" are "burned" in the conflagration of sexual ecstasy, signals the death of "this foul world" and the beginning of eternity. The poem's humour comes from Solomon's recognition that the "little death" of love is only an image of apocalypse, and from Sheba's comic eagerness to repeat the experiment in search, literally, of the ultimate orgasm: "O! Solomon! let us try again".

The wit and urbanity of "Solomon and the Witch" suggest that the relaxation of tension brought by Yeats's marriage allowed him to mock his own preoccupation with sex, death and the violence of apocalypse. These obsessions return, however, as the basis of the historical philosophy expressed in "The Second Coming". The symbols of *A Vision*, Yeats wrote, can all be thought of as "symbols of the relations of men and women and of the birth of children". His Great Wheel is "an expression of alternations of passion" (*AV*[*B*] 211), and the conflict between the gyres is a repetition on a cosmic scale of the old battle between the sexes. In *A Vision* Yeats attributes his conception of the gyres to Blake's poem "The Mental Traveller", in which a man and a woman who are bound to one another in unending sexual strife grow alternately old and young: "The woman and the man are two competing gyres growing at one another's expense, but with Blake it is not enough to say that one is beauty and one is wisdom, for he conceives this conflict as that in all love . . . which compels each to be slave and tyrant by turn" (*AV*[*A*] 134). "The Second Coming" focusses on a crucial moment in the sexual-historical struggle: the moment when slave becomes tyrant. The "rough beast", god of the new antithetical era, is the male sphinx of Egypt rather than the female sphinx of Thebes. Although the god he replaces is also male, the "rocking cradle" of Christianity suggests the feminine nature of the ebbing primary civilization, for it is women who traditionally rock cradles:

A *primary* dispensation looking beyond itself towards a transcendent power is dogmatic, levelling, unifying, feminine, humane, peace its means and end; an *antithetical* dispensation obeys imminent power, is expressive, hierarchical, multiple, masculine, harsh, surgical . . .

> . . . Somewhere in sands of the desert
> A shape with lion body and the head of a man,
> A gaze blank and pitiless as the sun,
> Is moving its slow thighs, while all about it
> Reel shadows of the indignant desert birds. (*AV*[*B*] 263)

The feminine gyre is "dogmatic" and "levelling", while the masculine is "expressive" and "hierarchical". Women are opinionated, democratic, pacifist, interested in the welfare of others. Their peace will be destroyed by male violence in the interests of an era that will replace the levelling tendencies of the present with hierarchical structures. In "Leda and the Swan" the process of the new annunciation is explicitly described as a rape.

Yeats's detractors insist that he approves of this transition, and that the beast symbolizes his own desires:[22] his dislike of "feminine" democracy leads him to long for the authority of the masculine principle. Yet the beast, with his slouching gait, his oddly sensual "slow thighs", and his "gaze blank and pitiless as the sun", is not a prepossessing advertisement for masculinity.[23] "The Second Coming" reflects the inexorability of historical evolution rather than the political or sexual prejudices of its author. Neither the "blood-dimmed tide" of European anarchy nor the "rough beast" of totalitarian authority are any respecters of the "ceremony of innocence". The fate of "innocence" concerned Yeats the more urgently because, at the time of the composition of "The Second Coming", his wife was expecting their first child. The poem's intensity reflects Yeats's new and terrified perception that the future he prophesies may be, by genetic extension, his own.

"A Prayer for My Daughter", written shortly after Anne Yeats's birth, is more than a Coleridgean meditation on the prospects of Yeats's child:[24] it is also a catalogue of the failures and mistakes of his own affective life. The "sweetness" that, in the drafts of the poem, Yeats invokes as an antidote to the hatred and bitterness of history, is a sweetness that he himself has known but rarely, as "Demon and Beast" makes clear. This poem, which immediately precedes "The Second Coming", argues that its speaker's moment of liberation from the demon of hatred and the beast of desire is only a temporary respite from the real business of living and creating.[25] Power is inextricably linked with hatred and desire; and the speaker is

> . . . certain as can be
> That every natural victory
> Belongs to beast or demon,
> That never yet had freeman
> Right mastery of natural things,

And that mere growing old, that brings
Chilled blood, this sweetness brought . . . (*VP* 401)

"A Prayer", therefore, shows its speaker overtly longing to protect his
vulnerable child, to free her from the tormenting polarities of hatred and
desire, while the poem's allusions and much of its imagery combine to
suggest that such protection entails the loss of independent creative
power, that the price of "sweetness" is the extinction of strength.[26]

The central subject in Yeats's mind is his daughter's sexual identity.
He makes a direct transition from the child asleep in the cradle to the
woman in front of her looking-glass: the intervening years of childhood
innocence are ignored. In three cancelled stanzas he talks to her as a girl
of twenty-four or twenty-five, two or three years younger than her
mother was at the time of the poem's composition;[27] and the burden of
the poem's prayer is, "May you, daughter, grow up to be like your
mother, and not like the other women in my life." In this sense "A Prayer
for My Daughter" has a conjugal as well as a filial bent, and is a tribute
to a woman who, though not "entirely beautiful", had "earned" Yeats's
heart through her courtesy and charm:

Yet many, that have played the fool
For beauty's very self, has charm made wise,
And many a poor man that has roved,
Loved and thought himself beloved,
From a glad kindness cannot take his eyes. (*VP* 404)

Those who are too beautiful,

Consider beauty a sufficient end,
Lose natural kindness and maybe
The heart-revealing intimacy
That chooses right, and never find a friend. (*VP* 403–4)

This speaker contradicts the position of Michael Robartes in the first
poem of the collection, where the woman is advised to concentrate on her
own image in the looking-glass, and, since she is not permitted to develop
her personality in any other way, must perforce "consider beauty a
sufficient end". Kindness, intimacy and friendship are values seldom
associated with the image of the femme fatale, and their appearance here
carries all the force of a lesson newly learned. This mellowness, however,
does not pervade the whole poem. With the eagerness of a convert, Yeats
begins to tear down the idols of his youth. Helen and Aphrodite are
invoked only to be derided, Helen in language as "flat and dull" as the
life Yeats attributes to her:

> Helen being chosen found life flat and dull
> And later had much trouble from a fool . . .

Bathos and anti-climax converge in this description of events that had
formerly stirred Yeats's imagination. Aphrodite gets equally dismissive
treatment:

> While that great Queen, that rose out of the spray,
> Being fatherless could have her way
> Yet chose a bandy-leggèd smith for man. (*VP* 404)

Both the passive and the active beauties, the chosen and the chooser, find
inappropriate mates. Yeats is probably thinking here of Iseult Gonne
and Maud Gonne, who has passed on to her daughter the Helen symbol
while acquiring a new and more powerful persona herself.[28] The fact that
Aphrodite rises out of the spray connects her with the murderous
instability of changing winds and tides rather than with rooted peace,
and her lack of a father sets her in opposition to the young Anne Yeats.
Yeats's stress on Aphrodite as "fatherless" may be ironic: one of the
legends about her origin tells how Cronos castrated and killed his father
Uranos and threw his member into the ocean: out of the blood and semen
which spread out on the surface of the water the goddess was born.
Aphrodite is thus the perfect image of the Fatal Woman, the daughter
who takes life from her father's castration, and who exemplifies the union
of blood and seed, sexuality and violent death. She is hardly the model
that a nervous father would choose for his own female offspring. Her
affair with Vulcan is explained by Yeats in his description of Maud
Gonne's phase from *A Vision*: "perhaps if the body have great perfection,
there is always something imperfect in the mind . . . Venus out of phase
chose lame Vulcan" (*AV*[A] 74). The perfect beauties, supercharged
with the freight of sexual desire, are dismissed from Anne Yeats's world:
and we remember Prospero, who in supervising and manipulating his
daughter's marriage, banished Venus and Cupid from the courtly
Masque. Something of Prospero's concern for his daughter's chastity
creeps into the subtext of the poem via the allusion to Apollo and Daphne
in the lines:

> May she become a flourishing hidden tree
> That all her thoughts may like the linnet be,
> And have no business but dispensing round
> Their magnanimities of sound,
> Nor but in merriment begin a chase,
> Nor but in merriment a quarrel.
> O may she live like some green laurel
> Rooted in one dear perpetual place. (*VP* 404–5)

Daphne, fleeing from the lustful Apollo, cried for help to her father, the river god Peneus. Peneus responded by turning her into a laurel tree, thus preserving her chastity at the expense of her humanity.[29] Despite the last stanza, the prevailing tone of "A Prayer for My Daughter" suggests that sexuality is troublesome, dangerous, and best avoided if possible. The prayer is designed to forestall Anne Yeats's inappropriate violation by a god: if Aphrodite chose unwisely because she was "fatherless", Yeats does not intend Anne Yeats, being fathered, to make the same mistake.

The allusion to Daphne focusses the father's dilemma: to protect his daughter from rape he is forced imaginatively to sequester her from all human relations, to "hide" her. Joyce Carol Oates is outraged by what she takes to be Yeats's attitude: "This celebrated poet would have his daughter an object in nature for others' – which is to say male – delectation. She is not even an animal or a bird in his imagination, but a vegetable: immobile, unthinking, placid, 'hidden' . . . the poet's daughter is to be brainless and voiceless, *rooted*." [30] While male critics like Daniel Harris (p. 146) and Douglas Archibald (p. 8) make slightly uneasy references to Yeats's supposed "chauvinism" in "A Prayer", Oates mounts a full-scale feminist attack on Yeats's "crushingly conventional" imagination: an attack the passion of which frequently overwhelms its accuracy.[31] Yeats nowhere says that the "hidden tree" is to be an object for male delectation: indeed his identification of his daughter with the virgin Daphne and with the tuneful linnet suggests the opposite: the chastity of the cloister. In "The Green Linnet", which Yeats surely had in mind as a source for this stanza, Wordsworth praises his song-bird as much for its singleness as for its beauty:

> While birds, and butterflies, and flowers,
> Make all one band of paramours,
> Thou, ranging up and down the bowers,
> Art sole in thy employment:
> A Life, a Presence like the Air,
> Scattering thy gladness without care,
> Too blest with any one to pair;
> Thyself thy own enjoyment.[32]

Images of enclosure, singleness, self-sufficiency and virginity, therefore, dominate the sixth stanza of "A Prayer", which completes Yeats's attempt to vanquish on his daughter's behalf the "beast" of desire.

The "demon" of hatred still remains, however. There are many kinds of hatred, but the speaker's preoccupation with his daughter's sexuality and his own failed relationships leads him to focus specifically on the destructiveness of political and intellectual passions in women:

An intellectual hatred is the worst,
So let her think opinions are accursed.
Have I not seen the loveliest woman born
Out of the mouth of Plenty's horn,
Because of her opinionated mind
Barter that horn and every good
By quiet natures understood
For an old bellows full of angry wind? (*VP* 405)

Yeats is obviously thinking of Maud Gonne, the woman of Phase Sixteen whose False Creative Mind is "Opinionated Will", and in whom "all the cruelty and narrowness of . . . intellect are displayed in service of preposterous purpose after purpose till there is nothing left but the fixed idea and some hysterical hatred" (*AV*[*A*] 72). He may also have in mind Constance Markiewicz, jailed for her part in the rising, and castigated in both "Easter 1916" and "On a Political Prisoner" not because of her nationalism but because

    . . . her mind
Became a bitter, an abstract thing,
Her thought some popular enmity:
Blind and leader of the blind
Drinking the foul ditch where they lie . . . (*VP* 397)

In 1918, shortly before the composition of "A Prayer", Constance Markiewicz and Maud Gonne had been detained in London as suspects in the "German plot". Yeats and his wife, who were in Dublin, had borrowed Maud Gonne's house. When she evaded the British authorities and arrived on Yeats's – or rather her own – doorstep, he refused to let her in, because he feared the effect of military searches upon the health of his wife, who was both pregnant and suffering from pneumonia (*Hone*, pp. 313–14). The result of this highly symbolic choice, the protection of wife and unborn child against the "stormy" incursions of his former Aphrodite, was a spectacular quarrel in which most of Dublin seems to have taken sides. "A Prayer" both reflects Yeats's bitterness about the highly-publicised disagreement and reaffirms the validity of his declaration of family loyalty.

In his poem Yeats's response to the "storm" of outward circumstances (political, historical, and personal) is therefore to turn inwards towards the family and towards the self, for

If there's no hatred in a mind
Assault and battery of the wind
Can never tear the linnet from the leaf. (*VP* 405)

As he was later to argue in "The Tower", external reality is created by the soul itself:[33] to rediscover "innocence" and "sweetness" and to dispel the storm Anne Yeats has only to realize that her soul is

> . . . self-delighting,
> Self-appeasing, self-affrighting,
> And that its own sweet will is Heaven's will . . . (*VP* 405)

One of Yeats's strongest statements about the autonomy and creative power of a woman,[34] however, is followed by what seems to be a conventional subordination of her previously liberated soul. The father-daughter dialectic is interrupted by a bridegroom who appears unannounced, like an afterthought, at the end of the poem. Harold Bloom (p. 327) wonders wryly how bride and bridegroom will get on if both have thoroughly absorbed the lesson that their own sweet will is Heaven's will; and the poem indeed contains an unresolved tension between female autonomy and female subordination, between chastity and matrimony.[35]

Something of Yeats's uneasiness in the face of this paradox is revealed in the drafts of the poem. As late in the process of composition as the typed fair draft Yeats had still not brought himself to imagine a real man as his daughter's husband: he wrote "And may she marry into some old house" (*Stallworthy*, p. 43). It is as though he were metaphorically wedding her to the stability of bricks and mortar rather than to the frailties and desires of the flesh. The hypothetical son-in-law who finally emerges is clearly chosen because of his aristocratic social status and ownership of landed property rather than because of his sexuality. The wedding "ceremony" implicit in the poem's last stanza, however, does suggest that Yeats is imaginatively relinquishing exclusive control over his daughter, giving her, however hesitantly, to a younger man:[36]

> And may her bridegroom bring her to a house
> Where all's accustomed, ceremonious;
> For arrogance and hatred are the wares
> Peddled in the thoroughfares.
> How but in custom and in ceremony
> Are innocence and beauty born?
> Ceremony's a name for the rich horn,
> And custom for the spreading laurel tree. (*VP* 405–6)

Since Anne Yeats was only a few months old when the poem was written, Yeats has performed a prodigious feat of projection, enacting the various stages of the father-daughter relationship: the paternalistic desire to protect her, seclude her, and guard her chastity; the recognition of her spiritual autonomy; the realization that his claims upon her must eventually be superseded.[37] The fact that the future to which he consigns her is one of his own choosing, and one, moreover, which seems to be at odds with the dignity and independence of women, should not obscure the generosity of his achievement.

Yeats's treatment of women reveals a striking split between theory and practice. Despite his poetic advocacy of the woman who "gives up all her mind" (*VP* 345) and concentrates on the culture of the body, many of the women he admired and loved were of a very different stamp. Maud Gonne, Constance Markiewicz, Eva Gore-Booth, Florence Farr – political revolutionary, socialist bohemian, trade union organizer, and actress – all these were emancipated women, and Yeats in theory did not like emancipated women. By what sexual alchemy, then, was he drawn to them in the first place? His social conservatism must have been defeated by the radicalism of his early reading, for Yeats notoriously took his passions from literature and only subsequently applied them to life. As a youth his thoughts of women "were modelled on those in my favourite poets and loved in brief tragedy, or like the girl in *The Revolt of Islam*, accompanied their lovers through all manner of wild places, lawless women without homes and without children" (*Au* 64). Cythna, the heroine of Shelley's poem, is not merely "lawless": she is a feminist, an egalitarian, an atheist, and an advocate of free love. When separated from her lover Laon she mounts an independent feminist crusade: "Can man be free if women be a slave?" she asks rhetorically. Since Yeats was attracted by "wildness" in women it should have been no surprise to him that most of those he loved were unwilling to sit at home labouring to be beautiful. He said of Maud Gonne after a political arrest, "She had to choose (perhaps all women must) between broomstick and distaff and she has chosen the broomstick – I mean the witches' hats" (*L* 697). Political women are therefore defined as witches: but as "Solomon and the Witch" demonstrates, that word could have positive connotations for Yeats. There was a part of him that loved witches and lamented their departure:

> All the wild witches, those most noble ladies,
> For all their broom-sticks and their tears,
> Their angry tears, are gone. (*VP* 343–4)

In the same poem, "Lines Written in Dejection", he explicitly identifies his dominant lunar myth with the powerful feminine principle, and equates the debility of age with exile into the realm of masculinity:

> Banished heroic mother moon and vanished,
> And now that I have come to fifty years
> I must endure the timid sun. (*VP* 344)

Yeats was interested in power, and, as both his personal experiences and the numerous goddesses, queens and witches who populate his poetry suggest, he was also drawn towards powerful women.

NOTES

1. Donald Davie suggests that *Michael Robartes and the Dancer* is primarily concerned with "the matter of woman's role in society": "*Michael Robartes and the Dancer*", in *An Honoured Guest*, eds Denis Donoghue and J. R. Mulryne (London: Edwin Arnold, 1965) p. 73. Harold Bloom prefers the view that "the volume's unifying theme is hatred, political and sexual": *Yeats* (London: Oxford University Press, 1970) p. 313. (Hereafter cited in the text as *Bloom*.)
2. See Edmund Burke, *Works* (London: George Bell, 1882) II, 368; and *Ex* 270–1.
3. Richard Ellmann, *Yeats: the Man and the Masks*, 2nd edn (New York: Norton, 1979) p. xi. (Hereafter cited in the text as *Ellmann*.)
4. See Elizabeth Heine " 'W. B. Yeats' (sic) Map in His Own Hand' ", *Biography*, I (1978) pp. 48–9.
5. In assigning Iseult Gonne to the Fourteenth Phase I am disagreeing with *Ellmann*, p. x, who assignes her to the Sixteenth. See *AV*[*A*], Notes, pp. 19–20. For George Yeats as a representative of Phase Eighteen, see *AV*[*A*], Notes, p. 23.
6. See "A Bronze Head" for another use of the word "composite," which suggests that Yeats has changed his mind.
7. Joseph Hone, *W. B. Yeats*, 2nd edn (London: Macmillan, 1962) p. 306. (Hereafter cited in the text as *Hone*.) For a fuller account of Yeats's dealings with Iseult Gonne at this time, see also George Mills Harper, *W. B. Yeats and W. T. Horton* (London: Macmillan, 1980) p. 65.
8. Giorgio Melchiori, *The Whole Mystery of Art* (London: Routledge & Kegan Paul, 1960) p. 116.
9. For a general discussion of this tradition see Mario Praz, *The Romantic Agony*, 2nd edn (London: Collins, 1960), Chapters IV and V. (Hereafter cited in the text as *Praz*.) For a more specific discussion see Melchiori, pp. 114–30.
10. For an account of their courtship and marriage see Francis Stuart, *Black List/Section H* (Carbondale and Edwardsville: Southern Illinois University Press, 1971).
11. The identification was made by A. N. Jeffares, *W. B. Yeats: Man and Poet*, 2nd edn (London: Routledge & Kegan Paul, 1962) p. 244.
12. The poem "His Memories" (*VP* 454–5) may suggest that she overcame this terror.
13. For this insight I am indebted to Deirdre Toomey.
14. Frank Kermode, *Romantic Image*, 2nd edn (London: Routledge & Kegan Paul, 1961) p. 89.
15. W. B. Yeats, *John Sherman and Dhoya*, ed. Richard Finneran (Detroit: Wayne State University Press, 1969) pp. 54–5.
16. Percy Bysshe Shelley, *The Complete Poetical Works*, ed. Thomas Hutchinson, 2nd edn (London: Oxford University Press, 1943) p. 19. (Hereafter cited in the text as *Shelley*.)
17. For a full discussion of this poem and its influence, see *Praz*, Chapter 1. For another source (in a poem by J. S. Le Fanu) for "a terrible beauty" see G. F. Dalton, "The Tradition of Blood Sacrifice to the Goddess Eire" in *Studies*, LXIII:252 (Winter, 1974) 343–54. See also *infra*, p. 159.
18. The picture is not in fact by Leonardo: See *Praz*, p. 41.
19. Walter Pater, *The Renaissance*, ed. Donald Hill (Berkeley and London: University of California Press, 1980) p. 230. (Hereafter cited in the text as *Pater*.) The reference to Shelley was contained in all versions of Pater's work except the 1893 text.

20. F. A. C. Wilson suggests that Yeats's Sheba is a nineties figure who may derive in part from Arthur Symons's play *The Lover of the Queen of Sheba* and in part from Flaubert's *La Tentation de Saint Antoine*: *Yeats's Iconography* (London: Gollancz, 1960) pp. 276–9.

21. Information from Professor R. D. Ellmann.

22. See, for example, Yvor Winters, *The Poetry of W. B. Yeats* (Denver: Swallow Press, 1960) p. 10, and *Bloom*, p. 321.

23. See George Bornstein, *Transformations of Romanticism in Yeats, Eliot, and Stevens* (University of Chicago Press, 1976) p. 63.

24. For a discussion of Yeats's debt to "Frost at Midnight" and "Dejection: an Ode", see Beryl Rowland, "The Other Father in Yeats's 'A Prayer for My Daughter' ", *Orbis Litterarum*, 26 (1971); Daniel Haris, *Yeats: Coole Park and Ballylee* (Baltimore: Johns Hopkins University Press, 1974) pp. 147–8; Douglas Archibald, *Yeats* (Syracuse University Press, 1983) pp. 1–12.

25. For an excellent discussion of "Demon and Beast" see Peter Ure, "Yeats's 'Demon and Beast' ", *Irish Writing*, 31 (1955) pp. 42–50.

26. The same idea is suggested in the opening section of "Meditations in Time of Civil War".

27. See Jon Stallworthy, *Between the Lines* (Oxford: Clarendon Press, 1963) pp. 38–42.

28. Here I disagree with Archibald (p. 5) and Harris (p. 138), who reverse the identification.

29. Harris (p. 142) objects to the reference because of its latent incest-content: he sees Yeats as identifying himself with the rapist god rather than with the protecting father. While I agree that there may be something incestuous about a father's obsessive interest in his daughter's sexuality, I can see no reason to identify the aging Yeats with Apollo rather than with Peneus.

30. Joyce Carol Oates, " 'At Least I Have Made a Woman of Her': Images of Women in Twentieth-Century Literature", *Georgia Review*, 37 (1983) p. 17.

31. Oates (p. 17 and p. 18) twice refers to the Horn of Plenty as an "unintentional" phallic symbol, and describes the "betrayal of the Horn" as "the independent woman's most unspeakable act" (p. 18). But since the Horn, which traditionally represents abundance and fertility, was torn by Zeus from the she-goat Amalthea, who suckled him, its connotations are obviously feminine rather than masculine.

32. William Wordsworth, *The Poetical Works*, ed. E. de Selincourt, 2nd edn (Oxford: Clarendon Press, 1952) II, 140.

33. It has not, as far as I know, been pointed out that Yeats's belief echoes Coleridge's "Dejection: An Ode":

> We in ourselves rejoice!
> And thence flows all that charms or ear or sight,
> All melodies the echoes of that voice,
> All colours a suffusion from that light.

Yeats's lines seem to be a condensation of Stanzas III, IV, and V of "Dejection": S. T. Coleridge, *Complete Poetical Works*, ed. E. H. Coleridge (Oxford: Clarendon Press, 1912) I, 366.

34. Harold Bloom (p. 326) asks whether these lines reflect "autonomy" or "autism". Joyce Carol Oates thinks Yeats is recommending "a kind of autism of the spirit". If we see the lines in the context of "Dejection" and of "The Tower", however, it is clear that they refer to the soul's ability to construct its own world.

35. See Rowland, p. 289.

36. For a brilliant exploration of the wedding ceremony and its ritual importance in dissolving the father's quasi-incestuous "ownership" of his daughter, see Lynda E. Boose, "The Father and the Bride in Shakespeare", *PMLA*, 97 (1982) pp. 325–47.

37. Unlike Bloom (p. 326) I do not see the last stanza as an imaginary evocation of the marriage Yeats never made with Maud Gonne.

"Heirs of the Great Generation" Yeats's Friendship with Charles Ricketts and Charles Shannon

J. G. P. Delaney

"The Irish love what they see to be right, and the English hate it", Yeats remarked to the artist Charles Ricketts.[1] So impressed was Ricketts by this observation, which echoed his own feelings about some aspects of English life, that he invited the Irish poet to dine with him and his friend, Charles Shannon.

The occasion had been a chance meeting at a Dolmetsch concert in November, 1899 (BL Add.Ms. 46788 f.125v.). Yeats was with Arthur Symons, whom Ricketts knew, though not well. On the whole, Ricketts and Shannon had always eschewed contact with London's literary and artistic world, and made a virtue of knowing few people outside a small and select coterie of friends and admirers, though Wilde had described their home in the Vale, Chelsea, as "the one house in London where you will never be bored".[2] Their high-minded isolation had been preserved by moving to the suburbs as soon as they began to make a name for themselves. Invitations to 8 Spring Terrace, Richmond, were handed out sparingly.

Now in their mid-thirties, they had founded an occasional magazine, *The Dial* (1889–97), revived the art of original wood engraving in the splendid illustrations and decorations of *Daphnis and Chloe* (1893) and *Hero and Leander* (1894), and founded the Vale Press. While Ricketts had also produced many commercial book designs, notably for Oscar Wilde, Shannon had become known for his poetic lithographs and was just making his first appearances as a painter. The two men had already formed the basis of their magnificent art collections, which embraced Egyptian, Greek and Roman antiquities, Japanese prints, Persian miniatures, Old Master as well as Pre-Raphaelite and modern French paintings and drawings. Yeats rightly described Ricketts as "one of the greatest connoisseurs of any age."[3]

After Yeats's visit, Shannon noted in his diary (5 Dec. 1899): "W. B. Yeats dined with us in evening. He is very intelligent and entertaining,

53

apparently not gifted with much of the Irishman's fund of humour. I may be wrong. He talked greatly with Ricketts about management of stage scenery" (BL Add.Ms. 58111). The theatre was to be one of their most frequent and fruitful topics of conversation, but Ricketts also facetiously reported other bits of their talk on that occasion to Katherine Bradley and Edith Cooper, who wrote under the name "Michael Field".[4] Yeats had said that Shannon might see visions, but that Ricketts never should. "A course of treatment is necessary to see visions," Ricketts continued, "you must go to Ireland. If you shut your eyes in England you see darkness. In Ireland you see the light that shows you things. Yeats says that the beings seen in this Irish daylight have faces not quite so beautiful as Greek things, but more spiritual." When Ricketts pressed Yeats for details of their garb, Yeats was going to say they were all dressed in white, but paused "for the note of authentic quaintness – 'robes with a great many pleats round the neck and little wreaths of ivy'". Ricketts, who was an aesthete to his fingertips and an unabashed materialist, retorted characteristically: "It seems such a pity to seek visions, when you can make them, or see them all round – a carbuncle, a garnet giving themselves to your sight." What beauty could be made or found in the real world interested him far more than shadowy occult matters. Still, they had liked Yeats and told the Fields: "he is provincial in a nice way . . . giving you the name of an artist or writer if you pause for it, and overjoyed if you have read the book he has just been reading" (BL Add.Ms. 46788 f.133).

These were certainly not their first contacts. As early as 1896, Yeats had contributed a story, "Costello the Proud, Oona Macdermott and the Bitter Tongue", to *The Pageant*, an annual magazine edited by Shannon and Gleeson White, though the latter as Literary Editor may have been responsible for it. Yeats mentions Ricketts' and Shannon's work in two articles published in 1898.[5] They had a number of friends in common. Yeats suggested that Lionel Johnson, who had visited Ricketts and Shannon when they lived in the Vale, Chelsea, may have first taken him to the artists' studio (*Au* 169).

Yeats recalled that a "fanaticism" had at first delayed his friendship with Ricketts and Shannon. This was his hatred of the eighteenth century. The first thing he had seen on entering the studio was a painting by Shannon of a mother and child, "arrayed in lace, silk and satin, suggesting that hated century. My eyes were full of some more mythological mother and child and I would have none of it and I told Shannon that he had not painted a mother and child, but elegant people expecting visitors, and I thought that a great reproach" (*Au* 169). The most likely picture of this subject was one that Shannon had started on Feb. 6th, 1899, when he noted in his diary: "made a rough for new portrait of Mrs MacColl with baby." (BL Add.Ms. 58111) The beautiful Mrs MacColl, the French wife of the art critic, D. S. MacColl, had been sitting to Shannon for more than a year, but this is the first mention of a double portrait. Entitled simply *Mother and Child*, Shannon had been working on this on December 3, only three days before Yeats's visit.[6]

In time, Ricketts was to become along with William Morris and Gordon Craig, an important influence on Yeats's life and work. In the early 1900s he was visiting Ricketts at his magnificent new flat at Lansdowne House, Holland Park, every three or four days.[7] He described Ricketts as "a fine mind and man of great knowledge" (*LMR* 69) and "my education in so many things" (*AV[A]* 208). In artistic matters, Ricketts and Shannon were his "chief instructors" (*Au* 169).

It was, first of all, their artistic interests that gave them common ground. Ricketts, having divided his youth between France and England, had come to love the Pre-Raphaelites as much as he did the French Symbolist poets and painters. *The Dial*, devoted solely to expressing its editors' taste, was a curious blend of the two schools, with a strong Symbolist element in the writing and illustrations and a Pre-Raphaelite interest in wood engraving. Yeats could hardly have met two people whose aesthetic interests were closer to his own at that time.

Conversation often turned on the indifference to art that prevailed in England and the threat to the great tradition of European art that modernism represented. Ricketts like Yeats was conservative in these matters, a believer in the traditions that were handed down from generation to generation, to which each artist made a personal contribution "When we studied his art, we studied our double," Yeats wrote of Ricketts in 1936, "We too thought that style should be proud of its ancestry, of its traditional high breeding, that an ostentatious originality was out of place whether in the arts or good manners."[8] If a mind were devoid of traditional values, moral or literary, its only power lay in hating tradition, thought Ricketts. As a result of such hatred, artists, he felt, began " 'to hesitate to accept public tasks because the almost certain attack [might] ruin their reputation'" (*Mem* 181). On another occasion, in 1909, Yeats recorded how they spoke of:

> the disordered and broken lives of modern men of genius and the so different lives of the Italian painters. He said in those days men of genius were cared for, but now the strain of life is too heavy, no one thinks of them till some misfortune comes – madness or death. He then spoke, as he often does, of the lack of any necessary place for the arts in modern life and said, "After all, the ceiling of the Sistine Chapel was the Pope's ceiling." (*Au* 518)

Similarly, Ricketts felt that Oscar Wilde had been persecuted by a jealous and philistine society, which hated art and the artist. While he did not feel that Wilde's writings ever reached first class, the man was greater than his work and "in intellect and humanity he is the largest type I have come across", (*SP* 124). As with Yeats, Wilde became a symbolic hero and martyr to him.

So long as their conversation was confined to aesthetic matters, the English painter and the Irish poet had a great deal in common, but Ricketts did not share all Yeats's interests. The occult amused or bored him. He poked fun at this side of Yeats. Once, at a dinner with "the Fields", Shannon's plate began to rise mysteriously. One of the women was pumping up an air bladder under the plate, a trick that had sent a doctor flying from the table convinced of the presence of evil spirits. Shannon, however, behaved very sensibly, and the quick-witted Ricketts, "striking a finger-point against his cheek imitated the complacency with which Yeats would have received the attention spirits showed him" (BL Add.Ms. 46790 f.5v.). On occasion, he could be more sympathetic. When *The Shadowy Waters* was being presented to an audience of fifty Theosophists at the Court Theatre, Ricketts suggested using a glass harp lighted from within by electricity, "so that the lamp will seem to burn with supernatural power".[9] In the 1920s he consulted Yeats over a seance to which he had been invited to meet the ghost of Oscar Wilde.[10] However, when Yeats had Ricketts' horoscope cast by his uncle, George Pollexfen, who had foretold the death of Beardsley and York Powell, Ricketts wrote (30 May 1904) in a more characteristic vein to the Fields, "I am curious to know what the stars think of me. I have always been quite rude to them. You remember my description of them, 'that they looked like fleas' " (BL Add.Ms. 58088). Ricketts was more interested by Yeats's admission that he had tinkered with some of the details, than with the results, which were dull (BL Add.Ms. 46794 ff.78–9). Though he sometimes discussed spiritualism with Yeats, his real opinion of it was that it was "mere rot", just as he had felt about Rossetti's experiments with seances (*LTSM* 44).

Nor did Ricketts have much sympathy for Irish Nationalism. Though on one occasion (23 April 1904) he could record that Yeats "spoke intelligently about Ireland and the Irish stage" (*SP* 104), his usual reaction was one of exasperation. Hardly more than a year later (June 30 1905), he commented in his diary: "Yeats in evening, obviously discouraged by Ireland and things Irish. He got on my nerves once or twice in using the editorial 'we' over Ireland. When he started posturing over the Gorki manifesto, I flashed up and said it was a matter of common human and artistic interest, one which affected Europe and not to be confused with any local political point of view."[11] At the beginning of the year, Ricketts had been involved in attempts to rescue Maxim Gorki, who was under arrest and said to be in danger of his life. Here was an artist of international stature suffering persecution at the hand of the state, just as Wilde had done. As Ricketts was more European than

English, having had a French mother and spent part of his childhood in France, Irish politics seemed parochial to him, and he concluded, "The Irish are odious with their barn-door politics and hen-run ethics" (*SP* 121). After a visit (28 April 1905) from Lady Gregory's son, Robert, he commented: "Ireland I fear is only half-civilized, a sort of provincial Poland. I am inclined to think the Irishman a solemn sort of beast, provincial in temper, suspicious and quite lacking in humour" (BL Add.Ms. 58103).

Yeats, however, later showed he could amuse them. He told them (November 12 1904) of his interview with the Queen: "Out of innocence he disregarded all the conventions and spoke to her in the Yeats way. She knew nothing, of course, of Yeats's disloyal manifestoes when royalty was in Ireland, knew his poems and wished to hear when next he gave one of his plays".[12] An even more amusing story, told on the same occasion, made them shout with laughter. He was staying with his American agent at the Carlton Hotel. Earlier in the evening, a note had been delivered to his room, but as it was addressed to the singer, Jean de Reszke, he sent it away. During the night, on hearing soft knocking, he turned on the light and opened the door in the belief that it was his friend Shine getting him up early. In came a lady in a bright rose-coloured dressing gown. "Oh, I beg your pardon" and she laughed and fled. Ricketts admired the lady's laugh and rather wished she had kissed Yeats on each cheek "on each side the forelock" (*SP* 112; Bl Add.Ms. 46793 f.196v.).

Finally, Ricketts, the aesthete and connoisseur, deplored Yeats's lack of the "sense of beauty as an art in life". Yeats had given dinner to Shannon and another friend: "The plates of soup plumped down – the chops with a knife and a fork plumped down, potatoes in the middle of the table, then pastry, and then a portion of cheese all set down like an inventory before the guests," Ricketts told the Fields (BL Add.Ms. 46793 f.196v.). Such casualness offended him. At Lansdowne House, guests ate at a table of sea-green marble, at one end of which was an antique Greek torso amid banks of lilies. Every plate and utensil was rare or antique or of exquisite workmanship, and the table was laid according to an ideal arrangement. Everything had its right place. "Then comes Willie Yeats," Ricketts observed wryly, "and there is the confusion of the Balkan states!" (BL Add.Ms. 46803 f.71v.).

It is not surprising that Yeats should have distantly reminded Ricketts of Wilde, "a man who has general ideas, humour, keen business sense, seeming a fool to be wise, self-absorbed". When Edith Cooper protested that Oscar could make a genial atmosphere round him, while Yeats could not, Ricketts agreed that Yeats was "infinitely less and less human, but the likeness strikes" (BL Add.Ms. 46793 f.196v.). Ricketts often found Yeats's presence disquieting: "There is something paralytic about it. And it is so tiresome to hear him talk about 'Po-etry' and wave his hands round it." Because of this, he told the Fields in 1904, that he shrank from writing to Yeats lest he should call (BL Add.Ms. 46793 f.57). This however was something that Ricketts occasionally felt about almost every old friend. Ironically, his own presence was disquieting. When Yeats commented to him, "You are always in a state of rebellion against yourself", the "Fields" thought that Yeats's perception went very deep. They suffered from the contradictions in his character, "the lack of peace one feels with him". With all his generosity, wit and brilliant conversational gifts, they found he rarely left joy or peace behind (BL Add.Ms. 46798 f.7v.). Yeats, moreover, was reminded of Ricketts when reading Hall Caine's life of Rossetti, whom Ricketts admired greatly. "There is the same apparent lack of philosophy with the same occasional philosophic insight and there is the same occasional over-generosity of praise, but there is something beyond all that which I cannot get at" (*LTSM* 40). Finally, a curious insight into their behaviour together was recorded by Gordon Bottomley: "it was uncanny and impressive . . . to watch Yeats mask his vanity and get out of the limelight and be quiet when he turned up at that [Ricketts's] house. And it was on those nights that one could tell that Yeats was a biggish man himself – though not to compare with Ricketts who never thought of himself".[13]

Ricketts and Shannon followed Yeats's life and career with an affectionate, if sometimes amused, interest. "Have you heard the news that Maud Gonne has gone and left Yeats and the future of Ireland for matrimony and comfortable Catholicism?" Ricketts mischievously asked the Fields. "Yeats is unconsolable in sonnets of the 'Oh Thou' type to various little lilts and tunes" (BL Add.Ms. 58088). When Yeats married in 1917, Shannon mischievously suggested, "it all seems very sudden and suggests she is furniture for the castle",[14] Ricketts, who actually disapproved of marriage for artists as it distracted them from their work, wrote to Yeats, "It is bad and sad of you never to have announced your marriage to us, and I hope on your return you will bring your bride to see us some Friday afternoon."[15]

As Yeats regarded Ricketts and Shannon as "heirs of the great generation" (*Au* 169), the Pre-Raphaelites, he was deeply interested not only in the attitudes to painting but also in their work. On one of his visits to Lansdowne House, (4 November 1904), he took along John Quinn, who became an important patron of Shannon's. Not only did he buy three paintings but he also commissioned Shannon's portrait of Yeats. Though Shannon's preliminary drawing of him looked "most damnably like Keats" (*L* 502) Yeats complained, the oil painting completed in 1908 was a good likeness and a great success, and Yeats had it reproduced in the *Collected Edition* of his *Works*.[16] In the sittings for the portrait, the old problem of the hated century had cropped up again, as Shannon explained to Quinn (29 June 1911): "The Yeats I feel is really much too dark because it is lacking in contrast, but this is not quite my fault. Yeats insisted on what he called a XVth century portrait, black on grey, he accused me of being XVIIIth century, but I say I'm XIXth; in fact I rather think I'm XXth" (NYPL). Shannon also did the portrait of Robert Gregory which Yeats mentions in "The Municipal Gallery Revisited".

Over the years of their friendship, Yeats continued to consult Ricketts and Shannon on Irish art matters. Shannon was asked to design new judges' robes for the Irish Republic, and in spite of a fervent plea by Yeats in the Irish Senate, only the design for the District Courts was accepted, his impressive caps and gowns for the High and Supreme courts being rejected in favour of the traditional wig and gown.[17] Shannon had also been approached to design some of the new Irish coinage, and when he refused Yeats turned to Ricketts for advice about other possible artists (*SS* 163). Likewise, Shannon was invited to sit on committees, while Ricketts was consulted over the appointments to the Irish National Gallery. Till the end of their lives, they remained Yeats's mentors in the visual arts.

Though Yeats had outgrown his first dislike of Shannon's paintings, it was Ricketts' work that moved him most. This was dramatic and tragic. Even from the earliest days, Yeats had recognized the symbolic element in Ricketts' work. In "Symbolism in Painting" (1898), he had observed, "All art that is not mere story-telling, or mere portraiture, is symbolic," and he went on to point out how "Wagner's dramas, Keats' odes, Blake's pictures and poems, Calvert's pictures . . . Villiers de l'Isle Adam's plays, the black-and-white art of Mr Beardsley and Mr Ricketts, and the lithographs of Mr Shannon, and the pictures of Mr Whistler, and the plays of M. Maeterlinck, and the poetry of Verlaine, in our own day" go beyond literal meaning to accept "all symbolisms" and therefore reach a deeper level of meaning and significance (*E&I* 148–9). Yeats knew and admired Ricketts' illustrations for Oscar Wilde's *The Sphinx* (1894), which Ricketts considered his best and most characteristic work, though Wilde himself had told him "your drawings are not of your best. You have seen them through your intellect, not your temperament".[18]

Such early work must have been in Yeats's mind when he wrote: "Men like Sir Edward Burne-Jones and Mr Ricketts have been too full of the emotion and the pathos of life to let its images fade out of their work, but they have so little interest in the common thoughts and emotions of life, that their images of life have delicate and languid limbs that could lift no burdens, and souls vaguer than a sigh" (*UP2* 134). As Yeats suggests. Ricketts' drawings and woodcuts not only tell a story but also evoked his own feelings about man and his relationship with the universe. His paintings bring this out in a more vivid and passionate style. Yeats described Ricketts as, 'an artist whose woodcuts prolonged the inspiration of Rossetti, whose paintings mirrored the rich colouring of

Delacroix'.[19] In this, he rightly recognised that the inspiration of
Ricketts' woodcuts derived from the English Pre-Raphaelites while that
of his painting came from French sources. As with Yeats, certain
themes fascinated and held a special significance for him, and there was,
as T. R. Henn points out, "a certain community of outlook" between the
two men.[20] This not only includes such typical Symbolist themes as the
severed head in Salome, of whom Ricketts did three paintings and a
bronze, and Judith, which he not only painted once but staged twice as a
play;[21] but also the "common troubled concern with scenes from the
Passion", though Yeats was not a Christian (*LT* 252). Nor indeed was
Ricketts, who yet painted at least ten oils of Christ's Passion and Death.
Yeats owned a coloured photograph of one of the best of them, *The
Betrayal*.[22] Like Yeats, Ricketts tended to turn his favourite images into
symbols and express his own mythology in his work. Christ is seen purely
as a man who confronted his sufferings and death without losing his
sense of mission. It was while he was first exploring the Christ theme that
Yeats told him, "You *paint* the tragedy of Man, most people only
understand the tragedy of Woman, or the pitifulness of their tragedy", a
remark which pleased Ricketts (*SP* 126). According to Yeats, only
Michaelangelo, Durer and Blake among the world's greatest artists had
attempted this. In an unpublished letter now in Emory University to
Lady Gregory (4 November 1904) he described how the intensity and
originality of some of Ricketts' paintings moved him as did no other
contemporary work. In them, he saw the rarest kind of genius. In
Ricketts's vision, certain other figures had a personal significance. One
of these was Don Juan, who from 1905 appears in no fewer than eight
paintings, though some of these are versions of the same incident.
Ricketts saw the notorious lover as "a grand gentleman – the type of the
debauché which gives the world vast pleasure, and takes on himself
almost the pains of a saint. . . . Don Juan faced damnation for his dream
– he never recoiled fearful" (BL Add.Ms. 46793 f.23v.–4). One of the
paintings *Don Juan in Hell* (c. 1908) depicts the naked Don on a white
horse riding through the bodies of women he had seduced, who raise
their arms or, in one case, a baby, towards him[23] (Plate 4). Behind, on
the left, are three clothed figures, the eunuchs who guard this tragic
harem and watch the Don riding through Hell. Yeats wrote to Lady
Gregory (8 March 1909) that he had made some notes on the painting, in
one of which he had compared Arthur Griffiths and his like with the
eunuchs.[24] The point is carried further in a passage in the 1909 Journal.

> The root of it all is that the political class in Ireland – the
> lower-middle class from whom the patriotic associations have drawn
> their journalists and their leaders for the last ten years – have suffered
> through the cultivation of hatred as the one energy of their movement,

a deprivation which is the intellectual equivalent to the removal of the genitals. Hence the shrillness of their voices. They contemplate all creative power as the eunuchs contemplate Don Juan as he passes through Hell on the white horse.[25]

The image reappears in "On those that hated 'The Playboy of the Western World', 1907":

> Once, when midnight smote the air,
> Eunuchs ran through Hell and met
> On every crowded street to stare
> Upon great Juan riding by:
> Even like these to rail and sweat
> Staring upon his sinewy thigh. (*VP* 294)

A second version of the painting was exhibited in the year of Ricketts' death, 1931.

Yeats also refers to Ricketts, though not by name, in his seven poems about Mabel Beardsley, "Upon a Dying Lady". He describes the four dolls which Ricketts had made for her based on characters in her brother's work. In a letter to Lady Gregory, Yeats spoke of them as "[w]omen with loose trousers and boys that looked like women. Ricketts had made them, modelling the faces and sewing the clothes. They must have taken him days" (*L* 574). One of them, described in the poem as "our beauty with her Turkish trousers on" was based on the frontispiece of *Mademoiselle de Maupin*, and there was also a Japanese, a Venetian lady and a meditative critic.

Yeats rightly saw Ricketts within the classical tradition of European paintings of which Symbolism was the last great manifestation before the victory of modernism. With Impressionism something had been lost. In his appreciation of Robert Gregory, Yeats observed, "A man of letters may perhaps find . . . in old Chinese painting, in the woodcuts and etchings of Calvert and Palmer, in Blake's woodcuts to Thornton's Virgil, in the landscape background of Mr Ricketts' 'Wise and Foolish Virgins,' something that he does not find in the great modern masters, and that he cares for deeply" (*UP2* 430). This is a symbolic, as opposed to a realistic, treatment of landscape. Even after Ricketts' death, Yeats remembered this particular painting and hoped that it would be reproduced in a book that was being prepared on him by Sturge Moore, along with one or two of the first Sphinx drawings "and other things that I have longed to possess", (*LTSM* 169) but the painting could not be traced (Plate 5). In opposition to the Impressionistic masters, Yeats singles out artists whose work, like Blake and Calvert, was symbolic: "The great myth-makers and mask-makers, the men of aristocratic mind, . . . Ingres in the *Perseus*, Puvis de Chavannes, Rossetti before 1870,

Watts when least a moralist, Gustave Moreau at all times", and among
these he included Ricketts' painting *The Danaides* (Plate 6), which
depicted the daughters of Danaus who were doomed forever to fetch
water in jars that leaked, together with the early illustrations to *The
Sphinx* (*Au* 550). These are also mentioned again in *A Vision*, where Yeats
notes how often Ricketts' "imagination moves stiffly as though in fancy
dress, and then there is something, – Sphinx, Danaides – that makes me
remember Callimachus' return to Ionic elaboration and shudder as
though I stared into an abyss full of eagles" (*AV[A]* 208). The powerful
effect of some of Ricketts' pictures on him is echoed when, in classing
Ricketts among those like himself who are "the opposites of our times",
he observes that "Ricketts made pictures that suggest Delacroix by their
colour and remind us by their theatrical composition that Talma once
invoked the thunderbolt."[26]

Ricketts for his part found much to admire and praise in Yeats work,
though with some surprise at first. When he read *The Countess Cathleen*
Ricketts noted in his diary (22 July 1901) "to my astonishment and
against all my suspicions, I was greatly impressed with its effectiveness.
As an artist, his work is melodious, and greatly heightened by naif and
forcible images, sparks of Irish thought and compressed diction that in
emotional scenes and homely scenes have a great and refreshing quality.
– There is a directness of thought and diction that conveys an impression
of character in the persons, which I do not think quite intentional". The
play, moreover, was free from "the nagging tone one finds in all modern
plays" with the exception of Swinburne's *Atalanta in Calydon* and
"Michael Field's" *The Tragic Mary* (BL Add.Ms. 58099).

When the Irish players came to London, Ricketts assiduously
attended the performances. On 26 March, 1904, he and Shannon
attended *The King's Threshold* and *The Pot of Broth* along with Padraic
Colum's *The Broken Soil*. Ricketts' letter to Yeats about the play did not
merely say how much he had enjoyed it but typically went on to analyse
it with the quick responsiveness, perception and independent judgement
that characterised his criticism:

> I like the motive of The King's Threshold, the telling simplicity and
> effectiveness with which you develop your situation, and the sense of
> variety & progress, or should I say climax you put into each
> situation notably when the bride is brought on to the stage. I was
> charmed by many beautiful & fresh things by the way which I
> should like to quote, but I became so angry at the end with the
> exchange of compliments and protracted life of the poet that they
> have slipped my memory. – I like the touches of humour which are
> fresh & direct, I like the reference to leprosy over the white hands of
> the princess. I do not like the curses; curses are always conventional or

spoken conventionally. I like the poet's reference to a place in his world, instead of that more comfortable place his bride had in mind. – All through I found myself deeply interested; once or twice annoyed by the intoning of pieces which were quite delightful enough in themselves.... The King's Threshold suffered of course at the hands of your players who were mostly inadequate but never offensive, and that is a compliment when romantic play acting is concerned (*LTWBY* 141).

In spite of his criticisms of the acting, he thought that Frank Fay had excelled in *The King's Threshold*. To Sturge Moore (c. April 1 1904) Ricketts summed up *The King's Threshold* as "quaint and telling, with some charming things in it and tons of nonsense, notably at the end where it becomes quite foolish and like a bad Oscar sentence. The actors were inadequate and quite intolerable when they indulged in the 'leetle lilt'. They acted the comedies admirably, however, with genuine tact and feeling" (BL Add.Ms. 58086). Though more succinct, this does not differ from what he had told the author.

Ricketts and Shannon were in Lady Gregory's party at the London performance of Yeats's *Where There is Nothing* in June, 1904. "Yeats's play failed to strike the audience," Ricketts noted, "though it seemed to me to be written for effect, with striking episodes which should tell over the footlights. It is much too long and showed halts in construction, but it could be cut down to a telling thing." Yeats later called on Ricketts to discuss the failure of his play. "He showed himself critical and shrewd," thought Ricketts, "When he does not pontify he is all right" (*SP* 109). On such occasions, Ricketts would have been full of suggestions about how Yeats could improve his play. With his fine critical mind and enthusiastic sympathy, he had a passion for influencing people. Yeats for his part seems to have counted Ricketts as one of the arbiters of his achievement. With regard to *At the Hawk's Well*, he wrote to Quinn, "If when the play is perfectly performed.... Balfour and Sargent and Ricketts and Sturge Moore and John and the Prime Minister and a few pretty ladies will come to see it, I shall have a success that would have pleased Sophocles" (*L* 610).

After seeing Mrs Patrick Campbell's production of Yeats's *Deirdre* in 1908, Ricketts wrote to give his impressions with a full recognition of Yeats's stature as a playwright.[27] "I like it immensely, not so much as Baily's Strand, but very much indeed. If our Time had a sense for Tragedy and if we had actors capable of understanding it and with the gift to interpret it, Deirdree would be famous instead of a literary curiosity for a matinee." His own paintings suffered from this same lack of "a sense for tragedy" in the modern world. Of course, there were also things that Ricketts did not like in *Deirdre*, but these could not be blamed on Yeats's writing, for they concerned the abominable performances of the actors.

I believe the dreadful interpretations you have always met with (and to which you seem quite blind) have spoilt your chances, so far, as a playwright. I have always liked your sense of construction, your sense of the stage. Where I am hostile is to a certain vagueness of texture for which you receive praise and in which I detect a sort of hesitation and a bias towards rhetoric of a kind. (*LTWBY* 205)

By this time, Ricketts had become involved in one of the Irish productions. From the beginning, Yeats had recognised his potential as a theatre designer. As early as May, 1899, he had Ricketts "in mind", according to a note he added in 1924, when he wrote, "If one could call one's painters and one's actors from where one would, how easy it would be! I know some painters, who have never painted scenery, who could paint the scenery I want, but they have their own work to do" (*E&I* 170). Yeats had enlisted the help of Thomas Sturge Moore and Laurence Binyon, both close friends of Ricketts in promoting his dramatic theories of musical speech, rhythmical acting and symbolic scenery in London.[28] As early as 27 January 1901, Sturge Moore discussed with Ricketts "the possibility of the foundation of a Theatre society for Romantic Drama, etc. which would be managed by him, in which the scenery would be done on a new decorative, almost symbolic principle" (*SP* 52). This was an idea which had haunted Ricketts ever since his discussions with Wilde in the early 1890s about the staging of *Salome*,[29] and Ricketts had thought of writing a pamphlet on it. He had always thought that the theatre should occupy a high place in life and that it was "the least understood . . . of our arts".[30] While Yeats, Binyon and Sturge Moore publicised in lectures and articles the new theatre, the Literary Theatre Club began to plan and train for their first productions one of which Yeats wished to be his *Countess Cathleen*. An amateurish reading for copyright of Sturge Moore's *Aphrodite against Artemis* was organised on July 30 1901, which amused Ricketts greatly (*SP* 63–4). He and Shannon attended a lecture at Clifford's Inn on 15 May 1902 in which Yeats, Sturge Moore and Dolmetsch explained the theory of speaking to the psaltery, while Florence Farr and her two nieces gave practical demonstrations with the instrument. Yeats and Sturge Moore called on Ricketts on June 20 1902 for further discussions, (BL Add.Ms 58114), but it was not until January 1903 that these plans became practicable, for on that day Sturge Moore told Yeats that Ricketts hoped to raise £600 with which Craig could stage Yeats's play in London (*L* 394). Ricketts offered the profits from the Vale Press edition of Marlowe's *Faustus*, issued in a format uniform with the 39 volumes of the Vale Shakespeare. Yeats, however, hoped now to form a larger, more professional body than the club, which became "The Masquers". With this second society, Ricketts had little to do, for, though Yeats wanted him on the committee, Gordon Craig's sister objected on the grounds that he would be too extravagant, a charge that his later successful productions, done on a shoestring, soon showed to be as foolish as it was unfounded. Anyway, Ricketts's research and writing for his book, *The Prado* (1904), kept him busy for most of 1903. However, Yeats still hoped to attract his help and money, though the *Faustus* had only managed to raise £150. As the society had decided to put on Yeats's *The King's Threshold* and Gilbert Murray's translation of Euripides' *Hippolytus*, he wrote to Murray (21 July 1903): "Now if Ricketts, who could also raise more money, could be put to stage the *Hippolytus* . . . we would get a beautiful series of dresses and stage pictures. . . . With Ricketts behind us I have not the slightest doubt that we could get a good many subscribers."[31] "The Masquers" had earlier failed to get sufficient subscriptions to get off the ground. At the beginning of 1904, after "The Masquers" had finally folded, Yeats was still hoping to "get hold of that £170 [sic] Ricketts has for theatrical adventure. As soon as we feel strong enough to play non-Irish work, we should, I think, approach Ricketts and see if he will work for us" (*L* 420). However, as Yeats's attention had now been diverted to Ireland, his London associates, Sturge Moore, Binyon, Florence Farr, W. A. Pye and Gwendolen Bishop as well as Ricketts and Shannon formed the Literary Theatre Society, to which Ricketts gave the money he had raised. The Society opened with Sturge Moore's play on April 1 1905, and closed when their funds ran out in 1907. All of the five plays in their productions were designed by Ricketts.

Fortunately, not all planned collaborations between Ricketts and Yeats went unrealised. In July, 1904, Yeats thanked Ricketts for having sent "such admirable designs for the Black Jester". This character was apparently to speak the Prologue (never completed) for *The Shadowy Waters* and was also going to appear in a play Yeats was writing, so "for that too the design will serve" (Coll. Michael Yeats). Later in the year, Yeats went to see Ricketts who promised to do the scenery for a play and to advise Robert Gregory who was designing a set for *On Baile's Strand*. Lady Gregory came a few days later to discuss the scenery. Ricketts' promise was not actually fulfilled until 1908, and the play was not one by Yeats, but Synge's *The Well of the Saints*. Ricketts had met Synge through Yeats in April, 1904, and admired Synge's "strange, wistful, brutal, poetic and sordid Irish dialect plays" and considered his early death "a calamity to British letters", which upset him greatly (*SP* 187). There seems to have been some difficulty over the designs for this revival of Synge's play, as Robert Gregory had originally been supposed to be the designer. On April 10, 1908, Yeats wrote to Synge that he was going to Ricketts at once for "artistic knowledge" but was apparently going to undertake the designs himself.[32] On the same day he wrote again (on Ricketts' Lansdowne House stationery) to say that Ricketts was doing the designs at that moment (*TB* 275). He also sent careful instructions from Ricketts, who wanted his work to be anonymous, about the execution of the designs. Ricketts wanted a "vague spunged-out" effect and instructed the scene painter to "use blue & violet in the shadows as well as brown & make the base of all the stones and tree trunks green as if moss grows where they touch the ground. The scene would be improved by a green floor cloth green at the borders smudgy green" (*TB* 276–7). The designs were all done with great urgency, but this brought out the best in Ricketts who always threw himself into any production with great zest and often had to work into the small hours on successive nights in order to meet a deadline.[33] Yeats wrote (again on Ricketts' stationery) to Lady Gregory to say it had been very good of Ricketts "to give up his day to the work on such short notice" (NLI Ms. 18709). Ricketts himself wrote to Synge, "I am glad if I have been of use towards *Well of the Saints*, I wish I had been given the time to reason it out properly. I had to work from Yeats's descriptions of Ireland where I have never been."[34]

By the time that Ricketts came to work for Yeats himself, he had already acquired a reputation as a stage designer. After the collapse of the Literary Theatre Society, he had gone on to work for the commercial theatre, working with Mrs Patrick Campbell and Shaw and making his name with his splendidly barbaric designs, based on Stonehenge, for *King Lear* at the Haymarket Theatre in 1909. The following year, Yeats could write that "Only two artists have done good work upon the English stage during my time, Mr Craig and Mr Ricketts" and while he acknowledged that Craig had been the impetus behind the reform of stage decoration and mechanism, he went on to say "all that these artists have done has had beauty, some of it magnificent beauty" (*UP2* 383).

Finally, on May 1, 1914, Yeats asked Ricketts to do the dresses for a revival of *The King's Threshold* for the Abbey season at the Royal Court Theatre (*SP* 194). When Lady Gregory called on June 6th, Ricketts felt that she was "a little cowed . . . by the splendour of the dresses" he had designed for the production (*SP* 196). Two days later, she wrote and confirmed that she "really felt quite overcome when I saw the beauty and carefulness of your designs". However, they were also producing another play by Yeats, *Deirdre*, and having sent a copy for Ricketts' acceptance, she asked him if he might be able to make a simple design for *Deirdre* and make suggestions about "shuffling" some of the costumes from the other play to this one. She also hoped that Ricketts might be able to decide on material and colour and see the dressmaker, Mrs Champion, whom she had visited on his recommendation. Her letter concluded: "I feel you are giving us a new start in life. Yeats will enjoy seeing his plays, which he hasn't done for some time" (BL Add.Ms. 58090). In the days of the Literary Theatre Society, Ricketts had been obliged to work under pressure with little money, so he knew how to make money stretch. "The pattern seems absolutely right," wrote Lady Gregory again on June 11th, "and quite within our means" (BL Add.Ms. 58090). Yeats too was delighted with the magnificent designs, and after one of the rehearsals wrote to Ricketts, "I think the costumes the best stage costumes I have ever seen. They are full of dramatic invention, and yet nothing starts out, or seems eccentric. The company never did the play so well, and such is the effect of costume that whole scenes got a new intensity and passages or actions that had seemed commonplace became powerful or moving . . . You have done a great deal for us and I am very grateful" (*SP* 196).

What Ricketts had done was in fact by the use of colour and abstract design created costumes for types rather than for individual characters. As Liam Miller has pointed out, Ricketts' notes on the drawings indicate that the parts of each costume were "interchangeable between all the plays set in the 'Heroic Age' – a concept very much in accord with Yeats's ideas".[35] Ricketts' familiarity with Yeats's ideas and plays enabled him to give Yeats what he wanted in stage or costume design. He aimed at an effect that was selective, suggestive and decorative. Moreover, by "shuffling" the designs, he could not only make a costume for one play do for another, but also create new costumes by recombining parts of the old (Plate 7).

Ricketts, however, did not actually see the costumes he had designed, again anonymously, for *The King's Threshold* on the stage, for he missed the two performances. Shannon, however, had managed to go, and said they were superb. Ricketts had been absent because he had been at the Russian Ballet, which since its first arrival in London in 1910 had thrilled and enthralled him as nothing before.[36] This may explain why the Irish Players were losing some of their appeal for him. On June 17, 1914, he noted in his diary, "Evening to the Irish Plays, on the whole a poor performance, they are stagnating. I told Yeats so, and advised him to turn 'Costello the Proud' into a play and the study of the religious persecution periods, Elizabeth, Cromwell etc no necessarily big episodes, but smaller ones treated with plenty of character and tragedy" (BL Add.Ms. 58105).

For the Abbey's London season of 1915, Ricketts was asked to design *On Baile's Strand*. While he did some new sketches for characters unique to this play, he also did a good deal of "shuffling". Cuchulain's son, for instance, as he explained to Yeats, was put in the soldiers' costumes for *The King's Threshold* (Coll. Michael Yeats). From the same play, according to Ricketts's notes on the costumes, the pupil's caps would do for the caps of the Old, Middle-aged and Youngest King, the Chamberlain's tunic for the Youngest King, an underdress for the Middle-aged King, while the Old King's underdress would come from *The Green Helmet*, another play in which Ricketts seems to have taken a hand.[37] As Synge's *Well of the Saints* was also being given, Ricketts came up with some new designs for it, working at first from memory of the play which he had designed six years before. All the new costumes were carried out under his supervision and with his careful eye for economy. For Synge's play, he had the help of Mrs Edmund Dulac, wife of the artist whom Yeats had met and befriended at one of Ricketts' Friday evenings. She undertook the women's dresses: "The idea," Ricketts explained, "is to hire her seamstress to work in her house under her supervision and mine. This would save in cost and reduce to little more than cost of material" (Coll. Michael Yeats). The result was such that Ricketts told a friend, "I am dressing Yeats's *Baile's Strand* on £20 and with the overflow of that vast sum have redressed Synge's *Well of the Saints*".[38] Ricketts seems to have shuffled his costumes for Yeats's plays yet again for an improvised single performance of Synge's *Deirdre of the Sorrows* on 31 May 1914.[39]

So successful was Ricketts in designing costumes that they were not only noble and beautiful in themselves but also adaptable that they served the Abbey Theatre for many years as a stock of costumes in which any of Yeats's poetical plays could be performed. Moreover, they proved as adaptable as the famous screens that Gordon Craig did for Yeats and were perfectly suitable for plays that Ricketts had never dreamt of, such as Lady Gregory's fantastic play *The Dragon*.

In May, 1916, Yeats wrote that there was "a chance of Ricketts, Dulac and I running a season at the Aldwych Theatre next year with Beecham. We have been asked and have sent in statement of conditions – absolute control. I am keeping my responsibility as slight as possible. It may mean a fine performance of *Player Queen*" (*L* 612). However, this last project was never realised.

Ricketts shared Yeats's interest in Japanese theatre and as early as 1900 and 1901 had attended performances in London by the actors Kawakami and Sado Yacco (*SP* 39–40, 60–2). When the Japanese dancer, Michio Ito, gave some special performances of No dancing in October 1915, Ricketts designed a costume for him in "the Witch Dance" (Ashmolean Museum). When Oswald Sickert, brother of the painter, went to Japan, he sent Ricketts a hundred cards of leading No dancers and a long letter describing the Japanese theatre. Ricketts had promised a copy to Yeats, but in December, 1916, he told Gordon Bottomley, "Yeats has forgotten all about my promise . . . and for the moment our relations are getting rather rocky or strained, owing to a reflex action of political Irish folly on his temper and bearing, doubtless excusable since he knew the men who have been shot (I told him they would not be shot). Anyway, though he has given me his last book with its charming preface to the No plays, I feel what I would describe as a passionate indifference towards Ireland and the Irish and all friends of Ireland."[40] The book was *Certain Noble Plays of Japan* (Cuala Press, 1916).[41]

His tone may also be partly explained by a misunderstanding that had occured earlier in the year. On 26 March, Yeats had written to Lady Gregory: "A man has issued, by mistake he says, by design I suspect, a pirated edition of some of my recent poems. He had proposed to make technical publication as his magazine *Form* was delayed and the poems were coming out in America" (*L* 609). It was in fact Ricketts who in August 1915 had approached Yeats about the new magazine: "A group of youngsters of whom a clever draughtsman, Austin Spare, is the guiding spirit, are about to start a new quarterly (a sort of *Dial*). Shannon and I have promised to contribute prints etc, and I have been asked to approach you for a poem or some sort of literary contribution. I fancy they are more in need of names for list of contributors than hard actual work." Having seen some pulls of pages, Ricketts had found them better than similar recent publications of the sort, and no doubt mindful of his and Shannon's own early efforts for *The Dial*, he had said to Yeats "I should be pleased if you feel young enough to smile on this venture" (Coll. Michael Yeats). Sturge Moore, Masefield, Laurence Binyon and Sidney Cockerell had received similar letters from Ricketts. In a second letter to Yeats shortly after the first, Ricketts added: "I doubt if there is any money at the back of it, or if they are able to pay. These sort of things rarely have money. Money being a separate and admirable thing in itself, perfect, incommunicable, self-centred and immovable and never to be polluted by contract with the arts" (Coll. Michael Yeats). As the magazine was delayed and as the poems were being issued in America, the eight poems, which Yeats had given free, were first published in pamphlet form in an edition of 200 copies to secure Yeats's copyright. This seems to have been unauthorised by Yeats himself, who was so enraged that he limited Spare to 50 copies, but the young artist replied that this would ruin him and that he did not have enough to eat. Not believing any of this, Yeats stood firm. However, when Ricketts offered to pay any loss that Spare was under, Yeats gave way as he did not want his old friend to be out of pocket. Then, it turned out that Ricketts had misunderstood the situation (*Wade* 121–2). Yeats was particularly annoyed because he felt that he had injured not only the Cuala Press, which should have all his first editions, but also himself "because the pirated edition is pretentious and has a vulgar drawing (which Ricketts had not seen)" (*L* 609). Spare's drawing was of a female nude and printed in red. "The red woman is a brute", Yeats inscribed one copy (*Wade* 122). The magazine finally came out in April, 1916, published by John Lane and containing the promised prints by Ricketts and Shannon, poems by Binyon and Sturge Moore as well as Yeats.

Their friendship survived such misadventures and Ricketts "passionate indifference" to all things Irish. Early in 1918, after Yeats had sent him an inscribed copy of *The Wild Swans at Coole* (Cuala Press, 1917), which contained the No play "At the Hawk's Well", he wrote to thank Yeats "for your book of poems and No play which absorbed and interested me whilst I read it, and somehow made me muse about it afterwards. I was struck by its melancholy and, to appreciate this, outside music, is a new phase or sign of mental health, or perhaps indifference to the crash of actual events"[42] (Coll. Michael Yeats).

After the war, Ricketts embarked on a new and different collaboration with Yeats which took him back to his earliest career as a book designer. Since closing the Vale Press in 1903, he had been reluctant to return to book design. Yet, he agreed to do the cover for the Collected Edition of Yeats's work to be published by Macmillan. He envisaged a cover stamped in blind, a style, he told Yeats, that "requires a more formal or abstract treatment not to look poor and ambitious". It was the type of decoration he had chosen for the Vale Press edition of Shakespeare issued from 1900 to 1903, and to which he returned after the war due to the enormous increase in the cost of gold. "I had proposed", he told Yeats, ". . . a formal arrangement of lines enriched with small sprays of yew, trefoils, perhaps woodbine buds, or other quite meaningless spots & twiddles." (*LTWBY* 428). Yeats, however, preferred more meaningful symbolic decoration, such as their friend Sturge Moore had given his covers, and he "retarded" the work, Ricketts complained to Bottomley, "by requests for unicorns, fountains, hawks and caves, all delectable things in good sound gold blocking, but, somehow, unsuitable to blind tooling on the hideous coloured cloth of poor quality, which is all that Macmillan can afford" (Private Collection). The figurative elements Ricketts hoped to put in an end-paper. As for the cloth, he had chosen "much to Macmillan's avowed disapproval – a fairly sound green of the old Vale Press type" but not so good in quality (*LTWBY* 430). In the decoration of the cover, he aimed at what he called a "library effect". "The cover is quite abstract decoration in which you can detect (by the eye of faith alone) roses & sprays of Ewe with their berries. I found", he confessed to Yeats, "your preferences in Fauna, caves, fountains etc. beyond the range of an end paper so I have combined most of them in a sort of book plate design which is placed inside the cover, like an ordinary book plate, on this I have presented a unicorn couching on pearls before a fountain, backed by a cave full of stars. On the crest of the cave is what I believe to be a hawk contemplating the moon." (Earlier Ricketts had admitted "hawks I can't draw.") He concluded, "If not overprinted it will not look bad" (*LTWBY* 430, 428; *SP* 341).

The first two volumes were published on 3 November 1922. Two days later, Yeats wrote to thank his friend for the design, describing how his wife had brought the books up to his study and "not being able to restrain her excitement I heard her cry out before she reached the door 'You have perfect books at last' ". Yeats was equally enthusiastic, "Perfect they are – serviceable and perfect. The little design of the unicorn is a masterpiece in that difficult kind. You have given my work a decoration of which one will never tire and all I have done will gradually be put into this form" (*L* 691). It pleased Yeats to think that the younger generation would get to know his work in Ricketts design, but this hope was not to be fulfilled. Only six volumes were published in this format.[43]

Throughout the 1920s, Yeats attended the Friday evenings at their new house in Regents Park whenever he could. Ricketts remained one of his few links with the Nineties. In 1924, he managed to visit Ricketts and Shannon's own tower, the Norman keep which their patron Sir Edmund Davis had given them for life on his estate at Chilham Castle, Kent. (*LTSM* 55) Ricketts still stubbornly refused to take Ireland seriously, especially since the European cataclysm that had destroyed not only the world he knew but also a great deal of Europe's artistic heritage. In 1922, he had written to Bottomley:

> Apropos of Yeats, he has written interesting human letters about himself and the state of Ireland, he is broken-hearted that the old mediaeval bridge to his Tower has been blown up. Shall I send you his letters? In them, you scent the essential shallowness of Irish events, the tragedies that are comedies, possibly I exaggerate their purpose and merely quote my own belief that the Irishman of Ireland – who has not escaped elsewhere – is of shallower texture than other tougher and more evolved races. (Private Collection)

However, he had found Yeats's *Autobiographies* most interesting, which concerned so many men of the Nineties he had met but refused to know like Arthur Symons. Fortunately, Yeats was not one of them. Their thirty-year friendship was based on their devotion to the theatre and the artistic traditions, the Pre-Raphaelites and the Symbolists, that they both loved and valued, perhaps all the more so because they had passed out of fashion.

In Yeats's house, hung the costume designs that Ricketts had done for him, the "special beauty and purpose" of which he explained to at least one visitor.[44] There was also a "most lovely" window designed by Burne Jones which Ricketts had given him, (*L* 901) and a large Shannon lithograph of boys bathing, probably *The Breakwater* (1906) (*L* 865). When news reached Yeats of Ricketts's sudden death on 7 October 1931, he wrote to their mutual friend, Sturge Moore: "I know what a blow Ricketts's death must be to you. I, though he was less to me than to you, feel that one of the lights that lit my dark house is gone. . . . He was in our tradition its last great representative" (*LTSM* 168).

NOTES

1. B.L. Add.Ms. 46792 f. 21v. Ricketts' conversations were recorded in detail in "Works and Days: the Journal of 'Michael Field' " (i.e. Katherine Bradley and Edith Cooper), B.L. Add.Mss. 46776–46804A. I would like to thank Miss Riette Sturge Moore for

permission to quote from this journal, and from copyright material of both Ricketts and Shannon; Colin Smythe Ltd, on behalf of Anne de Winton and Catherine Kennedy, for permission to quote from unpublished materials of Lady Gregory; Anne Yeats and Michael Yeats for permission to quote from unpublished materials by W. B. Yeats. Unpublished materials of Gordon Bottomley are quoted with the permission of Dr Roger Lancelyn Green.

2. Charles Ricketts, *Self-Portrait, Taken from the Letters and Journals of Charles Ricketts, R.A.* Collected and compiled by T. Sturge Moore. Edited by Cecil Lewis. (London: Peter Davies, 1939), 16. Hereafter cited in text as *SP*. Ricketts' and Shannon's diaries and letters are in the British Library, (Add.Mss 58085–58118). I have silently corrected obvious errors in spelling and punctuation.

3. Quoted in Ann Saddlemyer, " 'The Heroic Discipline of the Looking Glass': W. B. Yeats's Search for Dramatic Design" in Skelton, R., & Saddlemyer, A., *The World of W. B. Yeats etc.*, (Seattle: University of Washington Press, 1967), 70. Hereafter cited as *Her. Disc.*

4. Miss Bradley and Miss Cooper were known to their friends and each other as "Michael", and "Field", or "Henry", respectively. Ricketts referred to them jointly as "the Fields".

5. "Symbolism in Painting" (*E&I* 149) and "A Symbolic Artist and the Coming of Symbolic Art" (*UP2* 134).

6. Not completed until 1902, Shannon's painting is reproduced in *The Studio*, 64 (May 1915) 229.

7. Joseph Hone, *W. B. Yeats: 1865–1939* (London: Macmillan, 1942) p. 179.

8. Quoted in *Her. Disc.* p. 69.

9. B. L. Reid, *The Man From New York: John Quinn and his Friends* (New York: Oxford University Press, 1968) p. 36.

10. C.R. to T. Sturge Moore (C. Feb. 1924) B.L. Add.Ms. 58086.

11. The manifesto had been organized by German intellectuals, among them Count Kessler, with whom Ricketts was in contact.

12. Nowhere in his writings does Yeats mention this meeting with the Queen, for which this is the only source. However, the Queen in question is most likely to have been Alexandra, queen-consort of Edward VII, although no date is given for this meeting.

13. Gordon Bottomley to W. Graham Robertson (10 January 1940). Private Collection.

14. C.H.S. to John Quinn (7 November 1917). Quoted Quinn p. 306. Shannon's letters to Quinn are in the Quinn Collection, New York Public Library, (Astor, Lenox & Tilden Foundations).

15. Ricketts' letters to Yeats are in the collection of Senator Michael Yeats, Dublin; he rarely dated his letters, and I have silently corrected any obvious errors or spelling. I am grateful to Mr Yeats for access to these materials.

16. The drawing is now lost; the oil, which is in the Houghton Library, Harvard, was reproduced as frontispiece in Vol. 3 of the *Collected Works* (1908).

17. *The Senate Speeches of W. B. Yeats*, ed. Donald R. Pearce (London: Faber & Faber, 1961) pp. 125–32. Hereafter *SS* in text.

18. Jean Paul Raymond [i.e. Charles Ricketts] and Charles Ricketts: *Oscar Wilde: Recollections* (London: Nonesuch Press, 1932) p. 38.

19. Quoted in *Her. Disc.*, 70.

20. T. R. Henn, *The Lonely Tower: Studies in the Poetry of W. B. Yeats* (London: Methuen, 1965) p. 252. Hereafter cited in text as *LT*.

21. T. Sturge Moore's *Judith*, Queen's Theatre, January 1916; Arnold Bennett's *Judith*, Kings Theatre, 30 April 1919.

22. Information supplied by William H. O'Donnell.

23. Reproduced in *The Studio*, 43: (1908), 58.

24. *L* 525. See also A. Norman Jeffares: *A New Commentary on the Poems of W. B. Yeats*, (London: Macmillan, 1982) pp. 115–16.

25. *Mem* 176. See also *Au* 486.

26. *Ex* 418. See also *E&I* 529 and *VP* 625. Delacroix, of course, painted Talma in one of his stage roles.
27. Robert Gregory is listed as the designer of this production (New Theatre, 27 November 1908), but Ricketts may have had something to do with it. See Ifan Kyrle Fletcher, "Charles Ricketts and the Theatre", *Theatre Notebook* 22: No. 1 (Autumn, 1967) 6–23.
28. Ronald W. Schuchard, "W. B. Yeats and the London Theatre Societies, 1901–1904" *RES* NS 29 (1978) 415–46.
29. Charles Ricketts, *Pages on Art* (London: Constable & Co, 1913) pp. 243–4; hereafter *PA*.
30. C.R. to Gordon Bottomley (29 January 1919) Private Collection. See also C. J. Holmes, *Self and Partners (Mostly Self)* (New York: Macmillan, 1936) p. 165.
31. Gilbert Murray Papers, quoted by Schuchard *op. cit.*, 440.
32. Ann Saddlemyer, ed., *Theatre Business: The Correspondence of the First Abbey Theatre Directors: William Butler Yeats, Lady Gregory and J. M. Synge* (Gerrards Cross: Colin Smythe, 1982) p. 275; hereafter *TB*.
33. See J. G. P. Delaney, "Charles Ricketts and his Unlikely Friendship with George Bernard Shaw", *PEN: the Broadsheet of the English Centre of International PEN* 15 (Autumn 1983) pp. 3–5.
34. C.R. to Synge (c. May 1908), Trinity College, Dublin. Quoted *TB* 276.
35. Liam Miller, *The Noble Drama of W. B. Yeats* (Dublin: The Dolmen Press, 1977) p. 182.
36. C.R. to "Robbie" Ross, n.d., Coll. Mrs. Mary Hyde, New Jersey, USA.
37. George Sheringham and R. Boyd Morrison, eds., *Robes of Thespis: Costume Designs by Modern Artists* (London: Ernest Benn Ltd., 1928) p. 37; hereafter *Thespis*.
38. C.R. to Gordon Bottomley (19 May 1915), Private Collection. The sum may be £80.
39. C.R. to Lillah McCarthy (Aug./Sept., 1918), Humanities Research Centre, University of Texas, Austin, to which I am grateful for access.
40. C.R. to Gordon Bottomley (19 December 1916), Private Collection.
41. Sold (lot 294) at the sale of Ricketts's books, Christies, 5 December 1933.
42. Sold in the same lot as the previous book.
43. Ricketts' cover was however used again for The Collected *Poems* (1933) and *The Collected Plays* (1935), both published in New York. The design of the unicorn and the fountain were stamped in gold on the spine of the Macmillan *Collected Poems* (1950) and *Collected Plays* (1952). By chance, another of Yeats's books was issued in a binding by Ricketts, when Yeats's *Selected Poems* (1929) was one of several books issued by Macmillan in a blind-stamped cover that Ricketts had originally done for Laurence Binyon's anthology, *The Golden Treasury of Modern Lyrics* (1924).
44. Nancy Pyper, "Four O'Clock Tea with W. B. Yeats", *W. B. Yeats: Interviews and Recollections*, ed. Edward H. Mikhail (London: Macmillan, 1977) I, p. 163. Yeats showed her a design for *The Countess Cathleen*, which must have been one of the shuffled costumes.

Olivia Shakespear and W. B. Yeats

John Harwood

Olivia Shakespear was born on 17 March 1863, at Southlands, Chale, on the Isle of Wight. Her father, Major-General Henry Tod Tucker, C.B. (1808–1896), was commissioned into the Bengal Infantry in 1824 and served on Headquarters staff in both Sikh Wars. In 1856 he retired with the rank of Colonel, owing to ill-health, and was subsequently given the honorary rank of Major-General.[1] He married Harriet Maria Johnson, second daughter of Sir Henry Allen Johnson, at St. James's, Piccadilly in May 1857. Harriet Maria Johnson was the sister of Captain William Victor Johnson, Lionel Johnson's father.[2]

Major-General Tucker, at the end of his military career, engaged in controversy regarding the role and direction of British rule in India, and contributed to the debate over the events leading up to the Indian Mutiny. He wrote to *The Times* on 24 June 1857, to say that he had advised the Government against greasing the new Lee-Enfield cartridges with beef or pig fat, or indeed anything that might offend "the caste or religious prejudice of the natives". His pamphlet, *A Glance at the Past and the Future in Connection with the Indian Revolt*, is not as liberal in its sentiments:

> The authority of which the officers were so unwisely deprived, of administering a sound, severe flogging to high-caste Brahmins and others . . . would have been far more conducive to the stability of our power and authority than all the silly petting which originated in the weakness and fears of philanthropic rulers. Even the re-introduction of flogging by Lord Hardinge was thus rendered useless, for it was felt that mere child's-play was contemplated. When only fifty lashes were permitted to be administered, the cat lost its terrors, and the disgrace of punishment under such circumstances only incited to a desire for revenge, and to disaffection.[3]

The rigours of service, indeed, forced the Major-General into early retirement:

The simple fact is (and I apologise to the reader for stating it, being only of personal concernment), that the prostration of health and strength which forced me, in the spring of last year [1856], to quit India and relinquish an honourable and lucrative appointment, has rendered quiet and repose absolutely necessary to me.[4]

Major-General Tucker was 49 when he married; Harriet Maria Johnson was between 34 and 35. Their first child, Florence, was born at Niton, Isle of Wight, on 6 August 1858. Florence Tucker was still alive, and unmarried, when the Major-General made his last will in August 1889; that is all I have been able to discover about her. It seems reasonable to assume that the Tuckers remained on the Isle of Wight until some time after the birth of Olivia in March 1863, but this is by no means certain. Their third and last child, Henry Tudor Tucker, was born at Wharton Grange, Framfield, Sussex, on 7 March 1866. The Major-General was then 58; Harriet Maria was between 45 and 46. The Tuckers had left Framfield by 1871 at the latest. It is probable that they lived in a series of substantial country houses taken on short leases, given that the three children were born in three different houses.

In 1878, the Tuckers moved to London, where they leased a house (now demolished) at 3 Leinster Gardens, Bayswater. Florence was then twenty, and the search for an eligible husband was presumably under way. In 1881 they moved to 51 Gloucester Gardens, Hyde Park, and this became the family home until Harriet Maria's death in 1900.

Unless a cache of family papers is discovered, these few facts, augmented by a full list of addresses for the years 1863–77, must provide the basis for any reconstruction of Olivia Shakespear's early life. Much can be inferred from general social history. The Major-General was, as will be seen, a wealthy man. In the absence of further material, we could assume that the Tuckers lived the country-house life of well-to-do, conservative, unintellectual (though not uneducated) people of their day. But there is further material, of a kind. Olivia Shakespear published six novels between 1894 and 1910, together with the substantial short story, "Beauty's Hour", which appeared in two parts in *The Savoy* for August and September 1896.[5]

It is not part of my purpose here to undertake a critical study of Olivia Shakespear's work. The novels have never been reprinted. They are unpretentious, strangely naive in some respects, simply and elegantly written; well worth reading for their own sake. Two things, however, must surely strike any reader in search of biographical illumination. Firstly, the novels are not directly autobiographical. There is an element of *roman-à-clef* in *Rupert Armstrong* (1898). (Rupert Armstrong is a once gifted painter who has betrayed his talent in order to make money. His daughter Agatha, the narrator, engages in a struggle with her conventional and feckless mother for possession of Rupert's artistic soul). The poet "John Mordaunt" has certain mannerisms in common with Lionel Johnson; the down-and-out painter "Isaac Isaacson", ("a drunkard who will inherit the Kingdom of Heaven," as John Mordaunt describes him) resembles Simeon Solomon (*Au* 168). Maurice Wootton, one of the central characters, a painter who has had to abandon his art because his right arm is paralysed, has an old brown velveteen coat like MacGregor Mathers' (*Au* 182). Maurice's study contains a Crivelli, a Calvert pastoral, an unfinished head of Leonardo, and "the head of a Rossetti's inscrutable Assyrian goddess" (p. 47): objects with strong Yeatsian associations. His circle of friends includes the following:

> Harry Yorke, the painter; Guillaume D'Avarre [cf. Henry Davray, an early translator of Yeats], a young French critic and poet, whose upstanding hair gave to my unaccustomed eyes an impression of abiding terror; John Mordaunt, a writer of verse, whose first book, dedicated "To my dear friend Maurice Wootton," had been remarkable enough to excite my grandfather's ardent disapproval; and lastly, one of those long-eyed, pale-brown Hindoos, whose society . . . set me dreaming of ivory-coloured palaces . . . (p. 51)

This promising field of reference is, however, as close as we come to any direct treatment of "the tragic generation". There is no character resembling W. B. Yeats anywhere in Olivia Shakespear's fiction. No episode corresponding to their relationship as it developed during the years 1894–97 is to be found. Families with an Indian Army background appear, but the background is vague and generalised. There is no mother/daughter relationship corresponding to the close and affectionate relationship between Olivia Shakespear and her daughter Dorothy.

But to have said this much only makes the second point more striking. No reader could, I think, fail to be struck by certain recurrent motifs: the child brought up in isolation from the parents by a benevolent aunt or guardian; the passion (usually disastrous) of a young woman for a much older man; the heroine's characteristic lack of interest in men of her own age, who are often presented as either empty-headed or sexless, and sometimes both; the beautiful but destructive mother who abandons or destroys her children and/or her husband; the child obsessed with and psychologically enslaved to the parent of the opposite sex. This cluster of linked motifs occurs so often that some basis in experience seems overwhelmingly probable. But in the absence of further biographical material, the nature and status of the experience must remain undefined.

A letter from W. B. Yeats to Olivia Shakespear shortly after her mother's death on 14 May 1900 confirms the impression that the novels are not directly autobiographical. The theme of the "bad mother" in *Rupert Armstrong*, *The Devotees*, and *Uncle Hilary* is too striking to ignore. But, at the end of a very moving letter of condolence, Yeats says:

I sympathise with you very deeply, for I know that you cared for nobody else as for your mother, & when a mother is near ones heart at all her loss must be the greatest of all losses.[6]

Many of Olivia Shakespear's heroines grow up at odds with their surroundings. They read extensively in a world where reading is considered slightly eccentric or even positively discouraged; they are interested in art and ideas despite the indifference of those around them. There is nearly always a much older, affectionate guardian (never a parent: the central characters are either orphaned, or cast off by their parents, at the beginning of the narrative) who provides support and security, but is powerless to stop the approaching disaster – a consuming passion for a much older man, or for a lost parent who reappears after a long absence. There are resonances with Olivia Shakespear's own situation: the advanced age of her parents; her intellectual isolation in the Tucker household; her being trapped in a loveless marriage – but, on the available evidence, no simple one-to-one correspondence between life and fiction. The novels could be described as "latent autobiography": explorations of possible rather than actual experience which is nevertheless of immediate relevance to the writer.

The novels provide the most vivid account of Olivia Shakespear's imaginative life that we are ever likely to have. But there are a few glimpses of her, during the eighteen months before her marriage, in the Winchester letters of Lionel Johnson. Writing to "B" on 15 June 1884, Johnson asks about a portrait of Shelley:

Can you tell me where I can get a portrait of him, not unworthy of his name? I have hunted all London, and can't light upon what I want. It is for a cousin who almost literally prays to Shelley, having lost all her other gods.

Writing to "C" on 29 December 1884 he says:

My miserable play is now being copied into legible MS. by the loving labour of a cousin, the only member of my family to whom I can really disclose myself: when it is finished I shall send it the round of the Publishers: by the time it returns to me like Noah's dove, my self-conceit will, let us hope, have been disillusioned.

And to "A" on 15 May 1885 he remarks:

I had a letter from a cousin lately in which she says, "you live artificially, naturally, I live in chaos." That was true: my life is a study.[7]

Johnson was eighteen at the time of this last reference. It is clear that he and Olivia Tucker were already friends; not unnaturally, as they were evidently the eccentric members of their respective families. The "chaos" in which Olivia Tucker saw herself as living remains a matter for speculation, but it produced a tangible result: her marriage to Henry Hope Shakespear in December 1885. The notice in *The Times* read as follows:

On Tuesday the 8th Dec., at Holy Trinity, Paddington, by the Rev. J. L. Evans, B.A., HENRY HOPE SHAKESPEAR, of 8 John St. Bedford Row, eldest son of the late Alexander Shakespear, of the Indian Civil Service, to Olivia, second daughter of Major-General Henry T. Tucker, C.B. of 51 Gloucester Gardens W.

Henry Hope Shakespear has always been what biographers call "a shadowy figure". Given Yeats's impression of him in *Memoirs*, it is not surprising that a vague tradition has evolved in which Henry Hope is already an old man, or even a chronic invalid, when Olivia Shakespear and Yeats first met in 1894. In fact he was 36 at the time of the marriage; 14 years older than she was. The difference in age was the same as that between Olivia Shakespear's parents.

Lieut.-Col. John Shakespear's history, *John Shakespear of Shadwell and his Descendants 1619–1931*,[8] gives the following information. Henry Hope Shakespear was born in India on 19 February 1849. He was the second child of Alexander Shakespear, born 18 July 1821 in Calcutta, and Catherine Mary Taylor, born 13 October 1827. "Aleck" and "Kate" play a considerable part in Lieut.-Col. Shakespear's account of the family's contributions to various Indian campaigns.[9] Henry Hope, however, was left in London in 1855 and brought up there, his parents having returned to India after two years' leave in England.[10] He was

educated at Harrow and Trinity Hall, Cambridge, of which he was a scholar. Became a solicitor after trying for the Indian Civil Service. He was very fond of music and played the 'cello and sang. He also was a water-colour painter and a skilful carpenter, in which capacity he did good work during the War [i.e. World War I] working in the Kensington Square depot for artificial limbs, etc.[11]

The relative social and financial standing of the Tuckers and the Shakespears deserves some comment. When Major-General Tucker died in 1896, the total value of his estate was £35,000, and there are many indications both in his will and in his controversial writings of the 1850's that his wealth was of long standing. By contrast, Alexander Shakespear, who died on 5 July 1884, left a total of £7900, to be divided among the five surviving children after his wife's death.[12] The Tuckers, in their move to

London in 1878, immediately established themselves at a fashionable address. Henry Hope Shakespear, in the same year, was living at 12 Cambridge Terrace, Edgeware, listed in Kelly's street directory as "Lowe Miss Sarah lodging house" until 1880, whereafter Henry Hope is listed alongside Miss Lowe as a separate occupant until 1885.

He was, in 1885, a partner in a firm of solicitors: Lambert, Petch and Shakespear, at 8 John St. Bedford Row.[13] His prospects were secure but unexciting. Olivia would undoubtedly have provided a considerable dowry; she could also expect to inherit (and in 1900 did inherit) one third of the proceeds of a trust fund in which £35,000 was invested. She and Henry Hope set up house at 18 Porchester Square, Bayswater, only a few minutes' walk from the Tucker establishment in Gloucester Gardens.

The inference is inescapable. Henry Hope was not only marrying a beautiful, intelligent and cultivated girl fourteen years younger than himself; he was also marrying money. His motives for marrying Olivia seem obvious in all respects; hers, in marrying him, remain obscure. The Indian background of distinguished service on the part of both families provided a kind of equality which might, in the eyes of the Tuckers, have overriden the financial difference. Florence Tucker, at the time of the marriage, was 27 and still unmarried. Presumably the Major-General, and perhaps still more Harriet Maria, were relieved to see at least their younger daughter married off to someone who was, in their terms, a safe and solid prospect.

Yet the marriage failed immediately. "He ceased to pay court to me from the day of our marriage," Yeats reports Olivia Shakespear as saying to him (*Mem* 87–8). Dorothy Shakespear was born on 14 September 1886; there were no other children. Taken literally, Olivia Shakespear's words imply that the marriage was "white" within days of its having begun, and everything in Yeats's account reinforces this reading. But in one of her few published letters to Yeats, dated London, 14 April 1929, there is a reference to a miscarriage. She is speaking of Omar Pound:

> Omar is well & jolly. . . . He reminds me oddly of *Hope* in many ways – I read somewhere that a grandson is often a re-incarnation of the grandfather! Do you think there can be anything in this? My own impression (*now don't repeat this*) is that he is the child I didn't have, because of a miscarriage. That child was re-incarnated in a cat – which I really *loved*, & it loved me – and now Omar is another try at incarnation of the same soul. Needless to say these theories have not been imparted to the Pounds! (*LTWBY* 495)

This passage will bear at least two interpretations, the obvious one being that the child who miscarried was Henry Hope's. But there is a slight change of direction which allows an alternative reading in which the child was by another man. It would be futile to push the matter any further. In any case, the question is academic. Olivia Shakespear married Henry Hope, and discovered more or less immediately that he did not love her. He was, on every indication, a dull and lifeless man, prematurely old, basically indifferent to her. Here the evidence of the novels is both indirect and unmistakable. Every one of them deals in some way or other with the plight of a woman trapped in a loveless marriage. The situation is inhabited from every possible angle: the woman's, the man's, the outside observer's, the child's. The novels are imaginative projections of various forms of escape – and of the price of escape. And in every case but one (Clare and Maurice in *Rupert Armstrong*), the price is too high. The melancholy conclusion is that there is, in the world of late Victorian middle-class society, no escape for the woman who has married the wrong man. The only solution is a wry, philosophic resignation.

The exception proves the rule. Clare, in *Rupert Armstrong*, is in love with her tutor, Maurice Wootton, who also loves her. Agatha, the narrator, sees this clearly. But Maurice (who is twenty-three years older than Clare) does not declare himself, believing that he cannot make her happy and does not deserve her. In despair she marries Sir Lewis Wentworth, a jealous character (also much older than she is) with "an exceedingly tiresome passion" for her, as she remarks to Agatha. In the end Clare does leave him and goes to live with Maurice in the only enduring happy sexual relationship in the whole *ouevre*. Agatha comments: "Clare had no child; if she had had a child, she would have had to stay" (p. 251).

Rosalind, the heroine of the last novel, *Uncle Hilary* (1910), is a quiet, studious girl who falls in love with a much older Colonel Henry from India. She marries the Colonel, only to discover that he is in fact her stepfather, and that her mother is still alive, so that the marriage is not only bigamous, but also within the prohibited degrees. She leaves him immediately, discovers that she is pregnant, and goes through a form of marriage in name only with her benevolent old guardian, Uncle Hilary. Later, compelled by her feeling for Colonel Henry, she returns to him, only to discover that their passion burns itself out. She therefore resolves to leave him once again, and to return to her guardian:

She smiled to herself, as her thoughts unravelled themselves; seeing man as the eternal child; woman, in her ultimate relations with him, as the eternal mother. She would have found it hard to define her actual feelings towards Colonel Henry. She had loved him, and she would never love any other man; she had given herself to him, wholly; to find the gift was one no man really desires. She had recovered possession of herself, as it were, and could look on him now with tranquil eyes, unmoved by passion. Perhaps love, stripped of its glamour, was nothing but a matter of the senses, which are in women especially, immensely subtle and capable of turning the intellect and the emotions to their own uses. (pp. 295–6)

This is, in essence, the final statement of Olivia Shakespear's fiction, and it corresponds, on all the available indications, to the solution she accepted in life. She stayed with Henry Hope. There are many ways of making the best of things; she did so with humorous resignation and generosity, by turning her attention outwards and away from herself. Yeats's end of their extensive later correspondence, together with those few of her letters so far published, provides strong and obvious testimony here. It is a tribute to her natural warmth and lack of egocentricity that she remained so clearly unembittered. The novels speak, though indirectly, of the cost. But "indirectly" is the word. The older men who cause so much havoc are not Henry Hope; they are simply too energetic, too involved in the action, to correspond to the inert figure we glimpse from time to time on the sidelines of her life.

Much can be inferred, from the novels together with Yeats's account in *Memoirs*, about the early years of Olivia Shakespear's marriage, but the next recorded reference is in a letter from Ernest Dowson to Arthur Moore, dated 19 September 1890:

I went up & had "five o'clocque" with Missy, this afternoon: she was very charming: with much regret I had to refuse an invitation to a like ceremony at Mrs Shakespeare's [*sic*] yesterday (Johnson's beautiful cousin with filia pulchriore).[14]

This suggests that Olivia Shakespear had already established the pattern of her outward life in Kensington: that of the hostess who provided a salon for artists, writers and musicians of all persuasions.[15] Yeats's impression remains vivid:

She had profound culture, a knowledge of French, English, and Italian literature, and seemed always at leisure. Her nature was gentle and contemplative, and she was content, it seems, to have no more of life than leisure and the talk of her friends. Her husband, whom I saw but once, was much older and seemed a little heavy, a little without life. As yet I did not know how utterly estranged they were. (*Mem* 74)

This brings us up to the time covered by Yeats's *Memoirs*.[16] Yeats first saw Olivia Shakespear sitting opposite him between two distinguished novelists, at "a literary dinner where there were some fifty or sixty guests":[17]

Her face had a perfectly Greek regularity, though her skin was a little darker than a Greek's would have been and her hair was very dark.

She was exquisitely dressed with what seemed to me very old lace over her breast, and had the same sensitive look of distinction I had admired in Eva Gore-Booth. She was, it seemed, about my own age, but suggested to me an incomparable distinction. I was not introduced to her, but found that she was related to a member of the Rhymers' Club and had asked my name (*Mem* 72).

The conventional photograph which appears in the Wade edition of the letters and in other places gives little idea of Olivia Shakespear's appearance at this time; the photograph which appeared in *The Literary Yearbook* for 1897 (Frontispiece), makes Yeats's remarks far more vivid. Many years later, he came upon this photograph again:

> I came upon two early photographs of you yesterday, while going through my file – one that from *Literary Year Book*. Who ever had a like profile? —— A profile from a Sicilian coin. One looks back to one's youth as to [a] cup that a mad man dying of thirst left half tasted. I wonder if you feel like that (*L* 721).

In 1894, writes Ian Fletcher,

> Johnson performed another decisive introduction. He was much attracted to a beautiful, intelligent and not too happily married cousin, Olivia Shakespear. . . . A note survives in a long, rather excited hand, inviting Yeats to call on Mrs Shakespear.[18]

This is presumably the letter referred to by Denis Donoghue:

> A letter, undated but franked 30 May 1894, from Johnson to Yeats has a note added: "I shall be so glad to see you – Olivia Shakespear." (*Mem* 74n)

During January and February of 1894, Yeats was at work on *The Land of Heart's Desire*, which opened in London on 29 March 1894:

> When I went to see her she said, "So-and-so[19] seemed disinclined to introduce us; after I saw your play I made up my mind to write to you if [I] could not meet you otherwise" (*Mem* 74).

In the light of all this it is reasonable to date their first conversation, which took place at Porchester Square, in early June 1894. Yeats was, as usual, eager to pour out his trouble to a sympathetic confidant: "I told her of my love sorrow, indeed it was my obsession, never leaving by day or night" (*Mem* 74).[20] Olivia Shakespear, therefore, knew about Maud Gonne from the beginning. This may, paradoxically, have contributed to her attraction to Yeats; we may contrast the impoverished poet, celibate in the cause of unrequited love, with the empty-headed men about town who are treated satirically in several of the novels. His devotion to Maud Gonne must have seemed, to her, both moving and somehow unreal, a remote ideal rather than an actual force in his existence.

Olivia Shakespear's first novel, *Love on a Mortal Lease*, was published by Osgood & McIlvaine in June 1894. Yeats, writing to her on 6 August 1894, refers to *The Journey of High Honour*, though the novel was not published until November.[21] He also refers to "Beauty's Hour", which was by then virtually complete (though not published for another two years), offering suggestions for the occult reading of old Dr. Trefusis, the narrator Mary's confidant. Yeats in this letter looks forward to seeing Olivia Shakespear in September; to judge from the postscript she had been confined by illness (*L* 233–5). It is not yet possible to establish when she began writing seriously, but she was certainly in the middle of her most intense and productive phase when Yeats first met her. Intense imaginative activity often prefigures or accompanies some upheaval in outward life; in her case it seems reasonable to assume some relation between her writing and an increasing sense of crisis about her life with Henry Hope Shakespear. To say this is not merely to argue backwards from the fact of her relationship with Yeats, but to introduce a point which will be expanded later – that it was she who took the initiative in developing that relationship.

On 24 August 1894, Jack B. Yeats married. Biographers tend to pass over this event in silence, and yet it must have been of some significance to Yeats, "tortured by sexual desire" (*Mem* 71), nearing thirty, and still living at home. Whether he saw Olivia Shakespear in September 1894 we do not know; by October 11 he was in Dublin, on his way to spend six months with George Pollexfen in Sligo. He remained at Sligo until at least 3 May 1895; by 19 May he was back at Blenheim Road:

> I had received while at Sligo many letters from Diana Vernon,[22] kind letters that gave me a sense of half-conscious excitement. I remember after one such letter asking some country woman to throw the tea leaves for me and my disappointment at the vagueness of the oracle. . . . She was to tell me later on that my letters were unconscious love-letters, and I was taken by surprise at the description . . . (*Mem* 85).

Most of the letters referred to here seem to have been lost; in all probability Yeats destroyed some of them himself.[23] The five surviving letters from Yeats[24] certainly illustrate both the diagnosis and the reaction:

In a letter some time ago you said I complained that you wrote too exclusively of love. I did not mean to. I meant that the parts of your books which were not about love were not carefully studied enough, were not salient enough. I no more complain of your writing of love, than I would complain of a portrait painter keeping to portraits. I would complain however if his backgrounds were too slightly imagined for the scheme of his art. I have never come upon any new work so full of a kind of tremulous delicacy, so full of a kind of fragile beauty, as these books of yours however (*L* 257).

Yeats's comments are at once acute and interested (in both senses of the word). The impression left by his letters and the comment in *Memoirs* is of one slowly awakening from self-absorption ("youth's dreamy load") into "half-conscious excitement". But it was Olivia Shakespear who took the initiative:

I do not know how long after my return the conversation that was to decide so much of my life took place. I had found the Rhymer who had introduced me under the influence of drink, speaking vaguely and with vague movements, and while we were speaking this recent memory came back. She spoke of her pagan life in a way that made me believe that she had had many lovers and loathed her life. I thought of that young man so nearly related. Here is the same weakness, I thought; two souls so distinguished and contemplative that the common world seems empty. What is there left but sanctity, or some satisfying affection, or mere dissipation? – "Folly the comforter," some Elizabethan had called it. Her beauty, dark and still, had the nobility of defeated things, and how could it help but wring my heart? I took a fortnight to decide what I should do (*Mem* 85).

This is one of those crucial passages in Yeats's autobiographical writings which any biographer must confront. It is very much in the language of *Per Amica Silentia Lunae*: Olivia Shakespear auditioning for the part of tragic artist. The idiom of 1916 partly obscures the confusions of 1895; neither can be ignored. Yeats was either not listening very carefully to what Olivia Shakespear was saying, or else through sheer inexperience took her imaginatively "pagan" life (witness the world of the novels) to be her actual experience. Yet the impression she made upon him was profound, and remained vivid twenty years later. It is clear that she declared her love for him, and her despair over the sterile existence she had lived for almost ten years. She was the lover; Yeats the somewhat bewildered and yet deeply affected beloved.

Since this story has only been retold by Yeats scholars, from a Yeats-centred point of view, it is worth highlighting some of the implications. Olivia Shakespear had fallen in love with a penniless thirty-year-old Irish poet, a virgin with an idealised passion for "the most beautiful woman in the world". One might say that she loved him in spite of these disadvantages, but it would be truer, I think, to say that they contributed to her feeling for him.

The situation in which she thus found herself is explored in several of her novels. If she left Henry Hope, she would automatically lose custody of her daughter; if he chose to sue for divorce he could have claimed, and won, damages that would have ruined Yeats.[25] She must have been very confident that this would not happen. Henry Hope seems to have been an indifferent rather than a jealous husband; nevertheless, the risks were real. The Major-General was still alive, and might well have refused support in the event of a scandal.

Yeats was aware of the economic implications, at least:

I was poor and it would be a hard struggle if I asked her [to] come away, and perhaps after all I would but add my tragedy to hers, for she might return to that evil life. But, after all, if I could not get the woman I loved, it would be a comfort even for a little while to devote myself to another. No doubt my excited senses had their share in the argument, but it was an unconscious one. At the end of the fortnight I asked her to leave home with me. She became very gay and joyous and a few days later praised me [for] what she thought my beautiful tact in giving at that moment but a brother's kiss. Doubtless at the moment I was exalted above the senses, and yet I do not [think] I knew any better way of kissing, for when on our first railway journey together – we were to spend the day at Kew – she gave me the long passionate kiss of love I was startled and a little shocked (*Mem* 85–6).

The three-sided struggle between the obsession with a phantasmal Maud Gonne, a real if awkward beginning with an actual Olivia Shakespear (still very imperfectly known), and what might be called a typical young male Irish view of sexuality, is acted out sentence by sentence. The callous "if I can't have Maud I'll make do with Olivia – for a while" is set against the disturbing entry into the world of actual sexual experience – unknown territory.

Presently I told something of my thoughts during that fortnight, and she [was] perplexed and ashamed that I should have had such imagination of her. Her wickedness had never gone further than her own mind; I would be her first lover. We decided that we should be but friends till she could leave her home for mine, but agreed to wait until her mother, a very old woman, had died (*Mem* 86).

Harriet Maria Tucker was then between 72 and 73; it would have been a long wait.

It is fair to assume that Yeats's own fears and uncertainties played a considerable part in this decision. In the debate about escaping from disastrous marriages that recurs in Olivia Shakespear's fiction, the point is made that the woman is free to leave if she has no children and no close relatives likely to be distressed by the separation. In life she was faced with both obstacles; that she was prepared to leave at all is an indication of the strength of her feeling for Yeats – and of her despair over her marriage. It should be said that if all she sought was sexual gratification, there was a well-established code whereby affairs were tolerated (and to a considerable extent encouraged), provided they were conducted discreetly.

We decided to consult each a woman friend that we might be kept to these resolutions, as sponsors of our adventure, and for nearly a year met in railway carriages and at picture galleries and occasionally at her house . . . (*Mem* 86).

The sponsors of this somewhat curious arrangement have not yet been identified. Florence Farr seems one likely candidate. She was extremely tolerant in sexual matters, reserving her severity for the proper conduct of the rituals of the Golden Dawn.[26] Since the decisive conversation between Yeats and Olivia Shakespear took place no earlier than June 1895, the time described as "nearly a year" must have been less than nine months. Doubtless it seemed longer.

I wrote her several poems, all curiously elaborate in style . . . and thought I was once more in love. I noticed that she was like the mild heroines of my plays. She seemed a part of myself (*Mem* 86).

In this passage we see Yeats's image of Olivia Shakespear hovering on the boundary between the inner and the outer world. The word "noticed" is equivocal in its direction; here it means something like "unconsciously attempted to see her as". And which "mild heroines"? Certainly not the Countess Cathleen. Mary in *The Land of Heart's Desire* is a possible but strangely inappropriate reference. Though Dectora in *The Shadowy Waters* is far from mild, the image of the net of hair, which appears in the poems written to Olivia Shakespear in *The Wind Among the Reeds*, is also to be found in *The Shadowy Waters*.[27]

The dialectical play of image and reality is at the centre of Yeats's thought; at this stage of his career the two are so widely separated that it is often difficult to discern any transaction between them. To trace the influence of Olivia Shakespear on the iconography of *The Wind Among the Reeds* is a task which requires another essay with a different focus. In my judgement she is a far more significant presence in the lyrics than most critics have been willing to admit. But the traffic between image and reality is not one-way, and this is the great challenge, or test, which confronts any biographer of Yeats. It is often possible to follow the process by which life is transformed in the work. Here we have a glimpse of the opposite process: the images evolved through long meditation exerting pressure on Yeats's experience.

> I noticed that she did not talk so well as when I had first known her, her mind seemed more burdened, but she would show in her movements an unforseen youth; she seemed to have gone back to her twentieth year (*Mem* 86).

Yeats's whole account of their relationship is an extraordinary mixture (or perhaps uneasy alliance) of insight, wry comedy, naiveté, and blindness. It is not surprising that her mind seemed burdened. She must have wondered when this slow-moving courtship was going to gather momentum.

The chronology of events is perhaps inevitably vague; we can assume that most of Yeats's narrative so far relates to the summer of 1895. On 3 September 1895, Olivia Shakespear visited the Yeats family at Blenheim Road, and was described by Lily Yeats as "Willy's latest admiration, very pretty, young, and nice."[28] By 4 October 1895, Yeats had moved into Fountain Court with Arthur Symons; Lily recorded her displeasure in her diary.[29] Some time between October 1895 and February 1896, the disastrous tea at Fountain Court occurred, when Yeats managed to lock out himself, Olivia Shakespear and her sponsor while going to buy cake. Whether or not he was thinking of Maud Gonne at the time depends on whether one reads "Maud Gonne' or "three in the afternoon" at a key point in the manuscript. By 3 March 1896 he was writing to W. T. Horton from Woburn Buildings, though in all probability he moved in gradually over a period of a week or two, bringing furniture purchased from Symons' charlady and eventually the bed, purchased jointly with considerable embarrassment in Tottenham Court Road: "every inch increased the expense."[30]

Whether or not Maud Gonne was responsible for the lockout, she became an increasingly powerful force in Yeats's imagination as his relationship with Olivia Shakespear developed. Symons had called on Olivia Shakespear, not knowing her relation to Yeats, and "came back with her praises" (*Mem* 86). On the night of the lockout, Yeats sat up with Symons, and spoke of his love for Maud Gonne until two or three in the morning. Richard Ellmann comments on this episode: "With Maud Gonne never far from his mind, he must have had a strong half-conscious repulsion to the elopement."[31] But Yeats's long conversation with Symons can also be seen as an attempt at exorcism, a way of confronting the phantasm blocking the way forward to an actual relationship with Olivia Shakespear.

The word "phantasm" implies no judgement whatever of Maud Gonne; it is rather a judgement of her role in Yeats's emotional life. He had endowed her with superhuman attributes, and in doing so created a barrier between himself and any actual sexual relationship.[32] Attempts to deal with Yeats's psychological and imaginative makeup tend to become hopelessly reductive when they are not hopelessly theoretical.[33] But in this particular case, the image of Maud Gonne seems to have kept him bowed beneath "youth's dreamy load," whereas his relationship with Olivia Shakespear drew him forward, away from the emotional cul-de-sac of his obsession. The poem "Friends" unambiguously acknowledges his gratitude to Olivia Shakespear; equally, though more ambiguously, it insists on the importance of Maud Gonne.[34] All one can say here is that biography (and criticism) must confront the importance of both women in his life while recognising the utter unlikeness of the forces that, in Yeats's own terms, they embodied.

In the midst of this inner turmoil, Yeats was finally brought up to the mark:

> Presently I was asked to call and see my friend's sponsor. She condemned our idea of going away from home. . . . My sponsor came to see me and used the same arguments, and both, people of the world, advised us to live together without more ado. Then Diana Vernon tried to get a separation from the husband who had for her, she believed, aversion or indifference. "He ceased to pay court to me from the day of our marriage," she had said. He was deeply distressed and became ill, and she gave up the project and said to me, "It will be kinder to deceive him." Our senses were engaged now, and though we spoke of parting it was but to declare it impossible (*Mem* 88).

The arguments of the sponsors are somewhat contradictory, unless "live together" is read as sexual euphemism. It is again easy to overlook the strength of Olivia Shakespear's desire to be free of Henry Hope; Yeats's reluctance to take decisive action is also apparent. This is the only recorded occasion on which Henry Hope seems to have succeeded in surprising anyone.[35]

> At last she came to me in I think January of my thirtieth year, and I was impotent from nervous excitement. The next day we met at the British Museum – we were studying together – and I wondered that there seemed no change in me or in her. A week later she came to me again, and my nervous excitement was so painful that it seemed best but to sit over our tea and talk. I do not think we kissed each other except at the moment of her leaving. She understood instead of, as another would, changing liking for dislike – was only troubled by my

trouble. My nervousness did not return again and we had many days of happiness (*Mem* 88).

There is a finality about the last sentence which is strangely at odds with the elaborate explanation that follows:

> It will always be a grief to me that I could not give her the love that was her beauty's right, but she was too near my soul, too salutary and wholesome to my inmost being. All our lives long, as da Vinci says, we long, thinking it is but the moon that we long [for], for our destruction, and how, when we meet [it] in the shape of a most fair woman, can we do less than leave all others for her? Do we not seek our dissolution upon her lips? (*Mem* 88)

The da Vinci passage is one that resonates throughout Yeats's work. And yet I cannot see these remarks as other than equivocal. "I could not give her the love that was her beauty's right": that is the sad, but inescapable fact which seems to emerge. But in Yeats's own terms, the argument that he could not love her because she was too near to his soul is contradictory. His appeal to the power of *La Belle Dame sans Merci* strikes me as unconvincing. Yeats was hardly a paid-up member of the cult of dissipation and despair: his treatment of Maud Gonne is coloured, rather than governed, by the image of *la belle dame* in its fin-de-siècle form. His attempt at rationalisation on this level is something which itself requires explanation.

On the simplest level, we might say that he felt badly about the way in which his affair with Olivia Shakespear had ended, taking the straight-forward view that it ended because of his obsession with Maud Gonne. This, so far as it goes, is undoubtedly true. But it also appears that he had at last entered into a sexually fulfilling relationship, only to discover that this was not what he wanted. Yeats's explanation, in my view, only confronts us with his uncertainty about what he *did* want.

Something like the same pattern is repeated twenty years later in the events surrounding his marriage. Yeats, during the first few days of his honeymoon, was deeply unhappy, feeling that he had "betrayed three people" because of his attachment to Iseult Gonne. In this case, disaster was averted by George Yeats's mobilisation of the spirit world (*L* 633–4). Whether Olivia Shakespear could have achieved similar results in 1897 remains a matter for speculation. But in both cases it seems that an actual sexual relationship was threatened (and in one case destroyed) by something which cannot wholly be described in sexual terms.

All of this touches on larger questions. Yeats's repeated expressions of regret for his unspent youth, and indeed his tragi-comic, sometimes farcical attempts at compensation in his last decade, cannot be explained solely in terms of his barren passion for Maud Gonne. The awareness of what he had had, and lost, is equally part of that regret. In my judgement his "explanation" of the end of his affair with Olivia Shakespear is an attempt, twenty years later, to rewrite history in order to make it more bearable. In saying this I can appeal once more to his letter to her in December 1926:

> One looks back to one's youth as to [a] cup that a mad man dying of thirst left half tasted. I wonder if you feel like that.

The last sentence is half apologetic and yet close to unconscious cruelty, given the way their affair actually ended. The phantasm won; the reality lost; probably by March 1897 at the latest; Maud Gonne was by then back in London trying to raise funds for the Wolf Tone memorial project. Yeats had spent December and early January in Paris.

> Then Maud Gonne wrote to me; she was in London and would I come to dine? I dined with her and my trouble increased – she certainly had no thought of the mischief she was doing. And at last one morning instead of reading much love poetry, as my way was to bring the right mood round, I wrote letters. My friend found my mood did not answer hers and burst into tears. "There is someone else in your heart," she said. It was the breaking between us for many years (*Mem* 89).

Such was Yeats's perspective in 1916. But the following extract from the manuscripts of *The Speckled Bird* provides a disturbing comparison:

> He longed to live without strain, and said he thought that if he were to live with some woman whom he liked, he would begin to think of that great question of [BLANK]. He felt incapable of giving anyone any strong emotion and he did not wish to simulate what he had not. He knew that he had not even a shadow of love for this new friend, but this in itself attracted him to her; he would not put what he was quite determined could always be no more than a shadow in the place of a substance. This woman seemed so friendly and unexacting that he thought she would understand and demand nothing that he could not give and besides she had [BLANK]. Gradually they became closer and closer to one another, and after a time she became his mistress. This went on for two or three years, then they began to gradually drift apart. She began to seem unhappy, and he found it more and more difficult to reconcile this new relationship with the old unaltered feelings. Then, one day [she] told [him] with tears that [she] saw that she had failed to be anything to him and then [he] tried to convince her she was wrong. Their relations came to an end, and he found their coming to an end was a relief to his mind.[36]

This might be read as starker and more honest, but it strikes me as an even cruder form of rationalisation: an effort to minimise the significance of his relation to Olivia Shakespear, and to rewrite history so as to be able to say that he had never wavered in his devotion to Maud Gonne. But, in Yeats's defence, we must remember that he was attempting to write fiction. Apart from the letter of 1926, the simplest and most moving postscript is "The Lover mourns for the Loss of Love":

> Pale brows, still hands and dim hair,
> I had a beautiful friend
> And dreamed that the old despair
> Would end in love in the end:
> She looked in my heart one day
> And saw your image was there;
> She has gone weeping away (*VP* 152).

On 6 August 1896, shortly after Yeats's departure for Tillyra Castle, Major-General Tucker died at the age of 88. Harriet Maria Tucker lived on at Gloucester Gardens for another four years; she died on 14 May 1900 at Lyndhurst, Hants. Yeats's letter of condolence to Olivia Shakespear, quoted earlier, was probably the first contact between them since the breaking of their relationship early in 1897. Yeats himself left Woburn Buildings for Sligo in May 1897, and did not return until November. His first visit to Coole Park took place in August or September 1896: "I was never before or since so miserable as in those years that followed my first visit to Coole" (*Mem* 125).

It would be possible, given Olivia Shakespear's involvement in London literary life and the many letters written by Yeats to her in later years, to compile a fairly detailed diary of her activities in the years after 1900. But it is not my purpose to do so here. The outward facts can be briefly told. The Shakespears remained at Porchester Square until 1900, when, according to Noel Stock, they "had to move to something simpler when a partner in an earlier form absconded". "Dorothy Shakespear returned from boarding school to find they were living at 12 Brunswick Gardens." [37] She must have been away a long time, in that case, because the move in 1900 was to Pembridge Mansions, Moscow Road, Bayswater, where they remained until they moved to Brunswick Gardens in 1906. Lambert, Petch and Shakespear, the firm in which Henry Hope was first established, was dissolved in 1890; it seems unlikely that the financial consequences of any dereliction would have taken ten years to make themselves felt. Henry Hope, throughout the 1890's, is listed as being in practice on his own.

Richard Ellmann says that the affair between Yeats and Olivia Shakespear was resumed in 1903 (*MM*, p. 182). Presumably his authority for this was George Yeats. If he is correct, it is further evidence of Olivia Shakespear's generous nature, given that the occasion would have been Maud Gonne's marriage in February of that year. Certainly they were in regular correspondence again by 1904, when Yeats wrote to tell her how much he had enjoyed *The Devotees*[38] (Plate 8a).

Yeats's biographers have not, I think, made clear the fact Yeats would in all probability never have met George Hyde-Lees if it were not for Olivia Shakespear. All that is generally known at present is that George Yeats's mother married Olivia Shakespear's brother, and that Yeats was first introduced in the winter of 1911–1912 (*MM*, p. 222, *L* 632n). The story can be supplemented as follows.

Henry Tudor Tucker (known to the family as Harry) lived with his mother at 51 Gloucester Gardens until her death in May 1900. She left her entire estate (approximately £1800) to him. But at the same time he inherited one third of the income from the Major-General's £35,000 trust fund. He would have been well provided for even before this, and with his inheritance need never have worked for a living. So far as I know, he never did. He seems to have lived an itinerant life, moving around various seaside resorts, until at the age of 44 he married Edith Ellen Hyde-Lees on 1 February 1911, at a civil ceremony in St. George's, Hanover Square. The witnesses were Olivia and Dorothy Shakespear; the marriage was not advertised in *The Times*.

Edith Ellen Hyde-Lees was born Edith Ellen Woodmass, daughter of Montagu Woodmass, a manufacturer. She was 21 at the time of her first marriage to William Gilbert Hyde-Lees, on 19 December 1889 in Stockport, Chester. Their son, Harold Montagu, was born on 24 November 1890 at 40 Montpelier Road, Brighton; his father's occupation is given on the birth certificate as "Captain (Militia)". Bertha George Hyde-Lees was born in October 1892 at Hartley, near Wrexham in North Wales.

George Yeats's cousin, Grace Jaffe, provides a good deal of family background in her autobiography, *Years of Grace*. According to Mrs Jaffe, Edith Ellen Hyde-Lees quarrelled irrevocably with her mother, Edith Woodmass, shortly after her marriage to Gilbert Hyde-Lees.[39] The marriage lasted only a few years. Gilbert Hyde-Lees was regarded by Mrs Jaffe's parents as "a most undesirable character, but 'rolling in money' " (*YG*, p. 15). After the separation, George Hyde-Lees and her mother spent a good deal of their time travelling in Europe, presumably funded by the undesirable Gilbert, who died in Wimbledon on 18 November 1909, aged 45, leaving effects to the value of £845. The estate was then divided between the two children and one Arthur Tolfrey Christie of Fulham. Mrs Hyde-Lees is nowhere mentioned in the will. The following extract is of some interest:

I bequeath to my son Harold Montagu Hyde Lees all my jewellery family portraits and any of my books he may choose also my cabinet made out of the boat in which I rowed for Wadham College Oxford and all my private papers which papers I require him to keep in a place of absolute safety.

Edith Ellen Hyde-Lees ("Effie", as she was known to the Yeats family), married Henry Tudor Tucker fourteen months later. Mrs Jaffe, who describes Harry Tucker as an art collector, says that he suffered a serious mental breakdown late in life:

> He had always, I think, been a very shy, withdrawn man, and he lost his mental faculties not very long after I met him in Sidmouth [in the summer of 1934]. According to my Cousin Harold's gossipy account, he ended up in a mental hospital, where he distinguished himself by refusing to wear any clothes, and received visitors in a state of total nakedness. (*YG*, p. 120)

This might also be described as a last act of rebellion after a lifetime of conformity. He was still sufficiently in possession of his faculties to make a will on 11 November 1938. Harry Tucker died at Torquay on 15 September 1943. His estate amounted to £24,000 and was set up as a trust fund, the proceeds of which went first to his wife, then to Dorothy Pound, and eventually to Omar Pound. He also left Dorothy Pound a painting by Charles Conder, "The Bathers".

Henry Hope Shakespear died on 5 July 1923, leaving an estate amounting to £16,670, all of which went unconditionally to Olivia Shakespear. Six weeks later she made her last will. She left £10,000 in trust for Dorothy Pound, without power of anticipation, and £6000 in trust to Harry Tucker, which went to Dorothy Pound on his death, the entire trust fund to go in due course to Dorothy's children. The residue also went into the trust fund. The value of the estate at the time of Olivia Shakespear's death was £23,377.

By 1925, she had moved from the house in Brunswick Square to 34 Abingdon Court, Kensington, where she spent the remaining years of her life. Omar Pound was brought to England in 1926 when only a few weeks old, and remained in her care until her death (Plate 8b). Yeats's letters to her, together with those few of her letters to him which have been published to date, provide the best available picture of her life during those years. She died suddenly at home on 3 October 1938, aged 75. It may one day be possible to write a full biography of her, and to make the novels once more available.

NOTES

I would like to thank Deirdre Toomey for contributing the afterword upon *Rupert Armstrong* and for many suggestions which have greatly improved this essay. Such errors of fact and judgement which may remain are entirely my own.

1. *The Times*, obituary for Maj.-Gen. Tucker, 10 August 1896, p. 6.
2. For further information about the Johnson family, see Ian Fletcher, *The Complete Poems of Lionel Johnson*, 2nd rev. edn (New York: Garland, 1982) pp. xxi–xxii.
3. *A Glance at the Past and the Future in Connection with the Indian Revolt*, 3rd edn (London: Effingham Wilson, 1857) p. 20.
4. *A Glance at the Past* . . . , p. 45.
5. Olivia Shakespear's novels, in order of publication, are: *Love on a Mortal Lease* (London: Osgood, McIlvaine & Co., 1894), dedicated to "John Oliver Hobbes" (Pearl Craigie); *The Journey of High Honour* (London: Osgood, McIlvaine & Co., 1894), no dedication; *The False Laurel* (London: Osgood, McIlvaine & Co., 1896), dedicated to Lionel Johnson; *Rupert Armstrong* (Harper & Bros., 1898), dedicated "To My Friend Valentine Fox"; *The Devotees* (London: Heinemann, 1904), no dedication; *Uncle Hilary* (London: Methuen, 1910), dedicated "To My Friend Frederic Eden".
6. ALS Indiana. I am grateful to John Kelly, the Trustees of the Yeats Estate, and the Oxford University Press for permission to quote from this unpublished letter. Yeats's punctuation has been retained.
7. *Some Winchester Letters of Lionel Johnson* (London: Allen & Unwin, 1919) pp. 111, 168, and 203 respectively. "A" is Frank Russell; "B" and "C" are J. H. Badley and Charles Sayle. See Ian Fletcher, *The Complete Poems of Lionel Johnson*, pp. xxvi–xxx.
8. *John Shakespear of Shadwell and his Descendants 1619–1931* (Newcastle-Upon-Tyne: Northumberland Press, 1931), issued in a limited edition of 140 copies.
9. See ch. XXI, pp. 303–11. There is a portrait of Henry Hope Shakespear's father, "Aleck", facing p. 312. For further adventures of the Shakespear family, see H. V. F. Winstone, *Captain Shakespear: A Portrait* (London: Jonathan Cape, 1976).
10. Henry Hope Shakespear was left with two of his sisters in the care of "a lady named Russell" (p. 303). The younger of the two sisters, Agnes, died at Cannes in 1870 at the age of 19.
11. *John Shakespear of Shadwell*, pp. 381–2.
12. In a codicil dated 24 April 1875, Alexander Shakespear appointed Henry Hope as one of his executors. The family estate at Holly Lodge, Burnham, Bucks., went to the fourth son, Alexander Muirson, who worked in India all his life, never married, and outlived Henry Hope, dying in 1927.
13. Henry Hope remained at these chambers throughout his working life. The partnership was dissolved in 1889; Henry Hope then went into practice on his own, and eventually became Shakespear and Parkyn. Joseph Parkyn was still alive in 1938; he was one of Henry Tudor Tucker's executors, as well as being one of Olivia Shakespear's.
14. *The Letters of Ernest Dowson*, ed. Desmond Flower and Henry Maas (London: Cassell, 1967) p. 168.
15. Apart from the inferences which may be drawn from Yeats's end of their correspondence, there is a good deal of information scattered through Noel Stock's *The Life of Ezra Pound* (London: Routledge & Kegan Paul, 1970).
16. Large sections of the first draft of Yeats's autobiography were first transcribed by A. Norman Jeffares in *W. B. Yeats: Man and Poet* (London: Routledge & Kegan Paul, 1949). See especially Jeffares' extended transcript on pp. 100–1, corresponding to *Memoirs*, pp. 72, 74, and 85–7. The variations between Jeffares and Donoghue are such as to raise the possibility that there were two closely-related but separate drafts of the material published by Donoghue as "Autobiography". Consider, for example, the following:

Donoghue (86–7): "I do not think I had asked Symons, for I went myself to buy the cake. As I came home with the parcel I began to think of Maud Gonne till my thought was interrupted by finding the door locked."

Jeffares (101): "I do not think I had asked Symons for I went myself to buy the cake when I came in about three in the afternoon I found the door shut."

17. The dinner was the inaugural dinner for *The Yellow Book*, held at the Hotel d'Italie, 16 April 1894. Arthur Waugh describes the dinner: "Mr. George Moore, with his new collaborator, John Oliver Hobbes, at his side", near him was Theo Marzials and opposite Marzials was W. B. Yeats "whose earnest, clean-shaven face gave an air of seriousness to his corner". Next to Yeats was Lionel Johnson, "looking years too young for his critical utterances" ("London Letter", *The Critic*, XXI: 637 [5 May 1894], 312).
    However, when Arthur Waugh returned to this dinner in *One Man's Road* (London: Chapman & Hall, 1931), he remembered that "Mr George Moore was gaily conspicuous, with John Oliver Hobbes and Olivia Shakespeare, [*sic*] one on either side of him, and a bottle of vintage champagne on ice" (pp. 254–5).

18. *The Complete Poems of Lionel Johnson*, p. li.

19. "So-and-so" was presumably not Johnson, who seems to have been quite eager to introduce them; probably the person at the literary dinner of whom OS enquired about WBY (who was probably Pearl Craigie).

20. Cf. Yeats's remarks about Eva Gore-Booth on the occasion of his visit to Lissadell in November/December 1894: "Eva was for a couple of happy weeks my close friend, and I told her all of my unhappiness in love; indeed so close at once that I nearly said to her, as William Blake said to Catherine Boucher, 'You pity me, there[fore] I love you' " (*Mem* 78).

21. Both internal and external evidence suggest that *The Journey of High Honour*, which is only about 30,000 words long, may have been written before *Love on a Mortal Lease*. Wade infers, naturally enough, that Yeats saw *The Journey of High Honour* in manuscript, since he mentions it in the letter of 6 August (*L* 233n). But WBY's letter to OS dated 28 November 1894 (*L* 240–1), contains a detailed statement of his views about the novel, which suggests that he read it immediately after publication. OS may simply have referred to the novel by title in one of her letters.

22. Yeats remarked, of his choice of pseudonym: "Diana Vernon sounds pleasantly to my ears and will suit her as well as any other" (*Mem* 74). Scott's heroine has "sable" hair, but pale skin (cf. "A Poet to His Beloved" and "Aedh Gives His Beloved Certain Rhymes"). Though the original Diana Vernon is temperamentally unlike Olivia Shakespear, both are intellectually isolated in their family circles: "I am in this happy family as much secluded from intelligent listeners as Sancho in the Sierra Morena, and when opportunity offers, I must speak or die" (*Rob Roy*, ch. vi [Collins edition, 1953] p. 123). Yeats must have settled on "Diana Vernon" well before he began on his memoir, since George Moore makes some malicious play with "Miss Vernon" (whom he takes to be Florence Farr) in *Ave* (1911). It seems likely that Yeats was already speaking of "Diana Vernon" in 1895–96 during his time at Fountain Court, and that Moore overheard (and misconstrued) some exchange between Yeats and Symons on the subject.

23. "After Mrs. Shakespear's death in October 1938, her son-in-law, Ezra Pound, sent back to Yeats all the letters from him which she had kept, and these unfortunately reached him while he was staying away from home, and some of them he destroyed, apparently at random" (*L* 12). One may legitimately wonder how much attention Pound devoted to his part in the operation: "Pound was briefly in London to dispose of his mother-in-law's apartment after her death, a task he accomplished in part by giving away the furniture to such friends as Lewis" (Timothy Materer, *Vortex: Pound, Eliot and Lewis* (Ithaca: Cornell University Press, 1979), p. 123).

24. 6 August 1894 (*L* 233–5); 28 November 1894 (*L* 240–1); 7 April 1895 (*L* 255–6); 12 April 1895 (*L* 256–7); 11 July 1895 (unpub).

25. The Peregrine divorce case, reported in *The Daily Telegraph* for 10 and 12 August 1896, under the title "A Military Divorce", provides a good illustration. The Peregrines were living separately; Mr Peregrine had been away on the Gold Coast for some months endeavouring to make his fortune, while Mrs Peregrine remained in an apartment in Hyde Park, where Lieut. Lillington of the 1st Hyderabad Lancers became a frequent visitor. Abandoning themselves to passion, they left for the Shendon Hydropathic Establishment in Scotland, where Lieut. Lillington was seen emerging from Mrs Peregrine's room in the early hours etc. etc.: "They would walk about the grounds together and smoke cigarettes, and the proprietor was obliged to remonstrate with them with regard to their conduct." As a result of this escapade, the absent husband got custody of the child, and Lieut. Lillington was given a fortnight in which to pay £1,000 damages.

26. Florence Farr and Olivia Shakespear collaborated in the writing of two one-act plays in 1901–2. See Josephine Johnson, *Florence Farr* (Gerrards Cross: Colin Smythe, 1975) p. 90; also *L* 372.

27. See also *Druid Craft: The Writing of* The Shadowy Waters, ed. Sidnell, Mayhew, and Clark (Amherst: Massachussetts University Press, 1971) pp. 144–5.

28. See William R. Murphy, *Prodigal Father: The Life of John Butler Yeats* (Ithaca: Cornell University Press, 1978) p. 183.

29. Murphy, pp. 184, 581.

30. This may well be the bed referred to by Yeats in his letter to Lady Gregory dated 12 March 1900: "I have measured the breadth of the wire mattress part of the bed – it is 41¼ inches" (*L* 335). Perhaps the half-inch was allowed by the salesman at no extra cost.

31. *Yeats: The Man and the Masks* (1949; Faber and Faber, 1961) p. 159. (Hereafter cited in text as *MM*.)

32. Cf. his revealing early letter to Katherine Tynan, 12.2.1888: "I have woven about me a web of thoughts . . ." (*L* 58). See also Allen R. Grossman, *Poetic Knowledge in the Early Yeats: A Study of The Wind Among the Reeds* (Charlottesville: University of Virginia Press, 1969), especially ch. ix, "The Prior Love". Grossman argues that from 1893 until 1898 at least, Yeats was actively seeking an imaginative orientation which was likely to be disastrous for any actual sexual relationship, an orientation in which "poetry is the sexual act of the impotent man" (p. 163). There is much to quarrel with in Grossman's analysis, but the main line of his argument is in this respect persuasive.

33. See, as an instance of the hopelessly reductive, Brenda S. Webster, *Yeats: a Psychoanalytic Study* (Palo Alto: Stanford University Press, 1973).

34. Jeffares' *A New Commentary on the Collected Poems of W. B. Yeats* (London: Macmillan, 1984) is clearly wrong in maintaining that it was Lady Gregory whose hand "Had strength that could unbind . . . Youth's dreamy load." The tribute makes sense only in relation to Olivia Shakespear. See p. 123.

35. Apart from Ezra Pound, who when asked how he proposed to support Dorothy Shakespear, produced a fistful of banknotes, only to be told that this was not what Henry Hope had in mind. See Noel Stock, *The Life of Ezra Pound*, p. 108.

36. W. B. Yeats, *The Speckled Bird*, ed. William H. O'Donnell (Toronto: McClelland and Stewart, 1976), p. 105. This passage, from the "final version," was probably written early in 1902. Even more unpleasant is the following, from "Outlines". Michael takes a mistress while in Paris:

> She soon begins to weary him. Hitherto he has known, with increasing intensity, the persecution of sex, but its satisfaction ends the glamour as well as the persecution for a time. He sees the poorness of his mistress' nature and dislikes [her] the more because she is devoted to him. (p. 109)

O'Donnell dates this fragment somewhere between August and December of 1896. Making every allowance for fictional displacement, it still suggests that Yeats was attempting to rationalise himself out of the affair even before it ended. One might be tempted to relate the woman described in "Authorial Notes to pages 97–114" (pp. 230–1) to Olivia Shakespear, but she is in all respects much closer to Florence Farr.

37. Stock, *The Life of Ezra Pound*, p. 60.
38. WBY to OS, July or August 1904 (*L* 436–7). *The Devotees* was published in June 1904.
39. Grace M. Jaffe, *Years of Grace* (Sunspot, New Mexico: Iroquois House, 1979), p. 4. (Hereafter abbreviated as *YG* in text.) Omar Pound and A. Walton Litz also have much useful material in their biographical appendices to *Ezra Pound and Dorothy Shakespear Their Letters: 1909–1914* (New York: New Directions, 1984).

An Afterword on *Rupert Armstrong*

Deirdre Toomey

Olivia Shakespear's novel concerns itself with the career of an artist, Rupert Armstrong, formerly one of a group of painters with a common ideology, " 'It was a kind of double art – with an inner and an outer meaning' ". The group was founded by Maurice Wootton, who subsequently ceased to paint because of an injury to his right arm. Maurice's fiancée, Eve, jilted him and eloped with his friend, Rupert Armstrong. As a consequence of marriage to her, Rupert Armstrong has become a "merely popular painter".

One does not have to read more than fifty pages of this novel to realise that it is a *roman à clef* based upon the life of J. E. Millais.[1] Millais was an original member of the Pre-Raphaelite Brotherhood and was taken under the patronage of Ruskin. Millais fell in love with Effie Ruskin, whose marriage had never been consummated: she subsequently obtained an annulment and married Millais in 1855.[2] After a difficult period, Millais changed his style and subject matter and became an enormously successful, popular painter. He died, P. R. A., in August 1896: Effie Millais has been blamed, unfairly, for the deterioration in his work.

Olivia Shakespear has taken what she knew of Millais's life and career and made a highly charged fiction out of it. The Millais–Ruskin–Effie triangle is patently the model for the Rupert Armstrong–Maurice Wootton–Eve triangle, with an engagement substituted for an unconsummated marriage.[3] The closeness of the names "Eve" and "Effie" needs no further comment. The appearance of Eve is based upon that of Effie Millais: a striking portrait of her by Millais had been exhibited at the Grafton Galleries in 1896; both women are very attractive with golden hair and white skin.

The description of Rupert Armstrong merits quotation:

> a handsome, clean-shaven face, with features chiselled, not delicately, but with a bold, blunt touch; ruddy brown hair, that curled a little; the skin of a boy; a smile that came and went in a flash, and showed perfect teeth. . . . His chin, round, and rather short, had a dimple . . . this man with his easy air of fashion, was my father. (*RA* 66–7)

This is an exact description of Millais, down to the dimple in his chin. Other facts are pressed upon us: Maurice says of Rupert Armstrong, "he makes a good

income and has been knighted" (*RA* 77); by the 1880s Millais was making
£30,000 a year and he was knighted in 1885. Rupert Armstrong's "great,
beautiful house" (*RA* 32) is referred to: Olivia Shakespear would have been
familiar with Millais's *palazzo* in Palace Gate, not only from the illustrated
papers, but from her ordinary life – she lived on the north side of Kensington
Gardens.

When we move to the account of Armstrong's paintings, the parallels are
inescapable. A work called *The Reapers*, painted after his marriage, but still in his
earlier manner, is described:

> glorious in yellow corn, and purple distance, and perfect, delicately vivid
> flowers among the wheat.
>   Colour I saw, and again colour; and then a soul. There were figures of women;
> some old, who having sown tares, reaped now . . . in the midst was a young girl;
> her hands were idle; she looked at me with my own eyes, gray, wide open; she
> had my ruddy health, and red-brown hair . . . (*RA* 75–6)

The model for this is Millais's *Autumn Leaves* (with perhaps some symbolism
drawn from *Vale of Rest*) painted after Millais's marriage, but before the change
in manner: the reference to the portraits of "beautiful women in fine clothes"
(*RA* 35) offers direct comparison with Millais's later, facile portraits of society
women such as *Mrs Bischoffsheim*.[4] The landscape painting described (*RA* 36) –
"a lonely moor, stretching to a belt of trees and a gray sky"—is close to Millais's
Fringe of the Moor (1874). The pivot of the novel is the painter's descent into
facility: " 'He had a great birthright, and he has sold it for a mess of pottage' "
(*RA* 76). This last is a familiar response to Millais's career.

Even when the *roman à clef* intersects with the other motif, Agatha Armstrong's
obsessive, quasi-incestuous love for her father, there is a possible link with the
Millais circle. Agatha is the model for the central girl in *The Reapers*: the model for
the central figure in *Autumn Leaves* was Millais's sister-in-law, Sophia Gray, then
a child of twelve. There is a tradition in the Millais family that she and Millais
later fell in love, that she had a breakdown and was sent away for two years by
her sister.[5] The coincidence of this material is remarkable, given the repellent
Agatha's outburst against her mother, " 'I hate her because I love you' ", and
her departure for a year's exile in Paris.

Olivia Shakespear has included another figure who is intended to be identified
by the sophisticated reader. Rupert Armstrong has an "antitype" in Isaac
Isaacson, a drunken painter, described as a "genius of the pavement" (*RA* 148).
This is an overt, unmodified portrait of Simeon Solomon[6]: here the *roman à clef*
moves closer to Yeats's *milieu*. Olivia Shakespear's source for this material was no
doubt Lionel Johnson – John Mordaunt in the novel – who owned a painting by
Solomon (*Au* 305) and in whose rooms in Fitzroy Square Yeats met the "ragged
figure" (*Au* 168). Isaac Isaacson is used *passim* as a counterpart to Armstrong, to
whom he says "there is no crime but popularity" (*RA* 283), reminding us of the
outburst recorded by Yeats – " 'Sir, do you dare mistake me for that

mountebank?' " – when Solomon was mistaken for a successful Academy painter (*Au* 168).

In her description of the works in Maurice Wootton's room, Olivia Shakespear draws the two *milieux* together. The works largely express Yeats's tastes,

> A Crivelli . . . one of Calvert's pastorals . . . an unfinished head of Leonardo's . . . the head of a Rossetti's inscrutable Assyrian goddess, sad and voluptuous . . . two faces by an obscure artist, Isaac Isaacson; Love and Lust facing one another. (*RA* 47–8)

The Crivelli comes, perhaps, from *Rosa Alchemica* (*VSR* 127). Calvert is one of the painters discussed in "Symbolism in Painting" and Yeats had been intending to write a monograph upon him:[7] the Rossetti painting is *Astarte Syriaca*, which Yeats must have admired – he and Maud Gonne went to see it when they visited Manchester in 1897 (*L* 287). At this point a fictional presentation of the world of the Pre-Raphaelites meshes with Olivia Shakespear's private knowledge of Yeats's tastes, in a manner that is disorienting and disturbing. We are led to the obvious question – what was she doing?

Rupert Armstrong is an exceedingly strongly felt novel. Olivia Shakespear has made a tragedy out of what she knew of Millais's career and life: her sources no doubt included published material,[8] but she must have gathered some information from private sources. Her fictional vilification of Effie Millais involves her (and the reader) in an irony: Effie Ruskin's actual position, trapped in a loveless marriage was one which was the staple of Olivia Shakespear's fiction. She wrote no novel based upon or dealing with her affair with Yeats, but into this account of an artist's decline, there is surely a considerable transference of feeling.[9]

NOTES

1. This was apparent to the *Athenæum* reviewer who (4 March 1899) pointed to the parallel with the P.R.B., and continued "the author has got hold of some real persons, but she wastes them by making them do the wrong things – or, rather, she does not realise them fully, as she shows only the hard unsympathetic side of their natures". The precedent for such a novel is to be found in Vernon Lee's *Miss Brown* (1884), a *roman à clef* based on the life of Janey Morris. In this afterword, *Rupert Armstrong* will be referred to as *RA*.
2. For a full account see Mary Lutyens, *Millais and the Ruskins* (London: John Murray, 1967).
3. Although Rupert Armstrong is modelled upon Millais and Eve upon Effie Millais, Maurice Wootton is not a portrait of Ruskin; however we do encounter him as tutor to a pair of twelve year old girls, an activity congenial to the older Ruskin: the symbolism of the injured arm is also striking.
4. His many portraits of society women included a portrait of the Hon. Caroline Roche as Scott's "Diana Vernon", (1880): this handsome brunette bears no resemblance to the *Literary Yearbook* photograph of Olivia Shakespear (Frontispiece), but some to the later photograph (Plate 8a). Given the relative obscurity which surrounds Yeats's *choice* of this pseudonym for Olivia Shakespear, this possibility is worth presentation.

5. See Lutyens, op. cit., pp. 152–3.
6. For an account of the life of Simeon Solomon (1840–1905) see *D.N.B*. The aspects of his life of which Olivia Shakespear makes use are as follows. He had, as a young man, been an admirer of Millais's work and was further connected by the fact that his sister, Rebecca, executed replicas for Millais. However it was Burne-Jones, rather than Millais, with whom he remained in contact after his imprisonment. His drunken, dissolute character was well known: at the close of his career, he was an inhabitant of St. Giles's workhouse and he had at one time been a pavement artist in Bayswater – the "genius of the pavement" (*RA* 148). The work which Olivia Shakespear describes, "Love and Lust facing one another", is presumably *Love Dying by the Breath of Lust*, attacked by Robert Buchanan in *The Fleshly School of Poetry* and, according to Robert Ross, one of the most popular autotypes on the walls of Oxford undergraduates in the 1880s and 1890s (Robert Ross, *Masques and Phases* [London: Humphreys, 1909] p. 136). However, unlike Isaac Isaacson, Solomon did not preserve his genius as the expense of his life: after 1873, his work degenerated into feeble pastiche of his earlier work.
7. Yeats had intended to write a monograph on Calvert for Laurence Binyon's series, *The Artist's Library*; this is evident from an unpublished letter from Yeats to Binyon c. September 1899; the title was still being advertised in 1900. Yeats's interest in Calvert was of some standing; he is quoted in "The Tribes of Danu" (November 1897, *UP* 2, 57).
8. In 1896, for example, Sir Walter Armstrong's study of Millais was republished in the *Art Annual*; it possibly provided Olivia Shakespear with her protagonist's surname.
9. It is clear that Yeats and Olivia Shakespear spent much time together in Art Galleries (*Mem* 86). She possibly associated her response to painting, particularly Pre-Raphaelite painting, with her feelings for Yeats. Virginia Moore quotes Yeats's account of an episode of 1914, when both were looking at a Burne-Jones window in Rottingdean – presumably one of the four in St. Margaret's – "Don't think me a fool. It's the colour – it's like a sword. It has carried me back twenty years.' And when he looked at her she was in tears" (*The Unicorn* [New York: Macmillan, 1954], p. 235). This carries *us* back to *Rupert Armstrong* and to Agatha's response to *The Reapers*: "a great tide of emotion beat on me, and broke away my self-control. A desperate sense of tragedy, of something lost, made the beauty of the picture as a two-edged sword. I burst into sudden tears, and knew the throes of a great desire, a great pity" (*RA* 76).

The Secret Society of Modernism: Pound, Yeats, Olivia Shakespear, and the Abbé de Montfaucon de Villars

James Longenbach

In November 1913 Ezra Pound began the first of three successive winters he would spend at Stone Cottage in Sussex with W. B. Yeats, the man whom he had recently called "the greatest of living poets who use English".[1] The following summer, Pound composed "Vorticism", the manifesto he would publish in the September 1914 issue of the *Fortnightly Review*. In the essay, Pound situates Vorticism in the context of artistic movements past and present, and as a result, "Vorticism" emerges as a compact survey of Pound's own artistic development from 1908 to 1914; he even refers to the essay as his "autobiography".[2] Before the end of "Vorticism", Pound examines the growth of his own work from *Personae* and *The Sonnets and Ballate of Guido Cavalcanti* to "A Few Don'ts by an Imagiste" and the Imagist poems he would publish in *Lustra*. He contrasts Vorticism to contemporary movements that had captured his attention during his early London years: Symbolism, Impressionism, Futurism, Cubism, and Expressionism. He quotes or discusses the figures of the "tradition" who influenced his own aesthetic: Aristotle, Dante, Villon, Browning, Pater, Whistler, and Flaubert. And to reinforce the example of his own work, Pound invokes the work of his distinguished contemporaries: Apollinaire, H. D., Gaudier-Bzreska, Hueffer, Kandinsky, Lewis, and Picasso. The one figure whom Pound does not mention, oddly enough, is the man whose status as the "best poet in England" he had just reaffirmed in the May 1914 issue of *Poetry*: W. B. Yeats.[3]

Pound's remarks on Symbolism in the "Vorticism" essay not only betray his debts to Yeats, however, but also make a concealed reference to material that he and Yeats had studied at Stone Cottage during the previous winter. Pound writes that "one does not want to be called a symbolist, because symbolism has usually been associated with mushy technique". He also states that to hold a belief in a sort of permanent

103

metaphor is, as I understand it, "symbolism" in its profounder sense.
It is not necessarily a belief in a permanent world, but it is a belief in
that direction. (*G-B* 84–5)

Given the enigmatic style of this "autobiography", it is not easy to
determine what Pound means by " 'symbolism' in its profounder sense".
With the help of some new information about Pound's winter at Stone
Cottage, we can see that Pound was thinking of some occult material
that he had studied with Yeats – material that is crucial to our
understanding of the esoteric theology that lurks behind the clipped
precision of modernist poetics.

A letter that Pound wrote during his stay at Stone Cottage provides
the key to his special understanding of symbolism. Dorothy Shakespear,
Pound's future wife and the daughter of Olivia Shakespear, wrote to
Pound asking him to explain "symbolism" to her. Pound replied with
another question:

What *do* you mean by symbolism? Do you mean real symbolism,
Cabala, genesis of symbols, rise of picture language, etc. or the
aesthetic symbolism of Villiers de l'Isle Adam, & that Arthur Symons
wrote a book about – the literwary movement? At any rate begin on
the *"Comte de Gabalis"*, anonymous & should be catalogued under
"Comte de Gabalis." Then you might try the Grimoire of Pope
Honorius (IIIrd I think).

There's a dictionary of symbols, but I think it immoral. I mean that
I think a superficial acquaintance with the sort of shallow, conventional, or attributed meaning of a lot of symbols *weakens* – damnably,
the power of receiving an energized symbol. I mean a symbol
appearing in a vision has a certain richness & power of energizing joy –
whereas if the supposed meaning of a symbol is familiar it has no more
force, or interest of power of suggestion than any other word, or than a
synonym in some other language.

Then there are those Egyptian language books, but O.S. [Olivia
Shakespear] has 'em so they're no use. Ennemoser's History of Magic
may have something in it – Then there are "Les Symbolists" – french
from Mallarmé, de l'Isle Adam, etc. to De Gourmont, which is
another story. (*EPDS* 302)

There are two traditions of symbolism for Pound: the "literwary" and
the esoteric. As A. Walton Litz has remarked in a recent discussion of the
literary friendship of Pound and Yeats, Pound felt that literary
symbolism had run its course in England but believed that "the
'symbolism' of vision and the esoteric remained a powerful source of
poetic inspiration, and . . . had nothing but admiration for this aspect of
Yeats's work".[4]

This esoteric tradition is what Pound means by " 'symbolism' in its profounder sense." Postponing for a moment an investigation of Pound's reading list of esoteric texts, we can now see why Pound writes in "Vorticism" that this kind of symbolism is "not necessarily a belief in a permanent world, but it is a belief in that direction" (*G-B* 84). For Pound, true symbolism depends upon the artist's *visionary* power: "a symbol appearing in a vision has a certain richness & power of energizing joy" that a conventional "literwary" symbol does not, he writes to Dorothy Shakespear; the "literwary" symbol has lost its power to embody the divine or permanent world.

Pound wants to differentiate Imagism from this debased literary symbolism and align it with " 'symbolism' in its profounder sense'", with symbolism that appears in a vision. For Pound, the Image is not the simple word on the page, not a representation of the natural world: "The image is the word beyond formulated language", he writes in "Vorticism".

> Dante's "Paradiso" is the most wonderful *image*. By that I do not mean that it is a perseveringly imagistic performance. The permanent part is Imagisme, the rest, the discourses with the calendar of saints and the discussions about the nature of the moon, are philosophy. The form of sphere above sphere, the varying reaches of light, the minutiae of pearls upon foreheads, all these are parts of the Image. (*GB* 86)

These metaphysical statements about the Image have never seemed to fit comfortably with Pound's claim that the Image presents the "direct treatment of the 'thing' " (*LE* 3). Once we understand that "the thing" is not necessarily an object in the material world but usually an element of the artist's vision of the divine, we can see that for Pound there is no poem of more profound symbolism, Imagism, and vision than the *Paradiso*.[5]

The visionary foundation of Pound's art becomes even clearer when he describes the experiences that precipitated his Imagist poems. The vision of one "beautiful face and then another and another" that inspired "In a Station of the Metro" is well known (*G-B* 86). This poem was first published with eleven others as "Contemporania" (1913), Pound's first collection of Imagist poetry.[6] Another one of these poems, "Dance Figure, for the Marriage in Cana of Galilee", also had its origins in a visionary experience. In September 1912, Pound wrote to Dorothy Shakespear that he

> had last night a most gorgeous dream about the marriage in Cana of Galilee, it began in symbolical patterns on a rug and ended in a wedding dance to exceed the Russians both in grace, splendour & legerity – convincingly naive and oriental!! (*EPDS* 150)

"Dance Figure", Pound's "equation" for this dream-vision, begins in his best clipped, Imagistic style:

> Dark eyed!
> O woman of my dreams,
> Ivory sandaled,
> There is none like thee among the dancers,
> None with swift feet. (*Per* 91)

These Imagist poems, as Pound insisted, are not simply descriptive or "viewy" like the debased poems of "Amygism". Pound's Images point toward a permanent world, and the doctrine of " 'symbolism' in its profounder sense" lies behind their apparently "minimalistic" simplicity.

Like Pound, the Yeats of *The Wind among the Reeds* also valued symbols that arise from visionary experiences, symbols that are infinitely suggestive and suggestive of the infinite. The most powerful symbols, he wrote in "The Symbolism of Poetry" (1900), "call down among us certain disembodied powers, whose footsteps over our hearts we call emotions . . ." (*E&I* 157). When Yeats and Pound arrived at Stone Cottage in 1913, however, Yeats was already involved in the writing of his autobiographies and the "harder" poems of *Responsibilities* (1914), where "instead of 'vision'," he told his father, he "tried for more self portraiture" (*L* 583). Pound was also pushing for a harder idiom, but he was still using it to render his visions. As late as 1914, it was the Yeats of *The Wind among the Reeds* and not the Yeats of *Responsibilities* that held the greatest power over Pound.[7]

The early Yeats was not the only source of Pound's special understanding of symbolism, but the winter Pound spent with Yeats in 1913–1914 reinforced his belief in the esoteric and visionary aspects of the symbol. During the months that Pound was engaged as Yeats's secretary, Yeats was correlating Lady Gregory's collection of Irish folk-lore with other tales and myths from occult and esoteric literature. His work resulted in two essays, "Witches, Wizards and Irish Folk Lore" and "Swedenborg, Mediums, and the Desolate Places" as well as a collection of notes which were appended to Lady Gregory's tales. All this material was eventually published in Lady Gregory's *Visions and Beliefs in the West of Ireland* (1920). At the same time, Pound was working on his first translations of the Noh plays, and the two poets must have marvelled over the similarities of their projects. In *'Noh' or Accomplishment* (1916) Pound remarks that in Noh drama,

> The suspense is the suspense of waiting for a supernatural manifestation – which comes. Some will be annoyed at a form of psychology which is, in the West, relegated to spiritistic séances. There is,

however, no doubt that such psychology exists. All through the winter of 1914–1915 I watched Mr. Yeats correlating folk-lore (which Lady Gregory had collected in Irish cottages) and data of the occult writers, with the habits of charlatans of Bond Street. (*T* 236)

Pound and Yeats continued their cooperative investigations of Noh theatre, Celtic folk-lore, and the occult during their winters at Stone Cottage in 1914–1915 and 1915–1916. The product of these investigations for Yeats is well known: in the Noh theatre he found a model that rejuvenated his own plays, and in 1916 he wrote *At the Hawk's Well*. The effect of these investigations on Pound's work has seemed more ambiguous. Several critics have suspected that some form of Yeatsian mysticism is latent in Pound's poetics, but have assumed that Pound remained unsympathetic to Yeats's interest in symbolism and the occult.[8] We can now see, however, that the occult literature that Pound read during his 1913–1914 winter with Yeats actually helped him to focus his ideas about Imagism. Pound's statements about Imagism in the "Vorticism" essay, written just after the first winter with Yeats, are much more assured than the vague definitions given in "A Few Don'ts by an Imagiste", written just prior to that winter. Pound's earlier definition of the Image as "an intellectual and emotional complex in an instant of time" which gives "that sense of freedom from time limits and space limits" (*LE* 4) only hints at the visionary quality that becomes explicit in "Vorticism". Furthermore, while the 1913 list of "Don'ts" concentrates on the stylistic aspects of the Imagist aesthetic, Pound could write in the "Vorticism" essay of 1914 that Imagism "has been known chiefly as a stylistic movement, as a movement of criticism rather than of creation" and move on to discuss the creative, visionary process that gives birth to the Imagist poem (*G-B* 82). The growth of Imagism depended on Pound's reading of Montfaucon's *Comte de Gabalis*, Kirk's *The Secret Commonwealth*, and Ennemoser's *The History of Magic*.[9]

Pound's own interest in the literature of the occult was rekindled rather than initiated by Yeats. In "La Fraisne", a poem he wrote before he met Yeats in 1909, Pound linked the tales of spirits and fairies in Yeats's *The Celtic Twilight* with *De Daemonialitate, et Incubi et Succubis* by the 17th century Franciscan theologian Lodovico Maria Sinistrari. In his note to "La Fraisne" in *A Lume Spento* (1908) Pound writes that he found himself in the "mood" of "Mr. Yeats in his 'Celtic Twilight' " (*CEP* 8). "La Fraisne", a poem filled with echoes of the Yeats of *The Wind Among the Reeds*, tells of a man who takes for his "bride" a "pool of the wood" (*CEP* 9–10). The footnote to this "Note Precedent" to "La Fraisne" links Pound's Yeatsian "mood" with *De Daemonialitate*:

Referendum for contrast. "Daemonalitas" of the Rev. Father Sinistrari of Ameno (1600 circ). "A treatise wherein is shown that there are in existence on earth rational creatures besides man, endowed like him with a body and soul, that are born and die like him, redeemed by our Lord Jesus-Christ, and capable of receiving salvation or damnation." (*CEP* 8)

The Latin manuscript of *De Daemonialitate* was first discovered in 1872 and published with a French translation in 1875. Pound owned the 1879 edition which contained an English translation, and in his note to "La Fraisne", he quotes from the summary of the book printed on the title page of this edition.[10]

Pound must have remembered the connection he had made between Yeats's faeries and Sinistrari's demons during the first winter at Stone Cottage because he wrote to his father, "Yeats is doing various books. He wants my *Daemonalitas*. Will you try to find it along with the other thing I asked for" (*EPDS* 305). When the book arrived, Yeats made use of it in his notes for Lady Gregory's folk-lore. In a note on "the faery people" in *Visions and Beliefs*, Yeats asked,

> Were these beings but the shades of men? Were they a separate race? Were they spirits of evil? Above all, perhaps, were they capable of salvation? Father Sinistrari in *De Daemonialitate et Incubis, et Succubis*, reprinted in Paris with an English translation in 1879, tells a story which must have been familiar through the Irish Middle Ages, and the seed of many discussions.

Yeats goes on to paraphrase a tale that Sinistrari tells about a spirit who asks St. Anthony if his soul can be saved. He then remarks, "I heard or read that tale [in a different version] somewhere before I was twenty, for it is the subject of one of my first poems".[11] Yeats does not name the poem, but it is clear from his description of the tale that he remembers "The Priest and the Fairy", originally published in *The Wanderings of Oisin and Other Poems* (1889) and never reprinted in Yeats's lifetime.[12] The poem itself is a piece of juvenilia, but what is interesting is that Yeats has made the same connection between *De Daemonialitate* and his early "Celtic" work that Pound had made in his note to "La Fraisne" – and he probably did so at Pound's urging.

Pound also urged Dorothy Shakespear to read *De Daemonialitate*, but for an understanding of symbolism in its profounder sense, Pound suggested in his letter of January 14, 1914 that she "begin on the '*Comte de Gabalis*'" and by-pass the work of Mallarmé and Symons (*EPDS*, 302). *Le Comte de Gabalis, ou entretiens sur les sciences secrètes*, by the Abbé de Montfaucon de Villars (Paris, 1670) was frequently reprinted and expanded with notes and commentaries throughout the 18th and 19th centuries. Yeats read *Le Comte* at Stone Cottage as part of his effort to correlate Lady Gregory's folk-lore with the literature of the occult, and he shared the book with Pound. On January 6, 1914, a week before Dorothy Shakespear asked Pound for some help with symbolism, Pound wrote to her that he and Yeats had

> been reading The Comte de Gabalis – a charming and spritely book about Sylphs & Salamanders, you must read it when the Eagle [Yeats] lends it to O.S. [Olivia Shakespear] as I suppose he will sooner or later – tho' he borrowed it from somebody else.
>
> I have half a mind to translate only it seems too delicate to give to a profane english vulgo. (*EPDS* 293)

As important as *Le Comte de Gabalis* turned out to be for Pound, he did not translate it; however, he did persuade Dorothy Shakespear's mother, Olivia Shakespear, to translate it, and he published her translation in the *Egoist*. The five dialogues of *Le Comte de Gabalis* appeared in five issues of the *Egoist* from 16 March to 1 June 1914, running concurrently with *A Portrait of the Artist as a Young Man*.[13]

Like Sinistrari's *De Daemonialitate*, Montfaucon's *Le Comte de Gabalis* tells of the existence of a race of creatures that are neither human nor divine, neither corporeal or spiritual, but caught somewhere in between; in 1886, an English translation of *Le Comte* was published with an appendix from Sinistrari's work.[14] Although these two books treat similar material, they nevertheless differ greatly in scope and design. Sinistrari's *De Daemonialitate* is a rigorously argued "proof" of the existence of these creatures; it documents many accounts of their antics and cites numerous Biblical passages to show that commerce with these creatures is not sinful. *Le Comte de Gabalis*, on the other hand, is an occult romance complete with a wonderfully naive narrator, creatures called Sylphs, Gnomes, Nymphs, and Salamanders who inhabit the four elements, and sordid tales of their sexual relations with Adam and Noah. *Le Comte* is not the work of serious scholarship that Ennemoser's *History of Magic* or even Kirk's *Secret Commonwealth* or Sinistrari's *De Daemonialitate* is. Yeats read all these works, and the fact that he refers to them in *Visions and Beliefs* but not to *Le Comte de Gabalis* suggests that this work is less suitable to a serious investigation of occult phenomena.[15] Read not as a scholarly work but as a romance, however, *Le Comte* is the "charming and spritely book" Pound describes. The eternal pedagogue, Pound probably suggested that Dorothy Shakespear *begin* her investigation of esoteric symbolism with *Le Comte* in order to wet her appetite before moving on to the more rigorous but less spritely work of Ennemoser. He probably persuaded Olivia Shakespear to translate the book for the same reason: *Le Comte de Gabalis* provides a pleasant and diverting approach to the doctrine of symbolism in its profounder sense.

A certain mystery surrounds Olivia Shakespear's translations: although she published her novels under her own name and signed a review of "The Poetry of D. H. Lawrence" in the "Special Imagist Number" of the *Egoist* (1 May 1915) with "O. Shakespear", she signed her translations of *Le Comte* with "M. de V.-M.", the initials of the author, the Abbé de Montfaucon de Villars. Furthermore, in the pages of the *Egoist*, *Le Comte de Gabalis* is given a new title: "Memoirs of a Charming Person". While Pound suggested in a private letter that one should begin an investigation of symbolism with *Le Comte*, the title chosen for its public appearance seems to be designed to disguise its occult trappings and emphasize its "charming and spritely" character. In *'Noh' or Accomplishment*, when Pound notes the similarities between the spirits of Noh theatre and the doctrines of Western occultism, he adds that "If the Japanese authors had not combined the psychology of such matters with what is to me a very fine sort of poetry, I would not bother about it" (*T* 236). Pound's attitude toward *Le Comte de Gabalis* seems to be similar.

His attraction to its "delicate" prose (*EPDS* 293) did not overwhelm his interest in its subject matter, however. When Henry Bryan Binns wrote to the *Egoist* to object to "The Cabalistic extravaganza now appearing" in its pages, Pound replied,

> I trust no one will take Mr. Binns too seriously. Mr. Binns evidently believes in a general djinn like Jehovah having droits du Seigneur over all his female connections. . . . Mr. Binns objects to M. De Gabalis, permit me to object to Mr. Binns.[16]

Pound believed that the ethnocentricity of Christian monotheism was at the root of the disease of Western culture, and he approved of anything that undermined its power. Early in 1914, when Dorothy Shakespear's father objected to Pound's unwillingness to be married in the Church of England, Pound wrote to him,

> I have some religion. What you say about a priest's benediction is sound enough but I count myself much more a priest than I do some sceptic who is merely being paid for the public pretense of something he has probably never considered. . . . I think, seriously, that the spiritual powers are affronted when a person who takes his religion seriously complies with a ceremony which has fallen into decay. I can not find any trace of Christ's having spoken against the greek gods. . . . I should no more give up my faith in Christ than I should give up my faith in Helios or my respect for the teachings of Confucius . . . the whole sanity of classic religion was in their recognition that different men have different gods and that there are many sorts of orthodox piety. (*EPDS* 307)

Pound took his religion seriously. And as the priest of his own church, he sought the riches of many religious traditions, ancient and modern, orthodox and occult.

Pound's attraction to *Le Comte de Gabalis* and esoteric literature in general is further explained by "The New Sculpture", an article he published in the *Egoist* in February, 1914, the month before Olivia Shakespear's translations began to appear. In this review of lectures delivered by T. E. Hulme and Wyndham Lewis at G. R. S. Mead's theosophical Quest Society (where Pound himself had given his lecture on "Psychology and Troubadours" which was later published in the *Quest*), Pound laments the fact that "The artist has been for so long a humanist" and has had to "lead and persuade [humanity] to save it from itself". The solution to this problem lies in the new spiritualist emphasis of modern art:

> Humanism has . . . taken refuge in the arts.
>   The introduction of Djinns, tribal gods, fetiches, etc. into the arts is therefore a happy presage . . .
>   We turn back, we artists, to the powers of the air, to the djinns who were our allies aforetime, to the spirits of our ancestors. It is by them that we have ruled and shall rule, and by their connivance that we shall mount again into our hierarchy. The aristocracy of entail and of title has decayed, the aristocracy of commerce is decaying, the aristocracy of the arts is ready again for its service.
>   Modern civilization has bred a race with brains like those rabbits and we who are the heirs of the witch-doctor and the voodoo, we artists who have been so long the despised are about to take control.[17]

The introduction of elements drawn from spiritualism and the occult into the arts accomplishes three things for Pound: It enhances the artist's own visionary powers; it places the modern artist firmly in the aristocratic tradition of the divinely inspired bard; and most important, it provides the artist with an elite, esoteric language and practice that distinguishes him from the rest of humanity.

Le Comte de Gabalis gave Pound access to what he called in "The New Sculpture" the aristocratic tradition of "the witch-doctor and the voodoo". Like the work of Sinistrari and Kirk, *Le Comte* is about the "Djinns, tribal gods, fetiches, etc." that Pound wants to restore to the arts. Over the course of five "conversations", the narrator explains how the Count de Gabalis, a Cabalist and Sage of the Secret Sciences, came to tell him of "the existence of an order of beings between God and man, to whom everything can be attributed which is super-human, but less than divine". In order to provide an example of the kind of dialogue that characterizes *Le Comte*, I will quote Olivia Shakespear's translation at length: "When you are one of Us", explains the Count,

> ". . . you will discover, by the help of occult drugs, that living in the elements are most charming people, cut off from us by the sin of Adam:

you may think the air was made for birds and flies, the water for whales, and the earth for moles, and that fire is of no use at all. The air is really full of multitudes of beings, proud but friendly; fond of science, subtile-minded, and the sworn foes of the silly and ignorant; their wives and daughters are beautiful like Amazons."

"What," cried I, "do you mean to say these hobgoblins are married!"

"You needn't be alarmed," said he. "All this is only teaching from the ancient Cabala. You must put away all you have ever learnt, or you may have to acknowledge your own obstinacy, when you have had more experience. Let me tell you the rivers and seas also are full of Undines and Nymphs; very few of them males, of great beauty. The earth is full of little Gnomes, who look after treasure, and mines, and jewels; they are friendly too, ingenious, and easy to control: they have little wives, but pleasing, with curious habits."

He went on to tell me about the Salamanders, and when I disclaimed any wish to know such ugly creatures, he defended them ardently; saying that as they are made of the purest element, fire, they are all the more beautiful, besides being interesting in their minds, and attitudes towards life. They have, he said, laws and customs like ourselves, but their great grief is that they are mortal, though they live for many centuries. The Sages, it appears, interceded with God Himself on their behalf, and it was revealed to them that Sylphs, Gnomes, Nymphs and Salamanders were all capable of gaining an immortal soul by mating with a man, particularly if he were a Sage; whilst the males of these beings had the same advantages through marrying our daughters. ("Second conversation", pp. 153–4)

Le Comte de Gabalis is not only about the existence of these "elemental" people but about the necessity of having sexual relations with them. The Count explains that

If Adam had not grossly violated the command given him to have no relations with Eve, but had been satisfied with the Nymphs and Sylphs, the world would never have been shamefully peopled with imperfect creatures – almost monsters, compared with the children of the Philosophers. ("Fourth Conversation", p. 189)

The Count then documents the many church fathers who conceived children with the "elementals" and he tells the narrator that he must choose a Sylph, Gnome, Nymph or Salamander for his bride.

Le Comte de Gabalis is an amusing book, and the exchanges between the mysterious Count and the incredulous narrator are artfully turned; the narrator learns that "There was no use . . . in trying to reason with a Cabalist" ("Third Conversation", p. 171). Pound's attraction to a book about spirit-sexuality is not so absurd as it may seem when we recall that "Psychology and Troubadours", (1912; reprinted in *SR* after 1932) focuses on the influx of pagan sexual mysticism into Christian thought: when we examine Medieval mysticism, writes Pound, "we find sex" (*SR* 93). For Pound, however, the subject matter of *Le Comte de Gabalis* is not as important as the aristocratic attitude which the book projects toward its subject matter. Pound insists, as we have seen, on the superiority of a symbol that appears in a vision because he feels that a symbol should never be explained: "I think a superficial acquaintance with a sort of shallow, conventional, or attributed meaning of a lot of symbols *weakens* – damnably, the power of receiving an energized symbol" (*EPDS* 302). By the time Pound made this statement to Dorothy Shakespear, he had maintained this view of symbolism for several years. In a note to his prose poem, "Malrin", written while he was teaching at Wabash College in 1907, Pound said that "To give concrete for a symbol, to explain a parable, is for me always a limiting, a restricting . . ." (*CEP* 295–6). These sanctions are central to the snatches of Cabalistic doctrine presented in the fanciful conversations of *Le Comte de Gabalis*. Although Olivia Shakespear does not include it in her translation, the French text begins with an epigraph from Tertullian: "Quod tanto impendio absconditur etiam solummodo demonstrare destruere est" [when a thing is hidden away with so much pain, merely to reveal it is to destroy it].[18] When the narrator objects to the count's assertion that Adam's sin was that he had sexual relations with Eve instead of the elementals (" 'Then,' cried I, 'you think Adam's sin didn't lie in eating the apple?' "), the Count replies,

> Are you among those who take the story of the apple literally? . . . Do you not know that Holy Writ uses metaphorical language to express what could not otherwise be decently said? But the Sages have understood the mystery, and know that if Adam had had relations only with Sylphs, Gnomes, Nymphs, or Salamanders, the world would have been filled with a wonderfully strong, wise race. ("Fourth Conversation", p. 189)

This brief lesson in the interpretation of symbols contains the central tenet of Pound's understanding of esoteric symbolism: knowledge worth having can be expressed only in symbols that are unfamiliar and obscure. When the narrator of *Le Comte* objects that the oracles through which the "elementals" speak are too obscure to be understood, the Count replies, "As for the obscurity to which you object, isn't truth generally concealed by darkness – and isn't Holy Writ itself so obscure as to put off the haughty and presumptuous, and to guide the humble?" ("Third Conversation", p. 173). To explain a symbol is to destroy its ability to embody what Pound called the divine or permanent world;

knowledge that could be understood by the uninitiated masses would not be knowledge at all.

This attitude toward symbolism is mentioned only briefly in *Le Comte de Gabalis*, but it is central to most of the esoteric literature Pound was reading at Stone Cottage. In his *History of Magic* (1854) Joseph Ennemoser maintains that mythological symbols are not arbitrary fictions but originate in primitive man's attempts to use figurative language to explain visionary experiences he does not understand. Pound would have agreed with this theory: in "Psychology and Troubadours" he wrote that "Greek myth arose when someone having passed through delightful psychic experience tried to communicate it to others . . ." (*SR* 92). For the individual who undergoes this delightful psychic experience, Pound and Ennemoser agree, the resulting symbol is perfectly clear and intelligible. Ennemoser quotes Georg Friedrich Creuzer, the German classical philologist, to explain why these symbols become opaque: while the Greeks understood that art could intelligibly express the infinite, they also knew that "an expression of higher knowledge of the secret doctrine" as "an embodied enigma" could be even more powerful.

> Therein especially consists the temple symbolism of Greece and Rome. When the clearness of the scene is wholly annihilated, and only the astonishment remains, so that a certain religious instruction is implied, the symbolism is still more enigmatical, and the key to the mystery is in many cases lost.[19]

Those who possess the "secret doctrine" possess the key to the mysteries of its symbolism and establish themselves as priests – divinely inspired interpreters to whom the uninitiated public must turn for knowledge. At the beginning of *Le Comte de Gabalis*, the narrator says that he has heard that the Count "is dead of an apoplexy. The curious will not fail to say that such a death is usual for one who has failed to keep the secrets of the Sages . . ." ("Conversation the First", p. 112). It is imperative that the highest knowledge be veiled.

This attitude permeates the literature of the occult and justifies its obscurity. It also characterizes the sacred texts of literary modernism. In his initial editorial statement for the *Little Review* (1917), Pound surveyed his work with the *Egoist* and recalled Olivia Shakespear's translations:

> I do not think it can be too often pointed out that during the last four years *The Egoist* has published serially in the face of no inconsiderable difficulties, the only translation of Remy de Gourmont's *Chevaux de Diomedes*; the best translation of le Comte de Gabalis; Mr. Joyce's masterpiece, *A Portrait of the Artist as a Young Man*, and is now publishing Mr. Lewis's novel *Tarr*.[20]

Pound sets Olivia Shakespear's work among prestigious company here. Although *Le Comte de Gabalis* cannot stand in the same category as the masterpieces of literary modernism, Pound's juxtaposition is suggestive: in their readings in the esoteric and the occult, Pound and Yeats found a justification for the aristocratic, anti-democratic, willfully obscure attitudes of literary modernism. *Four Plays for Dancers* (1921) and "Three Cantos" (1917), the works influenced by their studies at Stone Cottage, are allusive and obscure for the same reason that occult literature conceals its secret knowledge in a language that only a small circle of initiated readers can understand: to explain their work to the public would be to destroy its beauty and undermine their priest-like status. In *'Noh' or Accomplishment* Pound wrote that "The art of allusion, or the love of allusion in art, is at the root of the Noh. These plays, or eclogues, were made only for the few; for the nobles; for those trained to catch the allusion" (*T* 214). Yeats remembered that with the help of Pound's translations of the Noh plays he "invented a form of drama, distinguished, indirect, and symbolic, and having no need of mob or press to pay its way – an aristocratic form". He wanted to create "an unpopular theatre and an audience like a *secret society*" (*E&I* 221, *Ex* 254; my emphasis). Pound was not joking when at the end of "The New Sculpture" he wrote that "the public will do well to resent these 'new' kinds of art" (p. 68).

Besides Yeats's own esoteric works, Olivia Shakespear's translation of *Le Comte de Gabalis* is one of the few works of occult literature we have that bears the personal stamp of a member of this "secret society" of modernism, and it provides a new opportunity to answer a question we have asked Yeats for years: how much of this did he actually *believe*? A comparison of Olivia Shakespear's translation with one published by "The Brothers" in 1914 offers clues about the attitude that she, Pound, and Yeats held toward the occult. In the first installment of "Memoirs of a Charming Person", the narrator says,

> As commonsense has always led me to suspect that there is much emptiness in what are called Secret Sciences, I have never been tempted to look through the books which treat of them; but, not thinking it reasonable to condemn, without knowing why, all those who are addicted to them, who are often otherwise clever men, mostly learned, notable in the service of the law or the sword, I have taken upon myself (to avoid being unjust, and not to bore myself with dullreading) to pretend that I am interested in all these sciences, when with anyone whom I have reason to suppose has enquired into them. ("Conversation the First", p. 112)

This passage is rendered faithfully from the French of the Abbé de Montfaucon de Villars: at the beginning of *Le Comte*, the narrator feigns belief in the secret sciences. Throughout the book, he expresses the same horror at the Count's teachings that one might even expect from a sensible reader of the *Egoist*. At the end of the original French text, however, the narrator's stance to what he has learned is much more ambiguous. Here is the final paragraph of the Abbé de Montfaucon de Villars's original text:

> Ainsi finit l'entretien du Comte de Gabalis. Il revint le lendemain, & me porta le Discours qu'il avoit fait aux peuples soûterrains; il est merveilleux! Je le donnerois avec la suite des Entretiens qu'une Vicomtesse & moy avons eus auec ce Grand homme, si j'étois seur que tous mes Lecteurs eussent l'esprit droit & ne trouvassent pas mauvais que je me divertisse aux dépens des fous. Si je voy qu'on veüille laisser faire à mon Livre le bien qu'il est capable de produire; & qu'on ne me fasse pas l'injustice de me soupçonner de vouloir donner credit aux Sciences secretes, sous le pretexte de les tourner en ridicules; je continuërary à me réjoüir de Monsieur le Comte, & je pourray donner bien tost un autre Tome.[21]

At the end of *Le Comte de Gabalis*, the narrator seems to discard his initial scepticism; he is much more enthusiastic about the Count's teachings. In the Brothers' translation of *Le Comte*, this final paragraph is faithfully, if heavily, rendered into English:

> Thus ends the Discourse of the Comte de Gabalis. He returned the next day and brought the speech that he had delivered to the Subterranean Peoples. It was marvellous! I would publish it with the series of Discourses which a certain Vicomtesse and I have had with this Illustrious Man, were I certain that all my readers would have the proper spirit, and not take it amiss that I amuse myself at the expense of fools. If I see that people are willing to let my book accomplish the good that it is capable of doing, and are not unjustly suspecting me of seeking to give credit to the Occult Sciences under the pretence of ridiculing them, I shall continue to delight in Monsieur le Comte, and shall soon be able to publish another volume. (p. 201)

For "The Brothers" the question of belief is obviously not the complicated issue that it is for Olivia Shakespear, Yeats, and Pound. Olivia Shakespear's condensed translation of this final paragraph of *Le Comte de Gabalis* is much more ambiguous, and seems designed to re-emphasize the scepticism that the narrator had professed at the beginning of the work:

> Thus ended our conversation. I had many others with him, and would give their substance were I sure that my readers would

recognize the fact that I am no believer in the Secret Sciences, whilst pretending to laugh at them. If I were certain of not being misunderstood on this point, I would go on amusing myself with the Count, and would soon give another volume to the world. ("V." p. 207)

Unlike the Brothers, Olivia Shakespear is not worried about the "proper spirit" of her readers or concerned that her book "accomplish the good it is capable of doing". Furthermore, her prose is constructed to make sure she *is* misunderstood on this point: "I am no believer in the Secret Sciences, whilst pretending to laugh at them". The awkward syntax and peculiar logic of this phrase obscure the issue of belief altogether. Even the endings of more famous books – "Shantih shantih shantih" or "yes I said yes I will Yes" – are, by comparison, less ambiguous because of the resonance of their incantatory power.

Olivia Shakespear's "Memoirs of a Charming Person" is designed to emphasize the essential levity of *Le Comte de Gabalis* – not the intricacies of occult philosophy. The Brothers' translation of *Le Comte*, like most French editions of the book, includes a detailed and oppressively serious commentary that doubles the size of the volume. When Pound suggested that Dorothy Shakespear read *Le Comte*, he was careful to warn her that the "first part only . . . is amusing" (*EPDS* 302); the appended notes were worthless to him. It is finally not the subject matter but the elitist attitude of occult literature that was most important for Pound. He did write to Dorothy Shakespear's father that he considered himself a priest, but he worshipped not in the Church of England or the Secret Commonwealth but in the society of the arts. Olivia Shakespear designed "Memoirs of a Charming Person" to introduce this secret society of readers to the doctrine of " 'symbolism' in its profounder sense" while requiring them to believe only in the sanctity of modernism.

NOTES

1. "Status Rerum," *Poetry*, 1 (January 1913) 125. Pound's praise of Yeats is qualified:

   > Mr. Yeats' method is to my way of thinking very dangerous, for although he is the greatest of living poets who use English, and though he has sung some of the moods of life immortally, his art has not broadened much in scope during the past decade.

2. "Vorticism" was originally published in the *Fortnightly Review*, xcvi, 573 (September 1914) 461–71. I refer to the more easily accessible reprint of the essay in Pound's *Gaudier-Brzeska* (1916; rpt. New York: New Directions, 1970). I will cite Pound's works in the body of the text using the following abbreviations:

   CEP   *Collected Early Poems* (New York: New Directions, 1976).
   EPDS *Ezra Pound and Dorothy Shakespear: Their Letters, 1909–1914*, ed. A. Walton Litz and Omar S. Pound (New York: New Directions, 1984).

G-B   *Gaudier-Brzeska*
LE   *Literary Essays*, ed. T. S. Eliot (New York: New Directions, 1968).
Per   *Personae* (New York: New Directions, 1971).
SR   *The Spirit of Romance* (New York: New Directions, 1968).
T   *Translations*, ed. Hugh Kenner (New York: New Directions, 1963).

3. In this article, "The Later Yeats", Pound's praise of Yeats is now unqualified:

> Whenever I mention Mr Yeats I am apt to be assailed with questions: 'Will Mr Yeats do anything more?', 'Is Yeats in the movement?', 'How *can* the chap go on writing this sort of thing?'
> And to these inquiries I can only say that Mr. Yeats' vitality is quite unimpared, and that I dare say he'll do a good deal; and that up to date no one has shown any disposition to supersede him as the best poet in England, or any likelihood of doing so for some time. . . . (*LE* 378)

4. A. Walton Litz, "Pound and Yeats: The Road to Stone Cottage", forthcoming in *Ezra Pound among the Poets*, ed. George Bornstein (Chicago: University of Chicago Press, 1985). This is the most comprehensive and incisive analysis of their early years. The two best examinations of the life-long relationship of Yeats and Pound are Richard Ellmann, *Eminent Domain: Yeats among Wilde, Joyce, Pound, Eliot and Auden* (New York: Oxford University Press, 1967) pp. 57–87 and Terence Diggory, *Yeats and American Poetry: the Tradition of the Self* (Princeton University Press, 1983) pp. 31–58. See also Thomas Parkinson, "Yeats and Pound: the Illusion of Influence", *Comparative Literature*, 6 (Summer 1954) 256–64; Herbert N. Schneidau, "Pound and Yeats: The Question of Symbolism", *ELH*, 32 (June 1965) 220–37; K. L. Goodwin, *The Influence of Ezra Pound* (London: Oxford University Press, 1966); and Thomas Rees, "Ezra Pound and the Modernization of W. B. Yeats", *Journal of Modern Literature*, 4 (February 1975) 574–92.

5. Herbert N. Schneidau, in *Ezra Pound: the Image and the Real* (Baton Rouge: Louisiana State University Press, 1969), has made a cogent although incomplete attempt to unify these two strains of Pound's thoughts about Imagism. See especially ch. 3, "Pound and Joyce: the Universal in Particular", pp. 74–109.

6. "Contemporania" was published in *Poetry*, 2 (April 1913) 1–12, and included "Tenzone", "The Condolence", "The Garret", "The Garden", "Ortus", "Dance Figure, for the Marriage in Cana of Galilee", "Salutation", "Salutation the Second", "Pax Saturni", "Commission", "A Pact", and "In a Station of the Metro".

7. Thomas Parkinson, in "Yeats and Pound: the Illusion of Influence", has shown convincingly that "Yeats himself – before meeting Pound – had outgrown the early Yeats". Parkinson errs, however, when he states that Pound "could not stomach Yeats's occult experiments . . ." (pp. 258–60).

8. Herbert N. Schneidau, in "Pound and Yeats: The Question of Symbolism", states correctly that Pound "developed a peculiar variety of metaphysical mysticism which . . . was to some extent shaped by Yeats" but like Parkinson is mistaken when he claims that "Pound was tying together spiritualism, suggestiveness and Symbolism in order to reject them more emphatically" (pp. 221, 232).

9. Pound mentions both *Le Comte de Gabalis* (1670) and *The History of Magic* (1854) in his response to Dorothy Shakespear's questions about symbolism. In Canto 83 Pound recalled that "at Stone Cottage by the waste moor" Yeats preferred "Ennemoser on Witches" to Wordsworth.
    Robert Kirk's *Secret Commonwealth; or, a treatise displaying the chiefe Curiosities as they are in use among diverse of the People of Scotland to this day* (1691) was another esoteric work that Pound and Yeats read during the winter of 1913–1914. On 21 November 1913 Pound wrote to Dorothy Shakespear that he had "started Kirk's 'Secret Commonwealth' which is diverting" (*EPDS* 276). Kirk justifies the existence of "SEERS, or Men of a 2d

or more exhalted Sight than others" (*The Secret Commonwealth*, ed. Andrew Lang [London: David Nutt, 1893] p. 28), and Pound no doubt found support for his visionary conception of symbolism in these doctrines.

In the 1920s catalogue of Yeats's library, a copy of *Le Comte de Gabalis* (1715) is listed. See p. 283 of this volume of *Yeats Annual*.

10. The title page of the edition Pound owned reads:

> DEMONIALITY / OR / INCUBI AND SUCCUBI / A TREATISE / *wherein is shown that there are in existence on earth rational creatures besides man, endowed like him with a body and a soul, that are born and die like him, redeemed by our Lord Jesus-Christ, and capable of receiving salvation or damnation.* / BY THE REV. FATHER / SINISTRARI OF AMENO / (17th century) / *Published from the original Latin Manuscript / discovered in London in the year* 1872, / *and translated into French by* ISIDORE LISEUX / Now first translated into English / With the Latin text. / PARIS / *Isidore* LISEUX, 2, *Rue Bonaparte.* / 1879

11. Lady Gregory, *Visions and Beliefs in the West of Ireland* (1920; rept. New York: Oxford University Press, 1970) p. 340.

12. Yeats's "The Priest and the Fairy" differs from Sinistrari's tale (as Yeats notes in Lady Gregory's *Visions and Beliefs*) in that the Priest declares that the souls of fairies are not redeemable: the fairy asks, " 'Man of wisdom, dost thou know / Where the souls of fairies go?" but "The father dropt his rosary – / 'They are lost, they are lost, each one,' cried he" (*VP* 729, 730).

13. On 21 March 1914, Dorothy Shakespear wrote to Pound saying that Olivia Shakespear "has done another Gabalis entretien which I shall bring back with me for you" (*EPDS*, 334). The five "conversations" of Olivia Shakespear's translation of *Le Comte de Gabalis* (retitled "Memoirs of a Charming Person") appeared in five issues of the *Egoist*:

> "Conversation the First", *Egoist*, 1 (16 March 1914) 112–13.
> "Second Conversation", *Egoist*, 1 (15 April 1914) 153–4.
> "Third Conversation", *Egoist*, 1 (1 May 1914) 171–3.
> "Fourth Conversation", *Egoist*, 1 (15 May 1914) 189–90.
> "V.," *Egoist*, 1 (1 June 1914) 207–8.

Olivia Shakespear translated only the original five dialogues by the Abbé de Montfaucon de Villars and included none of the appended notes and commentary that are present in most French and English editions of the book. In the "Third Conversation", p. 173, when the Count mentions the "Jewish Teraphim", Olivia Shakespear adds a footnote: "Translator's Note: Judges xvii.; Ezekiel xxi., 21; Hosea iii, 4". Further references to "Memoirs of a Charming Person" will be made in the body of the text.

Le Comte de Gabalis has made one other appearance in English literary history: it provided Pope with the Sylphs and Salamanders of his enlarged (1917) edition of *The Rape of the Lock*. In his dedication "To Mrs. Arabella Fermor" he describes *Le Comte* as a book "which both in its Title and Size is so like a *Novel*, that many of the Fair Sex have read it for one by mistake" (*The Poems of Alexander Pope*, vol. II, ed. Geoffrey Tillotson [New Haven: Yale University Press, 1962] pp. 142–3).

14. The title page of this edition reads:

> *Sub-Mundanes*; / or, / *The Elementaries of the Cabala*: Being / *The History of Spirits*, / Reprinted from the text of the Abbe de Villars, / Physio-Astro-Mystic, / wherein is asserted that there are in existence on earth rational / creatures besides man. / With an illustrative Appendix from the Work "Demonality," / or "Incubi and Succubi" by the Rev. Father Sinistrari, / of Ameno. Privately printed only for Subscribers / Bath / 1886.

When Montague Summers retranslated Sinistrari's book, he pointed out that it lay in a tradition which also included *The Celtic Twilight* and other writings by Yeats, who is cited as an authority in his introduction to *Demoniality etc.*, (London: Fortune Press, n.d., [1927]) pp. xxix–xxxii.

15. Even less appropriate for this work was the *Grimoire of Pope Honorius* which Pound also mentions in his response to Dorothy Shakespear's questions about symbolism (*EPDS* 302). This little book of black magic, falsely attributed to Pope Honorius III, was probably written in the 19th century. Both its claims for antiquity and its spells for mastering occult powers are spurious. Yeats's Hanrahan reads the *Grimoire* in "The Great Dhoul and Hanrahan the Red" (*VSR* 188–9) but no reference to the book is made in Yeats's notes for *Visions and Beliefs*. Dr Trefusis, in Olivia Shakespear's *Beauty's Hour*, speaks of Honorius as a "most absorbing old impostor" (*The Savoy*, V, Sept., 1896, 15).

16. Henry Bryan Binns, "The Dangers of Occultism", *Egoist*, 1 (15 May 1914) 200; Ezra Pound, "The Dangers of Occultism", *Egoist*, 1 (1 June 1914) 220.

17. Ezra Pound, "The New Sculpture", *Egoist*, 1 (16 February 1914) 67–8. Further references to "The New Sculpture" will be made in the text. Pound's growing interest in the aristocratic, priest-like role of the artist was probably enhanced by his association with Yeats. Before he met Yeats, Pound would have learned from *Ideas of Good and Evil* that "The arts are . . . about to take upon their shoulders the burdens that have fallen from the shoulders of priests" (*E&I* 193). But in addition, Pound admired the aristocratic attitude of the poems Yeats was writing at Stone Cottage for inclusion in *Responsibilities*. Reviewing this volume in "The Later Yeats" (May 1914), Pound wrote that in "The Grey Rock" he found "a nobility which is, to me at least, the very core of Mr Yeats' production, the constant element of his writing" (*LE* 379). As A. Walton Litz remarks in "Pound and Yeats: the Road to Stone Cottage", Yeats's *Responsibilities* "established a role for the poet and an attitude toward the social and literary values of the 'middle class' that would dominate avant-garde writing for the next decade".

18. I quote the translation of Tertullian from another English translation of *Le Comte de Gabalis* published in 1914: *Comte de Gabalis by the Abbe N. de Villars Rendered out of French into English with a Commentary, published by The Brothers* (London: W. H. Broome, 1914) p. [iii]. Further references to this translation will be made in the text.

19. Joseph Ennemoser, *The History of Magic*, trans. William Howitt (London: Henry G. Bohn, 1854) II, 8.

20. Ezra Pound, "Editorial," *Little Review*, 4 (May 1917) 5.

21. Montfaucon de Villars, *Le Comte de Gabalis*, ed. Roger Laufer (Paris: A. G. Nizet, 1963) p. 137.

Ezra Pound's Versions of Fenollosa's Noh Manuscripts and Yeats's Unpublished "Suggestions & Corrections" [1]

Yoko Chiba

I

The appointment by Mrs Fenollosa of Ezra Pound as literary executor of the Noh manuscripts of Ernest Fenollosa (1853–1908) took place in London in late 1913. There were at least two major incentives for her to entrust Pound with the documents: first, she had read and liked Pound's poems in *Poetry*, and secondly, she and Pound were linked by their association with a Japanese poet, Yone Noguchi (1875–1947).[2] After only three weeks' acquaintance, she asked Pound to edit and publish the manuscripts. Altogether there were about sixteen notebooks: some of them were handed to Pound personally and others were posted in London, presumably towards the end of 1913.[3] They contained draft translations of Noh dramas and Chinese poetry, and an essay on "The Chinese Written Character as a Medium for Poetry".

In 1962, Pound replied (in an interview for the *Paris Review*) to the question, "How did Mrs. Fenollosa happen to hit upon you?":

> "Well I met her at Sarojini Naidu's and she said that Fenollosa had been in opposition to all the Profs. and academes, and she had seen some of my stuff and said I was the only person who could finish up these notes as Ernest would have wanted them done. Fenollosa saw what needed to be done but he didn't have time to finish it." [4]

"My stuff" refers to some of *Lustra*, which first appeared as "Contemporania" in *Poetry* of April 1913.[5] Harriet Monroe had started *Poetry* in the previous year and from the outset she had shown interest in Japan.[6] Pound's poem "In a Station of the Metro" in "Contemporania", in

121

particular, shows strong Japanese influence,[7] which Mrs Fenollosa must
have easily discerned. Pound had read Noguchi's poems after 1911,
when he first wrote to Noguchi that "if the east and the west are ever to
understand each other that understanding must come slowly and come
first through the art".[8] It would never have occurred to Pound that he
would so soon find himself absorbed in that mediatory endeavour
through the editing of ancient Chinese poetry and medieval Japanese
drama.

In the opening Note of *'Noh' or Accomplishment* Pound described his
design in editing the manuscripts:

> The vision and the plan are Fenollosa's. In the prose I have had but
> the part of literary executor; in the plays my work has been that of
> translator who has found all the heavy work done for him and who has
> but the pleasure of arranging beauty into the words.[9]

The fact is that Pound's subsequent work was not so simple as it sounds
from the above, as I shall show. For the most part it was a total
reconstruction of Fenollosa's drafts written in pencil, and it took him
about three years to complete.

Fenollosa was not the first to translate Noh plays into English, but in
volume and concentration his work far surpassed that of his predecessors, as Pound recognized.[10] Fenollosa took chanting lessons from a
distinguished Noh actor, who had served the Tokugawa Shogunate in
the art which had come down to him through many generations. He
writes:

> For the last twenty years I have been studying the Noh, under the
> personal tuition of Umewaka Minoru and his sons, learning by actual
> practice the method of the singing and something of the acting; I have
> taken down from Umewaka's lips invaluable oral traditions of the
> stage as it was before 1868; and have prepared, with his assistance and
> that of native scholars, translations of some fifty of the texts.[11]

Fenollosa had ideal qualifications for a study of Noh as philosophy,
art, poetry, religion and music – as a total theatrical art form; one "of
which Mr. Yeats and Mr. Craig may approve",[12] as Pound rightly put it.
Fenollosa also "saw what the style in translation ought to be. He died
before he had been able to maintain this style for more than a few
sentences at a time".[13] To Pound, without knowledge of the language,
devolved the task of infusing poetry into Fenollosa's prose translations,
though he also wrote "the stuff as prose where the feet are rather
uniform".[14] The Fenollosa manuscripts amply demonstrate the eager
and efficient labour that he devoted to his notes in 1897–1900. Pound
studied them with equal care: in practical editing his "general principle"

was "not putting in mere words that occur in original when they contribute nothing to the SENSE of the translation".[15]

Only Yeats and Eliot had been inclined, according to Pound, "to estimate the general debt to Fenollosa", and "in both their cases they have show[n] a tendency to think that I did it all",[16] he said in an unpublished typescript note. Pound edited the manuscripts on the basis of Mrs Fenollosa's "conviction . . . that Fen. wanted it transd [sic] *as* literature not as philology".[17] The progress of Pound's work on the manuscripts is to be traced in his published letters written at Stone Cottage, Coleman's Hatch in Sussex. Pound was acting as private secretary to Yeats and they shared this winter retreat in 1913–16. Their close personal relationship in the cottage was an amicable one, though Yeats, as Pound wrote to his mother, would sometimes "bore me to death with psychical research".[18] Pound's first mention of his acquisition of the documents appears in his letter of 19 December 1913 to William Carlos Williams: "I am very placid and happy and busy. Dorothy is learning Chinese. I've all old Fenollosa's treasures in mss."[19] On 31 January 1914 he wrote to Harriet Monroe:

> I think you will agree with me that this Japanese find is about the best bit of luck we've had since the starting of the magazine. I don't put the work under the general category of translation either. It could scarcely have come before now. The earlier attempts to do Japanese in English are dull and ludicrous. That you needn't mention either as the poor scholars have done their bungling best. One can not commend the results. The best plan is to say nothing about it. This present stuff ranks as recreation. You'll find W. B. Y. also very keen on it.[20]

About this time Noguchi was back in England again to give lectures: on "Japanese Poetry" at the Japan Society, London on 14 January; and on "Japanese *Hokku* Poetry" at Magdalen College, Oxford on 29 January 1914. The latter was arranged by Robert Bridges, who asked Noguchi to show in his lecture "what Japanese poetry sounds like" and then to "transliterate it into English".[21] Between these two lectures Noguchi paid a visit to Yeats and Pound, who were spending their first winter in their cottage with the manuscripts.[22]

By the spring of 1914 Pound was so intent on his work as to write to Amy Lowell, "I am on my head with Fenollosa notes."[23] The exalting interactions between Yeats and Pound and Fenollosa's manuscripts continued until Yeats finished his first experimental play based on a new model in spring 1916. Yeats's "Swedenborg, Mediums, and the Desolate Places" (1914) was the immediate result of this stimulus of Noh; it had led him to a comparative study of psychical phenomena in East and West, as Pound reported the forming process of this essay to *The Japan Times* years later:

... Yeats, in my company, had spent several winters trying to correlate Lady Gregory's Irish folk-lore with the know[n] traditions of various myths, psychologies and religions.[24]

Thus, "Swedenborg, Mediums, and the Desolate Places" introduces Yeats's earliest mention of Noh with its spiritualistic connotations. Yeats accounts for his impression:

Last winter Mr. Ezra Pound was editing the late Professor Fenollosa's translations of the Noh Drama of Japan, and read me a great deal of what he was doing. Nearly all that my fat old woman in Soho learns from her familiars in there is an unsurpassed lyric poetry and in strange and poignant fables once danced or sung in the houses of nobles.[25]

In *'Noh' or Accomplishment* Pound echoes what Yeats said, but showed his simpler attitude towards Noh:

All through the winter of 1914–15 I watched Mr. Yeats correlating folk-lore (which Lady Gregory had collected in Irish cottages) and data of the occult writers with the habits of charlatans of Bond Street. If the Japanese authors had not combined the psychology of such matters with what is to me a very fine sort of poetry, I would not bother about it.[26]

Meanwhile Yeats, talking to Yone Noguchi about folk literature and Noh, said:

The folk element is, in my opinion, alone worthy of any poetry; by that I mean that the true literature should be a folk literature invigorated, not weakened, by the cultured elements. From such a view I am pleased with the Japanese No plays, specimens of which I have seen through the late Fenollosa's posthumous translation which my friend, Ezra Pound, is just now editing. I confess my mind is perfectly saturated now with the plays.[27]

The exact date of this meeting is not certain, but the report of it suggests how Yeats prepared himself for writing his Noh-influenced play. As Pound described it:

W. B. Yeats was at once enkindled by the imperfect versions of Noh which I was able to make from Fenollosa's notes. He started writing plays in Noh form for his Irish theatre and for performances where no western stage was available.[28]

The resultant play, *At the Hawk's Well*, was Yeats's "new start on the foundation of those Noh dramas" written for the "new theatre, or theatreless drama",[29] as Pound put it.

In the meantime, Pound had met another Japanese man who was in London at that time – Michio Ito. This occurred at the Café Royal, that "nest of artists", sometime after the outbreak of World War I, which had brought Ito to London from Germany.[30] In the early summer of 1915 Pound asked for Ito's help with the editing of the Noh manuscripts. Ito, who found "nothing more boring than Noh",[31] had two Japanese friends, painters trained in Noh chanting. He took them to Pound and Yeats so that they might get a feeling of Noh theatre. Pound listened to their chanting "inattentively".[32] On the other hand, Yeats who had not written any new plays since 1910, told Ito that he "had grown weary of realistic plays, and had already resolved not to write any more plays".[33] By August 1915, however, Yeats had renewed his enthusiasm for playwriting, as he wrote to Robert Bridges: "I shall be here till September I imagine. It is my one chance of finishing a new play."[34]

Yeats's confidence in this theatrical form is manifest in his letter to Lady Gregory on 26 March 1916: "I believe I have at last found a dramatic form that suits me . . .".[35] When the play came to production Pound was also involved, "bother[ing] a good deal about the production of Yeats's new play".[36] In fact, Pound was in the rehearsal, as Yeats records in "A People's Theatre": "Mr. Ezra Pound, who had never acted on any stage, in the absence of our chief player rehearsed for half an hour."[37] Yeats was "tired out with the excitement of rehearsing my new play".[38]

On 2 April 1916 *At the Hawk's Well* was played in Lady Emerald Cunard's drawing room in London to "delight", as Yeats says, "the best minds of my time".[39] A few hours before the performance, Yeats was more confident than ever, as he wrote to John Quinn: "I shall have a success that would have pleased Sophocles. No press, no photographs in the papers, no crowd . . . I shall be as lucky as a Japanese dramatic poet at the Court of the Shogun."[40] The performance was repeated on 4 April at Lady Islington's. To the first performance Pound took Eliot, who welcomed Yeats's emergence, as he felt, from being a "survivor of the '90's" and thereafter "saw Yeats as a more eminent contemporary than as an elder from whom one could learn".[41] Soon after these productions, *Certain Noble Plays of Japan*, the first publication in book form of Fenollosa's translations of Noh plays, appeared from the Cuala Press in Dublin.

II

As Pound's editorial work on Fenollosa's manuscripts inspired Yeats to write the new play, so Yeats exercised an influence on the Fenollosa–Pound translations. That Yeats gave assistance to Pound in the interpretation of the plays, in particular their mystical aspect, is easily recognized. Pound's English usage in the finished translations, too, was indebted to Yeats.[42] In his unpublished "Suggestions & Corrections", written in response to the galley-proofs of *Certain Noble Plays of Japan*, Yeats called Pound's attention to their earlier talks: "I have explained my objection to 'largess'. It does not mean 'thanks'."[43] This single comment implies that they had discussed the translations before they went to print. What and how much Yeats suggested and Pound accepted, before printing, remains a matter of conjecture. It is clear, though, that the editing was to a certain extent a collaboration between the two.

The Cuala edition contained *Nishikigi*, *Hagoromo*, *Kumasaka* and *Kagekiyo*, the first three of which had been published separately in American and English journals.[44] Yeats's essay, "Certain Noble Plays of Japan", which had introduced the Cuala volume, appeared by itself later in *Drama* in November 1916. *Kagekiyo*, whose translation by Fenollosa and Pound did not appear in any journal, had previously been translated by Marie C. Stopes in her *Plays of Old Japan* published in London in 1913.[45] While doing his editing, Pound referred to this book, which, though much neglected since, was one of the very few sources of Noh available in English at that time[46] (Gordon Craig, for instance, relied on this volume for information on Noh[47]). Stopes's version of *Kagekiyo*, translated in verse with elaborate archaic expressions and metrical devices, is academic. By comparison, Pound's rendition of *Kagekiyo*, a play "with Homeric force"[48] as he called it, is in modern free verse and a genuinely poetic work.

In all probability, the inclusion of *Kagekiyo* in the Cuala edition, not to mention *Nishikigi* and *Hagoromo*, reflected Yeats's preference. This inference may be drawn from the theme of the play. Based partly on the medieval Japanese epic, *The Tale of Heike*, *Kagekiyo* is a play about the brave warrior named in the title: his fighting in the battle between the two doomed clans, his destiny and paternal love. In its basic setting some parallelism with the great Irish saga of Cuchulain is plain. But Kagekiyo is now an old blind beggar in a hermitage, being sought by his daughter whom he had begotten on a courtesan. Like Cuchulain and his son, father and child have never met before. In *Kagekiyo* the father rejects his daughter, after they identify the other out of his sense of "shame". This "heroic" gesture, described by Pound, quoting from Fenollosa's notes, as the "stoicism"[49] of samurai ethics, contrasts with Cuchulain's more dramatic catastrophe. Nevertheless, Kagekiyo's paternal agony is as intense and tragic as the Irish hero's. *Kumasaka*, another of the four plays, is also reminiscent of Irish mythology with its heroic combats. The famous boy warrior, Ushiwaka, who kills Kumasaka and many of his followers with superhuman dexterity, recalls the young Cuchulain. As

Pound commented: "The ghost of Kumasaka returns not from a grudge and not to gain anything; but to state clearly that the very young man who had killed him had not done so by a fluke or slip, but that he had outfenced him."[50] All these correspondences must have left a strong impression on Yeats's mind.

Interestingly, the reviewer of *'Noh' or Accomplishment* in *The Times Literary Supplement* of 25 January 1917 identified in Noh "something not unlike Mr. Synge's divine savages". He goes on: "Change the deities and you will not be unpleasantly reminded of *The Well of the Saints*."[51] What is suggested is the type of character who represents spiritual nobility and freedom under the guise of physical defeat, common to both Noh and Synge. The sentiment of Noh is overwhelmingly human under its supernatural garb. As one of the exceptions to the general rule of Noh whereby the *shite* (main character) is the spirit of the supernatural or the dead, Kagekiyo is very much in the flesh, in beggarly modesty, throughout the play. Similar "divine savages" are to be found in *'Noh' or Accomplishment* in such plays as *Sotoba Komachi*, *Kayoi Komachi*, *Tamura*, *Genjo* and *Suma Genji*. In *Tamura* the Boy, who is the incarnation of the great ancient warrior, says, as Pound puts it, "You should think of me as some one of rank, though I am concealed in humble appearance."[52]

The similarities between Irish and Japanese themes and characters must have fascinated Yeats, not to mention other theatrical features of Noh – symbolism and simplicity – that embodied his ideals. And that his enthusiasm for the metaphysical aspect of Noh was equally great may be seen in the diction and phraseology used by Pound in his work under Yeatsian influence: (in the order of appearance) "ghost psychology"; 'the 'new' doctrine of the suggestibility or hypnotizability of ghosts"; 'astral body"; "séance"; "occult"; "supernatural manifestation"; 'spiritist doctrines"; "magic"; "ritual"; "the dance as symbolical of the daily changes of the moon"; "Sidhe"; "the first shadowy and then bright apparition" and so on.[53] Such words and expressions are consciously employed by Pound in his notes and stage directions to establish the affinity between Noh and Western esoteric spiritualism.

'Noh' or Accomplishment is full of pseudo-Irish, or Syngean, speech. For that matter, this volume of Noh plays is a curious mixture of at least four kinds of literary English: "English" English; Irish English; Japanese English; and "new" English. An analysis of this extraordinary fusion in the translated work unravels the subtle quality of the triple collaboration of Fenollosa–Pound–Yeats. It may also disclose these individuals' different attitudes towards Noh.

This significant linguistic aspect of the book was first mentioned by T. S. Eliot. In his review of *'Noh' or Accomplishment* in *The Egoist* of August 1917, "The Noh and the Image", Eliot points out the Irish–English usage. (He also gives the examples of Anglo-Saxon alliterative verse and a Provençal echo.) He quotes the same passage from *Kayoi Komachi* as is quoted by the *Times* reviewer:

> *Tsure*: I say they were very *fine* prayers. I will not come back without a
>   struggle.
> *Shite*: *I've a sad heart to see* you looking up to Buddha, you who left me
>   alone, I *diving* in the black rivers of hell. Will soft prayers be a
>   comfort to you?[54]

Here the Syngean Irish speech is undeniable in what Eliot calls "the semi-comic 'fine', the infinitive after 'I've a sad heart', and the Celtic present participle".[55] (To these we might add the flowing continuity of rhythmical speech.)

A comparison of the *shite*'s speech quoted with its original translation by Pound, as it appeared in *Drama* of May 1915, is illuminating. This earlier version goes:

> *Shite*: *It is a sad heart I have to see* you looking up to Buddha, you who left
>   me alone, *as I was diving* in the black rivers of hell. Will soft
>   prayers be a comfort to you . . . ?[56]

The first line already sounds Irish, while "diving" in the past progressive tense in the second line was changed later into the form we have seen. Excepting this revision, however, there are very few changes in *Kayoi Komachi*, none of which is serious, between the article and the book translations.

Of the fifteen Noh plays in *'Noh' or Accomplishment*, *Kayoi Komachi* has the most distinct Irish idiom, as Eliot rightly pointed out. In atmosphere, too, this play is strangely evocative of something like Irish mood. We may quote a few more lines from *Kayoi Komachi*:

> And *there's* an odd little woman *comes* here every day with fruit
>   and fuel.
> That's *queer*. I asked her her name . . . then she's gone *like a mist*.
> There's *a heap of good* in your prayers.
> I had my own rain of tears; that was the dark night, *surely*.
> *This night* is the *longing fulfilled*.[57]

This play is based on the celebrated ancient legend of Komachi. The heroine Komachi first appears as a hundred-year-old hag and wandering beggar. In her prime she enjoyed a fabulous life and reputation as a great poetess of unsurpassed beauty, followed by a train of suitors. Being haughty, she rejected them all. In the second part of the play, revealing her true self as this renowned lady, Ono no Komachi, her ghost meets the

ghost of her famed suitor Shosho. By a priest's prayer at the end of the
play both spirits are finally blessed with the liberation from their fixation
on unrequited love and are thus united. Pound wrote a note on the theme
of this play common to that of *Nishikigi*:

> There is nothing like a ghost for holding to an idée fixe. In *Nishikigi*, the
> ghosts of the two lovers are kept apart because the woman had steadily
> refused the hero's offering of charm sticks. The two ghosts are brought
> together by the piety of a wandering priest. Mr. Yeats tells me that he
> has found a similar legend in Aran, where the ghosts come to a priest
> to be married.[58]

Such phrases already mentioned as "the 'new' doctrine of the
suggestibility or hypnotizability of ghosts" and "astral body" come from
Kayoi Komachi.[59] The image of the old woman who has gone "like a mist"
and reappears as a young beauty, too, is remarkably reminiscent of
Yeats's Cathleen ni Houlihan, who, appearing first as a "poor old
woman", reveals her true self as a "young girl" with the "walk of a
queen"[60] at the end of the play. And, the down-to-earth reality of old
Komachi is comparable to that of some of Synge's plays.

The translation of *Kagekiyo* has relatively less Irish effect, despite the
afore-mentioned Irish–Japanese analogies. Nevertheless, the following
phrases have some Syngean ring:

> . . . the autumn *wind is upon us*.
> He begs *a bit* from the passers, and *the likes of us* keep him.
> . . . but oh, to tell them! *to be telling* them over now in his
>   wretched condition.[61]

In *Nishikigi* Irish idioms are few but we have:

> *'Tis a sad name to look* back on.
> There's *a cold feel* in the autumn.[62]

And a longer speech in prose from the opening scene of *Nishikigi* is
suggestive of Irish influence in its rich cadences:

> Times out of mind am I here setting up this bright branch, this silky
> wood with the charms painted in it as fine as the web you'd get in the
> grass-cloth of Shinobu, that they'd be still selling you in this
> mountain.[63]

The original translation of this passage by Fenollosa is in plain English,
implying nothing of Pound's flowing rhythm:

It is this very colored-branch, (set up) time after time, as if it were
brocade woven into the narrow fabric of Kefu, which shall set up the
rumor (of love) . . . (just as) the grass-patterns of Shinobu cloth in
Land's End . . .[64]

The poetic Irish peasants' speech dramatically intensified by Synge
was already sufficiently strange and exotic for the normal English ear to
get accustomed to. Moreover, this Gaelic-influenced English was "all
poetry" and an "imaginative tongue", as Yeats wrote in "Swedenborg,
Mediums, and the Desolate Places".[65] Hence, it would not be a
completely illegitimate vehicle for some of the characters of Noh. It
seemed particularly fitting for such roles as a poor old woman, two lovers
seeking to be united like the Aran lovers, villager, wanderer, fisherman,
and the like. The action of many of these Noh plays takes place in an
open-air setting just as in Synge's country scenes, and this may also have
encouraged a linguistic assimilation.

Such pseudo-Syngean cadences as those quoted are also found in
Sotoba Komachi and *Hagoromo*, and to a lesser extent in *Kinuta* and *Chorio*.
Here is an example from *Sotoba Komachi*:

You think, because you see me alone now that I was in want of a
handsome man in the old days when Shosho came with the others –
Shii no Shosho of Fukakusa (Deep Grass) that came to me in the
moonlight and in the dark night and in the nights flooded with rain,
and in the black face of the wind and in the swish of snow. He came as
often as the melting drops fall from the eaves, ninety-nine times, and
he died. And his ghost is about me, driving me on with the madness.[66]

Compared with Synge's intense vivacity and colour, the Noh character's
speech is no doubt much toned down, and yet its vibrancy echoes the
Irish model.

Eliot thought these "Irish lapses" served "only as a distraction". He
added: "One feels that the original is not rendered because the
translation is not English. I have no prejudice against the Irish
drama. . . . But . . . I prefer the Noh in English."[67] Eliot rightly finds in
Noh the nature of creating "image", which had been first pointed out by
Pound as "Unity of Image" in *'Noh' or Accomplishment*.[68] This quality
"makes the play brief", writes Eliot. "It also prevents rhetoric. And
another consequence is that the dialogue is never conversation."[69]
Indeed, the elusive speech in Noh is due to the image-producing power of
poetry and song as an expression of emotion rather than as a means of
communication. The dialogue is frequently interchangeable and taken
over between the *shite* and the Chorus, or the *shite* and the *waki* (side
character) or the *tsure* (the companion of the *shite*) and so on. All these
functions are quite incompatible with high-flown rhetoric. This incom-

patibility of image and rhetoric made Eliot demur at "making the personages talk like Irish peasants".[70]

Apart from his opposition to Irish speech in Noh, Eliot commends the "happy fusion of original and translator . . . most of the translation is quite as good". To him the "plays are real plays, with real personalities"; "the ghost lovers, with as fine a strangeness in their way as any lovers of Webster or Ford". Also, Pound "not only produces very fine poetry," writes Eliot, "but seems to bring us much nearer to the Japanese".[71]

Now, let us briefly look at the element of Japanese English in Pound's translated work and in his new style. Some of the Japanese remnants of Fenollosa's literal translation have inevitably crept into Pound's editing. Here are some of the obscure expressions of obviously Japanese descent which Pound left as they were: "drink a cup of moonlight"; "you drink from the lasting cup of the autumn"; "the rain walks with heavier feet"; "This dance is for the evening plays"; "remembering-grass"; "let him call in the deep of time"; "she entered the seed-pod of Butsu [Buddha]"; "Its colour-smell is mysterious"; "give it this side"; "piny wind"; "a green wife" and "I send the sleeves back to the city."[72] These Japanese–English expressions may be ascribed more to Fenollosa's assistant, Tokuboku Hirata, than to Fenollosa himself. Some of the phrases were questioned by Yeats in his "Suggestions & Corrections". Literal translation of Japanese phrases often results in nonsensicality. On the other hand, such unintelligible translations do sometimes create a strangely evocative, poetic effect. Pound probably retained them because of his experimental approach to translation.

Nishikigi is one of the few translations by Fenollosa in which he adopts a method of alloting three lines to each original line in the Noh text: in the first line he gives a romanized phonetic transcription of Japanese sounds; in the second line a word-for-word English translation with comments under (and sometimes above as well) each word when necessary; and in the third line a sentence thus derived. Fenollosa's main purpose in using this system was to convey the meaning of the text as faithfully as possible. For a Western translator with poetic ambitions this idea seems a very sensible one, and particularly efficient when it comes to chanting. The limited space for this article does not allow us to compare, in detail, Fenollosa's third line draft of a certain passage in *Nishikigi* with his own revision of it written as a synopsis, and further with Pound's rendition of the passage based on both. This three-stage development demonstrates how the original translation underwent poetic transformation from Fenollosa to Pound. Significantly, it is to be noted also how much skill Fenollosa showed in the polishing process.[73]

At the end of his review Eliot quotes from *Nishikigi* lines by the Chorus in which a ghost of the woman weaves cloth in her cave. This scene, as

Eliot says, is one of the most successful experiments of Pound's poetic recreation. It goes:

Kiri, hatari, cho, cho,
Kiri, hatari, cho, cho,
The cricket sews on at his old rags,
With all the new grass in the field; sho,
Churr, isho, like the whirr of a loom; churr.[74]

Compare this with its original by Fenollosa:

Kiri, hatari, cho, cho; Kiri, hatari, cho, cho,
Shuttle in the woof, insects in the pines; crickets as for this insect that sings "sew away on the old songs", for the sake of clothing is it – indeed never fear for that! (for) I will let you take *hosonuno*, weaving it of the thread of the many grasses (that grow) in the field when you yourself live.[75]

These unfamiliar words at the beginning are in fact onomatopoeic sounds in which Japanese is extremely rich. Fenollosa was the first to make, with his musical ear, imaginative and effective use of them in romanized transcription directly from the Noh texts. Just above the quoted lines Pound inserts, in parentheses, a stage direction, "mimicking the sound of crickets". More precisely, it is the noises of weaving which sound like crickets singing. Following Fenollosa, Pound transmitted Japanese onomatopoeia, and further created his own new, unJapanese forms, with eerie effect, such as "sho" and "isho", mixed with his English "churr". Evaluating Pound's rendition as a "remarkable triumph of translator's skill", Eliot writes, "it is certainly English, and it is certainly *new* in English".[76]

Being stimulated to further onomatopoeic experiment, Pound at times produced a "hit-or-miss" effect. For instance, in *Kakitsubata* there is a line, "And the wild ducks cry: 'Kari! . . . Kari!'"[77] Originally, *kari* is supposed to be *kake-kotoba* (double-meaning or pivot word) which technique is used in profusion throughout the Noh texts. *Kari* means, first, "temporarily" and, second, a "wild goose". Fenollosa put *kari* in parentheses after the bird's name, and Pound changed this proper noun into its crying sound.[78] On the other hand, in *Kinuta*, Pound changed Fenollosa's "*horo horo, hara hara*," suggestive of the mixed sounds of insects singing and sorrowful tears dropping, to "*hera, hera*",[79] which happens to be onomatopoeic mocking laughter. Perplexed as Pound was with Fenollosa's handwriting, which is difficult to decipher, it is quite a distraction to the Japanese ear.

On other occasions Pound put a Japanese noun, not onomatopoeic, side by side with its English translation for its poetic effect: "*Ari-*

aki, / The dawn! / Come, we are out of place; / Let us go ere the light comes."[80] All these attempts are consciously directed at what Eliot called "new" English. Pound was an audacious innovator in translation of Noh plays, searching for the possibilities of various elements in English usage for poetic purposes. It was, for the most part, in keeping with the treatment that Mrs Fenollosa wanted for her late husband's manuscripts.

III

Yeats's undated notes given to Pound concerning the four translations of Noh plays were written in London probably in May or June 1916. His detailed comments on a variety of linguistic aspects of the translations reveal the strong interest Yeats took in Pound's project. The suggestions range from the stylistic and the grammatical to the typographical, from rhyme to stage directions. Yeats is fastidious about punctuation marks. Vague, unintelligible phrases are questioned. One thing of some interest is also disclosed in his notes: about the word "shaft-bench" used in *Nishikigi*, Yeats writes that it is "not in my English Dictionary Chambers".[81] In fact, this word meaning a stand for a "thill"[82] was originally used by Fenollosa in his draft and Pound left it unchanged in his published work.

Yeats writes that the word "actually", in "can be seen actually before the eyes", is "curiously prosaic . . . journalism surely".[83] Meanwhile, about the phrase, "Look sharp then", Yeats says that it "checks me", and defines it as "the wrong sort of colloquialism". He goes on:

There is something in translation from asiatic tongues that tempts people to this. As in the first version of "The Post Office", there are a number of such phrases. This phrase is however also incorrect. "Look sharp" means hurry up. Your meaning is plainly "Use your eyes well" or "Well use you eyes" or "You will need good eyes".[84]

Eventually Pound accepted this advice, deleting "sharp", in his version of *Nishikigi* in *Certain Noble Plays of Japan*:

Shite: Look then, the old times are shown,
       Faint as the shadow-flower shows in the grass that bears it.[85]

It is of interest to note that Pound's work is compared with the modern Indian play in English translation by Rabindranath Tagore, first published in book form by the Cuala Press in 1914. Yeats was quite familiar with others of Tagore's translated works (such as *Gitanjali* [1912] to which he wrote an introduction), through his help with

corrections and revisions. Yeats assumed, apparently from his previous
experience with Tagore, that such colloquialisms as Pound used derived
from the oriental character of the original. However, the Fenollosa
manuscripts prove the contrary: he did not use that phrase at all.
Compare Pound's lines quoted above with Fenollosa's corresponding
passage in full three line form:

Shite: Ide   ide   mukashi   wo   arawa-san   to
        now   now   old times   show will   that
        Now, now, saying that we will show (you) the old times,
               (sometimes called *hotaru-gusa*)
        Yu(u)   –   kage   –   gusa   no   tsuki   no   yo   ni
        1. saying   shadow-grass   's   moon 's   night in
        2. evening(has a deep thin flower
                   grass in dark place)
                                      who relates to
        in the night when the moon (looks for) the shadow grass of
                                                                evening.[86]

From the above "Now, now", Pound drew his own "Look sharp then".
    In Yeats's notes there are several similar cases. He criticized such
words as "inexplicable", "ornate", "void", "tryst" and "largess" – all
Pound's choice. The first of them is from *Hagoromo*, on which Yeats
simply comments, "I do not understand 'inexplicable'."[87] Again a
comparison between Fenollosa's draft and Pound's version will be useful
to show the latter's transformation.
    Fenollosa:

From the clouds on the high mountain of thousand miles which had
risen one hardly knew how. The rain must be just now clearing, to
judge by the moonlight on yonder lone pavilion.[88]

    Pound:

Upon a thousand heights had gathered the *inexplicable* cloud, swept by
the rain. The moon is just come to light the low house. A clear and
pleasant time surely.[89]

To examine Yeats's objections to the other words mentioned may also
demonstrate something that characterized Pound's phraseology. These
three words are used in *Nishikigi* in the following contexts:

While he has a staff or a wooden sceptre
Beautifully *ornate*.

A seed-pod *void* of the seed,
We had no meeting together.

To dream under dream we return.
Three years. . . . And the meeting comes now!
This night has happened over and over,
And only now comes the *tryst*. [90]

Yeats gave a substitute for each of them: "painted", "empty" and
"marriage", respectively. But none was accepted by Pound. First,
regarding "ornate", the corresponding lines by Fenollosa are: "And, as
for the thing which the male carries, it is a piece of wood ornamented by
being beautifully painted." [91] It is clear from this that Fenollosa's
original did not have "ornate" and that Pound derived the word from
"ornamented" and "painted". Yeats's objection to "ornate" was subtle:
"I suggest 'painted' instead of 'ornate'. 'Ornate' I cannot quite explain
why does not seem to be good English in this sentence. It is probably a
word that 'has not yet got its soul'." [92]

Secondly, as to "void", Fenollosa's corresponding line is: "Yet we do
not meet, a seed (of something possible in future)." [93] In this ambiguous
and fragmentary line "void" is not used, while "seed" is euphemistically
used as Fenollosa explains it in the above parentheses. He defines it as
"origin" in his second word-for-word line. The quoted speech by the
shite, the man in *Nishikigi*, is typical of unconversational speech of Noh
as pointed out by Eliot. It is taken over by the *tsure*, the woman, who says,
"the famous poem that expresses (this constitution)", [94] as Fenollosa
puts it. These two speeches as a whole suggest that the couple are going
to make a poem in which their "not meeting" will be the central theme;
origin and "seed". The sheer vagueness in Fenollosa's translation
caused Pound to deviate from the original idea, and to recreate his own
image of "seed-pod" which is "void" due to their unrequited love. Here
Yeats's comment is: " 'Void' is I think a poorer word than 'empty'.
'Void' is literary. It is not speech." [95]

Thirdly, "tryst" was not used by Fenollosa, either. His translation
was: ". . . we just now return to dream after dream, and this evening to
the mysterious meeting of three years." [96] Pound's longer rendition of
these lines quoted before is far better. But Yeats's dissatisfaction with
Pound's "tryst" is severe: "Seven lines from bottom of page I suggest
'marriage' instead of 'tryst'. We have seen them together. So they had
not to wait for a 'tryst'." [97]

There is another word worth mentioning, that is, "deformed" in
Kagekiyo. Pound's version is:

A blind man without his staff, I am *deformed*, and therefore speak evil;
excuse me. [98]

Fenollosa's original is:

> . . . a blind man who has lost his staff. Being such a *deformed* person, I
> speak such passionate words. O pardon me![99]

In this case Pound concurred with Fenollosa's "deformed", against
which Yeats writes, " 'deformed' does not seem good English. 'Maimed'
seems the correct word".[100] But Pound did not change it.

Yeats's "objection to 'largess' " has been mentioned. The word
"largess" occurred in the galley-proof of *Nishikigi* in *Certain Noble Plays of
Japan*, as it had in *Poetry* of May 1914. It was Pound's own choice for the
speech of the *shite*:

> I give you *largess*,
> For this meeting is under a difficult law, . . .[101]

The equivalent Fenollosa passage reads:

> O how thankful is this mysterious meeting of the law which (meeting)
> it is difficult to have . . .[102]

Yeats's further comment, "It does not mean 'thanks' ",[103] is especially
appropriate in view of Fenollosa's draft. Pound eventually accepted
Yeats's advice and the first line became "Take my thanks"[104] in *Certain
Noble Plays of Japan*. But *'Noh' or Accomplishment*, which came out after the
Cuala edition,[105] retains "largess" (though "sharp," as mentioned, has
been deleted from both). It is quite probable that in proof-reading *'Noh'
or Accomplishment* Pound simply overlooked "largess".

Other minor "Suggestions & Corrections" made by Yeats include
grammatical ones, such as in *Kumasaka*: ". . . a wound is said 'to pierce'.
This raises an incorrect mental picture. A weapon not a wound
'pierces'."[106] Some of his other points need reference to the original
Japanese texts for further clarification. The phrases, "stand and
withdraw" and "give it this side" in *Hagoromo* and "evening plays" in
Nishikigi, all literal translations from Japanese, puzzled Yeats. As to the
first of them, for instance, he writes: "I do not understand 'withdraw'. It
shound [=sounds] like an echo of the melodramatic 'stand & draw'.
What does it mean? Is it to 'withdraw a statement'? No. If it is to go
away, it is an archaism & is contradicted by 'stand'."[107]

Yeats's bewilderment was due to the fact that Pound used Fenollosa's
transliteration superfluously. Pound took "stand" from Fenollosa's
second line to place it next to "withdraw" in the third line, where only
the latter sufficed. Underlying Pound's awkward phrase, "stand and
withdraw", was the peculiar convention of Noh in which the *shite*
describes his own action of "withdrawing" in the third person while

performing it.[108] Since this "self-descriptive" device was unclear to Pound, in this case, despite Fenollosa's correct translation, he obscured the point by using the contradictory words in juxtaposition, as Yeats mentioned. What seemed to be a set phrase to Yeats was not an idiom after all. Likewise, Yeats's question about "evening plays" can be fully illustrated with reference to classical Japanese prosody. Besides word play and allusions, of particular relevance to this phrase and its background is the chain reaction of images, so to speak, that recurs in Noh texts. These complexities being lost in another language, so remote from the original, the result tends to be a mere outline.

The final point under review is the matter of stage directions. Although Yeats's following comments on them for *Certain Noble Plays of Japan* are of relatively minor importance in themselves, they bring to our notice the whole question of Pound's idea of stage directions. Yeats notes: "In the last line I would like out '(the Tennin)'. It is not wanted. These stage directions in brackets as presented are a nuisance, for they read like text."[109] Against Yeats's suggestion, however, Pound retained "(the Tennin)" in *Hagoromo*.[110]

Throughout *'Noh' or Accomplishment* Pound frequently inserted stage directions even where Fenollosa did not indicate them. Pound added such directions as "ritual", "dance", "journey" and "exorcism", which are assimilated from the contexts of the manuscripts. Of these, his application of dance directions is the most irregular: he adds them to such plays as *Kayoi Komachi*, *Kumasaka* and *Awoi no Uye*, whereas their original texts do not specify them. The first two of them are missing in the Fenollosa manuscripts, preventing us from tracing Pound's fidelity to Fenollosa. However, the extant manuscript of *Awoi no Uye* has no indication of dance even in the climactic scene of exorcism, in which Pound added nine lines of his own stage directions, ending with the line, "Here follows the great dance climax of the play."[111] This is an example of his bent for overdoing the dance in his editing. Noh texts, when provided with dance directions, name the specific type of dance for each of them, as in *Hagoromo* and *Nishikigi*. But Pound omitted a dance direction from *Nishikigi*, in keeping with the manuscript, whereas in *Hagoromo* he gave one as in the original, yet disregarding Fenollosa.[112]

Yeats's predilection for Noh dance is expressed in his introduction to the Cuala volume. He writes, as he understood it from Fenollosa's comments: "At the climax, instead of the disordered passion of nature, there is a dance, a series of positions and movements which may represent a battle, or a marriage, or the pain of a ghost in the Buddhist Purgatory."[113] Yeats is fundamentally right in saying that the battle is expressed in stylized mimetic movements, which he might well have associated with *Kumasaka*, while he might have associated the marriage dance with *Nishikigi*. Yeats's description also echoes Pound's notes that *Kumasaka* is ". . . the Homeric presentation of combat. . . . all this is symbolized in the dance climax of the play".[114] Depending upon the nuance of the word "dance", there still remains some ambiguity in the English generalization of Noh dance: the specified dance in the text is not differentiated from other mimetic movements in the translations, since Fenollosa did not clarify them.

The above tendencies, coupled with other awkward insertions of explanatory remarks in brackets throughout the book, make Pound's stage directions the most precarious part of his editorial work. His weakness in theatrical awareness is further marred by the structural vagueness of many of the published plays which is due largely to Fenollosa's arbitrary drafts which lack sufficient clarification of complex dramatic construction and technical details peculiar to Noh. This basic, scholarly information, if given, would have enormously facilitated and improved Pound's work.

'Noh' or Accomplishment was never revised, although Pound grew dissatisfied with it. In his letter to John Quinn on 4 June 1918 Pound wrote:

> . . . I find *Noh* unsatisfactory, I daresay it's all that could be done with the material. I don't believe anyone else will come along to do a better book on Noh, save for encyclopaedizing the subject. And I admit there are beautiful bits in it. But it's all too damn soft. Like Pater, Fiona Macleod and James Matthew Barrie, not good enough.
>
> I think I am justified in having spent the time I did on it, but not much more than that.[115]

Nine years later, Pound's self-criticism was even more severe in his letter to Glenn Hughes on 9 November 1927:

> I wonder if Iwasaki is trained in No or if you and he want to undertake revision of my redaction of Fenollosa's paper on the Noh (or No; better I think spelled with the "h" to avoid homograph with simple Murkn negative) . . . I think Fenollosa did a lot that ought not to be lost. I had not the philological competence necessary for an ultimate version, but at the same time Mrs. F's conviction was that Fen. wanted it transd *as* literature not as philology. . . . At present it is the scattered fragments left by a dead man, edited by a man ignorant of Japanese.[116]

In 1921 Arthur Waley's more scholarly translation of Noh plays appeared. Waley had earlier assisted Pound in editing *'Noh' or Accomplishment*.[117] Not being a Japanologist as Waley was, Pound's aim was to make his own poetry out of the incomplete manuscripts in his typically laconic and wavering style. Waley evaluated this effort of Pound's in his work and remarked: ". . . wherever Mr. Pound had adequate material to work upon he has used it admirably".[118] If Pound's English rendition stripped away the subtleties and shades of the Japanese originals, this was also the case with Waley's.

Despite his diffidence and some of the results undreamt of even by the Fenollosas, Pound's editing of the manuscripts largely pursued Fenollosa's faith in translation as literature, not as academic reproduction. *Certain Noble Plays of Japan* and *'Noh' or Accomplishment* occupy a unique position as translations of Noh. The more academically oriented approach to Noh in recent years will scarcely allow imagination and linguistic experiment such free play as in these translations in which two of the great poets of our time were involved.

Pound's Noh translations should be evaluated in the light of their influence on Western theatre practice, *via* Yeats's achievement. They realized Fenellosa's dreams theatrically, beyond mere translation,[119] by the creation of an image whereby Noh can be used in Western drama.

NOTES

1. I am grateful to Mr Michael Yeats for his courtesy in allowing me to publish W. B. Yeats's hitherto unpublished "Suggestions and Corrections". Previously unpublished material by Ernest Fenollosa and Ezra Pound is used by permission of New Directions Publishing Corporation, agents for the Trustees of the Ezra Pound Literary Property Trust. Copyright © 1985 by the Trustees. Thanks are also due to the Beinecke Library of Yale University for permission to examine the Ezra Pound Archive, and to Michael J. Sidnell and Richard Taylor for their kind help.

2. Mrs Mary McNeil Fenollosa (c. 1865–1954) knew of Yone Noguchi through the *Ayame Kai* (Iris Club) which Noguchi had established as an International Poet's Club in Tokyo in 1906. See Shunsuke Kamei, "Yone Noguchi: An English Poet of Japan", *Yone Noguchi: Collected Poems* (Tokyo: Yone Noguchi Society of Japan, 1965) p. 69. Mrs Fenollosa, poet and novelist, was assistant to Ernest Fenollosa at the Boston Museum of Fine Arts in 1894–5. For her life and work, see Caldwell Delaney, "Mary McNeil Fenollosa, an Alabama Woman of Letters", *Lotus* (Tokyo: Fenollosa Society of Japan), No. 2 (1980) 27–36. Yone Noguchi went to London in late 1902 after making some reputation as a poet in America where he had studied the art of writing poetry in English under Joaquin Miller from 1895. With the private publication of *From the Eastern Sea* in 1903 (later republished by Unicorn, London in the same year), he had an immediate success in London. He made the acquaintance of Robert Bridges, W. B. Yeats, Arthur Symons, Laurence Binyon and W. M. Rossetti, among others. Soon afterwards, he returned to Japan via America, where he married an Irish–American woman, mother of Isamu Noguchi, sculptor and choreographer. After 1911 Noguchi had some correspondence with Ezra Pound and they met on Noguchi's revisit to England in 1913–14. Noguchi contributed poems and articles to *Poetry*, *Egoist* and many other English and Japanese journals early this century. Noguchi's *The Pilgrimage* (London: Elkin Matthews, 1909) introduced several *hokku* poems, and *Japanese Hokkus* (Boston: Four Seas, 1920) was dedicated to Yeats.

3. Noel Stock, *The Life of Ezra Pound* (New York: Pantheon Books, 1970) p. 148. Stock adds: " . . . in November 1915 she sent a further packet from Alabama". He then quotes from Pound's letter to John Quinn on 17 May 1917 that "Mrs. Fenollosa had not only given him a free hand to edit and publish the material but the right to any profit plus £40 to go on with."

4. David Ray, "Ezra Pound: An Interview", *Paris Review*, 7, No. 28 (Summer/Fall 1962) 38.

5. See also T. S. Eliot, "Ezra Pound: His Metric and Poetry", *To Criticize the Critic and Other Writing* (London: Faber & Faber, 1965) p. 177. He writes: "Mrs. Fenollosa recognized that in Pound the Chinese manuscripts would find the interpreter whom her husband would have wished: she accordingly forwarded the papers for him to do as he liked with. It is thus due to Mrs. Fenollosa's acumen that we have *Cathay*; it is not as a consequence of *Cathay* that we have *Lustra*. This fact must be borne in mind."

6. Harriet Monroe, "Nogi", *Poetry*, 1, No. 2 (Nov. 1912) 50.

7. Ikuko Atsumi, ed., *Yone Noguchi: Collected English Letters* (Tokyo: Yone Noguchi Society, 1975) p. 15. See also Stock, p. 136.

8. Atsumi, p. 211.

9. Ernest Fenollosa & Ezra Pound, *'Noh' or Accomplishment: a Study of the Classical Stage of Japan* (London: Macmillan, 1916), Note. In this article page references are to its New Directions paperback edition, *The Classic Noh Theatre of Japan* (New York: New Directions, 1959) (hereafter *CNTJ*).

10. *CNTJ*, 3.

11. Ibid., p. 62.

12. Ibid., p. 4. For a detailed study of Fenollosa's life and work, see Lawrence W. Chisolm, *Fenollosa: the Far East and the American Culture* (New Haven & London: Yale University Press, 1963).

13. Pound, "Fenollosa" (hereafter "F"), *Ezra Pound Archive* (hereafter *EPA*), file 51.

14. D. D. Paige, ed., *The Letters of Ezra Pound* (New York: Harcourt Brace, 1950) p. 31.

15. Ibid., p. 214.

16. Pound, "F".

17. Paige, *op cit.*, p. 214.

18. Ibid., p. 25.

19. Ibid., p. 27. See also Nobuko T. Keith, "Ezra Pound's Relationship with Fenollosa and the Japanese Noh Plays", *Markham Review*, 3, No. 2 (Feb. 1972) 21–7.

20. Paige, *op cit.*, p. 31.

21. Atsumi, p. 214. These lectures were included in Noguchi's *The Spirit of Japanese Poetry* (London: John Murray, 1914).

22. Atsumi, p. 15.

23. Paige, *op cit.*, p. 36.

24. Pound, "Study of Noh Continues in West" (hereafter "SNCW"), *Japan Times*, 10 December 1939. See also Yasunari Takahashi, *"Yeats to Nō"* (Yeats and Noh), *Sekai* (World), No. 451 (June 1983) 247–61.

25. *Ex* 64–5.

26. *CNTJ*, p. 26.

27. Noguchi, "A Japanese Poet on W. B. Yeats", *The Bookman* (London), 43 (June 1916) 431.

28. Pound, "SNCW".

29. Paige, *op cit.*, p. 72.

30. The exact date of their first meeting is unknown. World War I obliged Michio Ito (1894–1961) to leave Germany where he had studied dancing at the Jacques-Dalcroze School for two years. In London, in one evening in April 1915, Ito was asked by a friend to dance at Lady Ottoline Morrell's, where the guests included Lady Cunard, Yeats and Shaw. See Michio Ito, *"Omoide o Kataru"* (Reminiscences), *Hikaku Bunka* (Comparative Studies of Culture), No. 2 (1956) 68; & Helen Caldwell, *Michio Ito: The Dancer and His Dances* (Berkeley, Los Angeles, London: Univ. of California Press, 1977) p. 40. The performance was repeated the following night at Prime Minister Asquith's. This brought Ito fame and opportunity, thus making him a professional dancer in London. See Ito, *op cit.*, 57–76; & *Utsukushiku naru Kyoshitsu* (A Classroom for Beauty) (Tokyo: Hobunkan, 1956) 19–30. Also Ian Carruthers, "A Translation of

Fifteen Pages of Ito Michio's Autobiography '*Utsukushiku naru Kyoshitsu*' ", *Canadian Journal of Irish Studies*, 2, No. 1 (May 1976) 33–8.

31. Carruthers, 39.
32. Ibid., 35.
33. Ibid., 39.
34. *LRB* 41.
35. *L* 610.
36. Paige, p. 72.
37. *Ex* 256.
38. *L* 610.
39. Ibid.
40. Ibid.
41. Eliot, "Ezra Pound", *Poetry*, 68, No. 6 (Sept. 1946) 326.
42. Hugh Kenner points out in his Introduction to *The Translations of Ezra Pound* (London: Faber & Faber, 1951) p. 13, that in Pound's translations of Noh dramas "we are teased from time to time by traces of Yeats". See also Anthony Thwaite, "Yeats and the Noh", *Twentieth Century*, 162, No. 967 (Sept. 1957) 236.
43. W. B. Yeats, "Suggestions & Corrections" (hereafter "SC"), *EPA*, f. 2.
44. *Nishikigi* was the first to appear in May 1914 in *Poetry*. *Hagoromo* was published in October 1914 in *Quarterly Review*, together with *Kinuta*, in the context of a long article, "The Classical Drama of Japan," whose major part consisted of Fenollosa's essay on Noh. *Kumasaka* appeared in *The Drama* of May 1915 in "The Classical Stage of Japan", which contained, besides Pound's introductory reconstruction of Fenollosa's notes on the Noh programme, six other plays: *Sotoba Komachi* (fragmentary), *Kayoi Komachi*, *Suma Genji*, *Shojo*, *Tamura* and *Tsunemasa*. The *Quarterly Review* article eventually formed Part III of '*Noh' or Accomplishment*, with the addition of *Nishikigi* and *Kagekiyo* and the *Drama* article formed Parts I and II. In 1916, the translation of *Awoi no Uye* (also spelt *Aoi no Ue*) was published separately in *Quarterly Notebook* (1, No. 1 [June 1916] (10–16), and *Kakitsubata* likewise in *Drama*, No. 23 [Aug. 1916, 428–35). These two plays were incorporated into Part IV of the book, together with two other plays, *Chorio* and *Genjo*. '*Noh' or Accomplishment* was thus constructed gradually. The notes on the Noh programme were partly prepared by Tateki Owada, editor of the collections of Noh texts, *Yōkyoku Tsūkai* (1892) and *Yōkyoku Hyōshaku* (1907–8), 9 vols. Fenollosa had another Japanese assistant, Kiichi (Tokuboku) Hirata, who accompanied him to Noh lessons by Minoru Umewaka, as recorded in Umewaka's diaries, and helped him to translate the plays. See *CNTJ*, 27 & Hisashi Furukawa, *Meiji Nogaku-shi Josetsu* (A History of Noh Studies in the Meiji Period) (Tokyo: Wanya, 1969) pp. 180–97.
45. Marie C. Stopes, *Plays of Old Japan: The Nō*, assisted by Prof. Joji Sakurai (London: William Heinemann, 1913). The other three plays included are *Motomezuka* (The Maiden's Tomb), *Tamura* and *Sumida-gawa* (The Sumida River). Yeats refers to the theme of *Motomezuka* in "Swedenborg, Mediums, and the Desolate Places" (hereafter "SMDP"), *Ex* 65–6; and "The Soul in Judgement," *AV[B]* 231. It is likely that he read the play in Stopes's work. The Fenollosa manuscripts do not contain *Motomezuka* so far as the *EPA* goes. See D. J. Gordon, *W. B. Yeats: Images of a Poet* (Manchester: Manchester Univ. Press, 1961) p. 62; & Takahashi, 261, n. 13.
46. F. A. C. Wilson notes that Pound "had in fact at one time hoped that Dr. Stopes might collaborate with him in his own Noh translations": Wilson, *W. B. Yeats and Tradition* (1958; rpt. London: Methuen, 1968) p. 263, n. 8. Besides Stopes's volume, the other two sources Pound referred to are: Captain F. Brinkley, *Japan: Its History, Art and Literature* (1901–2; rpt. London: Jack, 1903) III, pp. 21–48; & F. V. Dickins, *Primitive and Medieval Japanese Texts* (Oxford: Clarendon, 1906) II.
47. *The Mask*, 6, No. 3 (Jan. 1914) 263–5.
48. Pound, "F". See also Pound, *Guide to Kulchur* (hereafter *GK*) (1917; rpt. London:

Faber & Faber, 1938) p. 81. He writes: "The play *Kagekiyo* has Homeric robustness. The Noh is not merely painting on silk or nuances *à la chas.* Condor."

49. Fenollosa & Pound, *Certain Noble Plays of Japan* (hereafter *CNPJ*), with an introduction by W. B. Yeats (Dublin: Cuala Press, 1916) p. 50; & *CNTJ* 112.

50. *GK* 81. See also *CNTJ* 37–8; & Nobuko Tsukui, *Ezra Pound and Japanese Noh Plays* (Washington: University Press of America, 1983) pp. 15 & 28.

51. "Japanese Mysteries", *TLS*, 25 Jan. 1917, 41.

52. *CNTJ*, 49.

53. Ibid., pp. 12, 18, 20, 26, 54, 56, 81, 98, 117 & 130.

54. Eliot, "The Noh and the Image" (hereafter "NI"), *Egoist*, 4, No. 7 (Aug. 1917) 103. My emphases.

55. Ibid.

56. *Drama*, No. 18 (May 1915) 215–16. My emphases.

57. *CNTJ*, 16, 17, 19 & 20. My emphases.

58. Ibid., p. 16. Yeats's own discussion of this appears in 'SMDP'', (*Ex* 68). See also *E&I* 232.

59. For a brief study, in Japanese, of Yeats's influence on Pound's editing of *Kayoi Komachi* from the occult viewpoint, see Toshimitsu Hasegawa, "Fenollosa, Pound and Yeats – an Attempt at the Interpretation of Noh Translations," *Lotus*, No. 3 (1983) 1–19.

60. Yeats, *The Collected Plays* (1934; rpt. London: Macmillan, 1972) p. 88.

61. *CNPJ* 42, 45 & 49; & *CNTJ* 106, 108 & 111. My emphases.

62. *CNPJ* 4 & 7; & *CNTJ* 78 & 80. My emphases.

63. *CNPJ* 1; & *CNTJ* 76. Liam Miller conjectures possible affinities in English expression between Pound's rendition of *Nishikigi* and Synge's *The Playboy of the Western World.* See Miller, *The Noble Drama of W. B. Yeats* (Dublin: Dolmen Press, 1977) p. 197.

64. Fenollosa, "Nishikigi" (hereafter "N"), *EPA*, file 42. In the *EPA* the number of the extant manuscripts of Fenollosa's handwritten translations and outlines of Noh and Kyogen (farce played between Noh plays) are as follows: seventeen Noh translations; fifteen Noh outlines; one Kyogen translation; and twenty-two Kyogen outlines. The manuscripts of seven Noh plays which first appeared in *Drama*, No. 18 (May 1915), are all missing in the Archive. (See n. 44.) According to Richard Taylor's examination of the material in 1975, "Internal evidence in the notebooks also points to the probable existence at one time of Englished texts" for three other Noh plays that cannot be found in the Archive at present (Taylor's letter to me dated 20 Feb. 1984). He also mentions that some of the materials were sent to auction by Mrs Fenollosa. All this shows that the Fenollosa manuscripts in the *EPA* are incomplete and that Fenollosa possibly translated more plays than those extant today. The others were either mislaid or lost over the intervening years.

65. *Ex* 43 & 46.

66. *CNTJ* 14–15.

67. Eliot, "NI", 103.

68. *CNTJ* 27.

69. Eliot, "NI", 103.

70. Ibid.

71. Ibid.

72. *CNTJ*, 20, 47, 56, 87, 90, 93, 97, 99, 101, 103, 116 & 126.

73. Fenollosa, "N", files 42 & 42a; *CNPJ* 1–2; & *CNTJ* 76–7.

74. *CNPJ* 12; & *CNTJ* 84–5.

75. Fenollosa, "N".

76. Eliot, "NI", 103. My emphasis.

77. *CNTJ*, 128.

78. This transformation curiously corresponds to the anecdote about Edmund Dulac and Michio Ito waiting to hear the cry of a hawk at the London zoo. Despairing of hearing it, Dulac asked Ito the Japanese word for hawk; thence '*taka*' was uttered by Ito in the

first production of *At the Hawk's Well*. This was recounted by Ito to John G. Mills. See
Mills, "W. B. Yeats and Noh", *Japan Quarterly*, 2 (Oct.–Dec. 1955) 500.
79. Fenollosa, "Kinuta", *EPA*, file 40; & *CNTJ* 94.
80. *CNPJ* 16; & *CNTJ* 87–8. "*Ari-aki*" is correctly "*Ariake*".
81. Yeats, "SC", f. 3.
82. *OED* defines "thill" as "The pole or shaft by which a wagon, cart, or other vehicle is
   attached to the animal drawing it, esp. one of the pair of shafts between which a single
   draught animal is placed."
83. Yeats, "SC", f. 5.
84. Ibid., f. 3. The punctuation marks in this quotation from Yeats are complemented
   and conventionalized, as in the other quotations from his manuscripts which follow.
85. *CNPJ* 11. Cf. *CNTJ* 83, in which the first line differs slightly: "Look, then, for the old
   times are shown." See also *Poetry*, 4, No.2 (May 1914) 44, in which the line is: "Look
   sharp then, for old times are shown."
86. Fenollosa, "N".
87. Yeats, "SC", f. 4.
88. Fenollosa, "Hagoromo" (hereafter "H"), *EPA*, file 40.
89. *CNPJ* 19; & *CNTJ* 98. My emphasis.
90. *CNPJ* 2, 4 & 9; & *CNTJ* 77, 79 & 82. My emphases.
91. Fenollosa, "N".
92. Yeats, "SC", f. 1.
93. Fenollosa, "N".
94. Ibid.
95. Yeats, "SC", f. 2.
96. Fenollosa, "N".
97. Yeats, "SC", f. 2.
98. *CNPJ* 46; & *CNTJ* 109. My emphasis.
99. Fenollosa, "Kagekiyo", *EPA*, file 43. My emphasis.
100. Yeats, "SC", f. 7.
101. *Poetry*, 4, No. 2 (May 1914), 42; & *CNTJ* 82. My emphasis.
102. Fenollosa, "N".
103. Yeats, "SC", f. 2.
104. *CNPJ*, 9.
105. *CNPJ*, dated April 1916, was finished on 20 July and published on 16 September
    1916. See Miller, p. 192; & *L* 612. '*Noh*' *or Accomplishment* is dated 1916 but was not
    published until 12 January 1917. See Stock, p. 199.
106. Yeats, "SC", f. 7.
107. Ibid., f. 4.
108. Mario Yokomichi & Akira Omote, eds, *Yōkyoku-shū* (The Collected Noh Plays), 15th
    edn (Tokyo: Iwanami, 1975) II, p. 327.
109. Yeats, "SC", f. 6.
110. *CNPJ* 27; & *CNTJ* 104.
111. Fenollosa, "Awoi no Uye", *EPA*, file 44; & *CNTJ* 120. For Yeats's comment on the
    play, see *Ex* 38, n.
112. *CNPJ* 15 & 25; & *CNTJ* 87 & 103.
113. *CNPJ* xii; *E&I* 230; & *CNTJ* 63 & 158.
114. *CNTJ* 38.
115. Paige, p. 137.
116. Ibid., p. 214. Y. T. Iwasaki and Glenn Hughes translated *Three Modern Japanese Plays*
    with an introduction by Hughes (1923; rpt. New York: Core Collection Books, 1976).
117. In *CNTJ*, Note, Pound extends due acknowledgement to Waley, "who has corrected
    a number of mistakes in the orthography of proper names from such Japanese texts as
    were available, and who has assisted me out of various impasses where my own
    ignorance would have left me".

118. Arthur Waley, *The Nō Plays of Japan* (1921; rpt. New York: Grove Press, 1957) p. 304.
119. The only published article on Noh by Fenollosa himself points out, as early as 1901, the necessity of treating Noh not merely as literature, but as theatre that approximates to today's familiar notion of a total theatre. See Fenollosa, "Notes on the Japanese Lyric Drama", *Journal of the American Oriental Society*, 22, first half (1901) 129.

"Do We or Do We Not, Know It?": an Unpublished Essay on W. B. Yeats

Thomas Sturge Moore

Before speaking of poetry which everybody is politely assumed to know, though certain facts suggest that several even of our professional critics have no more than a nodding acquaintance with it, I must humbly beg forgiveness of those whom this initial assumption wrongs. Like myself they will often have fumed to observe less central characters singled out as though they explained the success. I picture these, my fellows, in dispersed retreats, indifferent to noisy superficial fashions because

> They eat
> Quiet's wild heart like daily meat.

This vision of the veritable court of appeal urges me to attempt to aid not a few, who, through no fault of their own, may have failed to occupy their due seat in it.

My friendly acquaintance with Mr Yeats has lasted thirty years, and though I cannot claim to have studied all his work – much less to be familiar with all in the way which the ripeness of an aesthetic appreciation presupposes, yet I have been intimate with so much of it, as I could easily enjoy, after a fashion that no set purpose of studying would be likely to beget in myself or in anyone else.

On first acquaintance with his poetry I was in full reaction against those general characters to which critics then attached its value: and expressed this by scornfully asserting that my theory of poetry, was my theory of prose. This meant rejecting far more than I accepted in *The Wind among the Reeds* and in *Poems* (1901). Such work seemed too ornamental, too intentionally artificial. But those poems in these two books which I did not reject became for me profound and recurrent experiences, establishing themselves in spite of my prejudices. The same thing happened in respect of his conversation and occultism; much had at first seemed to prove charlatanism, nevertheless I was more and more attracted in spite of having assumed this bigoted attitude.

145

Yeats himself was then in process of purging his verse of those characters which offended me. He afterwards summed up this phase of his development in the witty lyric which every one will recollect. "I made my song a coat. . . . But the fools caught it, wore it . . . let them *take it*. For there's more enterprise in walking *naked*" (*Responsibilities* p. 80, *Later Poems* p. 233).

When we met, he might have been described as following an orbit which would bring him nearer to that I was launched on. Yeats was unfailingly generous; yet he probably studied my poetry if possible less than I studied his. No sort of collaboration in a movement or in furtherance of some poetico-political object existed between us. I mention this as some might conclude that our friendship must prove collusion, and so suspect anything I say about his poetry as dictated by ulterior motives. But we never meant the same by the nakedness of poetry and though our orbits may even have crossed we are still, both in our own and in others eyes, circling round quite different centres.

I have come to believe that general characters never account for value. Therefore that all criticism based on the discrimination of general characters is aesthetically futile. Of course it may be historically interesting. Does not the word beauty imply that the appearance commended is in some noteworthy degree unique? Unique in value even more than in identity, as cast and reproduction prove? The general characters of Mr Yeats's poems do not account for his felicities, nor do the general traits of Greek art raise the masterpieces above the remainder. This may sound too sweeping, but reflection assures us that the exception can never have the same cause as the rule. That the major half of modern criticism is based on the fallacy which supposes the contrary to be true, will also appear to anyone who reviews it, having lodged this extremely simple observation firmly in mind.

Every success in art has a particular character which proportions those elements it may share with other works, organizes them, and creates the health of a single whole. This bloom, this charm can no more be analysed than joy can.

We train the intellect; no trouble has been taken with taste till quite these last years. We used to train ethical discernment, but much new knowledge has rendered us shy of the old lessons, without discovering any practicable way of replacing them. Intellectual judgements are rife where the intellect has as yet neither road nor means of locomotion.

I think it was Yeats who first rendered me attentive to the blind temerity of our intellectuals. Though lacking any experience which would have enabled me to approach the subject from his angle, I perceived that he enjoyed a freedom of mind in certain directions from which my acceptance, shall we say, of Huxley's attitude debarred me. My study of Matthew Arnold had from another side been underlining a similar notion; very gradually I came to conclusions, which may be here applied to the appreciation of certain poems by Mr Yeats.

A true outline of the general characteristics of his verse might easily exclude all his best things. Call it "dreamy, arrogant, stocked with unfamiliar Celtic names and gradually becoming fantastically recondite and obscure"; no one could disprove the general assertion, though it flatly contradicts the experience of any one who loves his poetry. Only the mob, the hysterical, or pedants value poets in the lump, for them Keats, Wordsworth, Shakespeare are mythological figures, that neither have the same, nor similar proportions to those the same poets own in the eyes of any who habitually read their most perfect things.

I propose then to contemplate, as it were aloud, the beauty of a handful of Mr Yeats's poems. I shall not try to prove them beautiful, though I believe that poetry can have no excellence which is not essential to its beauty.

Pedants alone put faith in the reasons, that, by a silly foible, it has become fashionable to give for beauty, "A rose by any other name" . . . described or analysed in any other way . . . "would smell as sweet". Those who do not feel these poems beautiful will not understand me. I shall have to mention flaws which distress my admiration, therefore, profess myself unaware of any other poems published during the same period which rival these, for no flaw [,] yet detected, lessens my confidence in their towering eminence: neither do many appear more perfect, when I look back into the past,

> Lift up the white knee;
> That's what they sing,
> Those young dancers
> That in a ring
> Raved but now
> Of the hearts that brake
> Long, long ago
> For their sake.
>
> But the dance changes.
> Lift up the gown
> All that sorrow
> Is trodden down.

The unique cadence of this lyric so perfectly sustains the meaning of these forty five words, which convey so central an epitome of life in such a novel perspective, that even today tears of admiration moisten my eyes as I read. Lately I have often asked myself whether Paul Valery is anywhere so perfect; and have told myself that he is less human, less complex, more abstract. Do not even the most musical stanzas of

"Palme" exhort and encourage with an unction which is christian in the best sense of that word, and so may seem to reflect light that was more valid in another context?

> Patience, patience,
> Patience dans l'azur! etc.

But "the hearts that brake" are as far from any foreknown attitude as the Erickshay Love lilt and yet seem as old as the world. Even such perfect lines as

> Comme le fruit se fond en jouissance,
> Comme en délice, il change son absence
> Dans une bouche où sa forme se meurt,
> Je hume ici ma future fumée,
> Et le ciel chante à l'âme consumée
> Le changement des rives en rumeur.

may be too consciously subtle; they hover like the humming-bird's burning breast in the halo of its invisible wings, intensely intent. Whereas Yeats's lines remind me that my breath has been suspended as I watched the dip and rise of a water wag-tail's leisured descent from high on a building: something utterly unpreoccupied, dapper, clean and yet divine! The form remains, the inhabiting consciousnesses pass; the white knee is lifted in every generation. As we glimpse the agelong form, the agelong dance, we realize not only how all that sorrow has been trodden down, but that impersonal humanity, that faërie which haunts us as beauty, even as christlike kindness haunts our ethical consciousness. The aesthetic experience, the ethical experience, in such cases leaves the intellect far behind and appreciates that which reason can neither attack nor defend, nor explain, but must accept.

However, does not Mr Yeats too frequently use "that" not only for "which" but for "who"? I cannot help feeling that this song sounds ever-so-slightly more perfect when we substitute "who" for the second "that" – "who in a ring"; as does also the first line of perhaps his most beautiful love lyric "The Folly of being Comforted" (*Later Poems*, 73).

> One, who is ever kind, said yesterday

is surely better than

> One, that is ever kind, said yesterday.

The poignancy of the lines which follow this one, nowhere discommodes their exquisitely diversified lilt, though after every pause the address changes. The whole fourteen are spoken in that inner silence, which no accident troubles, and where the speaker is forgotten in the utterance.

I still croon the earlier version of this lyric which Mr Yeats has discarded for reasons which are easy to appreciate. It ran

> One, that is ever kind, said yesterday:
> "Your well-beloved's hair has threads of grey,
> And little shadows come about her eyes;
> Time can but make it easier to be wise
> Though now it's hard, till trouble be at an end;
> And so be patient, be wise and patient friend."
> But heart, there is no comfort not a grain;
> Time can but make her beauty over again
> Because of that great nobleness of hers;
> The fire that stirs about her, when she stirs
> Burns but more clearly. O she had not these ways
> When all the wild summer was in her gaze.
> O heart! O heart! if she'd but turn her head,
> You'd know the folly of being comforted. (*Poems* [1906] p. 164)

No doubt the repetitions of "wise" and "patient" seem lax in such fine spun verse as perhaps the first "heart" may lessen the effect of the second and third? But

> "Though now it seem impossible and so
> Patience is all that you have need of"

are the words, neither true, nor kind, attributed in his collected edition to the ever kind friend:

> "No
> I have not a crumb of comfort, not a grain"

answers the poet. The line has recently been modified yet again

> All that you need is patience.
> Heart cries "No"

The friend seems to have changed character, but, of course the poet is merely recollecting what was said yesterday, and wishes to make the words hurt him more than those actually used could. The new couplet is the least musical in the poem, and I prefer the more credible report of the kind friend's words, in spite of their possibly too facile melody, though I may be the richer for having read both.

The folly of being comforted afflicts, not only lovers, but humanity which allows the tune of life to inveigle it into dancing over its would-be and should-be unforgettable sorrows. In the moment of realizing their hugeness, mankind momentarily rebels and cries as this lyric does that to be reminded of such loss must always make consolation look foolish. No doubt the cross is for some the symbol and perpetual rebegetter of affliction over the actual world, though for most it may be only an assurance of escape – a permission to shirk an experience which they rightly feel would overwhelm them. Yet this common acceptance of comfort makes others feel

There's nothing serious in mortality.

And so we find Manley Hopkins jeering crabbedly but cogently at "carrion comfort" but he, for a christian, was amazingly outspoken. Possibly I am absurd to mention it but I have never discovered the meaning of

"The fire that stirs about her, when she stirs
Burns but more clearly."

As music and suggestion nothing could chime in more perfectly. But what is referred to? How can that burn *more clearly* which so far falls short of an earlier radiance? The hypothesis I should prefer, is that Yeats actually is one of those people who occasionally see aurae surrounding those they meet, and that the words referred to a sensuous experience of his in which I, like a colour blind person, am unable to share, but I am not convinced that this was implied.

"Never give all the heart" (*Later Poems*, p. 75) is all but as beautiful and certainly more flawless. For poetry is positive, not merely an absence of defect. So the more beautiful may also be the more faulty.

If beauty has ever been supreme, then the most that time can do, is to make it over again. The victim of an over-generous admiration, like the christ-lover [,] feels that eternity has beggared itself to produce that for which he gives his heart. And, as for those damned who were once all but saved, frustration becomes an incommensurable grief. "It is impossible to thought a greater than itself to know" said Blake and thereby suggests the possibility of there being a *greater* unknown. So worship always conceives a more perfect in losing that which had seemed perfect, and in consequence holds the complete gift of itself to have deserved better than to be rated cheaply by any object now perceived to have never been perfect.

"Adam's Curse" [*Poems* (1906) p. 170; *Later Poems*, p. 78] is very marrow of Yeats. The ease, simplicity, irony, and the imperceptible progress by which the tragedy is discovered without disturbing the tranquil plenitude of the mood, have no parallel and make the most complete, the most compact whole! The perfection of a masterpiece is not in any part; beauties often war with beauty, therefore surely a fullstop ought to have followed

Washed by time's waters as they rose and fell

instead of this rhetorical ornament

About the stars, and broke in days and years.

This line might have been left to those thieves who stole that first fine coat Mr Yeats wove for his song. Then, after the period and the break, might have come,

Desirous, yet not certain of your tears,
I have a thought for no one's but your ears;

Fascinated by a flaw in a pearl one worries and worries. Years passed before I hit on this remedy, which has now for some years seemed a possible one.

Are not the narrative portions of "Baile and Aillinn" completer without the interludes, lovely poetry though these contain? Certainly the poem reads far better aloud without them. This is the best of Mr Yeats's narratives and as poetry equals any in the language. The story is hardly more than a parable and there may be a too heavy insistence on Gorias, Findrias, Falias and Murias and the apples of the sun and moon. Such a passage cannot compare, as a decoration with Milton's best. The poems mentioned were I think the summits of Mr Yeats's production in 1906, few of the earlier poems compete with them in reflective richness or subtlety of cadence.

I have suggested more universal applications for some of their phrases. I do not wish to imply that Mr Yeats was or ever has been conscious of these or even that I myself was at first or that any one else should be. Perfect poetry resumes humanity's experience; the mere perception of the beauty of phrases, tempts us to fit them to endlessly diverse occasions, to see more and yet more reference to life in them. Are they not "Chockful of things" as Flaubert says that old professors of Latin find those of Virgil. So truly is poetry the servant of man and ready even to be his menial, that we all call on Shakespeare's phrases, as our need occurs, aptly if luck will, if not ineptly. Before some divine cadence will brim a thimble, either complete exhilaration or a manifold effort is needed for its distillation. The aging poet sits with idle pen before his table and says:

> Hands, do what you're bid,
> Bring the balloon of the mind
> Which bellies and drags in the wind
> Into its narrow shed. (*Later Poems* p. 285)

"The hungry thought that must be fed" also must be condensed; it grows like a cloud, when the poet walks, as he goes up and down stairs, when he lifts his eyes from the book, when his head turns on the pillow. Then the hands must scribble and cross out for hours before all that size will lie quiet once more in a few limpid lines like a gill of rain caught in a dent of rock. Others will unpack the balloon refill and go up to observe, and the cup in the rock is drained and fresh cloud woven. Yet the sun is no person, so the image of the balloon remains the more manifold.

Critics attempt an hopeless task when they judge poetry with which they have not lived year in, year out. For like reason, our would-be representative anthologists are bound to choose amiss. A rabid fury insists on their treating every line they read as though it were in for an examination, thus establishing a relation which destroys the possibility of intercourse. Approach to only one answer is listened for and that a foregone conclusion in the examining mind. Those who ride any theory as to what the only sound characteristics of poetry should be are almost sure to sniff at unrecognized masterpieces. The same is true of those who hunt faults, the teeth lining their jaws are preconceptions as to what can never be admitted into a poem. T. S. Omond, one of our most esteemed prosodists, actually asserted that dawn must not be rhymed with morn, because some thirty millions born south of the Humber would mistake it for a perfect rhyme. As if thirty millions had no right to a poetry of their own, especially when they include Keats, etc. The fatuity of prejudice can scarcely grow more dense. I have met poets who made sweeping distinctions between Caroline, Victorian, Georgian, Imagist and modern, so that one might have concluded the Muse was often a monarch's mistress or lady-in-waiting, yet who did not know work produced as it were under their noses by their contemporary of the most achieved reputation. The tilt of a nose can easily preclude sagacity. Long ago I met such a young dramatist who informed me that he regarded both Yeats and Shaw as "played out". Yet the event has shown that both were yet to produce much if not all of their most perfect work. His own name is now well-nigh as well-known as theirs. These ludicrous politics as to who is to be included in the successive cabinets of literary fashion can so easily pervert fine gifts or even genius.

"To a Child dancing in the Wind" (*Responsibilities*, p. 66) was possibly the high-water mark of Yeats's production (1916). Not that this has in any sense definitely receded but that here was an exceptional ninth wave.[1] But no! there is "Memory" (*The Wild Swans* p. 47, 1919) which though a mere ripple has surely run higher yet.

One had a lovely face,
And two or three had charm,
But charm and face were in vain
Because the mountain grass
Cannot but keep the form
Where the mountain hare has lain. (*Later Poems*, p. 272)

Complete homage to an apprehended value has never been more exquisitely suggested. Yet neither "The Child Dancing" nor "Memory"[2] is in the latest and most praised anthologies. But why waste words blaming the small crowds or the mighty herd? Has not the poet sung

"To a Friend whose work has come to Nothing:"
    Now all the truth is out,
    Be secret and take defeat
    From any brazen throat,
    For how can you compete,
    Being honour-bred, with one
    Who, were it proved he lies,
    Were neither shamed in his own
    Nor in his neighbours eyes?
    Bred to a harder thing
    Than Triumph, turn away
    And like a laughing string
    Whereon mad fingers play
    Amid a place of stone,
    Be secret and exult,
    Because of all things known
    That is most difficult. (*Later Poems*, p. 197)

Is that not rare as thought, rarer as temper, rarest as rhythm? Several of Yeats's masterpieces are about his friends. Though naturally a man knows his friends well, that is not what makes these poems so good. We do not seek knowledge in them. Greater poets have seemed better able to create with distant ill-known themes than with those which touched them; so when Yeats's life has entered into a subject, it is note-worthy that he has often been able to imagine and create beauty with it; not that power deserts him On Baile's Strand or in Conchubar's guest house. This reflection brings to mind an elegy that, alone of the many we have read since the war, holds its own with "Lycidas" and makes "Thyrsis" seem too long and "Adonais" ill put together. Nor do I think that any other poem of comparable length and written during my life-time has a chance of being in the end so profoundly appreciated as "In Memory of Major Robert Gregory" (*The Wild Swans*, p. 4).

Read it and let it soak in with its originality, its freshness of phrase and structure, width of reference, human weight, and flawlessly sustained mood. Imagination has become one with life complete, rich, affectionate, enquiring with a myriad roots, so the poem commences with ease and achieves most elegant proportions. Who else has done any comparable thing with half this felicity? Why in our threadbare famished world has it received so little praise? Ah yes! we have been down into the war and are still aesthetically recovering from shellshock, our children's children may be more able. Read it and tell me, you who read, could I quote from it without wronging you by breaking off before the end?

The poems I have named are untouched by that dreamy irresponsiblity which is a frequent weakness in Irish myth and folk story, and have that confidence in definite human relations which is held so great an asset in classic masterpieces. Yet this confidence is only sometimes an element in and not the cause of beauty since it also manifestly exists where there is none. The poet in "A Prayer for my Daughter" regrets that he had achieved this confidence so late in life. Less beautiful than the Elegy this Prayer permits of quotation

". . . many a poor man that has roved
Loved and thought himself beloved
From a glad kindness cannot take his eyes"

though it be not in other ways beautiful he attests, and ends

"And may her bride-groom bring her to a house
Where all's accustomed, ceremonious;
For arrogance and hatred are the wares
Peddled in the thoroughfares,
How but in custom and in ceremony
Are innocence and beauty born?
Ceremony's a name for the rich horn,
And custom for the spreading laurel tree."

Now that I have called attention to this handful of poems, I would fain gather another; but space forbids, though but two plays have been mentioned, and not even on "for Dancers". But I am not a professor and could not exhaust this subject even were it rational to try. Yeats, as a writer of great gifts who has followed his art studiously, must always fascinate the literary man even by his least inspired productions; they sparkle with technical suggestiveness, and many younger poets owe nearly everything they have to him. But excellent literary work even in fine verse, is not poetry, that name should be reserved for work which focussed the whole man, not the artist or the thinker alone, his body and complete being must contribute to that in which we enjoy everything and yet avert inquiry from nothing. No other statement of what carelessness might call the same thoughts, no other use of similar phrasing or cadences, can possibly share with this integrity which has come from Mr Yeats plentifully, while other men were making the world it appeared in more miserable than can be told, or were succumbing to the pessimism such misery evoked or, more childishly, were pretending to be superior to that despair. I noticed that some critics praised *The Tower* (1927) who had apparently never read *Responsibilities* or *The Wild Swans*, but though I rate "All Soul's Night" highly, and believe this volume proves that Mr Yeats's powers are undiminished I perceived no rival to the elegy on Robert Gregory, nor have I found a lyric to compare with those cited above. "Sailing to Byzantium" opens grandly, the first three stanzas maintain our expectation, but the fourth weakens to an ineffective and unnecessary repetition of "gold" four times in as many lines, while the meaning loses moment by implying that the contrast between artificial and natural forms is fundamental which is obviously not the case. Let me however end by quoting from The Tower (p. 100)[3] an altogether happy stanza in which the poet speaks of a dead but unnamed friend with an arch and tender consideration to be found in no other writer.

Two thoughts were so mixed up I could not tell
Whether of her or God he thought the most,
But think that his mind's eye,
When upward turned, on one sole image fell;
And that a slight companionable ghost,
Wild with divinity,
Had so lit up the whole
Immense miraculous house,
The Bible promised us,
It seemed a gold-fish swimming in a bowl.

May we not, by gliding over the reference to the "Bible house" as inapplicable, muse how closely appropriate to the poet this description of his friend becomes [?] "Rash" and "immoderate" might be substituted for "slight" and "companionable", but a woman's radiance would remain difficult to distinguish from that of the uncreated rose. And does not his more recent belief that the fifteenth life, or full phase of the moon, perfect beauty, never shines upon this earth, deepen the poignancy of the shadow that from some of these lyrics falls over our idea of their author? Time has substituted for a perfection he might have grasped, one that is beyond a mortal's reach.

NOTES

1. In Later Poems (pp. 222, 223), a mite of historical information *Two Years Later* has been allowed to intrude with all the pomp of capitals into a sequence which was perfect without it, even the dividing number was an impertinence, that in reading aloud could be completely ignored. The last line of the first division should be followed by the first of the second with no longer a pause than between two stanzas, if the full beauty of both is to be heard. In *Selected Poems* the first half is on recto the second on verso, so their divorce becomes complete: yet, why were they ever printed as parts of a single whole if sound and pleasure had not wedded them though reason and indifference may now part them.

2. *Memory* is in the Augustan Books selection though that includes no item from *Poems*, (1906), the book which perhaps contains more successful poetry than any Mr Yeats has published.

3. Also in "A Vision", 1925.

Thomas Sturge Moore and W. B. Yeats
– an Afterword

Warwick Gould

Thomas Sturge Moore wrote two essays upon Yeats. Better known perhaps than this one is his memoir published in *English*, 2:11 (Summer, 1939) 273–8, which contains Yeats's celebrated remark that Florence Farr had been a "chalk egg" that he "had been sitting on for years". The present piece is unpublished. A typescript and carbon are to be found among the Sturge Moore Papers in the University of London Library, (2/85 and 2/84 respectively). The text offered here is that of the top copy, as corrected by Sturge Moore, found in a binder of the A. D. Peters Literary Agency.

The only changes to the text are the regularization of the possessive, "Yeats's", and one or two other possessives, and new punctuational amendments which are offered in square brackets. The two footnotes are Sturge Moore's own. The carbon copy's uncorrected readings have not been collated, nor have certain of his instructions in the margin of the carbon copy – it was clearly used upon the podium – such as "Quote in full".

Dating the essay is not straightforward: there is no extant record of its composition or likely date (or place) of delivery. The newest collection named is *The Tower* published in London on February 14, 1928. Sturge Moore also utilizes *Selected Poems Lyrical and Narrative* (1929). The essay registers dissatisfaction with "Sailing to Byzantium" and is therefore likely to pre-date Yeats's despatch of "Byzantium" to Sturge Moore on 4 October 1930. In fact the wording of the essay (p. 155 above) is very close to that of the comment which prompted Yeats into the writing of the second poem:

> Your *Sailing to Byzantium*, magnificent as the first three stanzas are, lets me down in the fourth, as such a goldsmith's bird is as much nature as a man's body, especially if it only sings like Homer and Shakespeare of what is past or passing or to come to Lords and Ladies (*LTSM* 162:16 April 1930).

Certain points in the essay call for comment, particularly in the light of other papers in the University of London collection, as the following footnotes demonstrate. No attempt has been made to edit this essay fully, however.

157

p. 146 ". . . he probably studied my poetry if possible less than I studied his".
Sturge Moore presumably wants to provoke thought about that "study",
but Yeats's acquaintance with TSM's poetry was, as Ronald W.
Schuchard has reminded me, considerable. In "Friends of my Youth"
(as delivered on 9 March 1910), Yeats both praised and quoted TSM's
poems (*Y&T* 39–40), and his notes for these lectures expand upon his
estimation of TSM as the author of a poetry "so impersonal that it is like
some beautiful water plant sowing and re-sowing itself in the stillness of
his mind" (*Y&T* 78–9, 62). The lecture is referred to in *LTSM* 15–16 and
Yeats was later to acknoweldge his debt to "one of the loveliest lyrics of
our time", "The Dying Swan" (*VP* 826). His most extended comment on
the school of Binyon and TSM is where, in the Lecture notes for "Friends
of my Youth", he refers to TSM as "a really great poet", one "who does
not project" himself.

> I feel when I read Mr. Sturge Moore that he is so full of careless
> abundance because he welcomes every beautiful thought. It is enough
> if he believes in it for a moment, that it is part of the procession that
> passes his door. . . . He makes no selection amongst the beautiful
> things; and so there is through him a certain kindness and evenness, he
> is well content with his world, he has no personal tragedy, no personal
> delight. And so once more the great impersonal things, many
> landscapes, many ancient imaginings, Centaurs' forms, hurry about
> him. He creates myths and writes plays, and how well he sings of
> traditional virtues. He is so frank and simple in his pleasure that all is
> new and joyous where another found but platitude (Quote his poem
> called "Kindness") (*Y&T* 81).

p. 148 ". . . does not Mr. Yeats too frequently use 'that' not only for 'which' but
for 'who'?" Yeats, apart from one comment that Sturge Moore's poetry
was "somewhat difficult to read out" (*Y&T* 39–40) did not really
respond to TSM's work with technical criticism such as this. Many of
TSM's technical objections to Yeats's poems are taken up in an
extraordinary nine page draft letter, undated and possibly never sent
preserved in the University of London Library (26/179). It is referred to
in the description of that collection, *infra*, p. 176. TSM initially takes
issue with Yeats's dogmatic attitude to inversion of syntax in poetry, and
proceeds to analyze examples of inversion (and other syntactical
features) in *The Countess Cathleen*, elsewhere in the poems of Yeats, and in
the works of other poets, including Browning. Given Yeats's concern for a
"powerful and passionate syntax" (*E&I* 522; *LDW* 175), this documen
may bear upon their conversations and is worth quotation. TSM uses as
example the line "Terrible is your beauty to me" from his play *Judith*
which Yeats had seen prior to 26 January 1916 (*LTSM* 24–5). The line
which comes from the "sword episode" in the play (Lillah McCarthy

managed to please TSM but disappoint Yeats in the scene) may well be a source for the "terrible beauty" of "Easter 1916". See however *supra*, pp. 38; 51n.17 for Elizabeth Cullingford's discussion of other sources for this line. Judith, who "drives the steel into what has stirred [the] flesh" is later symbolical of judgment for Yeats in *A Vision* [*B*] (p. 38)

TSM also takes issue in the letter with Yeats's omissions of articles, relative pronouns and prepositions. He suggests that a refusal to utilize the beneficial effects of poetic inversion is "to cut off your nose to spite your face", and offers a reason why Yeats's poetry is becoming more obscure. Yeats, he says "compensates" himself

for the loss of inversions by omitting words which are rarely or never omitted in speach [sic] and never in prose.

TSM finds the lines following "Though pedantry denies" in "On Woman" unparaphrasable because of the omission of "transitions and connections . . . [n]othing in Browning is more obscure". Other examples discussed include the very line "That in a ring" from "Lift up the White Knee" under discussion above. The argument of the draft concludes:

Good and felicitous inversions help the sense to seize on the stirred mind as they present words in the order of the natural importance of their inherent meanings, as they would spring up in the mind before their syntactical relations could be ascertained. They are therefore not originally or when rightly used an artifice. There are always more of them in a rough draft or in unconscious poetry. But everyone must be judged by taste, and stand or fall like any other element of poetical language by success with the properly moved mind. Minds not properly stirred have no more say in these matters than the philistines; They are in this case and for these occasions philistine. To listen to the rough draft of a drama focusing the attention on the occurence of inversions, is I think a bad symptom of a theory ridden mind.

Nothing I have written here my dear Yeats in any degree lessens the great admiration I feel for much of your work or prevents me from concurring in many of your particular intuitions even when these may take the form of condemning this or that inversion, but the theory and the fanaticism which leads you to apply it out of season, seems to me rather characteristic of some vorticist or verslibrist than worthy of you.

I still croon . . .". In TSM's copy of *Poems 1899–1905* (*Wade* 64), described in this present volume, *infra*, p. 180, a fragment of this portion of the MS of this essay is tipped in at p. 150.

'It is impossible . . .'. said Blake". "Nor is it possible to Thought / A reater than itself to know" from "A Little BOY Lost". See Geoffrey

Keynes (ed.), *BLAKE: Complete Writings*, (London: OUP, 1966–9) p. 218.

p. 151 "Are not the narrative portions of 'Baile and Aillinn'. . ?" See *LTSM* 10 for TSM's mixed pleasure and criticism upon receipt of this volume. In it his responses are more vigorously recorded: the "interludes" are crossed through, yet an account of the legend upon which the poem is based, taken apparently from Yeats's verbal account, is tipped in at p. 151. Certain other pages of the volume reveal TSM trying out his own versions of Yeats's poems, while some pages of "The Shadowy Waters" have been crossed through.

p. 152 "T. S. Omond". Omond, formerly Fellow of St. John's College, Oxford, was well known for his books upon metrics, including *A Study of Metre* (London: Grant Richards, 1903 *et seq.*) and *English Metrists: Being a Study of English Prosodical Criticism from Elizabethan Times to the Present Day*. (Oxford: Clarendon, 1921.) Omond's assertion has not been traced. *English Metrists*, however, follows Thomas MacDonagh's *Thomas Campion and the Art of English Poetry* (Dublin: Hodges Figgis; London: Simpkin Marshall, 1913) in taking Yeats as an example of the "new blank verse, based upon the stress-rhythm theory" (pp. 258, 319). Mac Donagh, of course, had heard A.E. chanting Yeats's poems.

p. 153 ". . . 'Lycidas' ". The comparison is the more interesting in that TSM recorded in a letter to Trevelyan that "Yeats has made me very angry he *hates* Lycidas & The Ode to Autumn and talks utter nonsense for the sake of talking it. I'm afraid he won't be much use". (16/463.)

Note: The versions of Yeats's poems quoted by Sturge Moore are frequently incorrect: further evidence of his desire to revise Yeats's work.

Coming to Grips with Proteus

A. D. Hope

William Butler Yeats once remarked, "Swift haunts me; he is always just round the corner." I could very well say the same thing about Yeats himself. For most of my life he has been just round the corner. And although I am a poet of a very different kind and with not the slightest inclination to imitate and no hope to emulate him, he is rarely far from my mind. The nature of this haunting has never been clear to me. There are several contemporary poets to whom I feel more drawn than to Yeats, but I am free of their presences. Much as I admire them they do not lurk constantly "round the corner", and I do not feel the urge to write to or about them as I have about Yeats in recent years, verses in tribute to him and poking a little harmless fun which come almost spontaneously into my mind. Most of these, fortunately, remain unfinished but the five which I have completed are the occasion of the present article and I have brought them together as a sort of homage to a poet I so greatly admire.

I should add that my knowledge of the man and his work is extremely scrappy. I have known several people who knew him but I never met him except once and that was in a dream. It was a rather curious dream and may perhaps shed some light on the haunting.

In the dream I am visiting my friend the poet David Campbell at his property in the country about twenty miles from Canberra where I live. It is a cold and stormy night in winter and a number of people have gathered in a large room as though for a party. I am sitting at one end of the long room facing the door. At the other end a big log fire is blazing. There are drinks but no one is drinking; most are sitting round the walls and seem to be waiting. I turn to a man sitting beside me and say "I don't see David here; where has he got to?" "Oh, didn't you know?" he answers, "He's gone to the airport to meet W. B. Yeats and bring him here." Almost immediately after, the door flies open letting in a blast of wind and a flurry of snowflakes and David Campbell ushers in Yeats. It is the Yeats of later years, the tall and distinguished smiling public man of "Among School Children", his magnificent white hair blown about by the storm. David takes him round the room introducing him to the guests and he pauses for some time by the fire chatting with people while drinks are served, and finally David brings him up to me. "This is Alec Hope –" he begins. "I know!" says Yeats, "I have been hoping to meet you. May we sit down?" We sit and a long conversation about poetry ensues in which we find ourselves in perfect agreement and Yeats makes many interesting points which I recall when some time later I wake up. Unfortunately I did not follow up the urging of my mind to put on the light and make a note of the conversation and by morning it had all faded away.

Well, it was merely a dream though an unusually vivid and detailed one. I do not take it seriously but I recount it because I suspect Yeats himelf might have been inclined to take it quite seriously. Basically this difference of attitude between us is the occasion of the present piece of writing. Most of the things that Yeats took seriously, his engagements with magic, theosophy, spiritualism, various forms of the occult, automatic writing and so on, seem to me comic absurdities that could only argue a mind credulous to the point of silliness. Yet I known that Yeats was not silly. His avowed "monkish hatred" of science seems to me merely perverse. I am bored by his politics and can work up no enthusiasm for his theories of drama and find his plays dull and his excursions into Irish mythology and legend artificial. I could easily think of myself as his complete antithesis both as a man and as a poet. And yet I am forced to acknowledge him as the greatest poet, writing in English, of his day and perhaps the noblest mind of his time.

I have frequently tried to resolve the conflict of these attitudes by the method most natural and most appropriate to a poet, that is, by writing a poem about them. Most of these efforts came to nothing, were never finished and ended in the waste-paper basket, but the five quoted here have all been published before (except the last) and illustrate various ways in which I have tried at various times to come to grips with different shapes of this protean character. All five were written well after Yeats's death in 1939.

The first of them dates from 1948 when I was lecturing in the English department of the University of Melbourne, among other things on the poetry of Blake. This had led me to Yeats's study of Blake which I found quite fascinating despite the fact that I thought his theories and his interpretation untenable. It was what it told me about Yeats himself that interested me and led me to re-read the *Collected Poems* of 1939. These things may have led to the following poem. But I was unaware of it. What happened was that in the middle of a teaching term I suffered from what I call a "feeling of having a poem coming on". The only trouble was that in spite of all my encouragement it would not "come on", or even manifest itself or its subject. Finally I took a week's leave and borrowed a house by the sea where I sat for three mortal days in front of my blank paper – as bad a case of poetic constipation as I have ever experienced.

On the third evening I walked into the nearby town and bought myself a bottle of whiskey, swearing that if nothing came of my vigil next day I would return to my job. Either the threat or the whiskey proved efficacious. Next morning after a short show of obstinacy from the Muse I wrote two poems in an hour. They came quite unannounced. The first was consciously composed; the second, the Yeats poem, might almost have been dictated. It came as it were, ready-made, a most surprising thing to me, as I usually compose slowly with many erasures and second thoughts and revisions. Without premeditation on my part, the poem expressed for me at the time all that Yeats stood for in the world and in my own attitude to poetry. It still does.

This is the poem.

William Butler Yeats

To have found at last that noble, candid speech
In which all things worth saying may be said,
Which, whether the mind asks, or the heart bids, to each
Affords its daily bread;

To have been afraid neither of lust nor hate,
To have shown the dance, and when the dancer ceased,
The bloody head of prophecy on a plate
Borne in at Herod's feast;

To have loved the bitter, lucid mind of Swift,
Bred passion against the times, made wisdom strong;
To have sweetened with your pride's instinctive gift
The brutal mouth of song;

To have shared with Blake uncompromising scorn
For art grown smug and clever, shown your age
The virgin leading home the unicorn
And loosed his sacred rage –

But more than all, when from my arms she went
That blessed my body all night, naked and near,
And all was done, and order and content
Closed the Platonic Year,

Was it *not* chance alone that made us look
Into the glass of the Great memory
And know the eternal moments, in your book,
That we had grown to be?

This poem was later reprinted in the volume, *In Excited Reverie* edited by A. Norman Jeffares and K. G. W. Cross on the occasion of the hundredth anniversary of Yeats's birth in 1965.

The same celebration was the occasion of another poem on the same subject. David Campbell at the time was editor of the literary page of the newspaper *The Australian*. He had written to a number of Australian poets asking for poems paying tribute to Yeats on the occasion of the centenary. I was then on sabbatical leave in England, had been staying with Professor Jeffares and reading for the first time his study of the poet. When David Campbell's letter reached me I was at Cambridge working on a book and soon to go abroad. I was irritated by the extra call on my time but sat down attempting to see if I could set down an impression of those aspects of Yeats's life and character which I found irresistably comic and combine them with those which were undeniably noble and beautiful. As time was short I sent David the following verses, dashed off hurriedly and without the benefit of second thoughts or revision.

A Letter to David Campbell on the
Birthday of W. B. Yeats, 1965.

I

Well, I drink to you, David Campbell, but I drop a curse in the cup
For begging a poem on Willie Yeats that took so long growing up.
I thought myself safe from rhyming chores but see I've been sold a pup.

A poem for Yeats's birthday? You're organising a wake
For a boy that's been born a hundred years? Sure that's a piece of cake!
Write it yourself why don't you? Why don't you jump in the lake?

And then I begin to weaken as of course I always do.
It's hard to resist you anyway, but the subject tempts me too:
That marvellous, monstrous century Yeats didn't quite live through.

He was born to the swansdown feeling, when the world was wacky and wide;
Tennyson, Browning and Pinch-me went down to swim with the tide;
And the Wrath of God descended on Poetry when he died.

And in between there was Willie – indeed I loved the man;
Best thing out of Ireland since Tuath Dé Danaan
Back of me hand to the warty boys, but I'll write a piece if I can.

II

Sure I'll write a piece for Willie. It's a long time to be dead!
Madame Blavatsky's cuckoo clock, does he mind now what it said
'Never you rhyme to a ladybird; just keep her warm in bed!

See what a pig of a world it is, the bard was put upon:
Madam Blavatsky's cuckoo turned out to be a swan,
And the swan broke Willie's heart at last, and now he's dead and gone.

Now he sleeps with his fathers and minds his p's and q's.
(if it's some of those I could mention, it won't be much of a snooze);
But maybe he thinks of other things and cuddles up to the Muse.

Is it Dublin Senate he sits in? Does he walk through a Dublin school?
Dream of the green-room squabbles or the peaceful lake at Coole?
Does he lose himself in the mortal storm with King, beggar and fool?

Does he recall the politicos the day he explained his plans
For raising the ghosts of Ireland by spells and talismans
To drive the English into the sea and beat the Black and Tans?

Willie was often a prize galah. We mustn't say it aloud.
They wouldn't like it in Dublin and we've got to do him proud.
So let's dig him up for his hundred years and get him out of his shroud.

And not too solemn about it! I know the occasion's grand,
But after all it's his birthday or so I understand,
And a frock-coated speech to a tombstone was a thing he could not
stand.

III

What if he talked to the fairies? What if he talked through his hat?
The talk itself was magic, and musical magic at that!
And all of us sensible fellows, doesn't he leave us flat?

And you and I who are poets, we know the reason why
This is a day for a laughing, not for a weeping eye:
We go to waken our Master whose bones shall prophesy!

We go to conjure a creature that slouches from its den
Now that the time comes round for the word to be born again,
The word that a poet utters, and then becomes for men.

We are the earth's and of it, but his was the master's spell
That opens a pass to heaven and breaks the jaws of hell;
The tongues of men and of angels – and charity as well!

He was the golden candle that lights man's way to die;
The great shoulder of courage, that props a falling sky;
And the voice of intellectual joy we go on living by.

David Campbell only published the third section of the poem. I
imagine he though the first two were not serious enough or too

incongruous. Perhaps he thought the poem as a whole did not come off. But I had meant it to be taken as a whole and later on published it as such.

Three years later the urge to try again took hold of me because I had begun to see that what I had been viewing as two more or less contradictory and incompatible aspects of the poet's character and personality were in fact nothing of the sort, but parts of a complete and coherent whole, each drawing on the other and each essential to the other. The idea struck me after reading Oliver St John Gogarty's account, in *As I Was Going Down Sackville Street*, of how he called on Yeats at Rathfarnham with an invitation from the Governor-General for Yeats to attend the opening ceremony of the Spring Show. He found Yeats in bed and flatly refusing to go but cajoled him with an account of a butter-churning competition between young country lasses. They would, he said, be using the old-fashioned churns and singing the last remaining traditional song of buttermaking –

> Father Claude overheard it in Tipperary, when a buxom maid was churning as she thought all alone. She had buttocks like a pair of beautiful melons. Her sleeves were rolled up. She had churned from early morning. Her neck was pink with exercise. Her bosom laboured, but she could not desist, for the milk was at the turn. Up and down, desperately she drove the long handle. . . . In front of her ears the sweat broke into drops of dew. She prayed in the crisis to old forgotten gods of the homestead! Twenty strokes for ten! Gasping, she sang:
>
>> "Come, butter!
>> Come, butter!
>> Come, butter!
>> Come!
>> Every lump
>> As big as
>> My bum!"

Yeats was out of bed and reaching for his clothes before Gogarty had finished.

This enchanting tale should perhaps not be taken too literally. Gogarty calls his book "A Phantasy in Fact", and calls us to note that "The names in this book are real the characters fictitious"; but it provides just the insight into a relation between the two aspects of Yeats's nature and their interdependance that I was looking for and which became the source of a poem "The Apotelesm of W. B. Yeats" published in *Poetry* (Chicago) 1968.

> Such a grand story
> Of Willie Yeats
> Keeping his warm bed

Under the slates
To a tale of milkmaids
His friend relates:

"At churns in Sligo
The wenches hum:
Come butter, Come butter,
Come butter,
Come!
Every lump as
Big as my bum!"

A milkmaid mounting
The poet's stair;
A blackbird trilling
His country air;
Butter and bottom,
The Muse was there.

Sheep in the meadow,
Cows in the corn;
Come Willie Butler
Blow up your horn!
Out of such moments
Beauty is born.

I had used the word "apotelesm" designedly in both its senses: a summation, and the casting of a horoscope, but mention this only because it is so rare a word that it needs explaining.

It was some ten years before I returned to Yeats once more in verse. The occasion was my reading Robert Graves's attack on Yeats in his Clark Lectures at Trinity College, delivered in Cambridge in 1954 and 1955. I was in considerable agreement with Graves's aspersions on T. S. Eliot, Ezra Pound, W. H. Auden and Dylan Thomas, but the section of "These be your gods, O Israel!" devoted to Yeats seemed to me deliberately and vulgarly malicious. Unfortunately for Graves, in choosing an example to illustrate his thesis, he not only misquoted Yeats's lines but apparently picking a stanza at random from "Chosen", one of the series "A Woman Young and Old", he fell into one of those glorious howlers that delight authors when made by supercilious critics. The stanza in questions runs:

I struggled with the horror of daybreak,
I chose it for my lot! If questioned on
My utmost pleasure with a man
By some new-married bride, I take

That stillness for a theme
Where his heart my heart did seem
And both adrift on the miraculous stream
Where – wrote a learned astrologer –
The Zodiac is changed into a sphere.

Graves begins his assault by some pedantic strictures on the rhymes and having failed to reflect on the title of the whole series, interprets the speaker in the stanza as Yeats himself being asked about his pleasures of a homosexual nature in the presence of someone else's bride. He ends with a stern rebuke to Yeats for misinterpreting the words of Macrobius, the "learned astrologer" – Graves writes "astronomer" – in the second last line.

The temptation was too great: I could not resist inventing a reply from Yeats who at the time of the Clark lectures had been in his grave "Under bare Ben Bulben's head" for some years:

The Spectre of W. B. Yeats to Robert Graves.

My bones are stowed; my sleep is sound;
I know I lie in Irish ground;
What wretch, then, conjures me to come
Like Samuel's spirit from the tomb
And wakes the dead and turns the sod
To learn he has been cursed by God?

You Robert Graves, by Hare and Burke,
Why all this corpse and coffin work?
To be dug up in France and laid
Forever in Ben Bulben's shade
Is all an Irish poet craves:
He has no need of other 'graves'.

But speak, poor wizard, tell me true,
What was it could have prompted you
To stab dead poets in the back
With this mean-spirited attack?
Was it fierce envy, settled hate
Or a mere wish to demonstrate
To Cambridge dons and Cambridge dames
Your faculty for calling names?
What spurious goddess sent you down
From Sinai to play the clown
And make the undergraduates laugh
By proving me their Golden Calf

And smash the Tables of the Law
To raise a general guffaw?

And tell me, Robert, was it wise
To tilt at signs and mysteries,
My symbols, seances and spells
While warlock Graves in cap and bells,
Trumped up from folklore's bones and rags
White goddesses and triple hags?
Did you not recollect a knack
In pots to call the kettle black?
Nor, throwing stones at mine reflect
Your glass-house likelier to be wrecked?
For mine was honest nonsense, yours
Mad mumpsimus with Nancy's drawers.

Next who appointed you, I ask
To take your fellow bards to task,
Pontificate upon the times
And tell your peers to mend their rhymes.
Inventing rules to prove us wrong
About the finer points of song?
Or was your study to annoy
And prove yourself a warty boy,
And, with the jaw-bone of an ass,
Like Samson, slay the poets *en masse*?

But these are trifles: I'll be brief
And turn to your attack-in-chief,
That poem you laboured to discredit,
By showing that you had not read it.
Come Mr Graves, now don't be vexed,
But pay attention to the text.

Peruse your commentary! You note
In the first sentence you misquote
(Unless incumbent of a chair
In Cambridge, one must have a care.)
You then, deliberately no doubt,
Turning my syntax inside out,
Insinuate me to have been –
– with a fine nose for the obscene

And cocksure critical aplomb –
A sodomite and Peeping Tom.
Query: how could you think so? *Answer*:
You'd only read the second stanza

And, in your atrabilious rage,
Neglected to turn back the page.
Had you done so and read the title,
You might have learned – the point is vital
To one of your profound acumen –
The lines were spoken by a woman!

Fie, Robert, fie! Were these the ways
To add fresh laurels to your bays
And prove yourself a man of parts
Before a Faculty of Arts?

Robert, I have you on the hip!
Now will you prate of scholarship
And raise false witness from the dead
To teach us what Macrobius said?

Take my advice: In future learn
To read a text you mean to spurn,
And look more closely at the letters
Before you criticize your betters!

Yeats, I am sure, would not have met vulgarity with vulgarity in this way, but as he himself said, the prospect of a good row always cheered him up and put him in good heart – in any case it was a chance too good to be missed. I do not know whether Mr Graves ever saw those lines. I trust he did. But my own pleasure was chiefly in a chance to wear the mask of another poet without any pretence of parody. I have never really plumbed Yeats's theory of the mask and am suspicious of what his critics think he meant. To me he remains Proteus who when you attempt to sieze him turns now into a serpent, now to a lion, now to flame of fire and now to a wave of the sea. The questions you have come to ask him get different answers accordingly and sometimes none at all. But it is always worth while to try. You have always gained something unexpected. The question is often unanswered but it has rebounded on yourself in a way for which you did not foresee having to find an answer. Yeats himself had the same experience as Proteus reflecting on himself. "[A]s I look backward upon my own writing" he once wrote, "I take pleasure alone in those verses where it seems to me I have found something hard and cold, some articulation of the Image which is the opposite of all that I am in my daily life (*Au* 274)." That is one answer to a quite different question which I did find turned back on myself. At another time it was a statement about poetry which made me at last aware of what was the real bond between us.

All art is the disengaging of a soul from place and history, its suspension in a beautiful or terrible light to await the Judgement. . . .

1 Detail of Deidameia and the centaur Eurytion from the West Pediment at Olympia. From a photograph by Verlag Von Ernst Waspruth. Berlin, reproduced as Plate XV in E. Curtius, F. Adler *et al.*, (eds). *Die Funde von Olympia Ausgabe in einem Bande herausgegeben von dem Direktorium der Ausgrabungë zu Olympia* (Berlin, 1882).

2 Deidameia and the centaur Eurytion from the West Pediment at
Olympia. From a photograph by Alison Frantz, reproduced in
Bernard Ashmole and Nicholas Yalouris, *Olympia: the Sculptures
of the Temple of Zeus* (London: Phaidon, 1967), plate 111.

3 The *Medusa*. Flemish School, 17th Century. Uffizi, Florence.

4 *Don Juan in Hell* (c. 1908) by Charles Ricketts. Present whereabouts unknown. Photograph courtesy of the Witt Collection, Courtauld Institute, University of London.

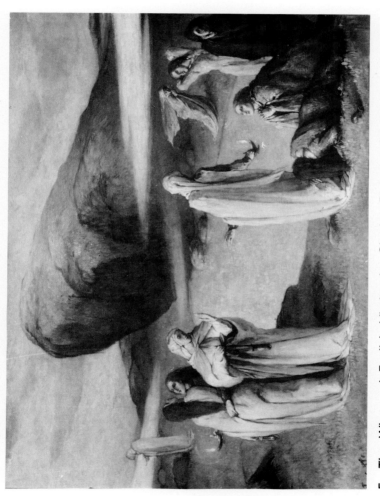

5 *The Wise and Foolish Virgins* by Charles Ricketts, Private Coll., London. Photograph courtesy of Sotheby's.

6 *The Danaides* by Charles Ricketts; 100.2×83.2 cm. From a photograph by Merrett & Harper, Montreal, of the original in the National Gallery of Canada, Ottawa.

7 Costume design by Charles Ricketts for *The King's Threshold*.
Courtesy of Victoria and Albert Museum, London.

8b *Olivia Shakespear, Dorothy Shakespear Pound and Omar Pound* (c. 1936), by courtesy of and © Omar Pound, and by courtesy of Ian Fletcher.

8a *Olivia Shakespear* (c. 1905), by courtesy of and © Omar Pound, and by courtesy of Ian Fletcher.

The almost illegible pencilled note by Thomas Sturge Moore reads, as far as can be made out "From the Latin Gospels at Paris / attested to have belonged to St Willebrord / who died 739 Irish work the oldest of which [?] / resemble [?] gospels of Lindisfarne". The design is a copy of Paris B.N. Latin 9389, *Evangéliaire de saint Willebrord* (f. 75). Late seventh century. The lettering in the original also reads "IMAGO LEONII". Thomas Sturge Moore has blocked in the title RESPONSIBILITIES in rough sketch, bottom r.h. corner.

9 A Tracing after the *"Latin Gospels at Paris Attested to Have Belonged to St Willebrord"*, with title RESPONSIBILITIES blocked in on bottom r.h. corner (13¾ × 10¼ in), by Thomas Sturge Moore. Courtesy of University of London Library.

"This design is the right size for a table centre / and suggests the right arrangement of colours for a / white ground./ The design is only suitable for lying flat like a table/centre or enlarged for a table cloth or bed spread. / it is not suitable for hanging perpendicularly." In hand of Thomas Sturge Moore.

10 A Table Centre Design Adapted from the Design shown in Plate 9, (15¾ × 10¼ in), by Thomas Sturge Moore. Courtesy of University of London Library.

"Block to be the same size Not at all reduced". Unknown hand.

11 Cover design for *Responsibilities* (deriving from two previous designs), (8¾ ×6½ in), by Thomas Sturge Moore. Courtesy of University of London Library.

"Spine & [   ] lettering gold" (bottom); "To be set in the same letters as LAST POEMS" (top l.h. corner). In hand of Thomas Sturge Moore.

12 Cover design for *Last Poems and Plays* (9 ½ × 6 ¾ in), by Thomas Sturge Moore. Courtesy of University of London Library.

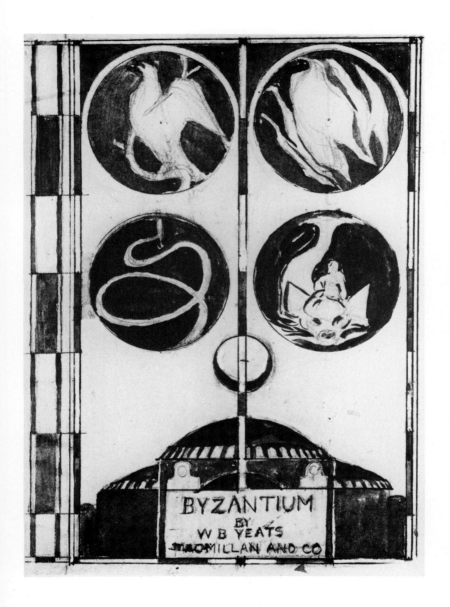

13 Early sketch for cover design of *Byzantium* (i.e. *The Winding Stair*), (8¼ ×5¾ in), by Thomas Sturge Moore. Courtesy of University of London Library.

"Drawing for book-cover to be cut in brass and printed in gold / on which buckram. The outside pencil rulings represent the edge / of the cover boards; lines that run out beyond them are intended to / continue beyond the edge." In hand of Thomas Sturge Moore. A note on a cover sheet to this design reads "This drawing to be returned with proofs of the cover printed / on several different kinds of white buckram". In hand of Thomas Sturge Moore.

14 Cover design for *Axel*, (12½ × 9¼ in), by Thomas Sturge Moore. Courtesy of University of London Library.

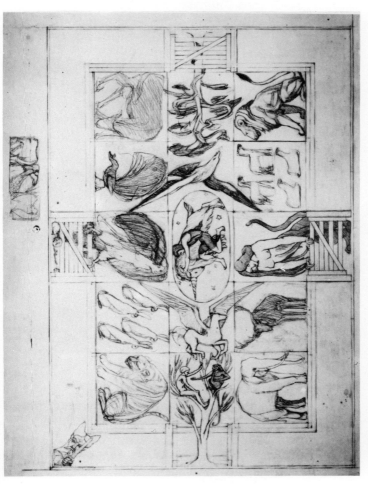

15 Design for table-cloth for the Yeats family, showing four gates and other symbols (22×30 in) by Thomas Sturge Moore. Courtesy University of London Library.

16 *King Goll*, by John Butler Yeats, employing W. B. Yeats as model.
From *The Leisure Hour,* September 1887.

It may show the crimes of Italy as Dante did, or Greek mythology like Keats, or Kerry and Galway villages, and so vividly that ever after I shall look at all with like eyes and yet I know that Cino da Pistoia thought Dante unjust, that Keats knew no Greek, that country men and women are neither so lovable nor so lawless as "mine author sung it me"; that I have added to my being, not to my knowledge (*E&I* 339–40).

That, I think, is the nub of the problem. What I have realized at last is that what I have received from Yeats has not added much to my knowledge, but it has profoundly added to my being both as a poet and as a man.

And now a valediction to which I have been prompted by the writing of these reminiscences.

Poet, farewell!
Everything ends.
Freed of your spell
I would part friends.
My hour draws on;
Time to depart.
Man dies alone,
So leave my heart.
Your part in me
I have repaid
Now I go free;
Your ghost is laid.
I foot alone
My road to die.
You, who rode high,
Horseman, ride on.

SIGNIFICANT
RESEARCH
COLLECTIONS

W. B. Yeats Material in the University of London Library

Pamela M. Baker and Helen M. Young

The material in the University of London Library relating to W. B. Yeats and his circle is mainly to be found in two of the Library's special collections: the Sturge Moore Papers and the Sterling Library. The former is a large collection of the correspondence, manuscripts and designs of Thomas Sturge Moore (1870–1944), poet, wood-engraver and man of letters, deposited in the Library by his son and daughter, Mr Daniel Sturge Moore and Miss Riette Sturge Moore, in 1964 and later. The collection is stored in some eighty-five large pamphlet boxes, many of which contain more than 300 items.[1]

Sturge Moore was trained as an artist at the Croydon School of Art, where he met Charles Shannon, and at the Lambeth School of Art, where Charles Ricketts was a member of the staff. In 1888 he joined them at the Vale, Chelsea, and worked with them on the Vale Press productions. Through Ricketts, Sturge Moore met Laurence Binyon who, late in 1898, introduced him to W. B. Yeats and so began the friendship which lasted until the death of Yeats in 1939.

Between 1915 and 1940 Sturge Moore designed the covers of twelve of Yeats's books and the original sketches for these designs, together with some correspondence with Macmillans about them, are probably amongst the most interesting items in the collection. This material would relate to holdings in the Macmillan archive in the British Library and in the University of Reading. Among the books concerned are *Responsibilities*, *Letters to the New Island*, and *Last Poems and Plays*. The correspondence concerning *Letters to the New Island* includes sketches, draft replies and part of the design for the spine. There are designs and proofs for covers for *Reverie over Childhood and Youth*, *Responsibilities* (Plates 9, 10, 11), *Per Amica Silentia Lunae*, *The Wild Swans at Coole*, *The Cutting of an Agate*, *Four Plays for Dancers*, *The Winding Stair*, *The Tower*, *Letters to the New Island*, and *Last Poems and Plays* (Plate 12).

A note in Sturge Moore's hand explaining the symbolism of this design runs, in part:

This design does not refer to any particular line or stanza but symbolizes the underlying theme of the book. Nut, the Egyptian goddess of the heavens is shown planted on and dominant over a lion while she lifts the starry sphere. (p. 47) Thus the royalty and ferocity of brute fact supports the intellect that projects a completed plan: or taken in an aspect that returns again and again in these poems; the goddess and the 'noble animal' are symbols for the fascination and ruthlessness of generation that raise above themselves the mind that "Michael Angelo knew". (p. 17) that by persistance discerns the truth as William Blake did ... creative pleasure crowns and causes life.... The brass should be cut a 12th of an inch smaller so as to exactly fit within the boards leaving merely a line of the cloth visible outside ... Generation ruthless majestic and terrible, causes life and supports its sublimations which in turn lifts the heavenly sphere both the astronomers map and the ... ideal astrological pattern of unembodied reality.

The Tower materials include the drawing, proof and two specimen covers, one with the design blind-stamped on the front cover and the other stamped in gold. Elsewhere in the collection there is a photograph of Yeats's tower at Ballylee which forms the motif for the cover of *The Tower*. On the back of the photograph Yeats has written: "The cottage at back is my kitchen. In front you will see on[e] parapet of the old bridge, the other was blown up during our civil war WBY." A small sketch-book contains designs for *The Winding Stair*: one of those not used was for the work under the title *Byzantium*, which Yeats had for some time considered for the book (Plate 13). There is also an interesting group of designs by Sturge Moore for the edition of *Axel* translated by H. P. R. Finberg and published in 1925 with Yeats's preface (Plate 14), together with a copy of the rare prospectus for that work, which contains quotations from Yeats and is not recorded in *Wade*. A selection of the Sturge Moore designs was displayed in a centenary exhibition at the University of Hull in 1970.[2]

Among other items are some embroidery designs by Sturge Moore for such articles as table-cloths and bed-spreads probably done for the Yeats family (Plates 10, 15), including silk panels to decorate a cupboard (now in the possession of Miss Anne Yeats) which were embroidered by Ethel Pye (*LTSM* 24, 159).

There are also several versions of two articles about Yeats by Sturge Moore, one published in English, II:11 (Summer 1939). The other, "Do we or do we not know it?" is published in this volume for the first time (see *supra*, pp. 145–56).

Unfortunately little of the personal correspondence between Yeats and Sturge Moore remains in the Papers: there are only two letters from Yeats to Sturge Moore. One, written in 1932 or 1933, concerns *The Conquest of Old Age*, by Peter Schmidt, Yeats's Steinach operation, performed by Norman Hare, and some letters of Charles Ricketts; the other, written in 1932, refers to Roger Ingpen, editor of Shelley, whom Yeats had met at Sturge Moore's house, and to the first volume of Sturge Moore's collected poems. Both appear to be unpublished. Sturge Moore's reply to the latter can be found in *LTWBY* 534.

There are also some drafts of letters from Sturge Moore to Yeats: in a nine-page draft (undated) Sturge Moore remarks "your poetry is tending to become more and more obscure" and "You also indulge in intollerably [sic] long sentences", but he stresses the "great admiration I feel for much of your work". This draft letter is further discussed in the present volume, on p. 158. Another (also undated) draft concerns a threatened charge of indecency by the Vigilance Society against one of Sturge Moore's stories, *A Platonic Marriage*, which was published in *The English Review* for January 1911. Sturge Moore and the editor, Austen Harrison, feared there would be a prosecution and the former asks Yeats "To save either me or Harrison from gaol I hope I may count on your bestirring yourself and the Academical Committee from which I have as yet heard nothing. He wants to get influential people like Gosse to come forward, if the Society prosecutes. This is a great nuisance though totally absurd". Letters from Yeats in reply were re-assuring: "Gosse has seen the Home Secretary . . . who is friendly and will do nothing", he writes, "but if the Vigilance people move on their own account they cannot be stopped. But I think nothing will be done" (*LTSM* 15). And in the event nothing was done. It is interesting to note that there are also letters to Sturge Moore referring to the affair from his friends, A. H. Fisher and R. C. Trevelyan, one from the latter mentioning that Yeats had been among several authors who had called at the offices of *The English Review*. This may serve as an illustration of the way in which a particular incident can be seen through the eyes of more than one member of the circle of friends to which both Yeats and Sturge Moore belonged, by reference to the letters exchanged between them and Sturge Moore himself. There is also a draft letter of condolence to Mrs Yeats on Yeats's death dated 3 February 1939, and further reactions to his death can be found in various parts of the collection.

At this point two items in the general manuscript collections of the Library might be mentioned: a letter from Yeats to Florence Farr in which he makes the request "Don't recite 'Bogland' " (1906?); and a draft from Sturge Moore to Yeats concerning the death of Lady Gregory (29 May 1932).

Occasional references to Yeats appear in the letters of other of Sturge Moore's correspondents and in the drafts and copies of his own out-going letters. The largest collections of the latter are those to Alfred Hugh Fisher, to members of the Pye family and to Robert Calverley Trevelyan. In his letters to A. H. Fisher Sturge Moore several times mentions Yeats, referring in one to the latter's visit in December 1925 to Hillcroft, the house at Steep in Hampshire where the Sturge Moores lived from 1919 until 1927, "We had Yeats here for two days last week he gave Bedale's a lecture which was very successful inspite of the hall being horribly cold. He is very delightful and has finished his philosophy, or at least all that he could get from the Spirits but the most important and fundamental idea remains unrevealed and now he is reading other philosophers to find out to what degree the spirits agree with them and is much smitten with an Italian Gentile who is Musolini's [sic] Minister of Education". The letters between Sturge Moore and Sybil Pye date from 1901 until 1943: in some he discusses his designs for Yeats's books, and in a letter of 8 March 1928 she gives particular praise to his design for *The Tower*. The correspondence with his friend Robert Trevelyan also stretches over many years and there are glimpses of Yeats in a number of letters:

one, written about 1901, includes an extraordinary account of a friend of Yeats, "an amateur murderer" (i.e. John Masefield) and his theories of re-incarnation; another (July 1902) contains important references to chanting:

> You know I have Dolmetsch here every week now for us to continue Yeats' chanting it is very interesting and I like him very much he is so enthusiastic and alive.
> He thinks I could learn to chant myself and Binyon also as we can both distinguish notes he says and usually in reading keep the musical intervals with correction. There is a Miss Owen who does it far better than Mrs Emery who comes here.

In yet another Sturge Moore describes meetings with Rabindranath Tagore (1912):

> Yeats and Rothenstein had a Bengalee poet on view during the last days I was in London. I was first priviledged to see him in Yeats rooms and then to hear a translation of his poems made by himself read by Yeats in Rothensteins drawing room. His unique subject is "the love of God". When I told Yeats I found his poetry preposterously optimistic, he said "Ah, you see, he is absorbed in God". The Poet himself is a sweet creature beautiful to the eye in a silk turban. . . . The elect like children play by the sea building castles making boats of leaves (their dreams & hopes) the sea goes on causing wrecks and disasters far & wide but they are always glad of him as a background to their play.

Other subjects of interest which appear in the Papers include *The Oxford Book of Modern Verse*; various responses to Yeats's publications and performances of his plays (in a letter to Sybil Pye of 25 September 1938, Sturge Moore wrote, "Gawsworth has been to Ireland and was very naughty over Yeats' last play 'Purgatory' given at an Abbey Theatre festival. . . . When the curtain came down everybody turned blankly to his neighbour 'what does it mean?' . . . after a little Yeats came on 'the best piece of acting of the whole evening' hanging his head and said 'I am an old man; *that* is what I think of life and death' and off he went"); and reactions to his marriage; in a letter of 14 December 1917, to Sturge Moore, Gordon Bottomley describes how he and his wife asked themselves:

> What has happened to the Phoenix he saw in his youth, and if the wind has ruffled away in the mountain grass all traces of the mountain hare. Do tell us.
> And what of La Beale Isoud with the White-Face whom we saw at your house, and to whom Yeats had such a charming and delicate avuncular bearing?
> And where, O where, is Ashdown Forest?

Bottomley's letters to Sturge Moore are noteworthy for their lively comments on Yeats: in one, dated 19 February 1913, he writes, "Damn Yeats in the past, the present, and the future; damn him from here to Dublin, from Dublin to the Seven Woods of Coole, from the Seven Woods of Coole to Baile's Strand, from Baile's Strand to the Shadowy Waters, from the Shadowy waters to Fiddler's Green (which is three quarters of a mile this side of hell) *and* for the rest of the journey. If you cut out Salamis from 'The Sea is Kind' you will break my heart for ever. I cannot afford to lose so much supreme loveliness. I don't feel I can defend the Arab God so wholeheartedly against the Erse attack, though I grew very much attached to it myself and should miss it a good deal . . ."; and in another, dated 15 January 1922, he condemns Gosse's "dastardly odious unpardonable and fundamentally unintelligent attack on Yeats . . . shameless to a man of Yeats's great position . . . especially as I believe that 'The One Jealousy of Emer' is the most magnificent thing that Yeats has ever done".

Sturge Moore's personal journals and diaries date from 1891 and contain comments on art, literature and philosophy, on his poems and designs and on his friends: entries in a diary between 13 and 17 May 1902, for instance, record conversations with Yeats, Binyon, Masefield and Shannon. There were many other notable men and women among Sturge Moore's friends and acquaintances so that his letters and papers may be said to form a window on the artistic and literary life of the period. Their names include Lascelles Abercromby, Granville Barker, Laurence Binyon, Edmund Blunden, Arthur Quiller-Couch, Walter de la Mare, John Drinkwater, T. S. Eliot, Michael Field (Katherine Bradley and Edith Cooper), H. P. R. Finberg, Roger Fry, John Gawsworth, Edmund Gosse, Thomas Hardy, Selwyn Image, Augustus John, Wyndham Lewis, John Masefield, Lady Ottoline Morrell, Esther and Lucien Pissarro, William Rothenstein, Bertrand Russell, Siegfried Sassoon, Rabindranath Tagore, Hugh Walpole, Emery Walker, Jack Yeats and Lily Yeats.

Most of the early Yeats printed material is in the Sterling Library, which was presented to the University Library by Sir Louis Sterling in 1956.[3] The collection mainly consists of first and early editions in English literature and at that time included about 20 Yeats first editions including some Cuala Press productions. Among these were sets of the Broadsides published between 1908 and 1915 and the Collections of 1935 and 1937. Since that time many additions have been made and there are now over 100 first and early editions of Yeats's works and an almost complete set of Dun Emer and Cuala Press books. They include some interesting association copies, mainly books from the library of Thomas Sturge Moore, some of which were gifts to him from Yeats. Nine of these contain the book-label, designed for him by Sturge Moore, on which he would sign his name and write a line of verse (Figure 1). There is also a proof copy of this label. Its design and printing was discussed in various letters exchanged by Yeats and Sturge Moore between July 1928 and March 1929.

Amongst other presentation volumes there is a copy of *The Green Helmet* inscribed to Yeats with a note almost identical to that in a copy of the same work presented to Allan Wade, reading, "The cover is the unaided work of the American publisher. He says it is he believes the kind of cover I like." There are also several books with pencilled notes and comments by Sturge Moore, including the copy of Yeats's Poems 1899–1905 (1906) given to him by the author (see pp. 159–60 of this present volume).

The Sterling Library also contains a number of books with illustrations by Jack B. Yeats, and also *A Broadsheet* for 1902, published monthly by Elkin Mathews, with illustrations by Jack B. Yeats and Pamela Colman Smith. Other Irish writers of the period, including J. M. Synge and Lady Gregory, are well represented in the Sterling Library. In the Library's Masefield Collection there is a copy of *A Mainsail Haul*, in which two autograph letters from the author to Jack B. Yeats have been inserted, written in 1907 before and after a visit to him in the Gara valley in Devon.

From this account it will be seen that, while having no claims to be a "Yeats centre", the University of London Library does contain in various of its collections material which has been and may continue to be of use to scholars and students engaged in research on many aspects of Yeats's life and work.

NOTES

1. *The Sturge Moore papers in the University of London Library. (Report on the papers of Thomas Sturge Moore, 1870–1944, poet and wood engraver, and his family.)* [Compiled] by M. J. Grant. Vol. 1, etc. [Unpublished typescript handlist.] London, 1973, etc.
2. University of Hull. *T. Sturge Moore (1870–1944): Contribution to the Art of the Book & Collaboration with Yeats. Catalogue of an Exhibition.* Compiled and edited together with an introduction by Malcolm Easton. Hull. 1970.
3. *The Sterling Library. A Catalogue of the printed books and literary manuscripts collected by Sir Louis Sterling and presented by him to the University of London.* Privately printed. Cambridge, 1954.

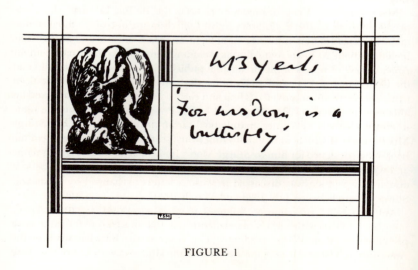

FIGURE 1

Some Notes on the Literary Estate of Pamela Hinkson

Peter G. W. van de Kamp

On 26 May 1982, Pamela Hinkson died at the age of 81. She had been a writer of some renown, whose autobiographically tinted novel, *The Ladies Road*, written under the pseudonym of "Peter Deane", was published by Penguin in 1932 and re-issued in 1946.

In Anglo-Irish studies Pamela Hinkson will be remembered for her devotion to her mother, Katharine Tynan, the poet and novelist who is perhaps more commonly known as K. T. – as she was dubbed by the Meynell family in 1884. She had been her mother's companion until the latter's death. In 1932, she edited a selection of K. T.'s verse for Benn's Series of Augustan Poetry, and contributed an introduction to the volume. She felt it her duty to protect her "dead mother from misrepresentation"; and for that purpose she published several sketches of her mother and of her mother's friendship with such prominent Anglo-Irish writers as Yeats and A. E.

In the 1950's Pamela Hinkson planned a full-scale biography of her mother. She never finished the work, perhaps partly because she was forced to sell a considerable amount of biographical material, including Yeats letters. Nonetheless, this unfinished biography remains of interest to any Yeats scholar. It is over a thousand – mostly typewritten – pages long, and adds to her mother's published reminiscences personal knowledge privately conveyed to Pamela Hinkson or stored in K. T.'s diaries and correspondence. The work forms part of Pamela Hinkson's literary estate which she bequeathed to the Right Revd. Richard Hanson D. D. and Canon Anthony Hanson D. D., sons of Sir Philip Hanson (1871–1955), K. T.'s good friend, private secretary to George Wyndham and one of the very few to receive favourable mention in George Moore's *Hail and Farewell*. In their capacity of literary executors of the estate they granted me permission to draw up a catalogue of the holdings in the estate.

In brief, the estate consists of some thirteen large trunks containing K. T.'s diaries, letters to and from K. T. and her daughter, first editions of K. T.'s and Pamela's works and of volumes sent to K. T. The latter are generally signed by the author. The estate furthermore comprises MS. poems and novels by K. T.

and Pamela Hinkson, in general from the holograph up to the final typewritten version, press cuttings of articles and reviews by K. T. and Pamela, and reviews of their works.

The correspondents include Jane Barlow, A. H. Bullen, Padraic Colum, Lord Dunsany, "George Egerton", John Galsworthy, Monk Gibbon, Lady Gilbert, Oliver St. John Gogarty, Eva Gore-Booth, Alfred Perceval Graves, Lady Gregory, Louise Imogen Guiney, the Gwynns, W. E. Henley, Douglas Hyde, Lionel Johnson, Rudyard Kipling, Alice, Wilfrid and Viola Meynell, G. B. Shaw, Edith Œ Somerville, H. G. Wells, and John and Jack B. Yeats. There are also about a hundred unpublished letters from George Russell.

The reviews of K. T.'s work include Yeats's famous contribution to *The Gael*, 11 June 1887 titled "Miss Tynan's New Book". This review was considered lost by Yeats scholars.

Among the type-written MSS. is an unpublished 429-page volume of reminiscences written by K. T., probably in 1930, dealing with the previous eight years of her life and featuring many of her prominent friends.

The handwritten MSS. comprise most – or perhaps all – of K. T.'s short stories, many of her novels, and virtually all of her poems. At present the archives are housed in 86, St. Stephen's Green, Dublin, Newman House, Room 18, the room occupied by Gerard Manley Hopkins, who once termed K. T. "small fry". K. T.'s correspondence in the estate, as well as Henry Albert Hinkson's, will become available in Manchester University Library. The remains of the estate, the MS short stories, novels, poems and reminiscences, a large collection of historical photographs and all the Pamela Hinkson material will be housed by the U.C.D. archives.

Unfortunately, progress in cataloguing was hampered by the disorderly state in which the material reached me. Moreover, some of the most important and intimate documents have been severely damaged by water, and some items, including early diaries and rare first copies, are beyond repair. A descriptive catalogue of the holdings in the literary estate was finished in October 1984, and is now available in the library of University College Dublin, The National Library of Ireland and the University of Manchester Library. This catalogue comprises the entire correspondence of K. T. and her husband, Henry Albert Hinkson that form part of the estate. It contains most of the letters that Pamela Hinkson received up to 1932, and includes several later letters to her, which are of literary interest. The catalogue furthermore lists all the clippings from K. T.'s reviews, short stories and articles, as well as all the review clippings of K. T.'s insofar as these form part of the estate. Mary-Ellen Fox has compiled a descriptive catalogue of the handwritten MS fiction and essays by K. T. that form part of the holdings. This catalogue is available in U.C.D. library.[1]

Surprisingly, the estate only contains two original Yeats letters and one telegram from Yeats to K. T. It seems that K. T. must have lost, or deliberately destroyed some of her correspondence. Pamela Hinkson, whom George Yeats in a letter praised for her discretion, did however make typed copies and some photo-copies of Yeats letters that she sold to two American universities in the 1950s.[2]

Miss Hinkson objected strongly to the one-sided attitude with which many scholars of Yeats approached his relationship with K. T., and was particularly appalled by the popularised misconception that Yeats had felt obliged to propose to her mother after he had overheard someone suggest that K. T. was the sort of woman who could make herself very unhappy about a man. She presented accounts of Yeats's friendship with K. T. in a lengthy article titled "The Fair Youth of Yeats",[3] and in *The House of Corn*, the unpublished biography of her mother. These, together with some other sources in and outside the literary estate, give a more balanced view of the friendship, extending over its early, intimate stages, which have been described by K. T. and documented by Roger MacHugh in his *W. B. Yeats. Letters to Katharine Tynan.*[4] In the confines of some notes a brief outline of the friendship must suffice.

When Yeats was introduced to K. T. in June 1885, he looked up to her as his senior. *Louise de la Vallière*, her first collection of poetry, had brought her instant acclaim that year, while as early as 1882 she had been described by the Irish press as one of Ireland's promising poetic talents. She was the daughter of one of Ireland's richest farmers, and could afford to hold a literary *salon* on Sundays in Whitehall, her father's house in Clondalkin. She was born on 23 January 1859[5] and thus was also Yeats's senior in age. Yet she instantly found him "very interesting" and "poetical looking".[6] He soon took over the special place in her affection that had been occupied by Charles Gregory Fagan, an Oxford aesthete and minor poet whose artistic fervour she had adored.[7] The nature of the close friendship which developed between Yeats and K. T. remains obscure.

From the letters recorded by MacHugh it appears that theirs was over all a working relationship. This is borne out by Yeats's first review of K. T.'s work. In 1887 he describes her in *The Gael* as "a fellow-worker", and he stresses that they have their "hands on the same plough".[8] In contrast, Tynan family tradition has it that they were "sweethearts"[9] and that "Willie Yeats proposed to . . . Katharine"[10] All in all it seems that, as Pamela Hinkson notes, there never was a suggestion even of romantic friendship, but Yeats "certainly thought at one time that he wanted to marry K. T. . . . made some sort of proposal and was refused."[11] The date of this legendary proposal, the first in a famous row, can only be conjectured.

K. T.'s initial awe for Yeats's poetic aura soon subsided and was substituted by motherly affections for his awkward boyishness and his disarming eccentricity.[12] As she gradually came to appreciate Yeats's poetic leadership, she more and more distanced herself from him. Early she had praised his rare judgment of character as "blindly illuminating". But in 1889 she declares him to be almost inhuman.[13] However, as K. T. distanced herself, he felt more and more attracted to her.

She spends the Summer of 1889 with the Meynells in London, staying at the Yeatses for a week in early July and occasionally throughout September, when the father paints a – forgotten – water-colour of her. Before the London visit

Wilfrid Meynell had facetiously suggested that K. T. was coming to London only to adore Yeats. She replies:

> Willie Yeats is not a swain of mine . . . but I have consistently bullied him for years and feel that he has so much claim upon me. If he were my young man – which Heaven forbid! – . . . I should be ashamed to summon him too soon.[14]

During and after K. T.'s Summer visit Yeats's letters to her grow slightly more personal and affectionate. He writes in August that he has started a poem for her, and asks in October if he could address her by her first name. One year later he goes so far as to express his wish to experience her "personally through ink and pen." During that year K. T., on the other hand, stresses her aloofness. She writes to Wilfrid Meynell that "Willie Yeats" is "not in her line", and that she does not "want a poet, anyhow".[15] Again, in June she pities "miserable Willie Yeats".[16] By the Winter of 1890 she is secretly engaged to Henry Albert Hinkson, student at the Royal University and Senior Classical Tutor at Clongowes Wood College, Kildare. She had fallen in love with him at first sight in September 1887 and they had started to meet regularly in the Autumn of 1888. Hinkson, a friend of the Meynells, had followed K. T. on her visit to London in 1889 and had met Yeats on 12 July, probably in the company of Horne of *The Hobby Horse.*[17]

Yeats, however, remained unaware of K. T.'s love affair; at least until 19 July 1891, when he spent a few days at Whitehall. It was probably on this day that he came into K. T.'s room, found Hinkson there with her and "the situation made plain".[18] Later he seems to have reproached her solemnly, exclaiming: "You should have warned me of this!"[19]

Yet he is back at Whitehall on 10 August and stays for a week, giving K. T. a "ghastly time".[20] His visits continue. He is, for instance, present on K. T.'s farewell party the day before she leaves Whitehall to marry Hinkson in London, in May 1893. And that year he often visits the Hinksons in their Ealing home.

The correspondence also continues, although now conducted in a more businesslike manner. He discusses their mutual reviews, despises "blackguards" of the "Taylor-type" for their condemnation of "log-rolling," praises the Gore-Booths and the "central fire" and lyrical beauty of O'Grady, whom he intends to run against Dowden. He criticises Mangan and DeVere for their limited output and Walsh, Callanan and Hyde for their lack of originality; he venerates Ferguson's *Conary,* soothes K. T. when she complains of being plagiarized by Nora Hopper in her *Ballads in Prose* by suggesting he and she should be proud for being taken as models, and he appeases K. T. when *The Irish Figaro* publishes a satire directed against their eclectic loyalty to each other's writings.[21]

There is a lull in the correspondence between 1895 and 1906, only interrupted by Yeats's formal complaint in 1898 about her intentions to publish verse under the title "The Wind Among the Trees", and by an apology in 1901 for his inability to visit K. T. From 1906 onwards his distanced and polite letters adumbrate the difference in their literary status. That year he discusses plans for the publication of twenty of her poems by the Dun Emer Press, and involves her, the friend of the family, in the family row about his veto-right as its editor. Two years later K. T. was to comment on payment for the selection: "To my amazement they sent me a £7 odd cheque. . . . The idea of a cheque signed by a Yeats nearly made me faint." [22] In 1906 he criticises Henry Albert Hinkson's plays, which K. T. had sent him, for their artificial dialect and emotions. He also writes a crushing letter about George Russell's lack of critical acumen, which he finds reflected in the self-conscious and vague work of the young Irish poets that A. E. surrounds himself with, and which make Yeats vent his wish to coach a generation of young Irish poets.

In April 1912, Yeats and K. T. meet again at a Dublin Royal Hospital Lunch, where K. T. found Yeats as amiable as of old. This occasion leads him to interest A. H. Bullen in publishing K. T.'s new collection of verse, which Yeats praises for its homely quality. In 1913 Yeats writes that he is not angry about her using his early letters without permission in her *Twenty-Five Years: Reminiscences*, although he would have asked her to delete his allusion to Shaw. [23]

The letters of the subsequent years are in the main taken up with K. T.'s work. He returns his letters, corrected, for K. T. to use in her *The Middle Years*, and comments on her poetry that it ought to lie upon many tables "between the photograph of a married daughter and the daughter who has taken the veil." [24]

The major threat to their friendly relations was effected by Yeats's reference in print to Lionel Johnson as a "dissipated . . . drunkard". K. T., not easily angered, was infuriated by this depiction of one who had been dear to her and her husband. [25] In *Studies*, March 1918 she reviews *Per Amica Silentia Lunae* and retorts: "Mr. Yeats might spare his friends . . . this is snobbish! . . . and it is painfully unlike the Yeats one remembers." (pp. 188–9) She reviles: "There is no poetry in this volume of strange speculation." The next year she condemns *The Wild Swans at Coole* for its "perverse mysticism" and rages: ". . . a plague upon what led him to those fountains of a fantastic and mudding philosophy". [26] Yeats completely disregarded these rebukes. In September 1918 he writes about his move into "Ballylee Castle", and in January 1919 he sends her a touching brief letter of sympathy on the death of Henry Albert Hinkson.

Throughout the twenties they continue to meet very occasionally. [27] He writes to her from Cannes on 25 November 1927, about his first serious illness, which had made him wonder if he had to leave the last word to George Moore. In his last letter dated 27 September 1929, he apologises for his inability to write an introduction for her *Collected Poems*. That introduction was written by A. E., "who never failed" K. T. [28] On 2 April 1931, K. T. died. The literary estate does not contain a letter of sympathy by Yeats on her death, and it seems unlikely that he ever wrote one.

NOTES

1. Mary-Ellen Fox, together with Pascale Jouenne helped me with the sorting of the material.

2. Southern Illinois, University at Carbondale, Special Collections, Morris Library and Humanities Research Centre, University of Texas Library, Austin, Texas. Other holdings of K. T. letters include the collections in the National Library of Ireland and the Central Catholic Library, Merrion Square, Dublin.

3. Typewritten MS. (75 pp) in the Literary Estate of the Late Pamela Hinkson, U.C.D. Archives, and in the Humanities Research Centre, Austin Texas.

4. Dublin, Clonmore and Reynolds: 1953.

5. As on baptismal certificate issued for "Catherine Tynan" by the Church of Our Immaculate Lady of Refuge, Rathmines, Dublin, 30 January 1859. For a long time, K. T. thought that she was born on 3 February 1861. She only discovered her real date of birth when P. J. Lennox checked her baptismal certificate in connection with some insurance. She reconciled herself with the date, but not with the year.

6. Letter to Miss Pritchard, 30 June 1859.

7. "Charlie" Fagan was the son of the Rev. Henry Stuart Fagan of Great Cressingham Rectory. K. T. had met him at the Irish Exhibition of 1882. He emigrated to India in 1884 and died there in August 1885.

8. "Miss Tynan's New Book", *The Gael*, 11 June 1887, p. 5.

9. Cullen Tynan O'Mahony to Sister Frances Ines Moloney, s.s.j., 28 August 1942. As in Moloney, "Katharine Tynan Hinkson: A Study of Her Poetry", Ph.D., University of Pennsylvania, 1952 [doctoral dissertations series, publication nr. 9684].

10. Nora Tynan O'Mahony to Austin Clarke, Huntington Library MSS. HM 26340.

11. Pamela Hinkson to Joseph Hone, 11 May 1943.

12. K. T. notes on a typewritten MS., titled *Yeats*, probably written in 1910: "There was a deal of the Don in his aspect – notably of the most famous Don of literature – but unlike the Don he has a half human, half elfin sense of humour." The Quixotic aspect of Yeats was stressed by K.T.'s husband in an unpublished satire, titled "Willie", which he submitted to *The Pall Mall* in the late 1890's.

13. See *The House of Corn*, i, p. 190.

14. *The House of Corn*, ii, p. 243 cf. *Yeats*, p. 9.

15. *The House of Corn*, ii, p. 323.

16. In a letter to Alice Meynell, ibid.

17. Entry in Hinkson's diary, 12 July 1889.

18. *The House of Corn*, ii, p. 426.

19. Ibid., p. 426.

20. Letter from K. T. to Alic Meynell, 22 August 1891.

21. *Irish Figaro*, 16 March 1895.

22. Letter to Frank Mathew, 11 March 1908.

23. In it Yeats suggests that Shaw is somewhat shallow. See *Twenty-Five Years: Reminiscences* (London: Smith Elder, 1913) p. 269.

24. Letter dated 13 January 1915.

25. In fact, K. T. appears to have been made aware of the allusion to Johnson by Frank Mathew, who wrote to her on 20 February 1918: "Can't you massacre Yeats? Yesterday I picked up a review of his last book and read an extract from it. . . . And Yeats can write this of his 'friends'! I have been boiling with rage ever since."

    Only five days later Mathew congratulates K. T. on her attack on Yeats, and adds: "How much better is the silence of the friendly Moon than the eloquence of a friendless lunatic. That title would have made Lionel smile tenderly: he found lots of fun in his beloved companion."

26. "A Strayed Poet", *The Bookman*, May 1919.

27. There is evidence that Yeats visited K. T. in August 1926 and on 25 April 1928. They also met more than once at A. E.'s.

28. K. T. dedicated her *Late Songs* "To A. E. who never fails."

SHORTER NOTES

A Source Note on "The Madness of King Goll"

Frank Kinahan

Few of Yeats's early lyrics escaped his later censorship, but the poem now known as "The Madness of King Goll" is notable for the frequency with which it attracted the young poet's blue pencil. First published in *The Leisure Hour* in 1887 (Plate 16), the poem appeared with a substantially revised first stanza in 1888s *Poems and Ballads of Young Ireland*. The opening stanza had been altered again when the poem resurfaced in 1889s *The Wanderings of Oisin and Other Poems*, and yet again when a more ambitious version of these verses reappeared, by now in an all-but-final form,[1] in the *Poems* of 1895. In this last case, the recastings effected in the opening verse can most readily be explained by reference to the changes that Yeats visited on the 1895 version of the poem's final stanza. The poet knew relatively little about Goll when he began to write about him, but he was willing to learn.

When Yeats decided to append a lengthy explanatory note to the *Leisure Hour* version of his poem, he no doubt did so because "The Madness of King Goll" was the first of his poems to appear in an English magazine. Unfortunately, the note opened with the observation that "Goll or Gall lived in Ireland about the third century" (*VP* 857), and thereby proved misleading from the outset. It was not that Yeats was wrong, but that he was right twice over. His earlier portraits of "Goll or Gall" inadvertently conflated two radically different characters, and the poet's confusion finds its explanation in the source from which he had quarried the narratives on which those portraits were based.

According to the *Leisure Hour* note, the primary source of "The Madness of King Goll" was Eugene O'Curry's *Lectures on the Manuscript Materials of Ancient Irish History* (1861). Even in old age, Yeats was to recall that O'Curry's "unarranged and uninterpreted history defeated my boyish indolence" (*E&I* 511). The defeats are evident enough in the versions of "The Madness of King Goll" that appeared in 1887 and 1888; but the text of 1889 stands as an even more direct testimony to the accuracy of the older Yeats's backward glance.[2]

As O'Curry had it, "Gall" was the son of the king of Ulster, a "youth of fifteen" who "obtained leave from his father" to go to the aid of Fionn at the

189

battle of Ventry – now Ventry Harbour, near the tip of Dingle Peninsula. Having arrived at the scene of the battle, and "after having performed astounding deeds of valour", his "excitement . . . increased to absolute frenzy" and he "fled in a state of derangement from the scene of slaughter" (O'Curry, p. 316). Thus a sketch of the central figure in both Yeats's lyric and his *Leisure Hour* note. But Gall was neither the powerful ruler that the opening stanza of the 1889 version of the poem describes nor, for that matter, was he even yet a king. What Yeats did in this case was to merge the figure of the third-century stripling from Ulster with a second and more eminent third-century figure from the *Manuscript Materials*: as O'Curry rightly describes him, "Goll Mac Morna, the great chief of the Connacht Fenians" (O'Curry, p. 302).

Renowned as the man who had slain the father of Fionn during the battle of Cnucha – now Castleknock, located at the western end of Phoenix Park – Goll was a figure possessed of strengths that O'Curry's Gall clearly lacked. By 1889, Yeats would have been familiar with many descriptions of Mac Morna, not only O'Curry's but those that appeared in the books from which he had culled the materials for his *Fairy and Folk Tales of the Irish Peasantry* (1888). William Carleton's *Tales and Stories* (1845),[3] for instance, included a note to the effect that "Gaul the son of Morni", though little known in Carleton's time, was once as legendary a figure as Fionn (Carleton , p. 98n); Patrick Kennedy's *Legendary Fictions of the Irish Celts* (1866) was to describe both Gall (Kennedy, p. 213) and Goll (pp. 216–17, 218, 221–2), naming the latter as "the best warrior in Connaught" (p. 216), an "amalgamation of Ajax and Diomed", "more redoubtable in fight than Fion himself" (p. 222). And the second volume of Standish O'Grady's *History of Ireland* (1880) assigned the same kind of pre-eminence to Goll's clan, noting that "the Clanna Morna" was "predominant" in Ireland "in the beginning of the third century", and that "their king always bore the title of Morna with a distinguishing epithet" (O'Grady, p. 168n).

In short, one of the questions that has most insistently confronted readers of "The Madness of King Goll" has to do with why a man of such apparent strength and self-possession is so abruptly transformed into a morbid haunter of forest solitudes; and one part of the complex answer is that the figure is schizophrenic in his literary origins, his poise the poise of the accomplished man and his weaknesses those of a boy. A concomitant, though less troubling, question turns on the extent of the dominion that this composite figure is said to command. In the opening lines of the 1889 text, Goll tells us that

> Mine was a chair of skins and gold,
>   Wolf-breeding mountains, galleried Eman,
> Mine were clan Morna's tribes untold,
>   Many a landsman, many a seaman. (*VP* 81–2)

The news that they were now being ruled by a fifteen-year-old prince from Ulster would have met with no glad welcome from the Connacht Fenians, so little glad that it is hard not to find a wry unintended irony in Yeats's description of the Fenians as "untold". But by 1895, the poet had the mere facts behind his lines more or less back in order. The Goll who appears in *Poems* remains the king that he never was; but the reference to "clan Morna's tribes" has been dropped, and his rule is now rightly confined to the North, "from Ith" in Donegal "to Emen" in Armagh (*VP* 81). Nor was this the only major alteration in the opening stanza. There was something else at work when Yeats was laboriously revising the lyrics that he allowed into the *Poems* of 1895; and in the case of "The Madness of King Goll", the shift once again has to do with the kinds of understanding that the poet brought to bear on his sources.

In the revised version of the poem that appeared in 1895, the final stanza opened thus:

I sang how, when day's toil is done,
    Orchil shakes out her long dark hair
That hides away the dying sun
    And sheds faint odours through the air: (*VP* 85)

In his 1899 note on these lines, the poet wrote that Orchil was "a Fomoroh and a sorceress, if I remember rightly. I forget whatever I may have once known about her" (*VP* 796). This lapse of memory cannot be faulted, since there wasn't a great deal to be known about Orchil in the first place; but what Yeats did know, he knew from his reading of volume two of O'Grady's *History*, wherein Oirchill (O'Grady, p. 150) or Orchil (p. 268) is described as an "earth-goddess" (p. 150) and a "sorceress" who rules "the realms of gloom" below the earth (p. 268). In the *History* she is pictured as summoning her fellow "earth-fiends", the "sisterhood of the deep, a dim consistory" (p. 268), to go out and do battle against Cú Chulainn. Yeats, whose early readings in comparative mythology – in this case, John Rhys's *Celtic Heathendom* (1888) may be the most relevant example –[4] had taught him to think of Cú Chulainn as a solar hero, could only have recalled the encounter between Orchil and the champion of the Red Branch as a mythic redaction of the war between the forces of darkness and light: hence the above-noted imagining in 1895's concluding verse of "how, when day's toil is done, / Orchil shakes out her long dark hair / That hides away the dying sun". What this more enterprising version of the poem is trying to suggest, then, is an image of Goll that lifts him out of Irish legend and into the realm of solar mythology; and it is at this point that the 1895 revision of the final stanza begins to explain the conclusive 1895 revision of the opening of the poem.

The concept of Goll as a dying solar hero had been latent from the first published version of the lyric; from 1887 through 1889, the poem's concluding lines had described an outcast whose final lines were addressed to the sun "in all his evening vapours rolled" (*VP* 86). In like fashion, the first three castings of the poem agreed in their depiction of a king whose rule has brought plenitude to his kingdom; " 'He brings the peaceful age of gold' ", says 1887's opening verse, and the line re-emerges in 1888 and 1889 as " 'This young man brings the age of gold.' " But by 1895, the stress of the line had shifted away from cliché:

> I sat on cushioned otter skin:
>   My word was law from Ith to Emen,
> And shook at Invar Amargin
>   The hearts of the world-troubling seamen,
> And drove tumult and war away
>   From girl and boy and man and beast;
> The fields grew fatter day by day,
>   The wild fowl of the air increased;
> And every ancient Ollave said,
>   While he bent down his fading head,
> 'He drives away the Northern cold.' (*VP* 81–2)

Speaking of the final version of this stanza – a version all but identical with that just cited – David Daiches notes that Goll "had power over men and animals: the fields grew fatter, 'the wild fowl of the air increased'. And the wise men flattered him by telling him that he had dominion even over the weather".[5] The remark is accurate, but falls short of the centre of what the stanza was meant to be driving at. What Yeats was seeking here was an opening image of the solar hero at the height of his power, an image that would ready the way for Goll's defeat by the powers of darkness – dark net cast on a dying sun – in 1895s concluding verse. The final proof of the poet's intent may be found in the final revision to be considered here, a revision that otherwise has no evident motive behind it. In 1888 and 1889, Goll's encounter with the marauders takes place "under the blink o' the morning star"; but by 1895 the reference to morning has vanished, and the battle is set, more simply, "under the blinking of the stars" (*VP* 83). It was Yeats's desire to cast Goll in the role of solar hero that impelled this shift to a night-time setting. Ultimately, Goll will fail both as man of action and as bard; and in the 1895 text, both of the events that are emblematic of the solar king's decline – the moment of vision that drives the warrior Goll from the battle, and his later discovery of the "tympan" that will break and leave him songless – take place at night, a time when his strengths are at full ebb.

There are other sources of "The Madness of King Goll" that might be considered here. Goll's description of "how I hear on hill heads high / A tramping of tremendous feet" (1887, 1888, 1889),[6] for instance, echoes lines from Sir Samuel Ferguson's *Congal* (1872), which depicts Congal and his men, encamped and awaiting battle, as hearing the footsteps of Manannán sounding through the hills around them: "for all the night, around their echoing camp, / Was heard continuous from the hills, a sound as of the tramp / Of giant footsteps".[7] More generally, one wonders if Yeats was familiar with Kuno Meyer's 1885 edition of the *Cath Finntrága*, which provides a detailed description of the bravery of the prince of Ulster during the battle of Ventry.[8] But in the absence of any reference by Yeats to the Meyer volume, the question of whether

Meyer's work should be numbered among the sources of "The Madness of King Goll" must remain an open one; and this essay has confined itself to works that Yeats certainly read and, just as certainly, sometimes misread. The point at which an author's sources begin to take on interest for the reader is the point at which they begin to reveal an author's intention; and on the strength of this count alone, the sources of this early poem are of no small interest. What they leave us with is an insight into the shiftings of what Yeats would later call the "secret working mind" (*VP* 639), and a means of tracing the slow veerings that an elusive poem charted as it worked its way up from confusion – "Goll or Gall"? – and sought out its present complexities.

NOTES

1. The closing lines of the third stanza of the poem were completely recast for 1899s revised edition of the *Poems* of 1895 (*VP* 83–4), but the current version of the text is otherwise much the same as that of 1895.
2. The 1887, 1888, and 1889 drafts of the poem all depict Goll as powerful and a king; but as my text will indicate, the 1889 version compounds the confusion by making him ruler over both Ulster and much of Connacht. There is no evident reason why this later revision of the text should have been more misleading than the earlier versions; but the interpolated 1889 reference to Connacht – "clan Morna's tribes" – might possibly be regarded as part of Yeats's determined attempt to make *The Wanderings of Oisin and Other Poems* as "Irish" in its "personality" as possible (*L* 66).
3. *Tales and Stories of the Irish Peasantry* is the short title of Carleton's *Tales and Sketches, Illustrating the Character, Usages, Traditions, Sports and Pastimes of the Irish Peasantry* (1845). Yeats did not include this work in the lists of Irish folklore "authorities" that he appended to both *Fairy and Folk Tales of the Irish Peasantry* and *Irish Fairy Tales* (1892); but the book nonetheless contains all eight of the excerpts from Carleton that appeared in those anthologies, six in *Fairy and Folk Tales*, two in *Irish Fairy Tales*.
4. The impact of Rhys's book on Yeats's early work has yet to be fully measured, perhaps because the poet sometimes failed to give Rhys's influence its full measure of credit. In discussing his "The Secret Rose" (1896), for instance, Yeats named Standish O'Grady as the likely source of his vision of Cú Chulainn and Fand "walking among flaming dew" (*VP* 169, and see note on 814). The source of the image had in fact been Rhys's *Lectures on the Origin and Growth of Religion as Illustrated by Celtic Heathendom*, which pictured Cú Chulainn as a solar hero and Fand as a demi-goddess of the waters (Rhys, p. 463), and which asserted that "the wooing of Cúchulainn by (Fand) is the sparkling of the pellucid drop in the sun's rays when he has reached the dark places of the earth" (p. 464). The collapsing of this idea into the image of "flaming dew" was a fine stroke; but it was a stroke for which the poet had Rhys, not O'Grady, to thank.
   This is not to say that Yeats swallowed Rhys's theories whole. In the essay titled "Away" (1902), for instance, the poet noted that "a story about Cuchullain in *The Book of the Dun Cow*" had been "interpreted too exclusively as a solar myth by Professor Rhys" (*UP2* 279). But it is also worth noting that the same essay later pays tribute to Rhys in a context that recalls the above discussion of the meeting of Fand and Cú Chulainn. Here Yeats points out that "Professor Rhys has interpreted both the stories of Cuchullain and the story of Pwyll and Arawn as solar myths, and one doubts not that the old priests and poets saw analogies in day and night, in summer and winter"; and immediately thereafter he adds that "it may be that the druids and poets meant more at the beginning than a love story, by such stories as that of Cuchullian and Fand" (*UP2* 282).

5. David Daiches, "The Earlier Poems: Some Themes and Patterns", in *In Excited Reverie: a Centenary Tribute to William Butler Yeats 1865–1939*, eds A. Norman Jeffares and K. G. W. Cross (New York: St. Martin's Press, 1964) p. 52.

6. In 1887, "A tramping" read "The tramping"; in 1887 and 1888, "hill heads" read "hill-heads" (*VP* 85).

7. See *Congal* (Dublin: Edward Ponsonby, 1872), p. 53; and for Yeats's early admiration of this poem of Ferguson's, see the first volume of *Uncollected Prose of W. B. Yeats*, pp. 84–5, 89, 99.

8. See *Cath Finntrága* (London: Oxford University Press, 1885) pp. 24–8.

The Systematic Rose

Donald R. Pearce

"What man is this", wrote Yeats to Olivia Shakespear after reading the proofs for the 1933 edition of his poems, "who . . . says the same thing in so many different ways" (*L* 798). It was a pertinent comment, repetition, transformation, renewal being the single most striking feature of that long poetical career. What the present note seeks to show, with the aid of some unpublished early materials, is that this principle – sameness in difference – can be seen operating in the case of the alchemical rose of the Nineties, which was reborn first as the visionary moon of the middle years, then as the privileged "antithetical" phases of the System, in short, that these seemingly divergent images are actually alternative forms and versions of each other.

In the two volumes in which the rose figures most prominently, *The Countess Kathleen and Various Legends and Lyrics* (1892), later entitled *The Rose*, and *The Wind Among the Reeds* (1899), as well as in stories in *The Secret Rose* (1897), it is pre-eminently the symbolic Western flower of the mystical life, proud, defiant, apocalyptic, violent even, yet at the same time the flower of perfect human discipline and peace. The physical appearance of the expanded Rose, with its overlapping, spiralling rings, layers, circuits of petals, made it an appropriate symbol of multiplicity in unity and of life conceived and lived (as Lionel Johnson had impressed on Yeats) "as ritual". The rose symbolized eloquently a synthesis which seemed at times to herald the arrival of a new life for Yeats himself, for Ireland, perhaps for all mankind:

> . . . I, too, await
> The hour of thy great wind of love and hate.
> When shall the stars be blown about the sky,
> Like the sparks blown out of a smithy, and die?
> Surely thine hour has come, thy great wind blows,
> Far-off, most secret, and inviolate Rose? (*VP* 170)[1]

At the very time during which the rose was at its apogee in Yeats's poetry and fiction, however, he was also "possessed", he tells us, by a notion that was precisely the opposite of everything symbolized by the rose. In a well-known passage on the decade of the Nineties, he remarks:

195

A conviction that the world was but a bundle of fragments possessed me without ceasing . . . I delighted in every age where poet and artist confined themselves gladly to some inherited subject-matter known to the whole people, for I thought that in man and race alike there is something called "Unity of Being" . . . I thought that the enemy of this unity was abstraction, meaning by abstraction not the distinction but the isolation of occupation, or class or faculty (*Au* 189–90).

Antagonism of rose and world received elaborate treatment in some of Yeats's early fiction. In "Out of the Rose" (1896), for instance, a knight of the Order of St. John confides in an uncomprehending country lad how he had

. . . seen a great Rose of Fire, and a Voice out of the Rose had told him how men would turn from the light of their own hearts, and bow down before outer order and outer fixity, and that then the light would cease . . . and none of those who had seen clearly the truth could enter into the Kingdom of God, which is in the Heart of the Rose, if they stayed on willingly in the corrupted world; and so they must prove their anger against the Powers of Corruption by dying in the service of the Rose. (*VSR* 22–3)[2]

It is clear from such passages that the mystic rose of the early poems and stories was Yeats's counter-symbol, in late Pre-Raphaelite manner, to that "bundle of fragments" he felt the modern world to be, or to be becoming; and this also connects it to that longed-for spiritual state or condition which, in *Autobiographies* and *A Vision*, he calls "Unity of Being" and "Unity of Culture." Indeed, in *A Vision* the central "antithetical" phases of the lunar system (12–18) are actually assigned most of the attributes and powers previously assigned to the rose, e.g. "imaginative", "emotional", "aesthetic", "violent", "dreaming", "solitary", "meditative", "aristocratic", "sensuous", "hierarchical", "traditional", "supernatural", "organic".

The affinity between the Rose and the "antithetical" phases of the system was more than one of terminologies, however. There were other, non-verbal, links between them. A comparison of four of Yeats's occult diagrams (reproduced below), two done during the Nineties, two many years later for *A Vision*, reveals the persistence of several important symbolic components, and suggests some of the evolutionary steps by which the earlier turned into, or, rather, begot the later. One of the pages in a notebook[3] kept by Yeats in the late 1890s contains a drawing of a 22-petalled cabalistic Rose, each petal inscribed with a letter of the Hebrew alphabet. At the centre, where the stamens would be, is a Rosicross. Next to this drawing Yeats has done a geometrical version, with wedge- or lozenge-shaped segments in place of petals, on which have been substituted Tarot card symbols for the Hebrew letters appearing on the other Rose. Following this is a table of occult equivalencies in which the meaning of each Tarot card is correlated with Greek and Roman deities, Celtic divinities and heroes, forms of evocation, magical rites, character traits, philosophical and religious notations concerning fate, death, birth, rebirth, occult colour symbolism, and other esoteric correspondencies, e.g.:

	Hebrew	Zodiacal	
Justice:	ך	⌒	: Eternal justice. Balance. Force arrested as in act of judging. Vulcan. Cap with serpent.
Hanged Man:	׆	△	: Enforced sacrifice. Punishment; fated not voluntary suffering.
Death:	⅂	∿→	: Involuntary change; sometimes death and destruction, but rarely. Mars. Wolf.
Devil:	ע	♑	: Materialist's temptation (material). Sometimes obsession (especially if with lover). Vesta. Lamp.

In compiling his Table of correspondencies, Yeats was probably drawing on one used by MacGregor Mathers in his Golden Dawn lectures on the Tarot and other occult themes. Thus, Mathers' explanations of the above four cards are as follows (R = reversed card):

8. *Themis, or Justice.* Equilibrium, Balance, Justice; R. Bigotry, Want of balance, Abuse of Justice, Over-severity.
12. *The Hanged Man.* Self-sacrifice, Sacrifice, Devotion, Bound; R. Selfishness, Unbound, Partial sacrifice.
13. *Death.* Death, Change, Transformation, Alteration for the worse; R. Death just escaped, Partial change, Alteration for the better.
15. *The Devil.* Fatality for Good; R. Fatality for Evil.[4]

Similarly, Yeats's matching of Hebrew letters and astrological signs, as well as of classical divinities and zodiacal symbols seems also to owe something to Mathers' lectures; in the section entitled "The Twenty-Two Atus of Thoth" (twenty-two trumps of the Tarot) Mathers lists, among others, the following equivalents:

	Hebrew Letter	Attribution	
11. *Justice* (Strength at one time)	ל	⌒	
12. *The Hanged Man*	מ	▽	
13. *Death*	נ	♏	
15. *The Devil*	ע	♑	[5]

He also lists several classical and zodiacal correspondencies (compare Yeats) including

⌒	*Vulcan*	The Cap with Serpent
♏	*Mars*	The Wolf
♑	*Vesta*	The Lamp [6]

This complex, symbolic rose was, of course, of central importance in Golden
Dawn rites and ceremonies, especially those of Stella Matutina, the G.D. order
into which Yeats was initiated in June, 1893. Indeed, on the ceiling of the
(reconstructed) burial vault of Christian Rosenkreuz, dramatically revealed to
the candidate for the grade "Adeptus Minor" at the climax of the ceremony, was
an elaborate twenty-two petalled rose, signifying (as Ellic Howe and others have
pointed out)[7] the twenty-two paths of the Cabalistic Tree of Life and the
twenty-two trumps of the Tarot. It seems apparent that the Rose diagram in
Yeats's 1893 notebook is, in fact, a copy of a Golden Dawn Rose, drawn no doubt
as part of his advanced studies in Golden Dawn and Rosicrucian symbology.

The significance of the rose, however, does not by any means stop here. There
are striking similarities not only between the two early Rose diagrams (Figs 2a
& b), but between them and two others appearing years later in *A Vision*:

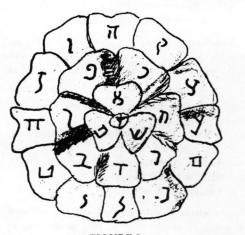

FIGURE 2a

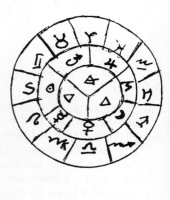

FIGURE 2b

The Great Wheel

FIGURE 2c

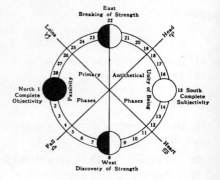

FIGURE 2d

So juxtaposed, the four drawings strongly suggest four successive steps in an evolving philosophic process, or series. It begins with the rather literally-executed cabalistic Rose, A, develops easily into the adjacent, geometricized (alchemical) version, B, with its table of occult values, mutates suddenly into the (pseudo-) medieval astrological moon-chart, or "Great Wheel", C, lunar phases replacing alchemical petals, to culminate in the much more stark mathematical diagram, D, of the finished System. What has been added at stages C and D are the all-important notions of "antinomy" and, via the lunar wheel, cyclic movement, by which the static early diagrams acquire interior tension and motion. Otherwise, the evolving series confirms visually the conclusion already suggested in our discussion of the early poetry and fiction, i.e. that in the symbolic Rose of the Nineties one undoubtedly finds the embryo of *A Vision*.

But the sources of *A Vision* may have been even earlier. How deeply the Rose was rooted in Yeats's poetic consciousness, particularly as regards the whole theme of magical vision, can be seen in the following two extracts from some of his earliest, unpublished work. In a notebook dating (according to Mrs Yeats)[8] probably from 1882, when the poet would have been turning seventeen, there is a little poem in which the speaker is imagined sitting on a gnarled root among pine trees talking to birds of their happy life. He is suddenly confronted by a spirit who rises "out of the soul of a wild rose" and with his golden lyre sings to him "of primal things". The vision fades. The speaker wonders whether a spirit really did appear and sing to him or only seem to have done so, and concludes:

Mayhap 'twas nothing at all
Only the clarion call
Of a far off water fall.

In a second poem, a visionary bard tells the young woodland poet of a high-born maiden who has wound a tress of her blazing hair about every man's heart. As in the case of the other poem, the vision fades, and the singer disappears. This time, however, the speaker is left with some tantalizing evidence: waking, he finds himself holding in his hand "a crumpled rose". The poem ends, questioningly:

What was he called?
Was he the mind of the rose?
——————— Who knows.
I heard the caw of a distant rook
And the gurgle of a far off brook.

Forty-five years later, when writing the Introduction for the 1928 edition of *A Vision*, Yeats asked himself the almost identical question – of literal belief in "the actual existence of my circuits" of sun and moon. The answer he gave, often considered hedging, seems in fact to recall, almost as if it were a kind of formula or ritual for dealing with that sort of question, the dilemma of those early poems:

. . . if sometimes, overwhelmed by miracle as all men must be when in the midst of it, I have taken such periods literally, my reason has soon recovered . . . I regard them as stylistic arrangements of experience . . . [which] have helped me to hold in a single thought reality and justice. (*AV[B]* 25)

Though Yeats is referring here to the symbolic machinery of the System, his words might equally well apply, as it has been the purpose of this note to show, to the visionary Rose of the early poems and stories.

NOTES

1. In Irish, Rus (Rose) signifies also "Tree", "Knowledge", "Science", "Magic", "Power".
2. That the "magical life" was a defeated thought is one of the themes of Yeats's novel *The Speckled Bird* (1896–1902). "The Rose of Battle" (*VP* 113) gives poetical expression to this thought.
3. A small white MS notebook, unpublished, formally identified as MBY 548, containing among other things occult, magical and celtic researches; begun "29 August 1893". Permission to quote from Yeats's notebooks and to reproduce tracings of diagrams for this article has been granted by A. P. Watt Ltd, Literary Agents. I mentioned, but did not reproduce, these drawings in "Philosophy and Phantasy" (*University of Kansas City Review*, Spring 1952, 177).
4. *The Sorcerer and His Apprentice, Unknown Hermetic Writings of S. L. MacGregor Mathers and J. W. Brodie-Innes*, ed. by R. A. Gilbert (Wellingborough: The Aquarium Press, 1983) pp. 61–2.
5. Ibid., p. 81.
6. Ibid., p. 82.
7. Ellic Howe, *The Magicians of the Golden Dawn* (London, 1972) p. 84; Israel Regardie, *The Golden Dawn; an Account of the Teachings, Rites and Ceremonies of the Order of the Golden Dawn*, 3rd edn rev. and enl., 4 vols (River Falls, Wis., 1970) vol. III, pp. 46–61.
8. So dated by Mrs Yeats in conversation, 1950.

Yeats and Heffernan the Blind

Nancy Rutkowski Nash

In the Special Collections of Emory's Woodruff Library is a presentation copy of *Poems* (1899) inscribed "To Lady Gregory/ May 10, 1899/ W. B. Yeats". On the preliminary leaves of this copy are two holograph poems, including an initialled quatrain, "The Song of Heffernan the Blind: a translation":

> I often am in Shrone hill, in Conroy is my bed
> I grind an old quern, I grind it for my bread,
> And Teig and Nora with me, no other souls than these;
> I grind an old quern & them I do not please.[1]

Though we know from Yeats's letters that his interest in Heffernan began as early as 1888, we have very little information concerning this poem. We also know from letters that Yeats adapted the poem from a translation by Douglas Hyde. The roughly ten-year interval between Yeats's first expressed interest in Heffernan and his gift to Lady Gregory suggests, at least, a recurrent attraction to a relatively obscure and minor Gaelic poet.[2] Such an attraction might well be accounted for by Yeats's developing interest in a half-anonymous yet wholly personal voice in his own poetry.

On 15 December 1888, Yeats wrote to Hyde, requesting information on "a gaelic speaking poet of the last century called William Heffernan or more usually William Dall or Blind William" (*Collected Letters*, vol. I, ed. Kelly & Domville, in press). Newly settled at Bedford Park in March of that year, Yeats "was greatly troubled", because he "was making no money" (*Mem* 31). The meagre compensation he received for compiling an anthology of Irish fairy stories and editing *Stories from Carleton* left little on which to live. His queries concerning Heffernan were prompted by the prospect of a job with the *Dictionary of National Biography*. William Henley, Yeats's new friend and "chief employer", had recently recommended Yeats to the editors of the *DNB*. Yeats advised Hyde not to trouble himself with his queries until he confirmed the commission, but the *DNB* never published Heffernan's biography, nor is such a biographical manuscript known to exist.[3]

201

Six days after the letter to Hyde, Yeats wrote to Katharine Tynan on the same subject:

> I am writing an article on an old blind Gaelic poet of the last century called Hefernan for the *Dictionary of National Biography*. He wrote the original of Mangan's "Kathleen Ny Houlahan." If this article does, I shall most likely do other Irish writers for them. (*L* 96)

That Yeats had to explain to Tynan who Heffernan was attests to his relative obscurity. In his letter to Hyde, Yeats acknowledges his own ignorance. He asks Hyde not only for any information he might personally have, but for any other possible sources and authorities for Heffernan's dates and for his current popularity with the people of Ireland, especially in Tipperary. Our best source of biographical information on Heffernan appears in two works mentioned by Yeats in his letter to Hyde: *Irish Popular Songs* (1847) and *Reliques of Irish Jacobite Poetry* (1844), both by Edward O. Walsh.

Walsh's account in *Irish Popular Songs* provides a sketchy biography of Heffernan. It identifies him as William Dall, or Blind William, the titles Yeats uses in his letter to Hyde. It gives his birthplace as Shronehill, in the county Tipperary. It indirectly suggests his dates by identifying his contemporaries, MacDonnell and Toomy (John MacDonnell "Clarach" 1691–1754 and John O'Tuomy 1706–75). Finally, it notes his life of poverty: "He was born blind, and spent the greater part of his life, a poor houseless wanderer, subsisting upon the bounty of others" (26). Throughout the remainder of the sketch, Walsh pays tribute to Heffernan's poetic powers without contributing anything further to our knowledge of the poet's life or Yeats's interest in him.

The biographical sketch in *Irish Popular Songs* appears to be an abbreviated version of an earlier account in *Reliques of Irish Jacobite Poetry*. This latter work by Walsh not only provides the source for Yeats's adaptation, but also gives information about the poet and his work. Heffernan combined the roles of the anonymous patriotic poet whose voice was the voice of his culture and the poet whose idiosyncratic voice revealed personal experience.

In his letter to Hyde, Yeats asks for translations of "some pieces of untranslated Irish of two and four lines each", referring Hyde to pages 15 and 16 of Walsh's text. The poem on which Yeats bases his adaptation, however, appears on page 17:

> Seal a Laition dam, aguṛ ṛeal a Spónaill,
> 'S ṛeal a meilt bṛóna a m-baile Loṅnaoi ;
> Ȝan do muintiṛ agam adt Caóȝ 'ṛ Nóṛa,
> 'S ní taitnigean leó maṛ do meilim í.

Therefore, Hyde probably translated more than Yeats had asked for. Yeats included in his version a recurrent line from the quatrain on page 16. In that poem a variation of the line "I often am in Shronehill" appears three times as the poet informs us that he often is in Cullen and Latten as well as Shronehill:

> 'S mịnịc me a ʒ-Cuịllịῄ 'ŗ m'uịllịῄ ŗŋe'm ċóca !
> 'S mịnịc me a Łaịcịon aịŗ uịŋeaŗba bŗóʒa !
> 'S mịnịc me a Sŋónaịll ʒo óúbaċ, 'ŗ ʒo bŗónaċ !
> 'S ŋaċaó aịŗ buịle maŋ a ʒ-cloịŗŗe mē cómŋaʒ ?

The "Song of Heffernan" thus appears to be a rather loose adaptation of one quatrain and a borrowing from another, all of which was originally translated by Hyde.

Less than a year after the letters to Hyde and Tynan, Yeats published "Popular Ballad Poetry of Ireland" in *The Leisure Hour*, where he again refers to the "old blind Gaelic poet". In this article, Yeats attempts to show that "behind Ireland fierce and militant, is Ireland poetic, passionate, remembering, idyllic, fanciful, and always patriotic". The Gaelic poets of the eighteenth century, including Heffernan, particularly suited his nationalistic stance:

> The poets of those days would make a long list – Andrew Macgrath, surnamed "The Merry Pedlar;" O'Sullivan the Red, pious and profligate; John MacConnell, of vision-seeing memory; John O'Cullen, who lamented in such famous words over the Abbey of Timoleaque; and Hefferman [sic], the blind, who in his old age loved to stand listening while the plough-boys in the hedge school droned out some Greek poet . . . (*UP1* 149).[4]

In his biographical account, Walsh says that Heffernan was distinguished by "unmitigated hostility to Damer, the celebrated usurer" who brought over with him to Ireland a colony from Scotland, usurped the land, and displaced the original inhabitants. Walsh recalls the elaborate court of "sculptured capitals and marble columns" built at Shronehill by Damer in the early eighteenth century and since "demolished to the ground" with no trace of the court's splendour or its people other than an unmarked grave. Heffernan was indeed a poet "fierce and militant . . . passionate, remembering . . . and always patriotic".

"For a popular ballad literature to arise", Yeats tells us, "firstly are needful national traditions not hidden in libraries, but living in the minds of the populace. . . . Secondly, it is needful that the populace and poets shall have one heart – that here shall be no literary class with its own way of seeing things and its own conventions" (*UP1* 147). Yeats's interest in a poetry of the people is a familiar one. He calls for a poetry in which the poet's voice merges with that of the populace. At the outset of his essay, he describes "a row of little blue-paper-poem books" calling attention to the obscurity of both the poets and their poetry:

> Every now and then the world may read in the accredited organs of enlightenment that the ballad or dramatic poem, or something else, is

obsolete. The writers of these little blue books wrote on regardless; but then, perhaps, the accredited organs of enlightenment never reached them or their barbarous mountains, or their readers, who read and sang, and delighted in what they wrote, as men delighted in poetry of old before organs of enlightenment were even heard of. (*UP1* 147)

To Yeats, the books present a poetry in which there is "no literary class with its own way of seeing things and its own conventions". While he emphasizes the anonymity of these ballad writers, he not only chooses to adapt a poem which calls attention to the poet's identity, he also underscores that identity by entitling his adaptation, "The Song of Heffernan the Blind." In *Autobiographies*, Yeats reconciles this apparent contradiction:

> I wanted to create once more an art where the artist's handiwork would hide as under those *half-anonymous* chisels, or as we find it in some old Scots ballads, or in some twelfth- or thirteenth-century Arthurian Romance. That handiwork assured, I had martyred no man for modelling his own image upon Pallas Athene's buckler; for I took great pleasure in *certain allusions to the singer's life* one finds in old romances and ballads, and thought his presence there all the more poignant because we discover it half lost, like portly Chaucer, behind his own maunciple and pardoner upon the Canterbury roads. (*Au* 150–1; my ital)

Heffernan's poetry not only preserved the history of Damer long after his "court" at Shronehill disappeared, it also immortalized the life of the poet who sang that history on behalf of his nation. As Yeats read in Walsh's *Reliques*:

> Every thing that fired the poet's fancy, or roused his passions, or filled his heart with indignant scorn of the miser and his *alien* horde, has disappeared; but the peasant's fame, the smallest traits of his character, the most trivial incidents of his life, and those rich and exuberant strains of Celtic eloquence, which came with the force and copiousness of a torrent upon his enemies, are remembered and recited by the people as if they were the productions of yesterday. (14)

Heffernan's poetry remains vital because of its successful blending of patriotic attacks on "the *alien* horde" with "the most trivial incidents of his life" and frequent self-references which he makes in his poetry ("I'm Heffernan of Shronehill", "I often am in ———").

> So masterful indeed was that instinct that when the minstrel knew not who his poet was, he must needs make up a man: "When any stranger asks who is the sweetest of singers, answer with one voice: 'A blind man; he dwells upon rocky Chios; his songs shall be the most beautiful for ever'." Elaborate modern psychology sounds egotistical, I thought, when it speaks in the first person, but not those simple emotions which resemble the more, the more powerful they are, everybody's emotion, and I was soon to write many poems where an

always personal emotion was woven into a general pattern of myth and symbol (*Au* 151).

Like the poets of the little blue books, Heffernan "had not the aid of early culture" nor was his mind "improved by education". While Walsh laments this fact, he also notes that "his compositions abound with so many elegant sentiments and frequent allusions to pagan mythology".

Although Yeats certainly adapted "The Song of Heffernan" while he was collecting information for the poet's biography in 1888, his inclusion of it in the copy of *Poems* presented to Lady Gregory in May 1899 is in all likelihood connected to the two recent summers he spent at Coole Park.[5] In 1897 Lady Gregory renewed her study of Gaelic first begun in 1880 (*Gregory* 318). Yeats was likely to have acquainted her with Heffernan. In the 1903 edition of *Poets and Dreamers*, she includes an essay on the Jacobite poets in which she not only mentions Heffernan by name, but translates lines from two of Heffernan's poems: these are clearly from "A Lament for the Gael" and "A Voice of Joy", *Poets and Dreamers*, pp. 70–1. As both of these poems are included in *Reliques of Irish Jacobite Poetry*, this work was clearly her source. Lady Gregory would have been interested in such a collection as early as 1897, when she renewed her study of Gaelic and it was the source of Yeats's adaptation. Whatever prompted Yeats to inscribe the quatrain in Lady Gregory's copy, it is clear that Heffernan's particular strain of ballad poetry informs his aims as a poet from 1888 to 1899.

NOTES

1. Ronald Schuchard discusses the other holograph, a sixteen line poem, "On a Child's Death", initialled and dated 5 September 1893, in "The Lady Gregory–Yeats Collection at Emory University", *Yeats Annual*, vol. III, 1985, where he also provides a transcript of the quatrain. Other works cited in this article are: Lady Augusta Gregory, *Poets and Dreamers* (Dublin, 1903), and *Seventy Years: Being the Autobiography of Lady Gregory*, ed. Colin Smith (Gerards Cross: Colin Smith, 1974); *Collected Letters of W. B. Yeats*, ed. John S. Kelly and Eric Domville (Oxford University Press, in press); *The Letters of W. B. Yeats*, ed. Allan Wade (New York: Macmillan, 1955); Edward Walsh, *Irish Popular Songs* (Dublin: Peter Roe, 1883), and *Reliques of Irish Jacobite Poetry* (Dublin: John O'Daly, 1866); W. B. Yeats, *Autobiographies* (London: Macmillan 1955), *Memoirs* (New York: Macmillan, 1973), and "Popular Ballad Poetry of Ireland", *Uncollected Prose of W. B. Yeats*, ed. John P. Frayne (New York: Columbia University Press, 1970).

2. Few translations of Heffernan's poetry exist, all published well after his death in 1803. The *Bibliography of Irish Philology and of Printed Irish Literature* lists five volumes which contain a total of nine translations by "O Hiffernain (Uilliam Dall)": James Hardiman's *Irish Minstrelsy*, vol. II (1831); John O'Daly and Edward Walsh's *Reliques of Irish Jacobite Poetry* (1844); Edward Walsh's *Irish Popular Songs* (1847); and John O'Daly's *The Poets and Poetry of Munster* (1850), as well as the second series of the same volume published in 1860. There are also four poems translated from Heffernan by James Clarence Mangan which first appeared in the *Dublin University Magazine* and the *Irish Penny Journal*. In a note to "Kathleen Ny-Houlahan", in the 1903 edition of Mangan's *Poems*, D. J. O'Donoghue writes, "The poems of Heffernan, one of the Munster poets, have never been collected or published" (325).

In fact the earliest appearance of a collection of Heffernan's original poetry is a 1939 edition of a volume of poems in Gaelic. The *National Union Catalogue* describes this work as "Poems, most of which are attributed to William Heffernan", and under the label "Contents", adds "Welcome to the Prince of Ossory from the Irish of William Heffernan the blind", by J. C. Mangan." While Mangan translated a single poem, the remainder of the volume contains Heffernan's original Gaelic. The editor, Richard Foley, supplies Heffernan's dates, circa 1720–1803. In a letter of 7 September 1902, Yeats tells Frank Fay that "Your brother must get some common air for 'The spouse of Naoise,' and sing it as much as possible as traditional singing. I adapted the words from 'Ben-Eirinn i' in Walsh's *Popular Songs*" (*Wade* 378).

3. Douglas Hyde refers to Heffernan in *A Literary History of Ireland* (1899) p. 604. Although Henley had brought Yeats's name to the attention of the editors of the *DNB*, Leslie Stephen and Sidney Lee, others associated with the project included Ernest Radford and A. H. Bullen, who became associates of Yeats in other contexts. By 1888, the *DNB*, started in 1882, had reached the stage where volumes covering the letter H (II & III) were being drafted (*Athenæum*, 20 October 1888). Although such Irish poets as Thomas Davis and Samuel Ferguson had been included in volumes already published, Carolan had not. The Welsh mediæval poet David ap Gwilym had however been included. Blind Raftery was later not included. Yeats's exclusion from the project may be connected with the fact that Dr Norman Moore, a Gaelic scholar, was already working for the *DNB* and had written the account of Ferguson. Stephen seems to have employed his authors upon the principle that "like wrote upon like": Catholic upon Catholic, Quaker upon Quaker and so on.

4. Yeats's source is again Walsh's *Irish Jacobite Poetry*:

> . . . there was a classical school conducted by a Valentine Roche, whither the blind wanderer [Heffernan] often found his way to listen with enraptured attention to those sublime lessons of poetry and eloquence bequeathed to us by the sages of Greece and Rome. (15)

"Ireland poetic, passionate, remembering" seems to have remained a touchstone for Yeats in matters of style. "I sometimes compare myself with the mad old slum women I hear denouncing and remembering; 'How dare you,' I heard one say of some imaginary suitor, 'and you without health and a home!' " (*E&I* 521). The blind man, of course, became for him a type of the poet. See "Why the blind man in ancient times was made a poet" (*E&I* 277–81), and *VP* 411, where Homer "that was a blind man", is recalled in "The Tower".

5. In the 1898 volume of the *Edinburgh Review*, a reference to a "rhythmical quern-chant" appears in a review of a book published in 1893 by folklorist Sidney Oldall Addy:

> Mr. Vigfusson added a reminiscence from his old home in the North, where he often heard the rhythmical quern-chant. Among the old Norsemen, he says, the bondwomen were employed at the mill, and the turning of the quern was then, as it still is in Iceland, "accompanied by singing a song". (440)

Yeats uses the word quern in two other works: "Fergus and the Druid" (1892) and *Where there is Nothing, there is God* (1896). The latter work suggests an acquaintance with quern chanting:

> The cold passed away, and the spring grew to summer, and the quern was never idle, nor was it turned with grudging labour, for when any passed the beggar was heard singing as he drove the handle round. (*VSR* 51)

Yeats, Clodd, *Scatalogic Rites* and the Clonmel Witch Burning

Genevieve Brennan

To Queen Anne's Mansions to dine with Lady Gregory, Mr. & Mrs. Fred. Harrison & Mr. W. B. Yeats there. Long talk with Yeats about Irish folk-lore & how rampant (when you can get it to confess itself) is the belief in fairies & witch-doctors. Yeats read to us some extracts from M.S. of examples of this.   [25 November 1897]

. . . then to Shorter's: Miss [Yeats] and W. B. Yeats there, talk re Folk lore and the Irish memorial of '98. Yeats spoke of P. Verlaine as looking like a Socrates who had been on the booze through the Christian Era.   [30 January 1898]

. . . after supper went to W. B. Yeats' diggings: good talk on Folk lore with him: he showed me his notes on the Black Pig & we discussed many things, chiefly the equation of the fairies with the dead: Irish belief in the body & soul as immortal . . .   [4 April 1898]

These extracts from Edward Clodd's pocket diary cover his early contacts with Yeats.[1] Yeats had encountered Clodd's scientific writings in his "materialistic" schooldays: Charles Johnston[2] recalls "Yeats, when he should have been studying the Olynthiacs pored instead over Grant Allen and Edward Clodd". The work which Yeats read as an adolescent was presumably *The Childhood of the World* (1873 and frequently reprinted). At the time of their first meeting Clodd had completed the manuscript of *Tom Tit Tot / An Essay on Savage Philosophy in Folk-Tale*, to be published by Duckworth in October 1898. This was a study of the Rumpelstiltskin tale; the study involved a tabulation of variants of the tale and a consideration of iron as a safeguard against the power of the fairies, but centred upon the "magic of names". One might have expected that this folk-motif was the matter of common interest between Yeats and Clodd, as Yeats had anthologised a curious version of the story, "The Rival Kempers", in *Irish Fairy Tales* (1892). But as Clodd does not include this version in his tabulation, one can only presume that Yeats had forgotten its motif. Yeats does however, appear in *Tom Tit Tot*:

207

> While these sheets are passing through the press, my friend Mr. W. B. Yeats
> hands me a letter from an Irish correspondent, who tells of a fairy-haunted old
> woman living in King's County. Her tormentors, whom she calls the "Fairy
> Band of Shinron," come from Tipperary. They pelt her with invisible
> missiles, hurl abuse at her, and rail against her family, both the dead and the
> living, until she is driven well-nigh mad. And all this spite is manifested
> because they cannot find out her name, for if they could learn that, she would
> be in their power . . . But the fairies trouble her most at night, coming in
> through the wall over her bed-head, which is no laughing matter; and then,
> being a good Protestant, she recites chapter and verses from the Bible to chase
> them away . . . (*Tom Tit Tot*, pp. 83–4)

Clodd's interest in this material is the power of the personal name; Yeats's, the
contact between the world of the living and that of the fairies and the dead. The
correspondent is presumably Lady Gregory, who had returned to Coole on 9
April 1898: Yeats must have handed this material to Clodd some time between
this date and 20 May, when Clodd completed the index to the book. Yeats later
refers to the haunted woman in "Ireland Bewitched" (*UP2* 175).

The next documented contact between Yeats and Clodd is in Autumn 1898. In
a letter of 10 October 1898, Andrew Lang gave Yeats a budget of folk lore, and
the letter was forwarded via Clodd (*LTWBY* 66, misdated 1899). In November,
Yeats wrote Clodd a series of letters dealing with some books which Clodd had
lent him. In the first he refers to Lang's letter, and also to a bundle of books which
Mrs Old, his housekeeper, had apparently returned to Clodd some months
before. It soon emerged that Mrs Old or her daughter had sent Clodd's books to
Dr Mark Ryan's surgery in Gower Street, from whence they were eventually
recovered. Clodd had received in their stead a medical book belonging to Dr
MacBride. The letters of 6 and 22 November 1898 give us some idea of the loan.
In the first, Yeats refers to a work "about excrement in folklore" and then later
identifies this as *Scatalogic Rites*, also mentioning some volumes of the *Archæological Review*. He also refers to other unidentified books which, in a letter of 27 July
1899, he indicates that he still retains.[3]

If Clodd was hoping to draw Yeats into the main stream of British Folk Lore,[4]
what kind of book was he lending to Yeats? The *Archæological Review* ran from
1888 to 1890, in four volumes, then merged with *Folk-Lore*. The Irish materials in
these volumes might not seem strong enough to justify a loan,[5] so perhaps it is
rather W. F. Kirby's article on the *Kalevala* (vol. I, pp. 376–84), which gives a
resumé of the poem and a critical commentary, which is the area of concern.
Clodd himself had written on the *Kalevala* and had intended at one time to
translate the work with Kirby.[6]

Given the nature of their reported discussions and the content of the first folk
lore articles, it seems likely that Clodd would have pressed upon Yeats E. S.
Hartland's *The Science of Fairy Tales*,[7] which includes forty-two pages on the
Changeling. Hartland discusses infant changelings and modes of ridding oneself
of them. Firstly, the device of making the changeling laugh.[8] Secondly, the more

sinister practices involving fire, dung and iron and the forcing, by actual or threatened torture, of the necessary exchange. He gives some Irish examples:

> It seems to consist in taking a clean shovel and seating the changeling on its broad iron blade, and thus conveying the creature to the manure heap. (*SFT* 118)

> Sometimes we are told of a shovel being made red-hot and held before the child's face: sometimes he is seated on it and flung out into the dung pit . . . (*SFT* 120).

Hartland, commenting on the horrible cruelty of these practices, reminds his readers that in 1884 two women had actually burnt a neighbour's child, by placing it naked upon a hot shovel, on the assumption that it was a changeling.[9] He refers to the hostile response of the Irish peasantry on this occasion:

> But we must regard it rather as a protest against the prisoners' inhumanity than against their superstition. . . . For if we may trust the witness of other sagas we find the trial by fire commuted to a symbolic act, as though men had begun to be revolted by the cruelty, even when committed only on a fairy who had been found out . . . (*SFT* 122).

Hartland also discusses adult changelings and it is here that we encounter solid evidence that Yeats had read this chapter before his 1901 revision of *The Land of Heart's Desire.* Hartland gives accounts of the wooden substitute which is left for the stolen person, "the image" is what he twice terms it: he further relates a "ghastly" tale of a coffin opened and a wooden figure found inside, another of "a withered leaf" found inside. In the revised *The Land of Heart's Desire,* Bridget says:

> Come from that image there: she is far away
> [Come from that image: body and soul are gone (errata)]
> You have thrown your arms around a drift of leaves
> Or bole of ash tree changed into her image. (*VPl* 209–10)

The repeated use of "image" as well as the motif of a substitution of leaves and wood brings us, I think closer to Hartland, than to Yeats's oral sources for such phenomena, such as

> The Irish country people always insist that something, a heap of shavings or a broomstick or a wooden image . . . is put in your place. (*UP2* 275)

Of course, Hartland's work may be behind both the revised play and "Away", the essay quoted here.

The book to which Yeats refers several times in the letters to Clodd and the loss of which clearly embarrasses him, is *Scatalogic Rites . . . A Dissertation upon the*

Employment of Excrementitious Remedial Agents in Religion, Therapeutics, Divination, Witchcraft, Love-Philters, etc., in all Parts of the Globe, by Captain John Bourke (Washington: Lowdermilk, 1891). In the 496 pages of this work, Captain Bourke, an enthusiast for his subject, documents the use of excrement in religion, sorcery folk custom and medicine. It is not a book which could be casually borrowed.

Turning aside from the broad sweep of Bourke's narrative and concentrating upon the Irish material[10] we find, on page 403, an account of the protective use of excrement by Irish peasants:

> Mooney relates an instance of the abduction of an Irishwoman by fairies. She managed to impart to her husband the knowledge of the means by which her rescue could be accomplished. "He must be ready with some urine and some chicken-dung, which he must throw upon her, and then seize her. . . . Soon he heard the fairies approaching and when the noise came in front of him he threw the dung and urine in the direction of the sound, and saw his wife fall from her horse" . . . The Irish peasantry firmly believe in the power of fairies to carry off their children; to effect a restoration, a "wise woman" is summoned, whose method is to "heat the shovel in the fireplace, place the changeling upon it, and put it out on the dunghill" . . . "Fire, iron and dung, the three great safeguards against the influence of fairies and the infernal spirits." (*Scatalogic Rites* 403)

Despite Clodd's interest in the protective power of Iron, one reason for directing Yeats to such a passage must have been the extreme similarity between the episode of the rescued wife detailed above, and a story used in "The Broken Gates of Death"[11] in which a man redeems his stolen wife by throwing "fowl droppings and urine" at her when she rides by: the story concludes "however it's well known that they will have nothing to do with iron" (*UP2* 99). The peculiar dependence of Irish peasants upon excrement as a magical safeguard is emphasised by Bourke, who refers to the use of excrement in "medicine bags" and amulets and to the sewing of dung into the garments of a bride – to protect her at this most vulnerable time. It is also possible that Clodd had reminded Yeats of a recent case, the "Witch Burning" near Clonmel. In December 1895, *Folk Lore* had published a long account of this case, drawn from Irish newspapers.[12] Briefly, in March 1895, in Ballyvadlea, a small village in Tipperary, a young married woman, Bridget Cleary had been tortured and burnt by her husband and others on the assumption that she was a changeling and that the "real" Bridget Cleary had been taken by the fairies. She died and her husband, father and several others were tried in July 1895 and were found guilty of manslaughter. Cleary received a sentence of twenty years imprisonment.

Cleary had become convinced that his wife had been stolen and that it was " 'with an old witch I am sleeping' " – ("to lie/ With a foul witch") – he succeeded in transferring his psychosis to a large group of friends and relations.

Cleary held "a lighting stick" near her mouth, threw lamp oil at her, " 'Then he caught her and laid her on the fire. Then she took fire . . . she blazed up' ". Cleary told her to "go up the chimney!". A sinister figure in the story is Denis Ganey, the "herb doctor" or "fairy doctor": he gave advice to Cleary and prepared various concoctions which the dying woman was forced to drink. Various witnesses testified to the fact that some fluid was thrown over her. *Folk Lore* footnotes this with a comment by Leland Duncan, the Irish folklorist: "I specially noted the phrase for enquiry this summer. I found the good folk of Leitrim full of the case . . . the great charm for getting people back from 'the good people' is to throw over them a concoction of strong urine and hen's excrement". Cleary believed that his wife was at a fairy fort and that, when the changeling was killed, he would meet her there, riding a grey horse: even after the murder he insisted that "She was not my wife. She was too fine to be my wife. She was two inches taller than my wife." This statement and some other aspects of the case, the young wife abducted, the fairy fort, the fairy doctor, bear an uneasy resemblance to materials and motifs used by Yeats in the six folk lore articles. His name was in fact brought into the *Cork Examiner*'s account of the "Tipperary Horror". The paper ran a short piece on Ganey, the Fairy Doctor (29 March 1895), describing his descent from a long line of Fairy Doctors, his use of a "bottle" which contained magical herbs, material of the sort that Yeats was to use in "Ireland Bewitched" and "Irish Witch Doctors". But on the previous day, the paper had carried a more theoretical discussion of the case: after a resumé of peasant beliefs, the writer refers to a story by Nora Hopper, a tale "founded on superstition, and told in a style which for lack of a better phrase, may be described as something like pagan appreciation of our folklore." The writer then continues

Now, the subject under discussion has very little relation with this story. Still it suggests it. This appalling episode proves that fairies are not everywhere discredited, that here and there in this storied island, with its large mass of heathen lore, a few people settled in some remote, wild region . . . whose image is that of the haunted past, blindly cling to old traditions, that old traditions die very hard indeed. To such few the good and the bad people hold the power we see [exemplified] in the legends which Crofton Croker and William Carleton have presented to a public which can enjoy the Celtic imaginativeness, seeing no harm in the elusive *leprechaun*, in the gambols on the forts (the fairy forts) by moonlight, even in the wicked fairy who bewitches the cow and stops the supply of milk. But when the interest passes from the literary or academic domain and becomes more real and active the aspect of the question changes, and changes so seriously that not even the most ardent folklorist amongst us – Dr. Hyde, Nora Hopper or Mr. Yeats, for example – could defend it, strong as is their attachment to the fascinating fairyland of our country. It is one thing to write fairy tales, telling us how "once upon a time" men and women, horses and cows were bewitched by the inhabitants of the Land of Shee; and it is patriotic to stimulate interest in our beautiful folk lore.

But when the fairies actually play pranks with people . . . when all the creatures of the imagination become practical agents of daily life, it is time to pause. Out of such a diseased spirit grew the tragedy of which Bridget Cleary was the victim. (*Cork Examiner*, 28 March 1895)

Then, with a brief sneer at *The Yellow Book* and the "Advanced Woman", the writer proceeds to the scene of the crime.

Yeats could hardly have avoided this case; he was staying at Thornhill at the time and in fact discussed the matter seriously with Mary Battle, his uncle's clairvoyant servant. The case must have been shocking and disturbing, presenting the dark side of peasant belief. It was many years before Yeats achieved a solution to the "practical" problem; the restriction of such beliefs to literary fancy and to folk lore urged by the *Cork Examiner* being, of course, unacceptable to him. The six Folk Lore articles deal *passim* with such phenomena as changelings, wives stolen by the fairies and magical remedies. The apotheosis of these concerns is the final article, "Away", published in 1902, and it is here, seven years after the event, that Yeats faces this ugly problem.

The country people seldom do more than threaten the dead person put in the living person's place, and it is, I am convinced, a sin against the traditional wisdom to really ill-treat the dead person. A woman from Mayo [Mary Battle] who has told me a good many tales . . . was very angry with the Tipperary countryman who burned his wife, some time ago, her father and neighbours standing by. She had no doubt that they only burned some dead person, but she was quite certain that you should not burn even a dead person. She said: "In my place we say you should only threaten. They are so superstitious in Tipperary." (*UP2* 277)

Mary Battle's solution is similar to that presented by Hartland; a superior stage of evolution is reached in which the cruel *act* becomes a threat or a symbol. In "Away", Yeats went on to instance other cases where a person, dead or otherwise, *has* been ill-treated. He then makes a more general statement:

I was always convinced that tradition, which avoids needless inhumanity, had some stronger way of protecting the bodies of those, to whom the other world was perhaps unveiling its mysteries . . . I heard of this stronger way last winter . . . "there was a girl used to be away with them. . . . And she told her mother always to treat kindly whoever was put in her place . . . for she'd say 'If you are unkind to whoever is there, they'll be unkind to me'". (*UP2* 278)

An admirable solution, were all peasants equally enlightened.[13] Earlier in this article, Yeats had discussed the "pagan mystery" of the "substitution of the dead for the living", suggesting a comparison with the mystery of transubstantiation: he continues "I will come to understand how this pagan mystery hides and reveals some half-forgotten memory of an ancient knowledge or of an ancient wisdom" (*UP2* 275). For this sacramental, sacrificial formulation of "away", Yeats is partially endebted to Alfred Nutt's discussion of the concept, in the second volume of *The Voyage of Bran*.[14] Yeats both refines and distorts Nutt's thesis by importing a very different belief-system. Nutt, in the course of his examination of the Celtic doctrine of re-birth, discusses changeling lore among the Irish peasantry and the relation of this folk belief to the ancient religion of Ireland:

> What was the root-conception of the antique agricultural worship? – that the Powers invoked were the lords and depositories of life; this they would dole out to their human worshippers, but on conditions; nothing is given for nothing, and if the Power of Life and Increase is to manifest himself, he must be fed, hence the necessity for sacrifice . . . I have purposely used crude, brutal terms for putting this theory, in order to emphasise the brutally practical nature of these antique faiths, the vigorous logic which boggled at no conclusion, however revolting. (*The Voyage of Bran*, ii, 231)

Nutt, having thus identified those who are "away", with those who were once sacrificed to the gods, continues:

> . . . the most popular incident of the fairy cycle, the Changeling story is found to be connected with the antique conception of life and sacrifice; how potent is the belief finding expression in this story may be gauged when we remember that only two years ago it induced a father, a husband and half-a-dozen cousins (all of them, save the husband, average representatives of their class, the small Irish peasant) to slowly roast an unfortunate woman to death because they suspected her of being a changeling. (*The Voyage of Bran*, ii, 232)

Nutt, in a footnote, refers the reader to the account in *Folk-Lore*, adding the eccentric judgement that the husband merely wished to rid himself of his wife, but that the others involved sincerely believed that Bridget Cleary was a changeling.

Yeats returned again to this problem and to the Clonmel Witch Burning about 1914, when he was writing the notes to Lady Gregory's *Visions and Beliefs in the West of Ireland*. In note 39, which glosses a story of remarkable kindness by a peasant to a changeling wife, Yeats represents the case:

> A man actually did burn his wife to death, in Tipperary a few years ago, and is no doubt still in prison for it. My uncle, George Pollexfen, had an old servant Mary Battle, and when she spoke of the case to me, she described that man as very superstitious. I asked what she meant by that and she explained that everybody knew that you must only threaten, for whatever injury you did to the changeling the fairies would do to the living person they had carried away. In fact mankind and spiritkind have each their hostage. These explanatory myths are not a speculative, but a practical wisdom. And one can count

perhaps, when they are rightly remembered, upon their preventing the more gross practical errors. The Tipperary witch-burner only half knew his own belief. (*VB* 360)[15]

NOTES

1. Edward Clodd (1840–1930), banker, folk-lorist, scientific writer: see *D.N.B.*, Joseph McCabe, *Edward Clodd, A Memoir* (London: John Lane, 1932) and Edward Clodd, *Memories* (London: Chapman & Hall, 1916). Clodd was a close friend of Meredith, Hardy and Gissing. He had been President of the Folk Lore Society in 1895 and 1896.
   Clodd had met Lady Gregory at Sir Alfred Lyall's on 11 November 1897; they discussed "Yeats' Irish F. lore" and peasant beliefs concerning the fairies. Clodd had no doubt read *The Tribes of Danu* (*The New Review*, November 1897), the first of the six major folk lore articles. Lady Gregory, at this time very anxious to provide Yeats with the best social contacts, invited him to dinner. I am grateful to Mr Alan Clodd for permission to quote from his grandfather's diaries.
2. E. H. Mikhail, *W. B. Yeats Interviews and Recollections*, vol. I (London: Macmillan, 1977) p. 7.
3. Unpublished letters from Yeats to Clodd, Brotherton Library, University of Leeds.
4. Clodd subsequently published Yeats's notes on traditions and superstitions in *Folk-Lore*, March 1899, (*UP2* 145–7).
5. Irish materials in these four volumes include discussion of polygamy in ancient Ireland (I, pp. 389–91), an Irish religious ballad on the Apocalypse (I, p. 147), a review article by Alfred Nutt on Irish myth and saga (II, pp. 110–42), an interesting discussion of totem names in Irish myth and history (III, p. 354).
6. Clodd had published a redaction of the *Kalevala* in *Knowledge* through 1885: W. F. Kirby's translation (verse) was finally published in Everyman in 1907.
7. Edwin Sidney Hartland, *The Science of Fairy Tales an Inquiry into Fairy Mythology* (London: Walter Scott, 1890). This influential work includes extended accounts of such themes as fairy births and human midwives, the supernatural lapse of time in fairyland: the discussion of this last is rich in reference and illustration, and is a key text for those interested in the concept "away". *SFT* in text.
8. Making the changeling laugh is a motif with which Yeats was familiar. See *Fairy and Folk Tales of the Irish Peasantry* (London: Scott, 1888) pp. 48–50. Hartland's extended discussion of this motif would naturally have interested Yeats.
9. At Clonmel, in May 1884, two women were prosecuted for "having on April 22 burnt a child three years old, named John Dillon, by placing him naked on a hot shovel. The act was a result of gross superstition on their part, the two women alleging that he was an old man left by the fairies" (*The Times*, 26 May 1884, p. 8, col. 2).
10. Bourke (pp. 58–9) gives a bizarre story about an Irish king called Aedh. Elsewhere (p. 393) he deals with the excremental aspects of the story of Dame Alice Kyteler (here Kettle). This was Yeats's first, but not last, acquaintance with Dame Alice.
11. This does not date for us Clodd's loan of *Scatalogic Rites*. It is clear from his diaries that Yeats or Lady Gregory might have read him extracts from "The Broken Gates of Death" well before its publication in April, 1898. The story as taken down by Lady Gregory can be found in *Visions and Beliefs in the West of Ireland* (Gerrards Cross: Colin Smythe, 1970) pp. 118–19. *VB* in Text.
12. "The 'Witch-burning' at Clonmel", *Folk-Lore*, 6 (1895) 373–84. This provides the fullest and most easily available contemporary redaction of the case.
13. Yeats and Lady Gregory collected this story in December 1897: it appears in *VB* 147, attributed to "An Old Woman at Chiswick" and from Lady Gregory's Ms. diary we know that they visited this old woman on 19 December 1897. Thus Yeats's "last

winter" suggests that the writing of "Away" was spread over many years. The majority of the changeling stories gathered by Yeats and Lady Gregory do involve a commutation of real violence into threatened or symbolic violence.

14. Kuno Meyer, *The Voyage of Bran Son of Febal . . . / With an Essay Upon . . . The Celtic Doctrine of Rebirth* by Alfred Nutt (London: David Nutt, 1895, 1897). Yeats reviewed both volumes in September 1898 (*UP2* 118–21), referring directly to "the powers of life and increase".

15. Mary Battle is here credited with both "solutions", having absorbed that recounted by the old woman at Chiswick. Yeats's formulation, with its sense of bargaining between the two worlds, recalls Nutt's remarks concerning "the brutally *practical* nature of these antique faiths" (my italics). One does perhaps, draw back a little, despite one's recognition of Yeats's beliefs, from a description of the killing of a woman (" 'Where was Bridget Cleary all this time? She was burning on the hearth' ") as a "gross practical error [ ]". Both Nutt and Yeats were directly influenced by J. G. Frazer's *The Golden Bough* (London: Macmillan, 1890, 2 vols). Nutt depends on Frazer's delineation of the link between agricultural religion and human sacrifice. Frazer had emphasized the sacramental aspect of killing the god "in the person of his representative" (Frazer, vol. 2, p. 67). Yeats had read at least part of *The Golden Bough* before November 1897, and half-quotes from it in "The Tribes of Danu": he did not, however, share Frazer's agnostic, scientific frame of reference.

"MASTERING WHAT IS MOST ABSTRACT": A FORUM ON *A VISION*

To "Beat Upon the Wall": Reading *A Vision*

Colin McDowell

To what extent may we consider that *A Vision* is a completed work? Numerous readers have come away from an attempt to read the book with the feeling that it is radically flawed. Perhaps this is the case. Perhaps the whole idea that geometry can lead to a truth worth telling about living creatures is misconceived. If so, Yeats is not alone in his misconception, and such a judgment does not appeal to my sense of adventure. Readers who feel that way about geometry should leave *A Vision* alone, as they will have left Plato's *Timæus* to those who prefer such things. Perhaps, though, *A Vision* is not wrong in its conception, but in its execution: the way in which Yeats has tried to capture his geometric "truth" on paper is not adequate to the subject. This idea is extremely problematic: if we find the work so flawed that it obscures its own exposition, we have no way of knowing what idea it is against which we are measuring the imperfections. Yeats's various statements about his intentions can be read in many different and contradictory senses, so they do not help in this matter.

An alternative assumption we might make is that *A Vision* is substantially complete, but that we have so far approached it in the wrong manner. This assumption grants that what Yeats is trying to tell us is worth the telling; it also grants that Yeats has, for the most part, adequately expressed his intentions. The belief that the book is a deliberate hoax on Yeats's part grants both of these conditions, and is not inconsistent with what we know of Yeats's sense of humour. Such a response would explain the almost universal experience everyone has when reading the book of insight in one sentence being taken away in the next. If we think of *A Vision* in architectural terms, it seems at times like a building from an Escher etching, where stairs which we had thought were leading upward suddenly debouche at a lower level. It might be possible to demonstrate that this experience of frustration is one of the structural features of *A Vision*, but such a demonstration would be laborious. We should be careful of coming to hold the view that *A Vision* is a hoax *because* it absolves us of work: it is too easy to think in that manner.[1]

My assumption is that *A Vision* is not a hoax, and that it is substantially complete. It tells us truths worth telling, and the difficulties of exposition are often, though not always, due to difficulties of subject matter. Several critics have raised the architectural metaphor. Richard Ellmann tentatively suggests that *A Vision* is a cathedral, which diminishes human presence with its "symbolic portentousness"; it can be seen as a "solipsistic structure" in which its creator is "cocooned", or into which he has been "ingested".[2] Hugh Kenner prefers a more martial metaphor than Ellmann: "a brief generation of critics assaulted the doors of that Gothic fortress, *A Vision*, or scrutinizing its interior by periscope reported that it was full of bats".[3] Both of these metaphors are useful. Certainly *A Vision* appears to be constructed in such a manner as to ward off extensive examination. Let us therefore assume that it is a cathedral. If so, is it consecrated to Yeats's own image, or can a larger congregation fit in? Let us assume the latter.

Before we can do this, however, we must dispose of the spectre of incompletion. It is true that Yeats published the book not once, but twice, and the American edition of the second version proclaims itself as "A Reissue with the Author's Final Revisions". Unfortunately, Yeats surrounded both versions of his book with alarming disclaimers about his ability to finish the work to his own satisfaction. These disclaimers may be due to an impossible perfectionism, or an old man's weariness, or they may accurately reflect an actual state of affairs: that the book is indeed incomplete. *AV[A]* is prefaced by Yeats's admission that "I could I daresay make the book richer, perhaps immeasurably so, if I were to keep it by me for another year, and I have not even dealt with the whole of my subject, perhaps not even with what is most important, writing nothing about the Beatific Vision, little of sexual love" (*AV[A]* xii). If Yeats treats these important matters in the second edition, it is not in an obvious manner. Various statements Yeats made about *AV[B]* suggest that these subjects are, for him, inadequately treated therein. Some of these statements occur in *AV[B]* itself. Even the admission that "All that is laborious or mechanical in my book is finished; what remains can be added as a momentary rest from writing verse" (*AV[B]* 7) can cut both ways. We should recall that this remark is dated "March and October 1928", that is, about nine years before Macmillan published the second version. The delay in publishing could mean that Yeats was tidying up odd corners, but nine years is surely a long time to take for the addition of curlicues. Alternatively, it could mean that Yeats was having doubts about some of the basic exposition. Some of Yeats's letters support this assumption.

In particular, there are the letters in which Yeats suggests that he had yet to construct his "private philosophy". In 1936 he writes to Ethel Mannin that *A Vision* is "my own book of mainly social philosophy" (*L* 865), and in 1938, to the same correspondent, that "The *Vision* is my 'public philosophy' ", whereas "My 'private philosophy' is the material dealing with individual mind which came to me with that on which the mainly historical *Vision* is based. I have not published it because I only half understand it" (*L* 916). Various critics, beginning with Richard Ellmann and Virginia Moore, would have us believe that the "private philosophy" is connected with, perhaps even identical to, the "Seven Propositions" which Yeats dictated to his wife in 1937 at Cannes. Ellmann in fact repeats as late as 1978 that "Yeats had begun to evolve a theory beyond *A Vision*, of how the varying panoply of the material world is really the reflection of spirits and their changing relations to each other".[4] This is a paraphrase of some of the "Seven Propositions". At least six of Yeats's "Seven Propositions" had been conceived as far back as 1929, and in fact *AV[B]* concerns very much "the reflection of spirits" into the material world.[5] It does not however do so in intimate detail, although it names names in several of its sections. One suspects, therefore, that "private" means "personal". Yeats's letter to Ethel Mannin of 9 October 1938, from which I have quoted Yeats's definition of "private philosophy", continues by discussing such things as *"Initiationary Moments"* and *"The Critical Moment "*, or the dissolution of the sensuous image leading to the "poverty" of "death" (*L* 916–17). Such topics, of course, should be treated in that section of *A Vision* called "The Soul in Judgment". That they do not immediately come at us "with staring eyes" in that section does not mean that they do not appear there. In fact, as such ideas occur in *Per Amica* and other places, it would be very odd not to have them treated in "The Soul in Judgment". Perhaps, then, the "private philosophy" ties parts of *A Vision* to Yeats's own life via a private code. Both George Harper's Editorial Introduction to *A Critical Edition of Yeats's* A Vision *(1925)* and his subsequent essay " 'Unbelievers in the House': Yeats's Automatic Script" show us several ways in which this might be the case.[6]

A letter from 1925 corroborates the suggestion that "private" is equivalent to "personal". Yeats describes *A Vision* as "exceedingly technical, a form of science for the study of human nature, as we see it in others", hence "less personal" than *Per Amica Silentia Lunae* (*L* 709). The phrase "as we see it in others" applies most strongly to the sections of *AV[A]* which survived almost unaltered in *AV[B]*, "The Twenty-Eight Embodiments" and "Dove or Swan", and reminds us that Yeats and his wife used to place people in their phases as a form of party-game, an entertainment.[7] Here, we must confront Yeats's ambivalence about these two sections. Does the fact that they are the sections least changed between publications mean that they are at the heart of the book? Alternatively, it could mean that they are peripheral to the main concerns, and hence were the easiest to write. Certainly both sections are adequately described as "public philosophy": both "The Twenty-Eight Embodiments" ("Incarnations" in *AV[B]*) and "Dove or Swan" possess some interest for those who wonder what a great poet had to say about well-known people and events. I suspect that these sections are a framing device, or bait to lure the reader into deeper waters. The fact that no one seems to have tested these deeper waters during Yeats's lifetime must have been very discouraging to him. It seems to have made him underestimate the amount of the system which he actually succeeded in putting into both editions, so that eventually he came to believe that "The Twenty-Eight Incarnations" and "Dove or Swan" represented the whole work, which henceforth became his "public philosophy". If so, then the details which he was constantly adding to the main outlines of *A Vision* assumed an importance for him which obscured what he had already accomplished. The pressure of constant discovery made him feel foolish because he had not noticed what should have been obvious to begin with. Such a feeling had no objective basis, but it did cause him to disparage what had been done, and to think that much more was necessary than was actually the case.

AV[*B*] is complete enough for detailed exposition to be undertaken: we do not have to wait for all of the unpublished drafts to be sorted, sifted and published. We do need to read the book in conjunction with *AV*[*A*], and some of the other published prose, but the main outlines are clear. There are several points which remain unclear, and I am sure that recourse to the drafts can assist in resolving these problems. But they are, I stress, problems on the periphery, or links which are missing, although we know where to postulate links. Remarkably, *A Vision* reveals consistencies which follow from its geometries, but which Yeats very probably did not know about – at least in the published versions.

I make several assumptions. The first is that "Stories of Michael Robartes and His Friends" is a covering device, a way to protect Yeats from the scorn of critics who find him endorsing outlandish things in the book proper. Given the choice of stories or doctrine, I would dispense with the stories, though fortunately we do not have to make that amputation. But perhaps, at least mentally, we do have to bracket off the stories in order to be able to take the rest of the book as a serious exposition of Yeats's philosophy. My second assumption, which is most important, is that the heart of *A Vision* is to be found in the section of *AV*[*B*] entitled "The Completed Symbol", and that our enquiries should therefore begin and end with that section. I assume this because of the word "Completed", which means "Having all its parts or elements; whole; entire", and because the title of the equivalent book in *AV*[*A*], "What the Caliph Refused to Learn", complements the title of the preceding book, "What the Caliph Partly Learned".

Yeats begins "The Completed Symbol", Book II of *AV*[*B*], with the statement "I knew nothing of the *Four Principles* when I wrote the last Book" (*AV*[*B*] 187). Whichever way we choose to understand the intentionally ambiguous "last Book", this is not quite true. It is a dramatic gesture to underscore the importance of the *Principles* to Yeats's system. It also refers to the fact that, although Yeats had been familiar with the *Principles* since 1920 (*AV*[*A*], notes, p. 69), the full force of the discovery did not become clear to him until after the publication of *AV*[*A*]. The alert reader of *AV*[*B*] will immediately relate "I knew nothing of the *Four Principles*" back to another passage in *AV*[*B*] where Yeats also tells us about the shifting state of his understanding of the *Principles*. Early in 1928, Yeats's instructors were constrained to return to improve Yeats's grasp of the system. "But now in a few minutes", he writes, "they drew that distinction between what their terminology calls the *Faculties* and what it calls the *Principles*, between experience and revelation, between understanding and reason, between the higher and lower mind, which has engaged the thought of saints and philosophers from the time of Buddha" (*AV*[*B*] 22). Yeats's rather careless use of parallelism here perhaps obscures the essential point. If we reverse the position of "higher" and "lower" the whole sentence may be read without obfuscation the *Principles* are "the higher mind".[8] Yeats's essential distinction is thus the traditional one between the material and the spiritual, the empirical and the mystical; and with the aid of this distinction one may make sense of other distinctions used throughout *A Vision*. A few pages before Yeats imparts the information about "higher" and "lower" mind, he admits to being ashamed of *AV[A]*, because "I had misinterpreted the geometry, and in my ignorance of philosophy failed to understand distinctions upon which the coherence of the whole depended" (*AV[B]* 19). These distinctions are those which follow from that major distinction between *Faculties* and *Principles*. Helen Vendler has said that the *Four Principles* are "irritatingly similar to the Four Faculties".[9] This may well be true of the *Four Principles* in *AV[A]*, where the *Four Principles* do not appear to have ordering capabilities, and are just another set of terms which Yeats feels he must expound. It is certainly not true of the *Four Principles* in *AV[B]*.

"The Completed Symbol" explains how the *Four Principles* have a movement comparable to that of the gyres in the *Faculties*, and how this movement gives rise to the twenty-eight incarnations. It also explains how the movement of the *Four Faculties* is only a small part of the wider movement of the cones of the *Principles*. The *Four Faculties* are however that part of man which is visible or palpable in incarnation, so Yeats has written of them at length in "The Twenty-Eight Incarnations" and "Dove or Swan". The geometry here is difficult but it is consistent. We need to follow Yeats's instructions when he tells us to draw diagrams. Sections VI and VII in particular are important. We need to distinguish between what Yeats calls "*Will* on the circumference", which is the *Will* of what *AV[A]* calls "Eternal Man" (after Blake), and the *Will* of the double vortex of the gyres. The latter is the microcosmic reflection of the former: it is the *Will* of the individual in the here and now. Geometry becomes mysticism with statements like "The union of *Spirit* and *Celestial Body* has a long approach and is complete when the gyre reaches its widest expansion" (*AV[B]* 198) and "at its gyre's widest expansion *Spirit* contains the whole wheel" (*AV[B]* 199). Perhaps more importantly, we need to follow up any suggestions Yeats gives us as to what his *Four Principles* are like in traditional terms. If they have no exact equivalents, at least a rough parallel may set us thinking. One such parallel given by Yeats is the Upanishadic states of the soul: waking, dreaming, deep sleep, and liberation from all three states. These are equated with *Husk*, *Passionate Body*, *Spirit* and *Celestial Body* respectively (*AV[B]* 219–223). This tetrad may be related without strain to other tetrads which belong to Yeatsian tradition: Blake's Ulro, Beulah, Generation and Eden, for example, or the Four Worlds of the Kabbalah, the Material, the Formative, the Creative and the Archetypal. Or else we can equate selectively: *Husk*, *Passionate Body* and *Spirit* appear to be very similar to the traditional division of man into body, soul and spirit; *Celestial Body* must therefore be a further extension of *Spirit*, perhaps the "Resurrection Body" of which G. R. S. Mead has written.[10] But what of the *Four Faculties*, that part of *Vision* most familiar to us? If the distinction between *Faculties* and *Principles* as a whole is the distinction between the material and the spiritual, how are we to reconcile what I have just said about the *Four Principles* with it? Well, in normal discourse we can either talk about body and soul, or else we can talk about body, soul and spirit, and we find no difficulty about it, although obviously the "soul" that is opposed to "body" must incorporate the "soul" and "spirit" of the more extended division. Similarly, I would suggest, we can change perspective readily enough with Yeats's terminology. We can think of the two lunar *Principles*, *Husk* and *Passionate Body*, as being material, with the two solar *Principles*, *Spirit* and *Celestial Body*, being spiritual; we can oppose the solar *Principles* as a whole to the lunar *Faculties* as a whole; or we can, I think, regard all of the "body" side as being summed up in the concept of the *Husk*: in other words, *Husk*, encompassing all *Four Faculties*, is the completed reflection of "spirits" into the material world, when viewed from an eternal perspective.

These equations are not offered in a dogmatic way. They may not be totally accurate; they do, however, have the merit of trying to fit *A Vision* into systems which at once have human relevance and which are not remote from Yeats's own concerns. For too long *A Vision* has been thought of as Yeats's private eccentricity. What I am suggesting is *not* that all of the pieces of *A Vision*'s jigsaw may now be put into place; rather, I am suggesting a likely base from which criticism may begin to work. It should not be forgotten that the Upanishadic parallels are Yeats's own: we should at least try to read the book against them to see whether they manage to clarify matters. Such a process of testing is how we come to understand anything that is confusing at first glance. We survey the material, seize upon something that seems relatively familiar, relate that something to the whole complex of the familiar idea, and then see if that *gestalt* helps us to explain the material before us. We tend to work from a whole to a part, even though the whole may have been suggested by a fleeting glimpse of quite a small part; we always use the familiar to explain the foreign.

One of the central passages of "The Completed Symbol" concerns a parallel which is rather more elusive than that of the Upanishadic states of the soul. Nevertheless, reference to this parallel may not be without its use here, offering as it does several possibilities for exploration: the parallel is with the philosophy of Plotinus. The editors of *A Critical Edition of Yeats's* A Vision *(1925)* are dubious about this parallel, as it occurs in *AV*[A], p. 176 and *AV*[B], pp. 193–95. However, an article[11] on this topic, by Rosemary Puglia Ritvo, who seems to read Plotinus much as Yeats would have read him, explains such hybrids of Yeats's as the "Authentic Existants". Ritvo's main conclusions appear sound, although I would query her statements about the Daimon. The diagram which Yeats provides for his Plotinian parallel is possibly even more eloquent than the prose passage which it accompanies:

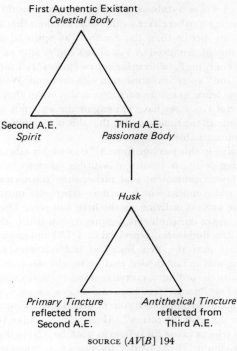

First Authentic Existant
Celestial Body

Second A.E.   Third A.E.
Spirit   *Passionate Body*

Husk

Primary Tincture   *Antithetical Tincture*
reflected from   reflected from
Second A.E.   Third A.E.

SOURCE (*AV[B]*) 194

FIGURE 3

As we can see, the upper triangle represents the spiritual, while the lower triangle represents the material. My suggestion about *Husk* encompassing the *Four Faculties* is not invalidated by the diagram. Interestingly, if we imagine that the triangles are in fact intended to represent cones, then we can see that the Great Wheel forms the base of the lower cone. We can, if we like, choose to emphasize the Great Wheel as the foundation upon which the edifice of *A Vision* is built; or, more fruitfully, we can see that the building does not stop at ground level. Then, perhaps, we shall begin to explore the upper storeys.

What may prevent this exploration, what I suspect has already prevented some exploration, is the statement Yeats adds immediately after giving his diagram. "But this diagram", he writes,

> implies a descent from *Principle* to *Principle*, a fall of water from ledge to ledge, whereas a system symbolising the phenomenal world as irrational because a series of unresolved antinomies, must find its representation in a perpetual return to the starting-point. The resolved antinomy appears not in a lofty source but in the whirlpool's motionless centre, or beyond its edge (*AV[B]* 194–5).

Yeats's system in *A Vision* symbolises the phenomenal world as irrational precisely for the reason given here. Are we therefore to take it that any suggestion that the *Principles* are better than the *Faculties*, as spiritual is better than material, has been discountenanced by Yeats? Is Vendler after all correct to find that the *Principles* are only the *Faculties* in fancy new clothes? Is Yeats wrong to use the terms "higher" and "lower" in connection with the mind? Well, in a way, but this does not give us leave to ignore such distinction when they are made. In order to understand *A Vision*, we have to imagine the waterfall, even climb the spiritual ladder, while all the time knowing that this is to impose a distortion on reality, which is unimaginable.

What Yeats is doing in this passage from *AV[B]* with his talk of "a perpetual return to the starting-point" is consistent with his religious beliefs expressed elsewhere, which favour immanent soul rather than transcendent god. Any intimations of the transcendent which we may experience must, of necessity, occur as part of the process of living, in the here and now. The transcendent experience solves none of our problems, leaving us still tied to the antinomies. Yeats's interest in Zen Buddhism, expressed in *AV[B]* and important essays,[12] arises from the fact that the Zen Buddhist did not seek salvation in a transcendent realm, and in fact denied that he sought salvation: the Buddha-mind is identified with the ordinary, everyday mind. *A Vision* expresses the same truth by having the *Four Principles* feed back into the *Four Faculties*, and vice versa: "How many times have you mortgaged your farm and paid off the mortgage?" "I take pleasure in the sound of the rushes" (*AV[B]* 214–15). Like Wittgenstein in the *Tractatus*, Yeats tells us to use his system as a ladder, but to throw the ladder away once we have climbed it: the reader, for Yeats too, "must transcend these propositions and then he will see the world aright".

NOTES

1. The idea that *A Vision* is a hoax solves many problems for Steven Helmling, in "Yeats's Esoteric Comedy", *The Hudson Review*, 30 (1977) 230–46.
2. Richard Ellmann, *Eminent Domain: Yeats among Wilde, Joyce, Pound, Eliot and Auden* (New York: Oxford University Press, 1967) pp. 80–1.
3. Hugh Kenner, "Unpurged Images", *The Hudson Review*, 8 (1956) 615.
4. Richard Ellmann, "Preface to the 1979 Edition", *Yeats: the Man and the Masks* (London: Oxford University Press, 1979) p. xxxii.
5. Richard Taylor, ed. *Frank Pearce Sturm: His Life, Letters, and Collected Works* (Urbana: University of Illinois Press, 1969) pp. 100–1.
6. George Mills Harper, " 'Unbelievers in the House': Yeats's Automatic Script", *Studies in the Literary Imagination*, 14: 1 (1981) 1–15.
7. To judge by the experience of Joseph Hone, in Hone, *W. B. Yeats, 1865–1939* (London: Macmillan, 1942 [1943]) p. 333.
8. The reader who is confused by the placing, by the supposedly anti-rationalist Yeats, of "reason" above "understanding", should read the excellent article by Grosvenor E. Powell, "Yeats's Second 'Vision': Berkeley, Coleridge, and the Correspondence with Sturge Moore", *The Modern Language Review*, 76 (1981) 273–90.
9. Helen Vendler, *Yeats's* Vision *and the Later Plays* (Cambridge, Mass.: Harvard University Press, 1963) p. 26.

10. Despite appearances, the suggestion of Mead's "Resurrection Body" is not a random casting-about. In "Swedenborg, Mediums, and the Desolate Places" Yeats used, as one of his main sources, two essays by Mead that later became part of his book *The Doctrine of the Subtle Body in Western Tradition* (London: J. M. Watkins, 1919). See *Explorations*, p. 61. Yeats's essay is of course acknowledged as one of the precursors of *A Vision*.

11. Rosemary Puglia Ritvo, "*A Vision* B: the Plotinian Metaphysical Basis", *Review of English Studies*, 26 (1975) 34–46.

12. See *AV[B]* 214–15, Yeats's Introduction to *Aphorisms of Yôga by Bhagwān Shree Patanjali*, tr. w. a commentary by Shree Purohit Swāmi (London: Faber & Faber, 1937), and "Bishop Berkeley" (*E&I* 410), with which one may compare "Pages From a Diary Written in Nineteen Hundred and Thirty" (*E* 304, 325). See also Gerald Doherty, "The World That Shines and Sounds: W. B. Yeats and Daisetz Suzuki", *Irish Renaissance Annual IV*, ed. Zack Bowen (East Brunswick, London, Mississauga [Ontario]: Associated University Presses, 1983) 57–75. Yeats owned three of Suzuki's books on Zen Buddhism, as we discover in Shiro Naito, *Yeats and Zen: a Study of the Transformation of His Mask* (Kyoto: Yamaguchi, 1984) p. 171. Naito reproduces some of Yeats's marginalia on pp. 27–8, 49–50, 53, 129, 149 and frontispiece.

REVIEWS

Karen Dorn, *Players and Painted Stage: the Theatre of W. B. Yeats* (Brighton: Harvester Press; New Jersey: Barnes & Noble Books, 1984) pp. xiv + 143.

David R. Clark

This short but solid book is a refreshing, egoless, excellent study of Yeats's theatre and drama, thoroughly grounded in past scholarship and criticism, but individual in viewpoint, with real insights, and a complete dedication to the art. Karen Dorn sees Yeats's development as a dramatist as one expression of "the wide range of interests that have animated twentieth-century theatre – the controversy surrounding naturalistic drama, the inspiration of classical Greek and Japanese dramatic forms, the shaping influence of new approaches to stage settings, and the fascination with the expressive figure of the dancer" (p. xii).

Yeats, as a poet, is "a maker of images" who, as a playwright, expands the poetic image into a dramatic image, "a whole built from language, actors' movements, and stage settings" (p. xi). Dorn describes "Yeats's long involvement in two aspects of nonnaturalistic theatre – the relation between stage performance and audience in the Greek theatre, and the nature of the poetic and dramatic image produced in that type of theatre" (p. 63). This quotation comes from her chapter on Yeats and the Greek theatre movement, but she sees Yeats's preoccupations with the dramatic image and with the relation of performance and audience as central concerns in each phase of his work.

Analyses of individual plays exemplify each phase, and these analyses are valuable in themselves and should be consulted by anyone studying or producing those plays. It is, however, difficult to excerpt analysis from the closely reasoned argument which is its context. The five chapters take us through five phases of Yeats's development, each leading logically to the next: his early attempts, as in *Deirdre*, "to create a nonnaturalistic drama based on Irish legend"; his work with the theatre designer Gordon Craig in new versions and productions of *The Land of Heart's Desire*, *The Countess Cathleen*, and especially *The Hour Glass*; his experimental dance plays based on the Ezra Pound/Ernest Fenollosa translations of Japanese Noh drama (This chapter deals not only with the *Four Plays for Dancers* but also with their emergence from the earlier *On Baile's Strand* and *The Green Helmet* and their assimilation in *The Player Queen*); "the

231

culmination [in his versions of Sophocles' Oedipus plays and *The Resurrection*] of his long involvement with the revival of Greek drama begun by Gilbert Murray and Granville Barker"; and, in *Fighting the Waves*, *The King of the Great Clock Tower*, *A Full Moon in March*, *The Herne's Egg*, and *The Death of Cuchilain*, his creation of "a new form combining dance, dialogue, and music in his collaboration with Diaghilev's dancer, Ninette de Valois, and the London experimental theatres of poetic drama" (p. xi). The line connecting these five phases is strongly drawn and Yeats is revealed as a leading theatrical thinker and experimenter of his and our times.

Although Karen Dorn says that her "emphasis is rather more on dramatic form than poetic language" some of her most valuable analyses demonstrate that "the two aspects are inseparable in Yeats's plays" (p. xii). Under the influence of Gordon Craig Yeats learned to create new stage space in which dialogue could be "enacted in performance" (p. 23). In the 1912 revision of *The Land of Heart's Desire*, the new stage space gives "greater coherence to metaphors in the dialogue" (p. 19), and the words are revised "towards a language that not only acts with the stage space, but grows from the movement within it" (p. 20). In the first version of *The Countess Cathleen*, Scene II, the stage was dominated by a tapestry picture of Fenian and Red Branch warriors, the pagan world which by the end of the scene the Countess has given up for Christian self-sacrifice. In the 1912 revision the "characters now move within a space, no longer dominated by the tapestry picture, which takes its meaning from their speech and movement." This is a "wood with perhaps distant view of turreted house at one side, but all in flat colour, without light and shade and against a diapered or gold background" (*VPl* 51). The characters' "words create the space": " 'when the moon's riding at the full,/ [Queen Maeve] . . . lies there/ Upon that level place' " (p. 21). But Aleel's tale of the legendary Maeve and her lost lover ends as the dialogue makes the space become the approach to Cathleen's castle and then turns that from a private refuge to a shelter for the poor: " 'all, all, shall come/ Till the walls burst and the roof fall on us./ From this day out I have nothing of my own' " (p. 22).

In the 1912–13 revision of *The Hour Glass* the play "changed not only from one style of theatre to another but from one style of language to another". The merely referential "even rhythms and repetitive logic" (p. 23) of the early prose gave way to a verse which "reflected the kind of movement made possible by the new stage space". In place of the "symmetrical set of the original production" (p. 24) Craig provided "a stage set composed of opposites – light, shadow, circle, square" in which "a corridor of screens" which "curves round to the left, disappearing back centre stage into light" suggests "that the Wise Man's place is at one point of a circular pathway, that his domain of learning is at the dark end of a path moving towards light" (p. 25). Dorn finds this "movement of perception" in the imagery:

> Reason is growing dim;
> A moment more and Frenzy will beat his drum
> And laugh aloud and scream;

And I must dance in the dream.
No, no, but it is like a hawk, a hawk of the air,
It has swooped down – and this swoop makes the third –
And what can I, but tremble like a bird? (p. 24; *VPl* 587)

"The images", Dorn points out, "are spatial: 'dance', 'swoop', 'tremble' ", and suggest "the energy displayed in an actor's voice and movement" (p. 24).

A remarkable quality of this book is Karen Dorn's awareness of the relationship between "Stage Images and the 'National Argument' ", not only in the first chapter, of which this is the title, but also here and there throughout the book in surprising contexts. If "declamatory, loose, and bragging," the Irish, Yeats felt, were "but the better fitted . . . to create unyielding personality, manner at once cold and passionate, daring long-premeditated act" (p. 7; *Au* 207). So Deirdre, too emotional at first to play chess calmly at a moment of danger, in the end moves from red heat to white heat, "from indecision to premeditated act" (p. 10) in her deception of Conchubar and her triumphant death. Thus Deirdre is for the Irish a "model of behaviour preserved in traditional literature" (p. 7).

Although Yeats claimed that the scene of *The Player Queen* was not laid in Ireland, "The controversy over the Irish national image reappears in Septimus' argument with the 'bad, popular poets,' while a rumour linking the Queen with a Unicorn provides the play with its own context of political interpretation" (p. 57).

The "slow low note and an iron bell" sung of in *The King of the Great Clock Tower* when the Queen dances with the severed head is related by Dorn to the "Fourth Bell" of Irish history, the death of Parnell, in Yeats's "Commentary on A Parnellite at Parnell's Funeral." This bell heralds "an Ireland that was 'passing through a phase of self-conscious violence' " (p. 87).

In a 1931 broadcast, Dorn says, Yeats placed the Oedipus of *Oedipus at Colonus* "at the centre of contemporary Ireland. For an audience living through the turbulent events of the Easter Uprising, the Troubles and the Civil War, Oedipus could be the image of intensity in the midst of disaster . . . " (81–2). Elizabeth Cullingford has written that "Yeats was essentially and not incidentally a political writer" (*Yeats, Ireland, and Fascism*, 1981, p. 235), and Karen Dorn seems to agree.

I have not room to mention the many passages which interest and please me in this book. In "An Intimate Theatre" Dorn draws an illuminating parallel between Yeats's attack on "vitality" – " 'It is even possible that being is only possessed completely by the dead' " – and Gordon Craig's essay "The Actor and the Über-Marionette": " 'Shades – spirits seem to me to be more beautiful, and filled with more vitality than men or women.' " Dorn saves both writers from a charge of morbidity by reminding us that "The emphasis on 'death' rather than 'life' is an emphasis on the convention of masks, costumes, and symbolic characters rather than the naturalistic mode of acting and stage setting" (p. 48).

In "Stage Production and the Greek Theatre Movement" Dorn shows that

Yeats's version of *Sophocles' King Oedipus* "transforms the tragedy of a community into that of the lone figure Oedipus, a modern 'tragic hero' " (p. 75). Because of the physical limitations of the Abbey Theatre Yeats reduced the Chorus to a Leader and five men and the choruses to lyrics. These choruses are no longer an integral part of the action, the responses of the *polis* to the King in their mutual crisis, but lyrical interludes to relax or shift the audience's attention. The final episode is shortened to focus on the lone Oedipus with his daughters and Creon rather than on the citizens' horrified revulsion from their king. Dorn also points out the similarity of *King Oedipus* to Yeats's dance plays when Yeats turns the last lines of the play into a song spoken by a single actor, the Chorus Leader, figuring forth again the isolation of Oedipus.

In "The New Dance Drama" Dorn has little to say about *The Death of Cuchulain*, but that little catches the tone of Yeats's last play as well as anything I have read: "The mood of *The Death of Cuchulain* is exuberant, from the impassioned bitterness of Yeats's comic self-portrait as the Old Man in the Prologue, to the absorption of the dancing Emer, the nonchalance of Cuchulain in his last 'gay struggle without hope,' and the lively song of the Street Singer" (p. 95). I should rather see a production that followed Dorn than one that followed Helen Vendler, perceptive as she always is: "I do not find tragic joy, or indeed joy of any description, permeating the play; weariness and indifference come nearer its note" (*Yeats's 'Vision' and the Later Plays*, 1963, p. 240).

The 32 illustrations are extraordinarily interesting and are well chosen to bear a direct relation to Dorn's argument. One has only to see Craig's wood-engraving of a feathered young man, "Hamlet: An Actor", to recognize Septimus of *The Player Queen* with his "breast-feathers thrust out and . . . white wings buoyed up with divinity" (plate 18).

But it is time to mention some minor faults. It is an inconvenience to the reader that there are no plate numbers under the illustratons, so that when the text refers to "Plate 18" the reader has to count them himself. One picture is mis-identified as "Robert Gregory's design for the 1906 Abbey Theatre production of W. B. Yeats's *Deirdre*" (after p. 50). And this identification enters Dorn's discussion (p. 5). But Colin Smythe has recently found this design to be "the backdrop for J. M. Synge's *Deirdre of the Sorrows* (not Yeats's play *Deirdre*, as has been thought)" (*A Guide to Coole Park*, 1983, p. 35).

Dorn's style is not always clear, and as a result what may not be errors appear to be so. When she writes "Describing the controversy surrounding Lady Gregory's *The Rising of the Moon* in 1907" (p. 2), the words do not immediately convey the fact that the description was written in 1907, whereas the controversy took place earlier (1904). Other errors may not be stylistic: "When the Abbey was established . . . Yeats's chief opponent was George Moore. . . . As Yeats wrote, 'I saw Moore daily, we were at work on *Diarmuid and Grania*' " (p. 3). But *Diarmuid and Grania* was finished and performed in 1901; the Abbey Theatre founded in 1904!

There are a number of misprints, and these are serious when they occur in quotations, as several do. Lady Gregory asked about "Image-makers",

". . . do we not live by the shining of those scattered fragments of their dream?" But in Dorn's book she is made to write "we do not live," the opposite of her meaning (p. 11). There are other examples, but misprints are disgracefully common nowadays as correcting them becomes more and more expensive for harried book publishers.

Sometimes one differs with Dorn's interpretations, or finds them too succinct, as when she refers to the Musicians' closing song in *The Only Jealousy of Emer* – the one beginning "What makes her heart beat thus?" – as "Emer's address to Fand" (p. 47). After the agonies of Wilson, Vendler ("Yeats at his most maddening," Vendler p. 230), Moore and others over the ascription of these lines, this is too concise.

These faults are minor. Karen Dorn's *Players and Painted Stage* is an essential book for the library of anyone seriously interested in Yeats's plays. It is one of the growing list of fine books which give Yeats his true place in the modern theatre.

Robert Hogan and Richard Burnham, *The Art of the Amateur, 1916–1920* vol. 5 of *The Modern Irish Drama*, (Mountrath: Dolmen Press, 1984) pp. 368.

Katharine Worth

In this latest volume of *The Modern Irish Drama* Robert Hogan and Richard Burnham trace the fortunes of an Irish theatre that was growing at a prodigious rate, though, in their words, "most of what was done was trivial, ephemeral and vulgar". The authors are highly conscious of the gulf between the trivial aspects of this "entertainment boom" and the seriousness of the times (The Easter Rising, Great War, Black and Tans). They often feel obliged in their summaries of plays to sound the "respectfully condemnatory" note so charmingly struck by the *Irish Times* reviewing Daniel Corkery's *The Labour Leader* at the Abbey Theatre in 1919:

> Daniel Corkery seems to be ill at ease when walking the common paths. His natural sphere lies in regions aloft, where he can indulge in fanciful flights to soothe his restless spirit.

The plays of the period under review did tend to walk the common paths: there was obviously a hunger among audiences for a sight of their own ways of life on the stage, for the ordinary life of Dublin as well as the peasant life which had long held sway on the Irish stage. Too long, said John MacDonagh, leading light of Edward Martyn's Irish Theatre, which was dedicated to the production of "nature plays, other than the peasant species", and also to foreign masterpieces. (They risked brave productions like that of Strindberg's *Pariah* in 1919, with their casts of "talented amateurs".)

Understandably, as they have to summarise or quote reviews of so many undistinguished plays, the authors tend to be somewhat apologetic about the whole subject, commenting, for instance, that there is not much in the diet of patriotic Irish melodramas enjoyed in those days at the Queen's Theatre to detain "the student of dramatic literature". This may well be, but there is quite enough to interest the student of theatre – and also, surely, Yeatsians; those who are intrigued by the "Theatre business" side of Yeats's life will relish these glimpses into the actuality of Dublin theatre business during five years notable for great diversity and energy, if not for masterpieces.

Only one new play of Yeats appeared during the period: *The Player Queen* was directed by Lennox Robinson at the Abbey in December 1919. A strange sport in a Dublin theatre increasingly devoted to realism on the one hand and musicals and farce on the other. Under a clever headline, "Villon at the Abbey", Joseph A. Power in the *Evening Telegraph* noted (conscientiously but without undue enthusiasm) interesting features of the production; Barry Fitzgerald and Philip Guiry as the two ancients conducting a conversation across the street ("Quite enjoyable") and the little girl from the Abbey acting school who played the "real queen" as a "frightened, anaemic-minded girl, anxious only for seclusion from the buffetings of the world".

There is always some interest in seeing how plays much studied for their author's sake, strike people when they make their first entrance on stage against a background of ordinary life. Suggestive outlines of performances and critical reception, as of personalities and theatre politics, do emerge from the scattered bits of correspondence, reviews and authorial comments which Hogan and Burnham have drawn together as the "voice" of the period. It is a curious perspective for Yeatsians, accustomed to see Yeats and the Abbey at the centre of things. The Abbey is still at the centre, in a way, but can no longer be so easily distinguished by its repertoire and style. A modern tide was flowing, as Yeats observed when writing to Lady Gregory about the odd changes taking place in the scenery of the Abbey Theatre:

. . . even the cottage in which *The Playboy* is performed, which we thought fixed to its type for ever, has got less cottage-like. It has now got a French window and something that evades all analysis has happened to the lintels of the doors.

A symbol of the times indeed! It sounds like a descent, but all these movements toward realism, from the Cork realists through the "foreign" imports advocated by Martyn and Yeats and harsh Irish plays like *Blight* ("the horrors of slumdom in the naked light of truth") were pushing the Irish theatre to the moment when the next great master would appear. In 1923 *The Shadow of a Gunman* would have its first performance on the Abbey stage and the era of Sean O'Casey would begin.

Richard Taylor, *A Reader's Guide to the Plays of W. B. Yeats*, (London: Macmillan, 1984) pp. 197.

Katharine Worth

Is the appearance of another book of commentary on Yeats's plays a sign that interest in them is spreading or even that they are becoming required reading for students as the poems have long been? That would be a welcome development, provided that it stimulated performances and gave more people the chance of experiencing these intensely theatrical works as they need to be experienced, through the physical medium which Yeats devised with such care.

Richard Taylor's guide is evidently designed for those coming to the plays without much or any knowledge of Yeats. For the use of these readers he supplies clear summaries of ruling themes, preoccupations and images – the gyres, masks, dreaming back – and gives an account of each play in relation to this context. This is not to say that his accounts are without theatrical reference: he finds some space in each for a brief mention of Yeats's ideas on staging, possible production effects and so on. But the emphasis is essentially on the dramatic working out of themes: *The Dreaming of the Bones* is introduced, for instance, as the play which has so many major themes that scholars have not been able to agree on the order of their importance and these are identified in the account that follows. The guide represents various critical interpretations without ascribing them to particular sources or entering into critical discussion. This is consistent with the aim of making a complex subject clear for beginners: readers are obviously expected to pursue ideas that have interested them, with the aid of the critical works listed for further reading. Since there is otherwise no way of identifying individual critical views, I hope that in any future edition the brief indication of contents attached to most of the critical works could be extended to all. (I speak with feeling as an author who suspects that her own book is in the wrong section of the bibliography!) There are one or two misprints, such as "Fargusson" for "Fergusson", which will already have been noted. The guide provides some useful information, and some very clear exposition of the complex material that makes up the plays. It should succeed in its aim, to "present the work and thought of an author as clearly and simply as possible".

A. S. Knowland, *W. B. Yeats: Dramatist of Vision*, Irish Literary Studies 17 (Gerrards Cross: Colin Smythe Ltd; New Jersey: Barnes & Noble Books, 1983) pp. xvi + 256

Richard Allen Cave

This is a disappointing volume, because it misjudges its line of approach to its intended audience and will quite likely alienate those it seeks to enlighten. Mr Knowland in his Epilogue claims he is trying to excite interest not only amongst students of Yeats's work, but in professional theatre circles, so that the plays may achieve production in a manner that meets with Yeats's exacting demands on the performer, designer, choreographer and director. Only then, he believes, can their lasting merits and theatrical viability be assessed. If this is his genuine ambition, then he falls short of his target by being himself in want of conviction that Yeats is unquestioningly a "dramatist of vision". It will not stir others to enthusiasm when so many of the commentaries on the individual plays (the study follows the ordering of the works in the *Collected Plays*) stress weakness, limitations, difficulties in interpretation and staging, failures of dramatic creativity. What this argues is a want of vision in the commentator, rather than the dramatist, in the sense of an ability adequately to visualise the plays in terms of performance against which to measure his responses. Wrongheadedness abounds.

Consider Knowland's view of Fergus in *Deirdre* as "naturalistically . . . implausible . . . in his complacent belief in Conchubar's promise of forgiveness . . . in his refusal to entertain seriously the possibility of the old king's jealousy, in his obtuseness in failing to recognise the purpose behind the presence of Conchubar's henchmen" (p. 100). In performance, in my experience, Fergus is invested with considerable pathos: he is a man willing himself to believe in the truth of Conchubar's word against every vestige of evidence to the contrary; to admit that the king is lying would be to undermine the whole structure of feudal loyalties, pledges and trust that Fergus lives by and that for him would be to contemplate the void where all decorum and courtesy are overthrown. Conchubar stakes all on this reading of Fergus's character as an innocent who lacks the courage it takes to view life with wary scepticism. Missing this, Knowland fails to appreciate the final irony of the play (he finds the conclusion "unsatisfactory") when Conchubar simply by reasserting the tone of command can achieve a free passage from the stage quite subduing Fergus's threats of rebellion: Conchubar knows his every reaction is conditioned by respect for authority, however profound his disillusionment with its representative. The nature of Fergus's character is beautifully judged by Yeats to create in his audience a sense of foreboding about Conchubar as a man of prodigious intelligence: the king is the evil genius who has shaped the action of the early part of the play yet he remains unseen till the trap is sprung on the lovers and Deirdre is, he believes, sufficiently prepared psychologically for his arrival. If Deirdre is to be brought to submission, then everything depends on Fergus's powers to allay her fears of a reprisal for her guilty love for Naoise and for that no suspicion must enter Fergus's mind of Conchubar's possible duplicity. Over the years the High King has become a consummate actor suppressing the force of his jealousy to realise his aim the better. His success is a tribute to the power of his will over his desire. If we do not sense this – and Fergus's characterisation is a major contributing factor in the theatrical realisation of Conchubar's power – then the climactic battle between two forceful wills, Conchubar's and Deirdre's, loses its dynamic momentum. Who will end the story rightly – he or she? Fergus's importance in the shaping of the psychological and theatrical climax of the play is testimony to Yeats's subtle but firm control of his dramatic structure. He is not deficient in the architectural aspects of playwriting.

One could go on listing examples of this kind where adverse judgements are not true to one's experience of the plays in the theatre. All but the Wise Man and the Fool are inadequately characterised in *The Hour Glass*, we are informed; but surely the Wife and Pupils are deliberately caricatured, rendered less than fully human, to show the damaging effect of the Wise Man's rationalism on the quality of their lives. *The Herne's Egg* (for Knowland) questions whether all "human gestures are futile"; humanity and God are mocked. But this is to miss the real mystery of the play in performance where the more cruelly Congal and Attracta are subjected to reductive farce, the more they are invested with pathos and dignity in their suffering; something of *human* worth is salvaged as they are whirled by circumstance into the void. The daring of Yeats's artistry here is remarkable: the dialogue in the closing scenes invites laughter, yet the situations for all their stylised presentation, actualise an intense awareness of pain that defies us to laugh. Or again Knowland suggests that in *Purgatory* the Old Man's madness "must be established in his very first speeches". But if that is so, an audience risks being complacently detached from the Old Man's predicament. The profound irony of the play is the man's belief in the power of reason; the audience like the Boy are swayed by the apparent logic of cause and effect as he tells of his past, only to discover too late that that logic is the expression of a total and lethal madness. To sense this too soon is to rob the play of the elements of shock and danger that make an experience of *Purgatory* as much a process of discovery for the audience as for the character. Knowland argues that Yeats's dramas should ideally act like epiphanies; if that is so, then the audience must never rest in a passive relation to the stage: the "reverie" must always be *excited*.

How can one treat seriously Knowland's insistence that performers should respect Yeats's prescriptions for the staging of his plays when in a Postscript to his essay on *The Words Upon the Window Pane* he suggests that the inner play of Swift, Vanessa and Stella be acted literally in period costume rather than be left to the resources of the actress playing the medium, Mrs Henderson, to conjure forth in the minds of the audience by her potent art? This shows a complete insensitivity to the demands of Yeats's style of theatre and to the actor's technique. If theatrefolk are to be attracted to the plays, a good line of appeal would surely be the challenge all but the earliest pose for displays of virtuosity. But simplifying and systematising is Knowland's customary approach. The remark, that Emer's dance with the severed heads in *The Death of Cuchulain* cannot convey the weight of meaning Yeats asks the dancer to express through it, is a similarly embarrassing lapse of appreciation of the possibilities of theatre.

It would be discourteous to suggest that there were not some random insights of value. There is a spirited defence of Conchubar's policy with Cuchulain in *On Baile's Strand* arguing that the King is not, as often interpreted, imperceptive and vicious (a view springing from drawing too close an analogy between Conchubar and the Blind Man), but sensitive rather to Cuchulain's predicament while acting out of prudence to safeguard the community. This reading gives the play a genuine tragic impetus: the conflict between King and Hero is between balanced but utterly irreconcilable principles of being; both men recognise the dilemma and their helplessness in the face of inevitability. Equally stimulating is the observation that in *The Death of Cuchulain* the hero's nobility is established through our growing perception that the identity of all the other characters is defined only through their particular relation to him: "all have had a relation with him in the past which still animates the present" (p. 244). Would that this quality of judgement and expression was sustained! Knowland can descend to the vulgar in an effort to be witty as when he refers to Swift as an "intellectual corner-boy" (p. 183) or remarks that *The Player Queen* shows Yeats "blowing a raspberry at his own thought" (p. 76); elsewhere the writing can be sloppy and even downright silly as when he claims that *The Only Jealousy of Emer* is "acted out in the deeps of the mind at the point between land and sea where they meet" (p. 122). Similarly trying for the Yeats scholar is the frequent reference with quotations not to precise sources but to their use in the author's previously published *A Commentary on the Collected Plays of W. B. Yeats*. Most irritating, though, is the tone in which most of the argument is conducted which implies that the case for the theatrical viability of Yeats's plays still has to be made; this is to ignore a wealth of excellent recent criticism, most notably by Katharine Worth, David R. Clark and James Flannery. These names appear in Knowland's bibliography of sources but their work seems to have had scant impact on the shaping of this study.

An Evening of Four Yeats Plays at the Peacock Theatre, Dublin, Opening on Monday 18 June 1984

Richard Allen Cave

It was a tall order facing Raymond Yeates in being invited to direct an evening of Yeats's plays at the Peacock Theatre that linked three of the dance dramas with the ever-popular *Cathleen Ni Houlihan*. On completing *The Cat and the Moon* Yeats had envisaged that it might be performed as an interlude in the manner of the Japanese Kyogen between two of his more ritualistic pieces such as *At The Hawk's Well* and *The Dreaming of the Bones*. But these three works have a common root in Yeats's fascination for styles of Japanese theatre; *Cathleen Ni Houlihan* belongs to a different tradition – a comic realism that Yeats steadily transforms into the symbolic. The director's success lay in seeing that each of the four plays is about a moment when character is transcended and a larger definition of the self emerges; and he drew our attention to this inner theme of the patterning of chance and choice that goes to the making of an identity by staging the plays in a manner that grew increasingly stylised and theatrical. Yeats asks for masks and mask-like make-up for his performers in the dance plays and Raymond Yeates chose to make this concern with the face as the index of identity the point of unity between all four plays: what the evening sought to define were the faces of Ireland.

We began with a powerfully allusive setting by Frank Hallinan Flood: a ramped stage marked out in concentric circles (portions of these were in perspex to allow for lighting beneath the actors which made for a particularly eerie ascent of the mountain in *The Dreaming of the Bones* as the turning figures seemed enveloped in vast, spectral shadows). About this structure, taut overlapping strips of gauze were hung, so that they seemed to shape a cross-section of a cone. In plastic terms Flood had realised Yeats's conception of the intersecting of the gyres at the point of tension, transition and change, when the pattern of destiny, be it historical or personal, momentarily shifts its course. From the pre-dominantly blue shadows the Musicians emerged – three women, their heads shaved bare, their faces whitened and impassive, ageless; as they turned their heads, the same faces – masks – stared out, Janus-like, from behind (the image called to mind, consciously or not, was of Shaw's all-seeing She-Ancients in *As Far As Thought Can Reach*). Throughout the plays they were to retain the note of authority as if the guardians and celebrants of some mystery; finally the Second and Third Musicians were to invest the First with the robe and mask of Cathleen Ni Houlihan ritually before our eyes to create for her that identity, the archetypal mistress of transformations, the old woman who is yet a young girl and she "with the walk of a queen". And it was with words from *Cathleen Ni Houlihan* that the performance began: as the women moved into the gestures of a ritual, a voice was heard intoning Cathleen's last song: "They shall be remembered for ever" – an apt introduction to Cuchulain's quest for immortality which is the subject of the first play *At the Hawk's Well*.

This, the most frequently performed of the *Plays for Dancers*, received the most orthodox treatment, with gold-painted masks and heroic costumes. Only the Old Man, his face heavily veiled, seemed of a different mould, cowering away from the light and Cuchulain's challenging stance as if dreading the dimension of reality the Young Man represented. The climactic moment of their encounter came with Cuchulain's searching and insistent question: "And who are you who rail / Upon those dancers that all others bless?" Impetuously tearing aside the Old Man's veiling when the only answer was silence, Cuchulain looked on a ravaged mask of himself, furrowed, dejected but recognisably the self he would become were he to pursue his ambition for an easy immortality free of the pain of daring. The hero's fearlessness was defined as a transcending of his care-worn, mortal self (Yeats seeing a revival of *On Baile's Strand* at the Abbey in 1938 was significantly to describe Cuchulain as a heroic figure because "he was creative joy separated from fear"). Yet the moment brought with it the recognition that such a choice had its cost: not for Cuchulain would there be a comfortable old age relieved by common pleasures – "human faces, / Familiar memories". The audacity of the choice (in the sense of Cuchulain's renunciation of normal human values and fears) made more startling his ensuing struggle to tame the hawk-woman to his will: the new-found identity had met its chance to prove its heroic status against a challenger of aptly mythological proportions. The Old Man may try to recall Cuchulain's attention to the well and the lost waters, but his concern is momentary, for this is no time to mourn; the hawk's cry has summoned Aoife's troop and Cuchulain's senses are attuned only to the thrill of battle. His departure is a confident assertion of his chosen self: "He comes! Cuchulain, son of Sualtim, comes!" Given the director's interpretation of the play with its stress on the hero's renunciation of human frailty and limitation, that depersonalised pronoun – "he" – carried an astonishing resonance, at once triumphant and awesome. As the characters withdrew from the stage and the women again entered their ritual, the intoning voice was now heard repeating Cathleen Ni Houlihan's song, "Do not make a great keening / When the graves have been dug tomorrow". Heroism, as the dance-play had shown, is its own reward and death a constantly-sought challenge to the extent that the eventual demise falls quite beyond the scope of conventional emotional responses: "They will have no need of prayers."

That idea of self-sufficiency proved a fitting introduction to *The Cat and The Moon* and the Lame Man's discovery of what it is to be "blessed". It was a vastly different world that the women conjured forth this time: the costumes were not naturalistic but the baggy, loudly patterned apparel of clowns. Rough but ingratiating rogues, Lame Man and Blind Man began their verbal sparring, calling vividly to mind the caricature Stage Irishman of tradition with the quick wits, face and posture of the fool. Establishing this travesty of a face of Ireland throughout the opening dialogue on the attraction of opposing temperaments to each other gave a surprising momentum to the advent of miracle: the conventional type-figure of the Stage Irishman does not normally encompass a capacity for religious commitment or for vision. While the miracle hardens the materialism of the Blind Man, in the Lame Man it releases a new dimension of being – the quick-wittedness is transformed into insight, the ingratiating into reverence, the knockabout into the ordered ritual of dance. The profane has magically opened out into the sacred and piety is revealed as the hidden essence of the Lame Man's temperament. Belief softens the contours of his face and invests the fool with dignity: in the visionary he has found himself. And we cannot mock or continue to take a patronising stance: he is not "cracked" but "blessed" in being *touched*.

One of the remarkable features of the production was the speed with which the action unfolded in each of the plays (the whole performance lasted little more than seventy-five minutes). Directors tend to aim for a hieratic mood with the dance plays inducing in characters and audience alike a vein of "excited reverie", but Raymond Yeates's approach, keeping the women's ritual and the play with masks and faces constantly in our minds, allowed for a different kind of intensity, one marked more by urgency than contemplation. This became especially true with *The Dreaming of the Bones*, where an elegiac lyricism was eschewed in preference for an attention to the surging rhythms of the verse which brought to the performance a driving force that made very real the Young Man's anxiety to traverse the mountain and find refuge by dawn and equally the ghosts' anxiety to find forgiveness and a different rest. This night on a bare mountain brought into confrontation two orders of perturbed spirits. The actors' focussing on the charged rhythm brought the desperation of the characters to find refuge from their inner turmoil to a pitch where their senses were at the quick of attention. Sights, sounds, nuances of feeling brought immediate responses as if the characters were living at their very nerve-ends. The intensity was heightened further by the decision to play with a kind of *mezza voce*, clamping down but not suppressing feeling – the Young Man dreads discovery of his whereabouts; the ghosts fear discovery too but must risk it to find release. The mode of production beautifully defined the intricate emotional structure of the play – the great wave of hope that propels all three characters onward and the gathering undercurrents of despair at the intuitive awareness that this is not the time nor the place where they will each find freedom.

It has often been argued that the Young Man's lack of a mask conveys the effect in performance that he is devoid of the heroic stature necessary to act independently of the way history has sought to condition his responses and to find in himself the means to forgive and so break the cycles of deterministic fate.

This production offered an alternative interpretation. The ghosts were not masked, but had whitened faces, painted only with a single, stylised tear; with costumes that, though threadbare and torn, carried suggestion of a pierrot's attire, the effect was of two faded images of pathos, wan and sentimental, embodiments of a dangerous self-pity. The temptation they afforded was a subtle emotional blackmail, appealing to the Young Man's sense of gratitude for kindnesses received, to his care for the distressed and benighted, to his fundamental humanity. To resist them he had to call on the race memory, a centuries-old pride in the nation's power to subdue the urge to place the personal before the patriotic. It was in embracing the national heritage that the Young Man found a new freedom and assurance, as if renewing a conviction sapped by the defeat of the Easter Rising to which he has recently been committed. The face lost its mesmerised, numbed look and the voice found natural timbres again in cursing Diarmuid and Dervorgilla, the architects of Ireland's continuing pain. The rebel, the champion of freedom was born anew, his clear-toned anger cutting a way straight through the toils and nets of despair that had beset him. Resisting the lure of doubt and self-pity had strengthened conviction. The figure that entered the action as little more than a frightened animal left it with the daring and resolute tread of manhood, having accepted the full burden of what it is to be Irish. And the ghosts, who, though they had till now addressed him, had never once looked at him but had sustained an infatuated gaze at each other (except when memory of the curse upon them turned their faces aside in shame), seemed positively driven from the stage by the firmness of his resolve that they should have no claim upon his sympathies. The play as Yeates directed it became not a study of defeat and self-betrayal but a rite of passage, centring on an act of choice which determines a man's future identity. Far from being elegaic, the performance was both frightening and exhilarating. It was apt that Cathleen's words, "If any one would give me help he must give me himself, he must give me all", provided the bridge between *The Dreaming of the Bones* and *Cathleen Ni Houlihan*.

By now a pattern had begun to emerge: the doubling of parts amongst the small cast – Cuchulain, the Young Man and later Michael Gillane (Maeloiosa Stafford); the Old Man with the Blind Beggar (Vincent O'Neill): Hawk Woman and Dervorgilla (Brid Ni Neachtain) – set up thematic parallels and resonances between the plays. All the dance-dramas demand a pared-down, stylised mode of performance and the stylisation as imitated by Yeats from the Japanese requires an extreme depersonalising of the actors involved; method and theme (the loss of self that accompanies the quest for identity) had found in this production a truly organic relationship. What was unexpected was that the director would reserve for *Cathleen Ni Houlihan* his severest exercise in stylisation yet. Cathleen's very dialogue stresses the timelessness of the play's central action, her wooing of Michael to Ireland's cause; placed as the climax of the evening's performance, the director was also stressing its representative symbolic quality as capturing an archetypal movement of the Irish conscious-ness in the conflict between self and soul. The original scheme had been to stage

Cathleen Ni Houlihan as a puppet-play, but rehearsal-time hardly allowed scope for the actors to master so demanding an art. The compromise was, if anything, more telling. The actors, clad from head to toe in black like stage-assistants in Chinese opera or Bunraku, carried aloft on their hands not puppets but life-size, detailed, naturalistic masks; with the entire source of lighting sharply angled from below and directed at these 'faces', the performers were quite eliminated from view. The dialogue was spoken naturally while the 'faces' dipped and turned animatedly in their chatter about the wedding clothes and the dowry. When the group parted to admit the Old Woman, she was the only full figure to be seen but she wore a mask denoting a face ravaged by age and sorrow. On her speaking apart with Michael however, the voice was of a sudden seductively young and vibrant. The process of transformation had begun. At the moment of commitment when Michael chooses to give his all, the actor tore aside the velvet hood to expose his own face, the eyes ablaze with conviction. It was the one genuinely human face in view, the one face where the eyes were not fixed and painted but alive with the tensions of fear and daring. Cuchulain, the Lame Man, the Young Soldier had each risked and found courage in the act of choice; now the momentous confronted Michael Gillane. It was such a simple effect, overtly theatrical; yet the whole production had worked to invest that gesture with profound symbolic meaning. Living in a "motley" world of puppet mentalities, a man had been visited by intimations of a richer mode of being and in pledging himself wholeheartedly to that way of life and its possibilities, fearless of whatever might be the cost, he had won access to a full humanity. That the First Musician, the Saint and Cathleen were played by the one actress (Maire O'Neill) carried the argument from the private sphere of reference to the public and national: the plays delineated the ideal aspects of the Irish consciousness, when the heroic spirit manifests itself.

This was a promising debut with Yeats's plays for the director who imposed his own cogent theatrical imagery on the sequence of plays to give them an artistic and psychological unity while scrupulously respecting the integrity of each individual work. His success came perhaps as a consequence of his discretion in selecting his primal images from the corpus of Yeats's preferred symbols – mask, puppet, the gyres. The production was rewarding because the direction showed a profound critical engagement with the texts and a sympathy with Yeats's theories of staging that recognised the value of the dramatist's passion for discipline and stylisation while never becoming merely derivative. On leaving the theatre one could not but recall Yeats's soul-searching in "The Man and The Echo":

> I lie awake night after night
> And never get the answers right.
> Did that play of mine send out
> Certain men the English shot?

Given such a performance, one could indeed appreciate Yeats's anxiety. And that is a fitting tribute to the excellence of Raymond Yeates's achievement.

Bramsbäck, Birgit, *Folklore and W. B. Yeats: the Function of Folklore Elements in Three Early Plays* (Uppsala: Acta Universitatis Upsaliensis, *Studia Anglistica Upsaliensia*, 51, 1984) pp. 178.

Genevieve Brennan

This monograph concerns itself with folklore elements in *The Countess Cathleen*, *The Land of Heart's Desire* and *The Shadowy Waters*. It covers traditional stories underlying these works, motifs common to all three, such as the use of the "Celtic Otherworld" and folkloric and legendary material pertaining to animals. The importance of folk music and poetry is also considered. The work is densely packed with references to source materials and should help to revive interest in this area of Yeats's concerns: in her preface, Professor Bramsbäck deplores the lack of interest in this aspect of Yeats's work; yet it is perhaps the very richness of folklore materials that inhibits research.

The way in which, at times, I tend to differ from Professor Bramsbäck in identifying sources is evidence of this richness. In her discussion of

> There have been women that bid men to rob
> Crowns from the Country-under-Wave or apples
> Upon a dragon-guarded hill . . . (*VPl* 91)

she seeks to identify these "vague allusions to myths and tales": "Crowns from the Country-under-Wave" she isolates as a somewhat garbled reference to the tale of Nera in the Underworld; she sees the dragon-guarded apples as an allusion to the apples of the Hesperides and concludes that this "myth has spread to many folk tales". Indeed it has: one of the tasks laid upon the Sons of Tuireann by Lūgh is to fetch three of the apples of the Hesperides. The most likely source for the first allusion is "The Three Crowns" from *Legendary Fictions of the Irish Celts*: in this tale we find a country which lies under a lake and is identified as Tir-na-nog; the hero of the tale wins his princess's hand by bringing a crown from the underworld. As he returns in the guise of a beggar, the Countess Cathleen's earlier speech, which refers to "old tales" in which "Queens have wed shepherds and kings beggar-maids" (*VPl* 89), is also pertinent. Bramsbäck points to the "mood of mystery" created by these allusions. I believe it comes from the fusion of such disparate elements. When Cathleen initially refers to the "old tales" she is evoking the optimistic world of the fairy tale, with its

247

domesticated supernatural; when she moves to the "dragon-guarded hill", she evokes the "unintelligible mysteries" (*E&I* 186) of a tragic myth, in which, though all debts are paid, redemption is only won by death.

Professor Bramsbäck includes a well researched section on "Bird Lore and Associated Beliefs in the Three Plays". Here and elsewhere in the monograph I felt that she might have been more helpful to those readers who are not folklorists. In her interesting discussion of the Fairy Child's revelation of her age by reference to the "eagle-cock" who is "the oldest thing under the moon" (*VPl* 203): she could have reminded her readers of more common examples of this formula. Yeats anthologised "The Brewery of Egg-Shells" (*Irish Fairy and Folk Tales*) in which the changeling says "I'm fifteen hundred years in the world": European versions use variants of the formula "I am older than the woods"; Yeats transforms this motif, eliminating the grotesque and introducing, as Professor Bramsbäck shows, a nobler, legendary element.

Noting that "a good deal still remains to be written" about the folkloric content of Yeats's work, Professor Bramsbäck warns that "to neglect the role of folklore in Yeats's work would be to deprive it of one of its greatest mysteries". The director of his plays in the theatre and the reader alike are challenged by her careful attention to the "mystery" of folkloric texture under the verbal surface of his plays.

LETTERS AND CRITICAL STUDIES

Norbert K. Buchta, *Rezeption und ästhetische Verarbeitung romantischer Poetologie im lyrischen Werk William Butler Yeats'* (Königstein, Germany: Forum Academicum, 1982) pp. v + 276.

K. P. S. Jochum

Buchta's book on the reflection and aesthetic assimilation of romantic poetology in Yeats's poetry consists of three long chapters. The first chapter discusses "backgrounds, connections, and patterns of experience"; in the second Buchta defines romanticism on the basis of the efforts of Frye, Langbaum, Rodman, and Wasserman and analyzes the idea of imagination in the works of Wordsworth, Coleridge, Shelley, and Keats; the third comes in two parts, one concerned with Yeats's "critical" prose and the other with some poems. The book's central thesis appears to be that Yeats was not only deeply influenced by the English romantic poets but that his whole outlook on life, society, and art was essentially romantic. This is true not only of his early derivative poems but generally of his entire work.

Yeats's problem, according to Buchta, was the incompatibility of romantic poetics with his own social reality. Yeats was out of tune with his time, unable to become a "contemporary" poet aware of the historical processes that had led to the present social conditions. A few quotations in translation will show the gist of the argument: "Yeats does not understand that the basis of the romantic concept of imagination, the belief in individuality as formerly maintained and carried to its extreme, was destroyed in the historical process, precisely because the historical development ran counter to its own ideology. Yeats's explanation, 'Confusion fell upon our thought,' reveals that the egocentric view of the imaginatively gifted individual. . . . does not correspond to anything in real life" (p. 214). "Easter 1916" is considered to be a "beautiful" poem, "but it is also, when measured against its subject matter, an empty poem because it attempts to understand real social phenomena from the romantic point of view of the private imagination, does not succeed, and offers instead compensatory magic of style" (p. 208).

These quotations should suffice to demonstrate Buchta's ideological concerns. He belongs to those critics who ask of a poet that he should justify his works to the society of which he is a part. Whether this will, of necessity, produce good poetry is a question which Buchta does not consider. He notes with approval that Ruskin engaged in economical analyses; to do something similar was out of Yeats's reach because it "would have transended Yeats's . . . purely aesthetic perspective" (p. 25). One is reminded of Pound who also wrote about economics; it did not always enhance his poetry. Elsewhere Buchta is less severe. He says that the last romantics failed by and large, but in an instructive way. "Defeat" and "disability", which result from the discrepancy between traditional literary forms and a reality that has developed away from them, are not terms of devastating criticism; instead they describe a specific quality of modern literature (p. 68). It seems to me that here and elsewhere Buchta cannot make up his mind whether to give way to his political thinking or whether to preserve his admiration for Yeats's poetry.

Buchta's difficulties, the impossibility to align his interpretative bias with Yeats's recalcitrant poetry, become all too apparent in the tortuous prose in which he presents his findings. The following unlovely passage is a fairly representative example: "Yeats, the private man, is incapable of identifying himself with what can also be discerned in his publications as writer and poet as an attempt that could not be brought to an end: to find a meaningful and valid logic which would render comprehensible his own historico-sociological status, inclusive of larger historical dimensions, and would provide, at least in a rudimentary way, the instruments with which to propel this status historically effectfully and according to an original ethical and moral intuition towards humanitarian progress" (p. 62). Now this is plainly wrong. Yeats was intelligent enough to know his position in contemporary society very well indeed. He was also capable of recognizing the historical events that had led to his somewhat anomalous position in Irish society. It is quite a different matter to say that Yeats's political choices, public, private, and poetical, did not coincide with the general opinion. But how should one define "humanitarian progress" in the Ireland of the early years of this century?

Buchta has a point when he notes the clichés, the empty phrases, the stillborn myths that can be found in Yeats's less successful poems and when he attributes them to an outmoded romanticism. He should have continued with this kind of investigation, yet as it is the book is unbalanced. Its title promises a thorough treatment of Yeats's poetry, but this is not what the reader gets. Buchta discusses, with notable intelligence and discrimination, "Politics", the last three stanzas of "Cuchulain Comforted", "The Lake Isle of Innisfree", "Easter 1916", "The Circus Animals' Desertion", "Long-legged Fly", parts of "Under Ben Bulben", and, more cursorily, a few other poems. All of this takes place on about 40 of more than 200 pages, and this is simply not enough. Other complaints have to be made. The first chapter, which in my opinion should prepare the argument, is full of conclusions, usually of the critical variety shown above, so that the reader feels hemmed in by circular reasoning when he has reached the last pages. The proofreading leaves much to be desired, especially in those very long sentences in which Buchta tries to define his own approach (see, e.g. p. 47).

Still, with all its imperfections, the book is not easily put aside. It points out the necessity to deal comprehensively with Yeats's romanticism in order to balance the more positive interpretations given by Bornstein (whose *Transformations of Romanticism*, published in 1976, Buchta inexplicably does not take into account) and others. Frequently Buchta makes one think that he could have done so with a much reduced ideological apparatus and more attention to Yeats's poems.

Alan Himber (ed.), *The Letters of John Quinn to William Butler Yeats* (Ann Arbor, Michigan: UMI Research Press, 1983) pp. xiii + 302.

James Pethica

As patron and above all as collector, the New York lawyer John Quinn became friend or helper to many of the major artists and writers of his time. B. L. Reid's Pulitzer Prize-winning biography, *The Man from New York: John Quinn and His Friends*, introduced him as a man of remarkable personal energy who, although an artist manqué himself, was a significant figure as "hodman to genius". In the process of acquiring his notable collection of art and literary manuscripts – which included the drafts of *The Waste Land*, *Ulysses*, much by W. B. Yeats and almost all of Conrad's writings – Quinn maintained a lively correspondence with those whose work he admired and owned. His enthusiasm and support for the cause of modern art won him appreciation from those he helped as more than a mere source of finance. "A great age of painting, a renaissance in the arts, comes when there are a few patrons who back their own flair and who buy from unrecognized men", Ezra Pound wrote to him, "If you can hammer this into a few more collectors you will bring on another cinquecento."

Of Irish extraction himself, Quinn's most sustained involvement in literary affairs began in 1902, when in the course of just one week's visit to Ireland he managed to meet and impress almost all the important figures of its burgeoning literary movement. He quickly made his presence felt by vigorously purchasing or commissioning numerous paintings by John and Jack B. Yeats, and in the company of the younger artist travelled to Co. Galway to be introduced to W. B. Yeats, Lady Gregory, Douglas Hyde and others. Recognizing a potential helper, Lady Gregory invited Quinn to Coole, along with Yeats and Hyde, and thus he found himself almost at once at the heart of Irish literary and cultural activism. The visit impressed Quinn deeply, and he revelled in the creative atmosphere at Coole and nights of conversation "about everything and everybody under the sky of Ireland, but chiefly about the theater of which Yeats's mind was full". By the end of his stay Quinn had been willingly enlisted as informal agent for Yeats and his friends in America.

The ninety-one letters from Quinn to W. B. Yeats which comprise this edition confirm the substantial range of his work on Yeats's behalf between 1902 and 1924. Besides arranging Yeats's American copyrights, organizing his lucrative lecture tour of 1903–4, acting as legal advisor, publicist and financial representative, Quinn also shouldered responsibility for the recalcitrant John B. Yeats, who came to New York in 1907 and spent his remaining years out-manoeuvring attempts to get him to return to Dublin. The letters themselves, however, are a disappointment. Alan Himber asserts in his preface that they "merit our attention primarily for the insight they give into Yeats's life and career," but the entire correspondence, of which ten letters were included in *Letters to W. B. Yeats* in 1977, adds little new to the established picture of Yeats's work.

The weakness of the letters stems partly from Quinn's utilitarian style. "Driven" (as he put it) by the pressures of his legal work and a multiplicity of demands made on him for artistic and other causes, Quinn was a man pressed for time. His letters to Yeats, dictated at speed, often resemble briefs, with points numbered or topics grouped under headings, such as "Re Your Father" or "Your memoirs". Treating matters from American royalties to such minutiae as Yeats's laundry arrangements while lecturing, their concern is dominantly of business affairs, and the personal dimension which might have been of most interest in such a correspondence is sadly submerged. A letter of 1921 detailing Quinn's exertions in care of the ailing Yeats père (and filled with grievances at his burden) is typical, with Quinn only remembering at the end of several pages to congratulate the poet on the birth of his son.

Quinn was aware of his epistolary failings. "You must overlook any jerkiness in the style of this letter or other faults" he writes at one point with a self-deprecation repeated in other letters. Yet his repetitive and often rambling style is perhaps as much a symptom as cause of the weakness of the correspondence; for with Quinn's self-conscious recognition of his deficiencies came an obvious timidity in broaching artistic matters with Yeats. His brief voicing of doubts over some revised lines in *The Shadowy Waters* is a telling example: "I can't make any rhythm out of these lines and they break the mood that the rest of the play brings on one. But you know and I don't." Again in a later letter we see the same apologetic reflex following a suggestion of minor stylistic changes for Yeats's memoirs: "You will probably think I am damned impertinent or cheeky to write all these things." Quinn's letters show many signs of an insecurity understandable in the artist manqué dealing with his peers, but also the insecurity of a man too frequently put upon by those he has helped to be entirely sure of his own worth. "One hates to feel that one is a friend only because one is useful or helps the other" he laments in one letter, impatient at being taken for granted by Arthur Symons. Nonetheless, perhaps in compensation for his artistic self-effacement, it is his utility and business prowess which Quinn most often stresses to Yeats.

His comparative reticence on personal and artistic matters in the letters is doubly unfortunate, then; partly in limiting the value of the correspondence to Yeatsian scholars, but also in presenting the writer as a somewhat one-dimensional figure, absorbed by business concerns. While the splenetic, "driven" Quinn is in evidence, railing variously against pacifists, politicians, Jews or, in his enduring love-hate relationship with Ireland, against the priest-ridden "pathriots" who so frequently burdened him with their expectations of help; the collector who was capable of brave critical judgements, and opinions sufficiently sanguine to earn thanks from Conrad, for one, for "the friendliness, the interest, and the wisdom" of his letters, is but fleetingly apparent here. So too, because of a five year hiatus in his friendship with Yeats following a misunderstanding in 1909, and because of the infrequence of their correspondence in Quinn's last years, there is but passing evidence of his finest hours, defending *The Playboy of the Western World* against obscenity charges in Chicago in 1912, or *Ulysses* in the *Little Review* court case of 1921. Indeed, rather than allowing him to reflect upon his artistic involvements, the letter form seems to have been for Quinn an opportunity to release some of the pressure in which he worked. The harrassed letters of his last years are a particularly sad record of decline: "I have had to squelch Pound for about the sixteenth time for unloading things on me" . . . "I am in no mood to have your father on my back again. I have had quite enough of him, in all fairness."

The edition, copiously footnoted, strikes a good balance between brevity in identifying peripheral figures and inclusiveness where external facts are necessary. Providing a complete record of Quinn's side of a substantial correspondence, it will be of most value when publication of Yeats's letters in their entirety allows a fuller appreciation of this uneven and rather functional friendship-at-a-distance. In being presented too-exclusively for its Yeatsian interest, however, the volume gives little suggestion of the wider context of the relationship, and lacks a depth which reference to Quinn's other correspondence – with John B. Yeats and Lady Gregory in particular – might have given.

Ann Saddlemyer (ed.), *The Collected Letters of John Millington Synge* 2 vols (Oxford: Clarendon Press, 1983, 1984) pp. 385 and 270.

Genevieve Brennan

We have in Ann Saddlemyer's edition of Synge's letters, the corrective to the "quasi-romantic, innocent and naive primitive" created by his friends and contemporaries. It is not possible for a collection of letters, deriving as Professor Saddlemyer explains, from an incomplete and distorted archive, to provide a portrait of the *whole* man: but here at last we have the *actual* man. The earliest letters have been reconstructed by Professor Saddlemyer, from drafts in his notebooks. No letters from Synge to Yeats survive before 1905: nine years of friendship thus go unrecorded, although Yeats's side of the correspondence has survived from 1898 onwards. Distortions were also deliberately effected: MacKenna, for example, censored, indeed vandalised, Synge's letters to him, limiting the documentation of what Yeats called the "brutal and outrageous" side of Synge. Fortunately MacKenna did not suppress Synge's story of the Abbey charwoman's account of him, "bloody old snot", although a subsequent page of this letter has been completely inked out by MacKenna, who comments "Some highly personal criticism of harmless and obscure people."

These *lacunae* produce an imbalance, given that the correspondence most fully preserved is that with Molly Allgood. The Synge who emerges is very human, though not always attractive. Rarely has the paradox of life and work been so fully expressed: the creator of Pegeen Mike and Nora Burke pleads with Molly Allgood not to allow an innocuous young man to teach her to ride a bicycle, nor to walk arm in arm with an actor, nor to allow medical students to talk to her in the Green Room. In a letter written after his mother's death, Synge refers to "People like Yeats who sneer at old fashioned goodness and steadiness in women." Here Professor Saddlemyer's annotations are most helpful: she quotes from an unpublished memoir by J. M. Kerrigan; "for a man of his experience and literary attitude to life [he was] *extraordinarily conventional*. He met me one day on the Dublin mountains linking a girl & was amazed to learn that I was not engaged to her". When Molly Allgood was finally admitted to Glendalough House he reminded her to "give a nice little double knock at the door": Professor Saddlemyer, in an excellent footnote, reminds *us* that ladies were taught to give double knocks to distinguish themselves from tradesmen and servants, thus economically directing our attention to Synge's social anxiety *vis-à-vis* Molly

Allgood. Self-pity plays a large part in his letters to her: at one point Synge apologises for this "whingeing" and later for his "selfpitiful" attitude. Yeats placed Synge at Phase 23, where the False Mask is Self-pity: yet when he writes to Molly Allgood during the Playboy riots, sick in bed, a more heroic figure emerges, closer to Yeats's stoical Synge; "You dont know how much I admire the way you are playing P. Mike in spite of all the row."

Professor Saddlemyer's annotation to material relating to Synge's private life and "Theatre business" is excellent. Annotation seems less consistent when it deals with certain literary or cultural references. Thus, when Molly Allgood goes to Glasgow in 1907, Synge urges her to see both a Rossetti and a Millet: the latter is glossed and two paintings by Millet are identified as being in the Glasgow Art Gallery at that time. The former reference is not glossed: the Rossetti was most likely to have been exhibited at the Royal Glasgow Institute of Fine Art in Sauchiehall Street; "The Bower Meadow" had been exhibited there in 1905. This, of course, still leaves us with the problem of Synge's *interest* in Rossetti; was it personal or merely casual, part of a desire to "improve" Molly Allgood? We do not know, because Synge died *aet*. 37, leaving insufficient documentation of his tastes and Professor Saddlemyer has been hampered by such *lacunae* throughout her task. Synge in 1906 urges Molly Allgood to read "your Arthur". Professor Saddlemyer identifies this as an edition of Malory and refers us to Synge's notebooks, but does not attempt to specify further. Given that Synge later refers to a "second volume" it seems possible that he had given her Ernest Rhys's two volume modern spelling *Le Morte D'Arthur*, which had come out in Everyman in February of that year. Here there is no doubt as to Synge's interest in Malory, his notebook entry and the letters themselves make this clear; "wild beautiful things like the beauty of the world". Professor Saddlemyer clearly decided not to annotate the folk lore background to *The Shadow of the Glen*: in her introduction to "1905" she refers us to Yeats's part in the controversy, available in *UP2*, but does not seek to annotate further Synge's assertion that the story he used was essentially different from any other version known to him. Yet there are many folk versions which resemble Synge's tale, rather than "The Widow of Ephesus", in that the husband merely pretends to be dead, to test his wife. Synge's presentation of folk tales in the *New Ireland Review* does not suggest an unsophisticated attitude to such materials.

As I have already pointed out, Professor Saddlemyer's annotation is at its best when dealing with Synge's private life and with "Theatre business": here her use of unpublished materials is exemplary. In a letter of January 1908, Synge tells Molly Allgood "Poor Yeats with his bad sight and everything is very helpless, and I have to look after him a bit". Professor Saddlemyer quotes a letter of MacKenna's which suggests a rather different picture; "[Synge] had . . . a curious admiration for Yeats on the practical side of things; he once said Yeats is a genius in bossing carpenters . . . S. pined for these powers." When we move to Synge's illness, the use of family mss. is extraordinarily effective, with Mrs Synge's letters providing a grim counterpoint to Synge's. In a letter to Yeats of April 1908, Synge remarks, quite casually, that he has a "nasty lump" in his side:

the footnote gives Mrs Synge's account "he had been getting steadily worse and lying awake till 3 with pains in his stomach . . . there is a small lump somewhere in his side". In May of that year he writes a brave, optimistic letter to Molly Allgood from the Elphis Nursing Home: "Dont be uneasy about me, I think I am over the worst now, but I have to stay very quiet indeed": Professor Saddlemyer annotates this with two letters by Mrs Synge; "Ball had no hope of our dear boy's life . . . the tumour or abscess is still there as it cannot be removed. . . . He has no idea he was in danger – the Drs. hid it from him completely."

Gloria C. Kline, *The Last Courtly Lover: Yeats and the Idea of Woman* (Ann Arbor, Michigan: UMI Research Press; Epping: Bowker Publishing Co., 1983) pp. 199.

Karen Dorn

"Knights, dragons and beautiful ladies" – W. B. Yeats's boyhood interest and indeed lifelong fascination with the literature of courtly love is the subject of Gloria C. Kline's study, *The Last Courtly Lover: Yeats and the Idea of Woman*. Offering a combination of literary criticism and biography, Dr Kline traces the transformation of a key cluster of images from the courtly love tradition: the knight, the lady, the troubadour, the witch, the mirror and the walled garden. Dr Kline's central concern is to give a feminist reading of the central unifying image of woman, or as she calls it, the "idea" of woman in Yeats's work and life. The sections of literary criticism are interspersed in part with an account of "the course of his great affair" with Maud Gonne, whom Dr Kline clearly admires and who emerges as a heroine. There are also accounts of his marriage and his friendships with Lady Gregory, Katharine Tynan, Olivia Shakespear, Florence Farr, Margot Ruddock and Dorothy Wellesley. These principal characters are further illustrated by a section of photographs.

This combination of literary criticism and biography is intended to illustrate the ways in which images drawn from the realm of the imagination can be seen to inform and shape our ordinary lives. Yeats's own life, seen in this light, becomes a type or representation of the radical changes in social and sexual behaviour which took place during his lifetime. Indeed Yeats is seen by Dr Kline as an example of Harry Slochower's notion of the mythopoet, a poet who re-creates the ideals of a "decaying social structure" and in so doing, offers a *critique* of "existing social norms" and points towards a new order (p. 1).

There is an illuminating account of the influential books that Yeats's father read to his son: *The Lays of Ancient Rome*, tales from Shakespeare, Chaucer and Balzac, Hans Christian Anderson, Sir Walter Scott, Rossetti, Blake, Shelley, Byron and William Morris. Here was more than ample material to encourage an interest in the characters and adventures of the courtly love tradition, and in particular, the image of the ideal woman as a source of inspiration. While Dr Kline has many stringent criticisms of Yeats's "attitude" towards women, she gives strong praise for his acceptance, especially as it appears in the late poems and plays, of the dual presence in women of the masculine and feminine aspects of personality. There is some contradiction though in her argument that on the one hand Yeats always acknowledged these complementary aspects of personality while on the other hand he achieved this understanding only after a lifetime of misguided idealism and personal failure.

This is an interesting and timely subject, of concern both to feminist critics and to a general public increasingly interested in the possible effects of the portrayal of men and women on television and in the cinema. Dr Kline marshalls support from anthropologists and psychologists for her view that the image of the ideal woman as found in the courtly love tradition is an image of confinement, an expression only of the man's "unity of being" and "unity of culture". As in all chivalric quests, however, there are obstacles that thwart the path, not least of which appears in the discussion of nineteenth century "middle class sexual attitudes" and "life-styles". Dr Kline sees these as determined by stereotypes of the ideal man and woman, but what would an anthropologist, or for that matter a psychoanalyst, make of an analysis of sexual attitudes and life-styles that is based upon evidence taken from literature, correspondence or autobiography? Surely this type of evidence, while not unrelated to ordinary behaviour, raises as many questions as it appears to offer answers.

Dr Kline is on firmer ground when she discusses the transformation throughout Yeats's work of those key images: the knight, the lady, the witch, the troubadour, the mirror and the enclosed garden. She does not manage, however, to escape the tendency to substitute paraphrase for a careful reading of the text. The result, in my view, causes some major distortions. An example appears early on in her feminist account of the historical and religious roots of the masculine and feminine types. The "objective" masculine is set against the "subjective" feminine. In Dr Kline's view, women have been forced by the traditional image of woman into accepting a passive and confining role, just as Cinderella "proves her identity . . . by having the foot that fits the Prince's slipper" (p. 32 – though any child would be quick to point out that the slipper was in fact Cinderella's). Yeats's ideas too are forced, by an unsuitable paraphrase, to fit into this feminine schema. His definition of the primary (feminine) and antithetical (masculine) dispensations in *A Vision* is interpreted as an example of the active/passive polarity. This is the point however at which the feminist map of polarities must be redrawn, for in no instance does Yeats offer passivity as the feminine ideal. His primary dispensation sets "transcendent power", not passivity, in opposition to "imminent power" (*AV[B]* 263).

Dr Kline's desire to find the aspect of passivity in Yeats's image of woman reappears to distort her interpretation of the poem, "A Prayer for my Daughter". Yeats's image of the rooted tree, taken from traditional political and religious imagery to signify organic growth, is here seen as "inseparable from complete passivity" (p. 96). Dr Kline appears to overlook the opposition in the poem between on the one hand the "soul's radical innocence" and on the other hand the mind's "arrogance and hatred": "Yeats would bring his lady in from the streets and enclose her like a tree within his garden wall" (p. 97). This misreading reappears in the summary of the book when Yeats is praised for abandoning his stance as the "patriarchal chauvinist who wants to enclose a bird-brained woman behind garden walls, praising her the more for the more of her mind that she gives up" (p. 163).

Yeats's own view of his youthful rebellion against the prevailing belief in progress would tend to support Dr Kline's judgement that he was a "reactionary" who "failed to move along with the maturing sexual concepts that began with the work of . . . his contemporaries in psychology, sociology, medicine and law" (p. 1). Yeats's interests lay not with progress, which he considered an illusion, but with the eternal recurrence of energies and emotions that might be summoned by those ideal images which feminist criticism has rejected. New images for women are emerging from the vast sea-change of education and opportunity. Feminists must surely acknowledge however that there are many uses for the image of the ideal woman. Yeats may well speak of a woman's opinionated mind peddling its wares throughout the thoroughfare of Irish politics, but he generally uses "mind" and "image" in a different sense. Dr Kline acknowledges Yeats's belief in the Anima Mundi, the "Great Memory passing from generation to generation", though she sees it only as dogma for his "new religion" (p. 30). Yet she quotes his view that "this great mind and great memory can be evoked by symbols" (*E&I* 28). Here is a use of ideal images and a spiritual dimension as yet unchallenged by current feminist debate. The gauntlet is there for the taking.

Gale C. Schricker, *A New Species of Man: the Poetic Persona of W. B. Yeats* (Lewisburg: Bucknell; London: Associated University Presses, 1983) pp. 214.

Jo Russell

Gale C. Schricker's book forms part of an extended interest in the nature of the persona as it develops through the whole of English Literature from Chaucer onwards. One might therefore suppose that she would take a disinterested line in her examination of Yeats: she proves, however, to be as thoroughly devoted as any Yeatsian. It is this devotion, however, that lends a sense of special pleading to her argument. A greater detachment might persuade more thoroughly.

Dr. Schricker's thesis is that the persona – the "I" of Yeats's work, carefully defined to exclude any "dramatis persona", can be traced as a single continuous and developing entity through all the works from *John Sherman* to "Under Ben Bulben". She postulates a Rembrandt-like series of self-portraits which are the constantly changing, but always recognisable faces of a persisting creation who is the "I", and who is and is not the poet. This interesting idea is pursued through close examination of the imaginative prose works and selections from the *Collected Poems*. Within separate chapters Dr Schricker makes close and perceptive analysis of individual uses of persona and clearly exposes the creative process in action, but it is hard to see exactly how she links them all together as a developing entity. It is not enough to say, – here they all are, see if they look alike; – similarity of features must be indicated or the reader will not be able to discern the family resemblance; and it is this indication that she fails to make.

Dr Schricker's method is sometimes disconcerting. Her competent analysis of individual works is occasionally marred by her eagerness to block up any holes in her argument. In her discussion of *Autobiographies* she is at great pains to justify Yeats's right to choose and shape the elements of his life he might seek to record, a right no one would deny him. She occasionally wrestles with objections to her own argument and subdues them by brute force rather than by logic. For instance, she observes: "Hugh Kenner has noted the influence of a transcendent poetic structure on the Yeatsian persona within a volume of poetry: '[Yeats] was an architect, not a decorator; he didn't accumulate poems, he wrote books. . . . It is a radical mistake to think of Yeats as a casual or fragmentary poet whose writings float on a current discoverable only in his biographable life'." Dr Schricker is really taking Kenner's name in vain here, since her thesis is that the persona draws a pattern out of the "current discoverable in his biographable life", whereas Kenner refutes this and concludes "we misread him [Yeats] if we suppose – that in each poem he was trying for a definitive statement of all that, at the time of composition, he was." She does the same thing with Ernest Dowson, detecting an influence on Yeats in the theories of persona contained in his work on George Eliot. She recognises, however, the objection that "Yeats did not always approve of Dowson's critical opinions" and most especially with Dowson's opinions on George Eliot. Nevertheless Yeats was (or probably was) exposed to them and ideas are of course contagious. Hard luck on a poet who has to write all possible *caveats* into his utterances.

All this gives a clue as to Dr Schricker's critical technique, which is good scientific method: postulate theory and design experiments to prove theory. The results of the experiments should be predictable if the theory is good. However the temptation is to make the results fit the thesis, or to skip stages in the argument. Dr Schricker's analysis of *A Vision* tends towards this approach and offers a dangerous conclusion: each reader interprets *A Vision* as he may and all these differences affirm the success of Yeats's venture, and take their places within the Great Wheel. There is no counter to such an argument: if *A Vision* creates a system so universal that all judgements reinforce its universality then no criticism can validly stand outside it. It is a "so-there" argument, and as such devalues Dr Schricker's otherwise respectable integration of *A Vision* into the pattern of Yeats's work.

The examination of the *Collected Poems* provides the bulk of the work and in the main Dr Schricker offers sensible readings of the poems on which she concentrates, even though sometimes she tries too hard to make a case. She strains to include the poems of *The Wind Among The Reeds* in her thesis, expressing surprise that the I-persona occurs only in one poem and there in a form which does not accord with the personalised development she postulates. She wrestles hard with this "problem" to come up with the surprising conclusion that "the poems are consequently valuable for the insights they provide into this conflict of internal and external, or objective and subject, aspects of the poetic identity.": these fine poems should mean more to her than that.

That the "scientific method" that Dr Schricker adopts tends to the undervaluing of extraneous findings, becomes clear in the examination of the *Collected Poems*, where she begins to examine the interesting relationship between the mediaeval Quest-romance and the integral structure of the *Collected Poems*. This is left tantalisingly unexplored, though it promises to lead to a possible heroic identity for the persona.

Dr Schricker's book proves, in the end, to be a respectable, adequate if inconclusive exploration of one of the back alleys of Yeatsian criticism.

Michael Steinman, *Yeats's Heroic Figures: Wilde, Parnell, Swift, Casement* (London: Macmillan, 1983) pp. 197.

Richard Burton

It is difficult to ascertain what, precisely, Michael Steinman sets out to achieve in this study. He claims, in an introduction of only two pages, that the four men of his title were the Anglo-Irish historical figures that dominated Yeats's life and art "because they resembled [his] heroic conception of himself, and in the artistic ways he chose to re-create their images" (p. 1). The four are linked by their martyrdom at the hands of the mob, and Yeats's refashioning of their images, the transcendence of history "to create heroes who were true to character, not fact", constitutes an attempt by Yeats to "understand men acting in history's drama", and so "to understand himself and the art, politics, and Ireland they shared" (p. 3). I take this to be the germ of Dr Steinman's thesis, and it is, perhaps, the sole merit of this book that if it delivers little, it promises less.

The faults of the book are too numerous to itemize, but three in particular cannot pass unremarked. The first problem is methodological. The chapters begin with the first reference in Yeats's writings to its subject, proceed in strict chronological order through (it seems) all such references, and end with the last. There is nothing particularly wrong with this approach, if handled sensitively, and, indeed, it is useful to trace the development of Yeats's response to the figures Dr Steinman has selected. It would appear, however, that the author's only guides have been the concordances and a comprehensive list of prose references. He does not seem to have trifled with Wade or Jochum, and *Yeats's Heroic Figures* reads, in parts, like a catalogue. There is little enough critical interest, and one must wonder, for instance, if it is really crucial to our perception of Yeats's response to Swift to be reminded that William Carleton was the only man of genius since the Dean to have satirized the Irish Established Church (p. 103). The failure to select material of critical import results in a swamp of citation.

The second problem is critical. The catalogue is punctuated by a sequence of assertions and assumptions that require much justification if they are to convince. Sadly, Dr Steinman does not linger over knotty issues. Can it *really* be said that "Wilde was always Yeats's first model for the artistic man" (p. 2)? I should have thought that, say, Dante, Blake, Shelley and Morris deserved at least a mention. Is *The Picture of Dorian Gray* the source of 'Easter 1916' (p. 32)? Is it true that Wilde's philosophy of art "almost conquered the British" (p. 53)? Dr

Steinman confidently concludes that the qualities Yeats "prized *most*" were "proud intellect and *heroic dalliance*" (p. 86, my italics). It might be that closer attention to the writings would have uncovered virtues more valuable to Yeats than real or alleged promiscuity, adultery and homosexuality.

The chief problem, however, and the one that infects this study most deeply, is the title. Do these four include *all* of Yeats's heroes, or is this a selection? Are they equally "heroic"? What, precisely, do we mean by "hero"? Dr Steinman sticks at these questions, and his failure to confront the essence of his thesis seriously diminishes it. I cannot see Yeats differing greatly from Carlyle's view that heroes are "the leaders of men, these great ones; the modellers, patterns, and in a wide sense creators, of whatsoever the general mass of men contrived to do or to attain" (*On Heroes, Hero-Worship, and the Heroic in History*, 1841, pp. 1–2), and I cannot see Roger Casement, for one, being comfortable in such a role. It would appear that Dr Steinman agrees with me, for the influence of that particular great Yeatsian hero is examined in an appendix of only twelve pages. Why not *Yeats's Heroic Figures: Synge, O'Leary, Blake, Mathers*, or . . . *Morris, Swedenborg, Berkeley, Shelley*? Dr Steinman does not say, but I doubt that he would have made a significantly better book even if he had.

Graham Hough *The Mystery Religion of W. B. Yeats* (Brighton: Harvester Press; New Jersey: Barnes & Noble Books, 1984) pp. 129.

James Lovic Allen

Graham Hough's short book on Yeats's religion is based largely on the Lord Northcliffe Lectures in Literature which he presented at University College London in February, 1983. As he indicates in the brief preface, dealing with Yeats's philosophical and occult interests before an audience of non-Yeatsians was an undertaking inevitably beset with problems, but he seems to have resolved or transcended most of those reasonably well. Apparently the first three chapters of the book were taken from the lectures in nearly unaltered form. The fourth chapter was written as an addendum to treat more technically some of the difficulties in both editions of *A Vision*.

If the book receives negative responses or little notice because of its "popularized" nature, that will be an unfortunate turn of events. For, in it a distinguished literary authority – now Emeritus Professor at Cambridge – takes seriously Yeats's involvements in various occult activities and relates these meaningfully to the poetic canon. Although critical attitudes towards Yeats's esoteric interests have become less derogatory since the availability of his unpublished papers on microfilm in 1976 and the publications on or editions of the poet's occult materials in recent years by George Mills Harper and others, a frank and overt acceptance like that in Hough's volume is more than overdue. Nor does Hough stoop to niggling and arguing with predecessors of different mind at any significant length. For the most part, he merely puts the facts – long deprecated, ignored, or distorted – as they should be put, usually in engaging and readily comprehensible prose. The title of his second chapter, for example, is simply "Yeats's Beliefs", suggesting as almost axiomatic an unruffled position which stands in sharp contrast, on the one hand, to Richard Ellmann's contention in *The Identity of Yeats* that the poet declined to commit himself to credal allegiance at all and, on the other hand, to critical exchanges on the subject described by Weldon Thornton as "vexed" and "highly charged" (in *Studies in the Literary Imagination*, special issue on Yeats's occult and philosophical backgrounds, 1981).

Hough's book is not entirely flawless, however. Virtually all Yeatsians are familiar with the materials presented in the chapter on beliefs, for instance, whether they agree with Hough's assessments of them or not. Similarly, the first part of chapter three is just one more in a long series of efforts to paraphrase or elucidate *A Vision* in reasonably understandable terms. And in the more technical concluding chapter on *A Vision*, Hough falls into a trap which has victimized all too many of his forerunners – a tendency to treat that late volume as though it alone constitutes an adequate articulation or delineation of Yeats's "religion", with far too few references to the extensive collection of other doctrinal prose pieces and with no allusion anywhere in the entire book to Yeats's various symbolic and thematically esoteric plays, such as *The Shadowy Waters*, *At the Hawk's Well*, *The Dreaming of the Bones*, *A Full Moon in March*, or *The Herne's Egg*.

On the brighter side, the first chapter of *The Mystery Religion of W. B. Yeats* fills a void long inadequately addressed in Yeats scholarship and criticism. In his book *The Rhizome and the Flower: The Perennial Philosophy – Yeats and Jung*, James Olney concedes that lack of time and space precluded two chapters, one each on the exoteric and the esoteric "tradition of Platonism from the fourth century B.C. down to Yeats". Even in its form tailored to an audience of non-Yeatsians, Hough's first lecture, entitled "The Occult Tradition", deals with that subject more fully and informatively than the introductory section of F. A. C. Wilson's *W. B. Yeats and Tradition*, more concisely and coherently than Virginia Moore's *The Unicorn*, and more specifically and uniformly than any of my own publications on the same and related topics. One wishes, indeed, that Professor Hough might consider developing that valuable chapter into a fully-fledged essay directed expressly to an audience of his fellow Yeatsians.

Another positive feature of Hough's examination of Yeats's heterodox religion is its recognition of the fact that there is little or no moral component involved. This point is voiced in several places. The poet's esoteric vision may be in part aesthetic, in part cosmological, and in part experiential, but it is not, to any significant extent, ethical. What Yeats seeks, Hough says quite accurately, is communion between heaven and earth, not a marriage of heaven and hell.

Finally and most importantly, in the second half of his third lecture Hough undertakes what should be ultimately the primary endeavour of any book or essay like his – an effort to relate meaningfully Yeats's occult pursuits to the body of his poetry. Generally speaking, the enterprise seems to be successful, although Hough's failure to include folk and fairy lore as part of the occult, in contrast to others like Moore, Thornton, and even Yeats himself, is a bit unsettling. The thesis is that Yeats's esoteric ventures and adventures accreted over the years, in his syncretic imagination, into a "vast design" or unified history of the soul that holds in interrelationship with each other what would otherwise be essentially discrete and independent lyric utterances. Of course, Donald Stauffer articulated a somewhat similar theory as long ago as 1949, though without emphasis upon occultism as the foundation of continuity and unity. But probably that difference in emphasis is little less than crucial. The numerous "clusters", "congeries", or "ganglions" of images and mythologems in Yeats's work identified and explicated by Stauffer, Henn, Ellmann, Melchiori, Wilson, me, and others *are almost all* drawn from one cranny or another in that great storehouse of symbology known variously as the perennial philosophy or the occult tradition, which embodies a given complex of meanings. Most of the commentators just enumerated have acknowledged as much, explicitly or implicitly, but some of them – along with many others – have boggled at the idea of Yeats's literal belief in the psychic or spiritual phenomena represented by those same esoteric emblems. Equable acceptance of such belief as a fundamental feature of Yeats's creative vision, as found in Graham Hough's study, has been long, long overdue.

Editorial Miscellany

One pleasure of compiling a miscellany such as this is that as well as reviewing what is passing or *passim*, one can occasionally cope at the last minute with what is to come. Edward O'Shea's *A Descriptive Catalog of W. B. Yeats's Library* (N.Y.: Garland Reference Library of the Humanities, 1985) reached me in page proof. Here is a research tool which will transform and strengthen whole areas of research, as well as, one imagines, simplifying life for Miss Anne Yeats, whose custodianship of Yeats's books is as helpful and informative as it must also be onerous. But from now on, scholars have not only a catalogue, but what will pass muster as an *ad hoc* marginalia for those who have at hand a good reference library. Transcriptions are offered, as is information about passages which have been marked and pages turned down.

Those who have used the library know how much they owe to those who have worked there before them. Not only to Mrs Yeats and to Miss Yeats, but to those such as the late Glenn O'Malley, and Roger Nyle Parisious, whose archival work in xeroxing marked pages and cataloguing the collection must have assisted Professor O'Shea to bring this work to completion. When this catalogue is set alongside the list of currently missing books from the "old" catalogue (see pp. 279–90 below) there is enough to keep scholars busy for years. Yeats's library, as those who have used it know, neither fulfills fantasies nor disappoints the enquirer. It is consistently challenging to preconception even when it rewards hunches.

The books and their provenance form a spiritual autobiography and, because Professor O'Shea has also included and annotated the entries for Yeats's own copies of his own books, the catalogue is indispensable for the editor of Yeats's works. Donald Torchiana's article (pp. 3–11 above) shows the kind of reading Yeats gave to his philosophical books, and his occult books will also be found to be annotated in detail. His Balzac collection shows his preoccupation with the order in which the *Comédie Humaine* should be read, even in English. While areas of his youthful reading in the British Museum will never be easy to map or to quantify, there are signs that the Nobel money went at least in part upon the purchase of old favourites he had not been able to buy as a young man.

If I could make one modest contribution to the sort of work Professor O'Shea's standard work will now inaugurate, it would be to provide the correct identification of a fugitive item, No 1649. *Prophetia et Alia*, bought by George Yeats in June 1915 and provisionally attributed to Silvestrus Mencius, is in fact the work of Silvestro Meuccio. Meuccio, of Santo Cristoforo della Pace in Venice, was an Augustinian who set out to edit the works of Joachim de Fiore, and this work is the second (1516) printing of his first Joachimist compilation *Expositio magni prophete Ioachim in librum beati Cirilli de magnis tribulationibus et statu sancto matris ecclesie*. There are several *lacunae*, in fact it is lacking the woodcuts of Abbas Joachim magnus propheta from the titlepage and it is lacking the great seven headed *draco magnus et ruffus*. Its nineteenth century owner, Count Vimercati-Sozzi, or some previous owner, has indicated inside the front cover that it has been assigned the title *Prophetia et Alia* on the spine because of the slimness of the spine and that it has been catalogued in that earlier library under the name of Telesphorus of Cosenza. Meuccio had added extra matter to a mid fifteenth century compilation by Rusticianus of Telesphorus's *Libellus . . . de causis, statu, cognitione ac fine instantis scismatis et tribulationum futurarum* (c. 1386), itself a Joachimst commentary upon a pseudo-Joachimist commentary upon the *Oraculum angelicum* attributed to Cyril the Carmelite. Layer upon layer one can peel away at a tract which, in its modern fragmentary form, comes to resemble a certain *Speculum Angelorum et Hominum*. Mrs Yeats may have been led to buy the work by reading "The Tables of the Law" which sent Joyce into Marsh's Library in quest of Joachim, but then at the time she did buy it, Yeats was busily encouraging others in the Stone Cottage circle to read his favourite occult books. Roger Nyle Parisious first directed my attention to this "quaint and curious volume of forgotten lore," one of the oldest books in the library.

La Rose Secrète (Lille: Presses Universitaires de Lille, 1984) follows *Le Crépuscule Celtique, Per Amica Silentia Lunae* and *Explorations* in the series of Yeats's works being collectively translated by the remarkable Centre de Littérature Linguistique et Civilisation des Pays de Langue Anglaise de l'Université de Caen. It is pleasing to note the use of the copy-text of the new *Variorum* edition as the basis for this translation. "Rosa Alchemica" offers the possibility of comparison with the 1898 translation by Yeats's friend Henry Davray. In a passage which differs only slightly from the copy-text here used, lines 322–42, Davray's attention to Yeats's syntax and tenses is loose: the Caen translators have been determined to reproduce Yeats's prose as closely as possible. Once or twice, however, Davray's translation seems marginally preferable. His "qui avait entrepris de lutter contre nos temps . . ." seems closer to "war upon" than "qui etait en conflit avec notre époque . . .". Both translations use "l'idée" for the "phantasy" which "possessed" the narrator: some loss of force is risked here; apparently "fantaisie" sounds "wrong" to the French ear.

In one respect the Caen translators have made a bold decision. All versions of this passage excluding the posthumous *Mythologies* utilise both "fantastic" and "phantastic" exactly in accordance with the distinction between them proposed in the *OED*. The context suggests that in line 330 ("fantastic") and line 340 ("phantastic") Yeats means "fanciful" and "visionary" respectively. (He is not wholly consistent: elsewhere in this section of the story he uses "fancy" in a manner indistinguishable from "phantasy") Davray in the lines just cited decided in favour of consistency, and opted for "fantastique" in both cases, but the

Caen translators have sought to preserve Yeats's distinction, rendering "phantastic" as "chimérique". *La Taille d'une agate et autres Essais* (Paris: Klincksieck, 1984) has an introduction by Pierre Chabert. The translation has been done by various hands at the Centre de Littérature, Linguistique et Civilisation des Pays de Langue Anglaise de l'Université de Caen under the direction of Jacqueline Genet, who has also provided the notes. The title may appear something of a misnomer to the reader familiar with *Essays and Introductions*, since it omits six of the pieces in *The Cutting of an Agate*, and includes twelve pieces from *Ideas of Good and Evil* and three from the later essays. But such a view would not reckon with the *Essais et Introductions: sélection* available from Presses Universitaires de Lille, which prior selection has obviously shaped this new one perforce. The French student is generously rewarded with Professor Genet's notes. However it must be said that Yeats's much repeated quotation from Blake "chaque moment plus bref que le battement d'une artère est egal . . . à six mille ans . . ." comes not from "The Everlasting Gospel" but from *Milton*. The sheer industry with which the French translation of Yeats is progressing is clearly a direct result of the drive and enthusiasm of Professor Genet, and French readers are greatly in her debt.

A selected Yeats is almost inevitably the student's introduction to the poet, though the *Collected Poems* in paperback now looks competitively priced. Those who encounter Yeats afresh via A. Norman Jeffares's *Poems of W. B. Yeats: a New Selection* are in for several surprises. The volume is extraordinarily generous for a selection——307 pp. of poems, an introduction, biographical summary, appendices upon Yeats's technique, Irish names and their pronunciation (helpfully supplied by Loreto Todd), maps, charts and a bibliography.

The selection at last does some justice to the narrative poems placing 30 pages from "The Wanderings of Oisin", "The Old Age of Queen Maeve" and "The Two Kings" (the last two entire) in a section devoted to "Irish Narrative Poems". Other sections include "The Craft of Poetry", "Love and Sex", "Politics and Polemics", "Idiosyncrasies and Grotesqueries" and so on – eighteen of them in all. These show Yeats's wide ranging competence by intentionally breaking up the order of his published collections, although every poem is clearly dated both as to publication and composition. Some will want to raise an eyebrow at this proceeding, but selections require renewal through such devices. It may even be interesting to see if students who confront the poems in this form for the first time are less prone to be led into biographically platitudinous responses than heretofore. One drawback is the use of the text from *The Poems a New Edition*, but such imperfections as this introduces into, e.g. "The Song of the Happy Shepherd" and "A Bronze Head" can be rectified in new printings.

Elizabeth Cullingford's Macmillan Casebook, *Yeats: Poems; 1919–1935* fills an obvious gap in the series and complements Stallworthy's well-known volume on the *Last Poems*. Its contents are more fully listed in our bibliography below (p. 325). The introduction is economical and accessible. Benedict Kiely's new introduction to the Macmillan (New York) reissue of the Colin Smythe text of *Fairy and Folk Tales of the Irish Peasantry* and *Irish Fairy Tales* under the unchanged title of *Fairy and Folk Tales of Ireland* is anecdotal in tone. The English edition with its introduction by Kathleen Raine is still in print from Picador.

Celtic Dawn: a Portrait of the Irish Literary Renaissance by Ulick O'Connor (London, Hamish Hamilton) is a popular account setting its subject within the history of modern Ireland and it is largely compiled from secondary sources. It is not a reliable guide, but it is otherwise an innocuous work. O'Connor's subjection of his material to an easy flow of narrative results in error: Woburn Buildings has been transplanted to Bedford Park. Yeats sought, one feels, to preserve the distance between. The remarkable distortion of Yeats's own account of Mathers (from *Autobiographies*) diminishes confidence. According to O'Connor, Mathers walked the streets of *London* in highland dress, *yelling out* " 'I feel like a walking flame' ". O'Connor believes Yeats met Florence Farr through the Golden Dawn. However, he met Farr in late 1889, joined the G.D. in March 1890; she joined it in July, no doubt introduced by Yeats. The book's real interest lies in its reproduction of two rare photos of Maud Gonne; a studio portrait, and an unusually approachable Maud Gonne, presumably of the late nineties, with Dagda posing as Cerberus.

Colin Smythe's *A Guide to Coole Park Co. Galway Home of Lady Gregory* (Gerrards Cross: Colin Smythe, 1983) contains a foreword by Anne Gregory, sixty-nine pages of informative text, and an astonishing eighty illustrations, many never before published. It includes plans, maps, photographs of persons, places, pictures mostly unpublished, always appropriate. It also includes the first publications of a new quatrain by Yeats in honour of Lady Gregory, "The loud years come the loud years go". This revised and enlarged edition is the fruit of the last ten years' work by Colin Smythe among the Gregory papers and is invaluable.

Richard Cave's Chatterton lecture to the British Academy *Yeats's Late Plays: 'A High Grave Dignity and Strangeness'* (London: British Academy, 1983) is a densely packed commentary upon those plays of which he has been so successful a director. Doubtless his work in directing *The Herne's Egg* in particular initiated his concern with "strangeness". Tracing Yeats's misattribution (in 1905) of Bacon's "There is no excellent beauty that hath not some strangeness in the proportion" to Ben Jonson, he endeavours to discover traces of a link via Jonson's stage directions to *The Masque of Hymen*. The link between Bacon and Yeats is perhaps more easily made via a French connection. Bacon's quotation, the headnote to Poe's *Ligeia*, becomes in Baudelaire's hands the *symboliste* axiom "Le beau est toujours bizarre", but Dr Cave's concern is less with sources than with the theatrical realisation of such an aesthetic, and his commentary is pointed, documented in detail, and convincing.

Yeats: an Annual of Critical and Textual Studies, vol. I (1983) is edited by Richard J. Finneran and published by Cornell University Press. It is a new journal, handsomely bound and pleasing in format, with footnotes at the foot of the page. Perhaps the era of endnotes is passing away? The illustrations, which accompany Elizabeth Bergmann Loizeaux's article " 'Separating Strangeness': From Painting to Sculpture in Yeats's Theatre" are well-known and poorly reproduced straight on to the page. The contributors include George Mills Harper, Connie K. Hood, Brendan O'Hehir, Virginia D. and Raymond D. Pruitt, Stanley Weintraub and the editor, K. P. S. Jochum contributes a rational and easily used annual bibliography for 1981. There are some 43 pages of reviews and the recent crop from *Dissertation Abstracts International* (for 1982) is harvested by Carolyn Holdsworth. *YAACTS* will in future contain shorter notes and will consider readers' letters.

Unputdownable is the Pruitts' essay upon the Steinach operation. From "Goat Gland Brinkley" to Norman Hare in Harley Street is a large slice of a little-recalled area of surgical aspiration, but it would seem that unilateral vasectomies in the cause of rejuvenation spread among Yeats's friends and there may yet be more of them to write up. Certainly Yeats proselytised, apparently to Sturge Moore and Dulac, as unpublished papers show.

Stanley Weintraub's material upon the "Uneasy Friendship" of Yeats and Shaw is well-processed but familiar, whereas George Mills Harper leads the reader into the wilderness of the automatic script in quest of "Yeats's Theory of 'Transference' and Keats's 'Ode to a Nightingale' ". Connie Hood makes a determined assault on the textual history of *A Vision* [*B*]. The next issue of *YAACTS* will apparently contain many of the papers presented at the 1983 Winthrop symposium.

". . . works of art are always begotten by previous works of art, and every masterpiece becomes the Abraham of a chosen people" (*E&I* 352). Yeats's *dictum* is but one expression of the theme of Carlos Baker's *The Echoing Green: Romanticism, Modernism and the Phenomena of Transference in Poetry* (Princeton: Princeton University Press, 1984), which covers Wordsworth, Byron, Shelley, Coleridge, Keats as "ancestral voices" alongside their "modern echoes" in Yeats, Frost, Pound, Eliot, Stevens, and Auden. This is a book which seeks to absorb such *dicta* and the modern academic literary theory built upon them to a critical survey of a large field for a non-specialist audience. The aspiration is worthy and one would place this book in the hands of an undergraduate inclined to be overwhelmed by biographical criticism.

UMI Research Press have now published a couple of dozen titles in their Studies in Modern Literature series. The motive for it is obvious and straightforward. Young (American) scholars need *that* publication when seeking tenure. This series makes available, in unpretentious form, selected, revised dissertations to provide a quick way into print for the best postgraduate research.

Yet these imperatives are also the series' limitations. Having seen several titles (not all on Yeats), I suspect that theses are theses and books, books. Many of these dissertations have no obvious right to any wider circulation than is already provided by University Microfilms International. There are honourable exceptions, but the characteristic faults of the series are indulgent "commentary" and inadequate documentation.

Shorter than the thesis upon which it rests, Herbert J. Levine's *Yeats's Daimonic Renewal* retains what he calls the "most original" feature of that thesis, a "full-scale" commentary upon *Per Amica Silentia Lunae*. I think it an extended paraphrase of that work, which, section by section, praises Yeats for being worthy of this sort of treatment. The preface tilts at some venerable windmills, and skirts some newer ones, including Lawrence Lipking. The prospect of publication did not encourage Professor Levine to check some of the more recondite sources. It is not satisfactory to summarize Henry More from Basil Willey, for instance, and there are other problems. Yeats's "hollow image of fulfilled desire" (*Myth* 329) is remembered from Simeon Solomon's *A Mystery of Love in Sleep* (1871), where on p. 4 one finds "a hollow image of appeased desire". It is not misremembered, however creatively, from *A Vision of Love Revealed in Sleep* (1871) where the phrase reads "a hollow image of unappeased desire". That the earlier version is close enough to Yeats's recall seems to invalidate the theory, put forward by Levine, of "unconscious revers[al] . . . in order to validate [Yeats's] impulse to dismiss happy art".

The "passing bell" of the second best known sentence in the entire work is deliberately read as "fleeting" bell rather than as death knell; Levine seems unaware of any older, precise meaning of "apocalyptic" or "apocalypse"; his reading of "The Moods" (despite citation of its variants) seems to ignore the cyclical force of these immanent powers, and so on. But the quality of the writing and the nature of the biographical assumptions are the more worrying feature of its later "commentaries" on plays and poems, in the light of the commentary upon *Per Amica Silentia Lunae*. Yeats's foil in "Anima Mundi" XI is "phallic"; further, it is "significantly buttoned". We are here told that "the fragility of Yeats's relationship with Maud . . . could hardly have stood the shock of his virtually incestuous liaison with her daughter". Georgie Hyde-Lees becomes "an old occultist flame, Georgie Hyde-Lee [sic]". Yeats and his wife, according to Levine, "dreamed together of monstrous new births for the modern world" as "they conceived and gave birth to Anne Yeats". "*Per Amica* helped Yeats clean house in middle age. . . . marriage unleashed a flood of new subconscious material that became *A Vision*, and Yeats once again had to sweep the untidy room."

The book concludes with a section which would have been pleasing if it were not beside the point. "On reading Yeats without *A Vision*" is provocative and lively and critical, but it concludes (as I understand it) in a partisanship for *Per Amica* which seems both unnecessary and yet inadequate; although it is probably true that Yeats never found final form for his "private philosophy" and it also seems true that that aspect of his thought finds its earliest full expression in "Anima Hominis".

Levine and others in the series seem caught in an unfortunate double standard. What is selected for the series is a thesis, yet what is published must be judged as a monograph. It hardly seems fair to the young scholar.

Also noticed in page proof is *Ezra Pound and Dorothy Shakespear: Their Letters, 1909–1914* (N.Y.: New Directions, 1984), edited by Omar Pound and A. Walton Litz. Theirs is an exemplary treatment which abundantly demonstrates that full annotation of apparently ephemeral or intimate material can conjure up a consistent and forgotten world. It begins with a besotted Dorothy Shakespear confiding to her journal

> Listen to it – Ezra! Ezra! – And a third time – Ezra! . . . he began to talk – He talked of Yeats as one of the Twenty of the world who have added to the World's poetical matter – He read a short piece of Yeats, in a voice dropping with emotion, in a voice like Yeats's own – He spoke of his interest in all the Arts, in that he might find things of use in them for his own – which is the Highest of them all.

Thus the "forgotten school of 1909" in intimate record. The volume culminates with the marriage and gathers in along the way footnotes lavish with anecdote. Thus Yeats at the award of the Polignac prize to James Stephens:

> Mr Yeats? Ah, Mr Yeats. Mr Yeats explained with Dublin Theatre gestures and parsonic elocution that he had no manuscript to read from. He had given his to the press. He smiled benignly, and recited his memorised speech perfectly. He spoke in his beautiful voice; he expressed Celtic lore with his more beautiful face; he elevated and waved his yet more beautiful hands. He blessed us with his presence. He spoke of spirits and phantasmagoria. He spoke of finding two boots in the middle of a field and the owner of the boots listening for the earth-spirits under a bush. He said that in Ireland the hedge-rows were rushing upon the towns. He praised Mr Stevens' Crock of Gold. He read one of Mr Stevens' poems, which was admirable as he read it.
> Mr Yeats concluded the performance by giving Mr Stevens a hundred pounds. We could not hear Mr Stevens promising to be a good boy and not spend it all on toffee and fairy-books.

The Olivia Shakespear who occasionally appears is no more a figure of "pale brows" and "dim hair" but a somewhat world-weary *femme du monde* who tries to curtail Ezra Pound's wooing with a merciful brutality.

> . . . she isn't the least likely – she can't in decency – "transfer her affections" to anyone else whilst you are always about – & you'll be doing her a great injury if you stand in the way of her marrying – She *must* marry – she & I can't possibly go on living this feminine life practically *à deux* for ever, & we haven't money enough to separate – & should have less than we have now if her father died – indeed, in the latter event I should probably marry again, & she wd be very much de trop – raison de plus for her marrying.
> You ought to go away – Englishmen don't understand yr American ways, & any man who wanted to marry her wd be put off by the fact of yr friendship (or whatever you call it) with her.
> If you had £500 a year I should be delighted for *you* to marry her. . . . I've seen too much of girls wasting their lives on men who can't marry them, & they generally end by being more or less compromised demivierges . . . she can't go

about with you American fashion – not till she is 35 & has lost her looks. Dear
Ezra – I'm sorry for you – really – but you are a great trouble . . . I wish she had
never been born. She chose her parents very unwisely.

She had become a Balzacian heroine. Omar Pound's unrivalled knowledge of the
milieu of Kensington and Ashdown Forest is directed towards allowing the
literary issues buried in the material to emerge unobtrusively. Important new
letters about Pound's concept of "phantastikon", and the "chronological table of
emotions" being shaped into *Canzoni* are cases in point. In the latter instance
once can see how Pound comes to apply Hugo's *Légende des Siècles*, probably with
the encouragement of the "eagle" who in 1909 had written of *his* ambition to be
the Hugo of Ireland, and whose own *légende des siècles* issued in *The Secret Rose*.
Omar Pound and Walton Litz have laid before us in the best possible fashion
material which is already proving invaluable to new thinking about the period –
(see p. 103 above).

Warwick Gould

BIBLIOGRAPHICAL AND
RESEARCH MATERIALS

The 1920s Catalogue of W. B. Yeats's Library

Edward O'Shea

What follows is a partial listing of a catalogue of Yeats's private library (including some of Mrs Yeats's books) as it existed in the year 1920 or shortly thereafter. Intentionally *excluded* are titles from the 1920s catalogue which are *presently* in the poet's library as maintained by his daughter, Anne Yeats, in Dalkey, Ireland. These titles are included with full particulars in *A Descriptive Catalog of W. B. Yeats's Library* (Garland, New York: 1985) where they are designated by an asterisk before the item number. The 1920s catalogue consists of a file of 4 × 6 inch cards with holograph entries recording, typically, author, title, date of publication, format, and a shelf designation. The compiler is unknown (the hand unidentified), and the year 1920 is derived from the latest publication date in the entries. The complete 1920s listing contains 1159 entries, in some cases recording multiple copies or runs of serials. Of these 1159 entries, 521 are not found in the present library, and it is these "missing" items that follow. Nothing is known conclusively about their disposition. Anne Yeats speculates that whole cartons of books may have been lost in frequent removals. Other items were likely lent out by the poet, a largesse that Mrs Yeats discouraged but apparently never stopped completely. An examination of the titles that follow also suggests that certain kinds of books may have been intentionally "weeded out": novels (the existing library contains very little fiction, with exceptions like Balzac and some Irish writers), the occult (although the library is still exceptionally rich in this area), and "faded enthusiasms." An example of the latter may be the work of Katharine Tynan. Eight of her 10 books listed in the 1920s catalogue are missing from the library, including three presentation copies. While this may have no significance, it is a fact that Yeats's interest in her poetry diminished after the 1890s. Other "casualties" are two writers as different as William Wordsworth and G. R. S. Mead. In marginal comments in Wordsworth's books in his library, Yeats records his impatience and exasperation with what he takes to be Wordsworth's sentimentality and prosaicism, and this kind of criticism may explain the four missing titles in the 1920s catalogue, or they may simply have been considered redundant – or were lost. Also missing, for whatever reason, is a collection of 15 titles, mostly theosophical works, by G. R. S. Mead.

Other items are noteworthy because they fill obvious gaps: the Dalkey library contains no books by John Ruskin or Sigmund Freud and only one by Tennyson. The 1920s catalogue records multiple titles by all three. Other authors well represented in the 1920s catalogue but sparsely represented or missing altogether in the library are Strindberg, Schopenhauer, and Jessie Weston, and the catalogue contains a surprisingly large number of titles on Mormonism.

The file cards indicate that the books were ranged in six bookcases, lettered A to F. While there seems to have been some attempt to arrange books by subject (e.g. religion, English literature), no clear system is apparent, and in some cases an alphabetical system seems to have been used. The following entries are arranged by author where applicable, otherwise by title. Compilations and anthologies are generally listed under editor's name, but translations appear under title or main author, whichever is appropriate.

Abercrombie, Lascelles. *Emblems of Love*, designed in several discourses. 1912. 12mo

About the Farm, an illustrated description of the New Boston Dairy. 1910. 8vo

[Achilles Tatius]. Achilles Tatius, with an English translation by S. Gaselee. 1915. 12mo

Addison, Joseph. *The Spectator*. Edited by G. A. Aitken. Vol. 6. 1898.

[Aeschylus]. *Aeschylus*. Translated by E. H. Plumptre. Vol. 1. 1868. 12mo

Aids to Irish Composition by the Christian Brothers. n.d. 12mo

Ancoats Recreation [Committee?]. Winter Programme, 1911–12. 1911. 8mo

Anderson, J. Redwood. *The Mask*. 1912. 12mo

——. *Walls and Hedges*. 1919. 12mo. Presentation copy.

Andreieff, Leonid. *The Seven that were Hanged*. 1909. 12mo

Anwyl, Edward. *Celtic Religion in Pre-Christian Times*. 1906. 12mo

Ariosto. *The Orlando Furioso*. Translated by William Stewart Rose. 2 vols. 1905. 12mo

Armitage, Ella S. *An Introduction to English Antiquites* [sic] with illustrations. n.d. 18mo

Arnold, Hugh. *Stained Glass in the Middle Ages in England and France*. Painted by Lawrence B. Saint. 1913. 4to

Arnold, Matthew. *Poetical Works*. With an Intro. by Sir Arthur Quiller-Couch. 1913. 12mo

Aston, W. G. *Shinto. The Ancient Religion of Japan*. 1910. 12mo

Atlas of Ancient and Classical Geography. n.d. 12mo

Aucassin and Nicolette: A Play from the 12th Century French Song-Story. 1913. 8vo

B., J. T. *Brian Boru*. A tragedy. 1879. 12mo

Baedeker's Guide to Central Italy and Rome. 1909. 12mo

Baedeker's Guide to Northern Italy. 1906. 12mo

Barrett, Sir W. F. *Swedenborg. The Savant and the Seer*. 1912. 12mo

Bartholomew, Dr J. G. *A Literary and Historical Atlas of Europe*. n.d. 12mo

Bennett, Edward T. *Automatic Speaking and Writing*. A Study. 1905. 8vo

——. *The Direct Phenomena of Spiritualism*. n.d. 8vo

Besant, Annie. *The Ancient Wisdom, an Outline of Theosophical Teachings*. 1897. 12mo

——. *Esoteric Christianity or the Lesser Mysteries*. 1901. 12mo

——. *The Seven Principles of Man*. 1892. 18mo

Besier, Rudolf. *The Virgin Goddess*, a tragedy. 1907. 12mo

Biagi, Dr Guido. *The Last Days of Percy Bysshe Shelley*. New details from unpublished documents. 1898. 12mo

Binyon, Laurence. *The Death of Adam and Other Poems*. 1904. 12mo

——. *First Book of London Visions*. 1896. 12mo

——. *Odes*. 1901. 12mo Presentation copy.

Black's Guide to Galway, with maps and plans. 1912. 12mo

Blagdon, Claude. *Episodes from an Unwritten History*. 1920. 12mo

Blake, William. *Exhibition of the Works of William Blake at the Grolier Club New York*,

with a catalogue of Books, Engravings etc. 1905. 12mo
——. *His Lyrical Poems*. With an intro. by Walter Raleigh. 1905. 12mo
——. *Selections from his Works*. By Mark Perugini. 1901. 18mo
Blavatsky, H. P. *The Stanzas of Dzyan*. From *The Secret Doctrine*. 1892. 18mo
Blunt, Wilfrid Scawen. *Love Poems*. 1902. 18mo
Boehme, Jacob. *Dialogues on the Supersensual*. Edited by B. Holland. 1901. 12mo
——. *The Nature of All Things*, with other writings. n.d. 12mo
Bolton, Gambier. *Ghosts in Solid Form*. 1914. 12mo
Bond, F. B. and Lea, T. S. *The Cabala Contained in the Coptic Gnostic Books and of a Similar Gematria in the Greek text of the New Testament*. 1917. 8vo
Borrow, George. *The Zincali*, or an account of the Gypsies of Spain. 1902. 12mo
Bosschère, Jean de. *The Closed Door*. Translated by F. S. Flint. 1917. 8vo
Bottomley, Gordon. *Laodice and Danaë*. 1909. 8vo. Presentation Copy.
Bourgeois, Maurice. *John Millington Synge and the Irish Theatre*. 1913. 8vo
Bowker, James. *Goblin Tales of Lancashire*. n.d. 12mo
Boyd, Ernest A. *Ireland's Literary Renaissance*. 1916. 8vo
Boyesen, H. H. *A History of Norway*. 1900. 12mo
Bragdon, Claude. *The Beautiful Necessity*. Seven essays on theosophy and architecture. 1910. 8vo
Breasted, J. H. *A History of the Ancient Egyptians*. 1912. 12mo
Bridges, Robert. *The Humours of the Court*. n.d. small folio.
——. *Nero*. Part 2. n.d. small folio
——. *Palicio*. A drama in five acts. 1890. small folio
——. *Poems*. Including the eight dramas. 1912. 12mo, bound in leather
Brill, Dr A. A. *Dreams and their Relation to the Neurosis*. 1910. 8vo
A Broadside. First year. 1908. Missing numbers 3 and 7.
——. 1909. Missing numbers 8 and 10.
——. 1910. Missing 4 and 5.
——. 1911. Missing 2, 4, 5, 10.
——. 1912. Missing 3.
——. 1913. Missing 3, 4, 5, 7.

A Broadside. 1914. Missing 8 and 12.
Brooke, Rupert. *Poems*. 1917. 12mo
Brotherhood of the New Life. Numbers 1, 3, 5. 1896. 8vo
Browning, Robert. *Poetical Works*. 4 vols. Tauchnitz. 12mo
Buchanan, Meriel. *Petrograd, the City of Trouble*. 1914–1918. 1818 [sic]. 12mo
Budge, E. A. Wallis. *Egyptian Ideas of the Future Life*. 1900. 12mo
Burke, Edmund. *Works*. With an intro. by Judge Willis. 6 vols. 1906. 12mo
"Burlington" Art Miniatures. No. 4. The Louvre, Paris. n.d. 18mo
Byron, Lord Gordon. *Poetical Works*. With an intro. by Arthur Symons. n.d. 12mo Presentation copy from Arthur Symons.
Byron, William A. *A Light on The Broom*. 1904. 12mo
Campagnac, E. T. *The Cambridge Platonists*. 1901. 8vo
Campbell, Nancy. *Agnus Dei*. Illustrated by Joseph Campbell. n.d. 18mo
Carr, H. Wildon. *Henri Bergson, the Philosophy of Change*. 1911. 12mo
Carson, Thomas. *Church of Humanity*. Some sentiments of the South American Brethren. 1886. 8vo
Carus, Paul. *The Bride of Christ*. A study in Christian Legend Lore. 1908. 8vo
Celtic Association of Philadelphia, U.S.A. Contributions. 1904. 8vo Presentation copy.
Charles, Dr R. H. *The Book of Enoch*. Intro. by Dr W. O. E. Olsterley. 1917. 12mo G[eorge] Y[eats]
Chattopadhyay, Harindranath. *Poems. The Feast of Youth*. 1918. small 4to
Chaucer. *The College Chaucer*. Edited by H. N. MacCracken. 1913. 12mo
——. *Complete Works*. Edited by W. W. Skeat. n.d. 12mo
——. *The Riches of Chaucer*, in which his spelling has been modernised etc. Edited by Charles Cowden Clarke. 1896. 12mo
Childers, Erskine. *The Framework of Home Rule*. 1911. 8vo
Chrestomathie du Moyen Age. 1897. 12mo
Clarke, Joseph I. C. *Robert Emmett*. A tragedy of Irish History. 1888. 4to
Claudel, Paul. *Autre Poëmes durant la Guerre*. 1916. royal 8vo
Cleather, A. L. and Basil Crump. *The Ring of the Nibelung*, an interpretation embodying Wagner's own explanation. 1903. 12mo

Clodd, Edward. *The Story of "Primitive" Man.* 1897. 12mo

Clutton-Brock, A. *William Morris,* his work and influence. 1914. 12mo

Coffey, George. *Prehistoric Cenotaphs.* 1896. 8vo

Colvin, Sidney. *John Keats.* 1916. 12mo

———. *W. S. Landor.* 1888. 12mo

Connolly, James. *Labour in Ireland, Labour in Irish History, the Re-conquest of Ireland.* 1917. 12mo

Conrad, Joseph. *The Children of the Sea.* 1897. 12mo G[eorge] Y[eats]

Contemporary Belgian Poetry. Selected and translated by J. Bithell. 1911. 18mo

Converse, Florence. *Long Will.* A Romance. 1903. 12mo

Cooke, John, ed. *The Dublin Book of Irish Verse,* 1728–1909. 12mo

Coomaraswamy, Ananda. *Art and Swadeshi.* n.d. 12mo
Another copy.

———. *Indian Music.* 1917. royal 8vo
Another copy.

Cowper, William. *Poems.* Edited by J. C. Bailey. 1905. 8vo

Coxon, H. B. *Roman Catholicism.* An explanation of Catholic Belief. n.d. 12mo

Crashaw, Richard. *Poems.* Edited by J. R. Tutin. n.d. 12mo

Cromartie, The Countess of. *The End of the Song* and other stories. 1904. 12mo

———. *The Web of the Past.* 1905. 12mo

Cronyn, George W. *The Path on the Rainbow.* An anthology of songs and chants from the Indians of North America. 1918. 12mo

Crowley, Aleister. *Mortadello or the Angel of Venice.* A comedy. 1912. small 4to

Curtis, Elizabeth Alden. *The Norseman,* a drama. 1912. 8vo Presentation copy.

Cushag. *The Peel Plays.* Sketches of Manx Life. 1908. 18mo

Dallas, H. A. *Across the Barrier.* With an additional chapter by H. B. M. Watson. 1913. 12mo

D'Annunzio, Gabriele. *Gioconda.* Translated by Arthur Symons. 1901. 12mo Presentation copy.

Dante. *The New Life.* Translated by D. G. Rossetti. 1899. 12mo

———. *Purgatorio.* In English. 1902. 12mo

Dasent, George Webbe. *The Story of the Burnt Njal from the Icelandic.* n.d. 12mo

Davis, A. J. *Answers to Ever-recurring Questions from the People.* 1911. 12mo

———. *Arabula:* or the divine guest, containing a new collection of Gospels. 1911. 12mo

———. *Events in the Life of a Seer,* being memoranda of authentic facts. 1911. 12mo

———. *The Harmonial Philosophy,* a compendium and digest of the works of A. J. Jackson.

———. *The Principles of Nature,* her divine revelations and a voice to mankind. 1911. 8vo.

———. *A Stellar Key to the Summer Land.* 1910. 12mo

Davis, H. W. C. *Medieval Europe.* n.d. 12mo

Deeney, Daniel. *Peasant Lore from Gaelic Ireland.* 1900. 12mo
Another copy.

De Flagello Myrteo. Preface by "Neva." 1906. 12mo

Descartes, René. *Discourse on Method and Metaphysical Meditations.* n.d. 12mo G[eorge] Y[eats]

Dhar, M. Mohan. *Krishna the Charioteer.* 1917. 18mo

Dickens, Charles. *Barnaby Rudge.* n.d. 12mo

Digby, Sir Kenelm, Knight. *The Closet of Sir Kenelm Digby, Knight, Opened.* Edited by Anne Macdonald.. 1910. 8vo G[eorge] Y[eats]

Dobbs, M. E. *Side-lights on the Tain Age* and other studies. 1917. 8vo

Donne, John. *Poems.* Edited by E. K. Chambers. Intro. by George Saintsbury. 2 vols. n.d. 12mo

Donoghue, D. J. *Life and Writings of James Clarence Mangan.* 1897. 8vo

Dostoevsky, Fyodor. *The Brothers Karamazov.* Translated by Constance Garnett. 1913. 12mo

———. *Crime and Punishment.* Translated by Constance Garnett. 1916. 12mo

———. *The Possessed.* Translated by Constance Garnett. 1913. 12mo

Dowden, Edward. *A History of French Literature.* 1897. cr. 8vo

Duffy, Sir Charles Gavan. *A Short Life of Thomas Davis.* 1896. 18mo

Dunsany, Lord. *Plays of Gods and Men.* 1917. 12mo

———, *Time and the Gods.* Illus. by S. H. Sime. 1906. SM 4to

Duquet, Alfred. *Ireland and France*. Translated by J. de L. Smyth. 1916. 12mo

Dutt, Romesh. *Ramayana, the Epic of Rama, Prince of India*. Condensed into English verse. 1899. 12mo

Dyer, Louis. *Studies of the Gods in Greece at Certain Sancturies Recently Excavated*. 1891. cr. 8vo

Dyer, T. F. Thiselton. *The Ghost World*. 1898. 8vo

Echegaray, Jose. *The Great Galeoto [and] Folly or Saintliness*. Two plays. Translated by Hannah Lynch. 1895. sm 4to G[eorge] Y[eats]

Eder, Dr M. D. *War-shock*. 1917. 12mo

Emerson, P. H. *Welsh Fairy-tales* and other stories. 1894. 12mo

The Equinox. The Review of Scientific Illuminism. Vol. 1, no. 3. 1910. 4to

Ervine, St. John G. *Sir Edward Carson and the Ulster Movement*. 1915. 12mo

Eschenbach, Wolfram von. *Parzifal*, a knightly epic. Translated by Jesse L. Weston. 2 vols. 1894. 8vo

Evans, John Henry. *One Hundred Years of Mormonism*, a history of the church of Jesus Christ of latter-day saints: 1805–1905. 1909. 8vo

Fairclough, H. R. *The Connection between Music and Poetry in the Early Greek Literature*. 1902. 8vo

Fielding, Alice. *Faith-healing and 'Christian Science.'* 1899. 12mo

Ferguson, Lady. *Sir Samuel Ferguson in the Ireland of his Day*. 2 vols. 1896. 8vo

Ferguson, Sir Samuel. *Congal*, a poem in five books. 1907. 12mo

Festing, G. *When Kings Rode to Delhi*. 1912. 8vo

Figgis, Darrell. *George W. Russell*. A study of a man and a nation. 1916. 12mo

Finlay, George. *History of the Byzantine Empire*. 1906. 12mo

First Irish Grammar by the Christian Brothers. n.d. 12mo

Fitzgibbon, H. Macaulay, ed. *Early English Poetry*. 1887. 18mo

Fitzpatrick, Samuel A. Ossory. *Dublin*, historical and topographical account of the city. Illus. by W. Curtis Green. 1907 12mo

Fletcher, John. *The Two Noble Kinsmen*. 1897. 18mo

Folk-lore and Legends of Ireland. 1889. 12mo

Forel, Dr August. *The Sexual Question*, scientific . . . study for the cultured classes. Adapted into English by C. F. Marshall. 1908. 8vo

Forman, Alfred. *The Nibelungs Ring*. English words to Wagner's Ring des Nibelungen. 1873. 12mo

Freud, Dr Sigmund. *The Interpretation of Dreams*. Translated by A. A. Brill. 1913. 8vo

——. *Totem and Taboo*. Resemblances between the psychic lives of savages and neurotics. Translated by Dr A. A. Brill. 1919. 12mo

Furst, Herbert. *J. B. S. Chardin and His Times*. 1907. 12mo

[Gabalis, Le Comte de]. *Le Comte de Gabalis, ou Entretiens sur les sciences secretes*. 1715. 12mo

Galton, Francis. *Hereditary Genius*, an inquiry into its laws and consequences. 1914. 12mo G[eorge] Y[eats]

Gardner, Edmund G. *The Story of Florence*. Illus. by Nelly Ericksen. 1905. 12mo

Garnett, Edward. *The Breaking Point*. With a preface and a letter to the censor. 1907. 12mo

Garnett, Porter. *The Green Knight*, A Vision. Privately printed for members of the Bohemian Club. 1911. royal 8vo

Gautier, Theophile. *Charles Baudelaire, His Life*. Translated by Guy Thorne. 1915. 8vo

Georgian Poetry: 1918–1919. 1919. 12mo

Gibson, Wilfrid Wilson. *Livelihood*, Dramatic Reveries. 1917. 12mo

Gill, Dr W. W. *From Darkness to Light in Polynesia*. With illustrative clan songs. 1894. 12mo

Goblet D'Alviella, Count. *The Migration of Symbols*. 1894. 8vo

Goethe. *Faust*, Parts 1 and 2. Translated by Albert Latham. 1912. 12mo

——. *Wilhelm Meister*. Translated by Thomas Carlyle. 2 vols. 1895? 12mo

Gomme, G. L. *Ethnology in Folklore*. 1892. 12mo

Goncourt, E. L. A. and J. A. Goncourt. *The Journal of the De Goncourts*. Edited by Julius West. n.d. 12mo

Gorky, Maxim. *Reminiscences of Tolstoi*. 1920. 12mo

[Gosse, Edmund]. *Edmund Gosse, His Collected Poems*. 1911. 12mo Presentation copy.

Grant, Sir Alexander. *Aristotle*. 1910. 12mo

Graves, Alfred Percival. *The Irish Fairy Book*. 1909. crown 8vo

Graves, Arnold F. *Clytaemnestra, a tragedy*. 1903. 12mo

Gregory, Padric. *Old World Ballads*. 1913. 12mo

Grierson, Herbert J. C. *The First Half of the Seventeenth Century*. 1906. cr. 8vo

Guide to Dublin and the Wicklow Tours. n.d. 12mo

A Guide to Penzance. With maps and illustrations. n.d. 12mo

Guthrie, James J. *The Elf*. n.d. 12mo

Hallam, Henry. *Introduction to the Literature of Europe*. 4 vols. 1882. 12mo

Hare, Augustus J. C. *Guide to Florence*. With maps and woodcuts. 1896. 12mo

———. *Paris*. Vol. 1. 1900. 12mo

Harper, Charles G. *The Hardy Country: Literary Landmarks of the Wessex Novels*. 1904. 8vo

Hasell, E. J. *Calderon*. 1898. 12mo

Henry, Victor. *Éléments de Sanscrit Classique*. 1902. royal 8vo G[eorge] Y[eats]

Herbert, George. *Poetical Works*. Introduction by Arthur Waugh. 1913. 12mo

Hewlett, Maurice. *Pan and the Young Shepherd*. A pastoral in 2 acts. 1898. 12mo

Heydon, John. *The Holy Guide*, leading the way to the wonder of the world (A Complete Physitian). Teaching the Knowledge of all things past, present, and to come etc. 1662. 12mo

Higginson, Thomas W. *Tales of the Enchanted Islands of the Atlantic*. 1899. 12mo Presentation copy.

Hitchcock, F. R. Montgomery. *The Midland Septs and the Pale*. 1908. 12mo

Hoernle, A. F. R. and H. A. Stark. *History of India*. 1909. 12mo

Homeric Hymns. Translated by Andrew Lang. 1899. 12mo

Horrwitz, E. *A Short History of Indian Literature*. n.d. 12mo

Howard, B. Douglas. *Life with Trans-Siberian Savages*. 1893. 12mo

Howard, Newman. *Collected Poems*. 1913. cr. 8vo

———. *Kiartan, the Icelander*. 1902. 12mo

Hudson, W. H. *Green Mansions*. 1910. 12mo

Hull, Eleanor. *The Cuchullin Saga in Irish Literature*. Being a collection of stories relating to the hero. 1898. 8vo

Hunt, Leigh. *Stories from the Italian Poets*, with critical notices and lives of the writers. n.d. 12mo

Huon of Bordeaux. Translated by Sir John Bourchier and retold by Robert Steele. 1895. 4to

Hyde, Douglas. *Beside the Fire*. A collection of Irish Gaelic Folk Stories.

Ibsen, Henrik. *Peer Gynt*. Translated by R. Ellis Roberts. 1912. sm 4to

Ikenio, Conrado. *Antiquitates Hebraicae*. 1741. 12mo G[eorge] Y[eats]

Improvisations from the Spirit. 1857. 18mo

Irish Art Gallery. *Ballymaclinton*, an illustrated catalogue. 1908. royal 8vo

Irish Texts Society. Vols. 1–3. 1899–1900. 8vo

Jacobs, Joseph. *Celtic Fairy Tales*. Illus. by John D. Batten. 1892. 8vo

Jastrow, Dr Morris. *Aspects of Religious Belief and Practice in Babylonia and Assyria*. 1911. 8vo G[eorge] Y[eats]

Jessop, Dr A. *The Coming of the Friars* and other historical essays. 1910. 12mo

Johnson, Lionel. *Selections from his Poems*. 1908. 18mo

Jones, Henry Festing. *Diversions in Sicily*. 1909. 12mo

Joyce, P. W. *A Short History of Ireland from the Earliest Times to 1608*. 1893. 12mo

Jusserand, J. J. *The English Novel in the Time of Shakespeare*. 1901. crown 8vo

———. *English Wayfaring Life in the Middle Ages*. Translated by Lucy Toulmin Smith. 1909. 12mo

———. *The Literary History of the English People*. 1907. 8vo

Kalidasa. *Sakuntala, or the Fatal Ring*, a drama. n.d. 12mo

Keats, John. *Poetical Works*. With an intro. by Robert Bridges. 2 vols. 1896. 12mo

———. *Poetical Works*. 1906. 12mo

———. *Poetical Works*. 1915. 12mo

Kempis, Thomas à. *Of the Imitation of Christ*. Rev. trans. 1909. 18mo

The Kensington. A Magazine of Art, Literature and the Drama. Vol. 1. 1901.

Ker, W. P. *Epic and Romance*. Essays on Medieval Literature. 1897. 8vo

Kirby, W. F. *The Hero of Esthonia*, and other studies in the Romantic literature of the country. 2 vols. 1895. sm 4to

Knight, Charles. *Shadows of the Old Booksellers*. n.d. 12mo

Knight, Joseph. *Life of Dante Gabriel Rossetti*. 1897. 12mo

Krans, Horatio Sheafe. *Irish Life in Irish Fiction*. 1903. 12mo

Kyd, Thomas. *The Spanish Tragedy*. 1898. 18mo

Lane, Sir Hugh. *French Pictures*. 1917. 8vo

——. *Sale Illustrated Catalogue of Old Masters*. 1917. royal 8vo

Lang, Andrew. *The Book of Dreams and Ghosts*. 1897. 12mo

Langbridge, Frederick. *Ballads and Legends*. 1903. 18mo Presentation copy.

Larminie, William. *West Irish Folk-lore and Romances*. 1893. 8vo

Latin Poems of the Renaissance. Translated by Richard Aldington. n.d. 20/50. 8vo Presentation copy.

Latter-Day Saints. 19th semi-annual conference. 1919. 8vo

Lawless, Emily. *Ireland*. 1891. 12mo

Lawton, Frederick. *Balzac*. 1910. 8vo

The Lay of Havelok the Dane. Re-edited from MS in the Bodleian Library by Walter W. Skeat. 1902. 12mo

Lecky, William E. H. *History of European Morals from Augustus to Charlemagne*. 1911. 12mo

Lee, Sidney. *The French Renaissance in England*. 1910. 8vo

Le Fanu, J. S. *The House by the Churchyard*. 1904. 12mo

Legouis, Emile. *Geoffrey Chaucer*. [In French]. 1910. 12mo

——. *Geoffrey Chaucer*. Translated by L. Lailavoix. 1913. 12mo

Leighton, Mrs *Mediaeval Legends*. Five legends, a gift-book to the children of England etc. 1895. 8vo

Lennius, Lavinus. *The Secret Miracles of Nature*. In four books. 1658. folio

Leo, Alan. *Horary Astrology*. 1907. 12mo

Leslie, Shane. *Verses in Peace and War*. 1916. 12mo

Levy, Oscar. *The Revival of Aristocracy*. Translated by L. A. Magnus. 1906. 12mo

Lewisohn, L. *The Modern Drama*. An essay in interpretation. 1916. 12mo

Liddell, Dr H. G. *Student's History of Rome*. 1885. 12mo

Light. A journal of psychical, occult, and mystical research. 37 (Jan. 1917–July 1917).

The Light of Egypt, or the Science of the Soul and Stars. 1889. sm 4to

Lillie, Arthur. *Madame Blavatsky and her "Theosophy,"* a study. 1895. 12mo

Linley, Laura. *Out of the Vortex*. The true record of a fight for a soul. 1916. 12mo

Livingstone, Dr David. *Travels and Researches in South Africa*. 1905. 12mo

A Living Theatre. The Gordon Craig School. 1913. 8vo

Lodge, Sir Oliver J. *Raymond, or Life and Death*. n.d. 8vo

Longfellow, H. W. *Poems*. With biographical note. n.d. 12mo

Lorris, Guillaume de. *The Romance of the Rose*. Translated by F. S. Ellis. 3 vols. 1900. 12mo

Lucas, E. V. *The Open Road*. A little book for wayfarers. 1899. 12mo

Ludovici, Anthony M. *Nietzsche, His Life and Works*. 1910. 12mo

The Mabinogion. Translated by Lady Charlotte Guest. 1913. 12mo

McDonagh, Thomas. *Through the Ivory Gate*, a book of verse. 1903. 12mo

McDougall, William. *Psychology*, the study of behaviour.

MacKayne, Percy. *The Civic Theatre in Relation to the Redemption of Leisure*. 1912. 12mo

Maclean, Magnus. *The Literature of the Highlands*. 1904. 8vo

MacManus, Seumas. *In Chimney Corners*. Merry tales of Irish Folk-lore. 1899. 8vo

Macrobius. *Somnium Scipionis and Pythagoras*. 1894. 12mo

Maeterlinck, Maurice. *Monna Vanna*, a drama in three acts. Translated by Alfred Sutro. n.d. 12mo

——. *Pelleas and Melisanda* and *The Sightless*. Translated by L. Alma Tadema. n.d. 12mo

Mair, G. H. *English Literature, Modern*. 1911. 12mo

Manning, Frederic. *Eidola*. 1917. 12mo

——. *Scenes and Portraits*. 1909. 12mo

Marie de France. *Seven of Her Lays*. Translated by Edith Rickert. 1901. 18mo

The Marionnette To-night [Florence?]. Novr. 5th at 12:30. 1918. 12mo

Martinengo-Cesaresco, Countess Evelyn. *Essays in the Study of Folk-Songs*. 1886. 12mo

Masefield, John. *My Faith in Woman Suffrage*. 1910. 12mo Presentation copy.

——. *Sea Life in Nelson's Time*. 1905. 12mo Presentation copy.

Mason, Redfern. *The Song Lore of Ireland*, Erin's story in music and verse. 1910. 8vo

Masterman, Lucy. *Poems*. 1913. 12mo

Mather, Marshall. *John Ruskin, His Life and Teaching*. 1900. 12mo

Maurice, F. D. *Mediaeval Philosophy*, a treatise of moral and metaphysical philosophy from the 5th to the 14th century. 1859. 12mo

Mayhew, A. L. and W. W. Skeat. *A Concise Dictionary of Middle English from 1150 to 1580*. 1888. 8vo

Mead, G. R. S. *The Chaldean Oracles*. 2 vols. 1908. 18mo

——. *The Doctrine of the Subtle Body in Western Tradition*. 1919. 12mo

——. *Fragments of a Faith Forgotten*. 2nd ed. 1906.

——. *The Gnosis of the Mind*. 1906. 18mo

——. *The Gnostic Cricifixion*. 1907. 18mo

——. *The Gospels and the Gospel*. 1902. 8vo

——. *The Hymns of Hermes*. 1907. 18mo

——. *The Hymn of the Robe of Glory*. 1908. 18mo

——. *A Mithraic Ritual*. 1907. 18mo

——. *The Mysteries of Mithra*. 1907. 18mo

——. *Orpheus*. 1891. 12mo

——. *Plotinus*. 1895. 12mo

——. *Quests Old and New*. 1913. 8vo

——. *The Vision of Aridaeus*. 1907. 18mo

——. *The Wedding-Song of Wisdom*. 1908. 18mo

Meredith, George. *The Ordeal of Richard Feverel*. 1909. 12mo

Mérimée, Prosper. *Love Letters of a Genius*. Translated by E. A. S. Watt. 1905. 4to

Mers, John Theodore. *Leibnitz*. 1914. 12mo

Meynell, Alice. *A Father of Women* and other poems. 1917. 12mo

——. *John Ruskin*. 1900. 12mo

Mignet, F. A. M. *History of the French Revolution, 1789–1814*. n.d. 12mo

Milton, John. *Paradise Lost*. Illustrated by William Blake. 1906. 4to

——. *Prose Works*. Edited by Richard Garnett. n.d. 12mo

Mitchell, Susan L. *George Moore*. 1916. 12mo

Monro, Harold. *Children of Love*. 1914. sm 4to

——. *Trees*. 1916. sm 4to Presentation copy.

Montague, E. R. *Tales from the Talmud*. 1908. 8vo

Moore, A. W. *The Folk-Lore of the Isle of Man*. 1891. 12mo

Moore, George. *Esther Waters*. 1899. 8vo

——. *The Lake*. 1905. 12mo

Moore, T. Sturge. *A Conflict*. 1911. 8vo

Mordell, Albert. *The Shifting of Literary Values*. 1912. 8vo

Moreau, Gustave. *Catalogue Sommaire des peintures, dessins, cartons et aquarelles* exposés dans les galeries du Musée Gustave Moreau. 1904. royal 8vo

[Morison, Eliz. and Frances Lamont]. *An Adventure* by two ladies. 1911. cr 8vo

Morris, Richard and W. W. Skeat. *Specimens of Early English*. Part 2. 1898. 12mo

Morris, William. *The Life and Death of Jason*. Introduction by John Drinkwater. n.d. 12mo Presentation copy.

Muhammad Riza Nau'i of Khabushan. *Burning and Melting*, being the Suz-u-Gundasz of Muhammad Riza. Translated by M. Y. Dawud and A. K. Coomaraswamy. n.d. 8vo

Murray's Guide to Ireland. 1912. 12mo

Myers, F. W. H. *William Wordsworth*. English Men of Letters. 1912. 12mo

Newbolt, Henry. *The Island Race*. 1899. 12mo

Nicoll, Maurice. *Dream Psychology*. 1917. 12mo

Nietzsche, Friedrich. *Thus Spake Zarathustra*. Translated by Thomas Common. n.d. 8vo

Nivedita [Margaret Eliz. Noble]. *The Master as I Saw Him*, pages from the life of the Swami Vivekananda. 1910. 12mo

Nivedita and Ananda Coomaraswamy. *Myths of the Hindus and Buddhists*. 1913. 8vo

Noguchi, Yone. *The Pilgrimage*. 2 parts. 1909. 12mo Presentation copy.

Northcote, Thomas W. *Crystal Gazing*, its history and practice. 1905. 12mo

Nutt, Alfred. *The Fairy Mythology of Shakespeare*. 1900. 12mo

The Old English Miracle Play of Abraham and Isaac. 1905. 18mo

Oliphant, Mrs and F. Tarver. *Molière*. 1898. 12mo

Ordish, Thomas Fairman. *Shakespeare's London*, a commentary on Shakespeare's life and work in London. 1904. 12mo

Ostrovsky, A. N. *The Storm*. Translated by Constance Garnett. 1899. 8vo

Ouspensky, P. D. *Tertium Organum*, a key to the enigmas of the world. 1920. 8vo. G[eorge] Y[eats]

Ovid. *Art of Love*. n.d. 12mo
——. *Ovidii Metamorphoses*. Edited by P. Rabus. 1735. 18mo old vellum
Pagan, Isabelle. *Astrological Key to Character*. 1907. 18mo
Papus [Gerald Encausse]. *The Tarot of the Bohemians*. The most ancient book in the world. 1892. 8vo
Paracelsus. *The Prophecies of Paracelsus*, made about 400 years ago. Translated by J. K. 1915. 8vo
Parker, E. H. *Studies in Chinese Religion*. 1910. 8vo
Parsons, John Denham. *Our Sun-God* or Christianity before Christ. 1895. 12mo
Pascoe, Charles Eyre. *The Joyous Neighbourhood of Covent Garden*. 1887. 12mo
The Pearl. Translated by Marian Mead. 1908. 12mo
Pearse, P. H. *Three Lectures on Gaelic Topics*. 1898. 12mo
Petrie, W. M. Flinders. *Religion and Conscience in Ancient Egypt*. 1898. 12mo
Pfungst, Henry J. *Illustrated Sales Catalogue of Pictures and Drawings*. 1917. royal 8vo
Phillips, Stephen. *Christ in Hades* and other poems. 1890. 12mo
Plato. *Selections from Plato*. n.d. 12mo
Pliny the Younger. *Letters*. Translated by John B. Firth. n.d. 12mo
——. *Letters of the Younger Pliny in English*. n.d. 12mo
Poems in Bengali.
Poems of To-Day. An anthology. 1919. 12mo
Pound, Ezra. *Hugh Selwyn Mauberley*. 1920. royal 8vo
Powell, G. E. J. and Eirikr Magnusson. *Icelandic Legends*. 2nd series. 1866. crown 8vo
Prasad, Rama. *Nature's Finer Forces*. 1890. 8vo
Pratt, P. P. *A Voice of Warning and Instruction to All People*. 1897. 18mo
Prel, Carl du. *The Philosophy of Mysticism*. Trans. by C. C. Massey. 2 vols. 1889. 8vo. G[eorge] Y[eats]
Proclus. *The Elements of Theology*. n.d. royal 8vo
Ragon, J. M. *Rituel de l'Apprenti Maçon contenant le Cérémonial*, etc. 1853. 8vo
Rajendra. *The Taking of Toll*, being the Dana Lila of Rajendra. Translated by A. Coomaraswamy. 1915. 4to
Ransome, Arthur. *Oscar Wilde*. A critical study. 1913. 12mo

Ransome, Arthur. ed. *The Book of Friendship*. Essays, poems, maxims, and prose passages. n.d. 4to
Raupert, J. Godfrey. *Christ and the Powers of Darkness*. 1914. 12mo
Reclus, Elie. *Primitive Folk*. Studies in Comparative Ethnology. n.d. 12mo
Redgrave, H. Stanley. *Alchemy, Ancient and Modern*. 1911. 8vo
Reichel, Willy. *Occult Science*. 1906. 12mo
Renan, Ernest. *Études d'Histoire Religieuse*. n.d. 8vo
Renaud of Montauban. Translated by William Caxton. Re-translated by Robert Steele. 1897. sm 4to
René, Francis. *Egyptian Aesthetics*. n.d. 8vo
The Return from Parnassus or The Scourge of Simony. Edited by Oliphant Smeaton. 1905. 18mo
Rhys, Ernest, ed. *Lyrical Poetry from the Bible*. Vol. 1. n.d. 12mo
——. *The Prelude to Poetry*. The English poets in the defence and praise of their own art. n.d. 18mo
Rhys, John. *Hibbert Lectures 1886* on the origins and growth of religion etc. 1892. 8vo
Ricci, Corrado. *Collezione di Monografie Illustrate*. Vol. 1: *Italia Artistica*. 1906.
Rimell, Eugene. *The Book of Perfumes*. n.d. 4to
Roberts, R. Ellis. *Poems*. 1906. 8vo Presentation copy.
Robinson, J. H. *An Introduction to the History of Western Europe*. 1903. 12mo
Ross, G. Campbell. *Municipal Gallery of Modern Art, Johannesburg*. Illustrated Catalogue with notes by G. C. Ross. 1910. royal 8vo
Ross, Ronald, *Philosophies*. 1910. 12mo
Rossetti, D. G., trans. *Early Italian Poets*. Parts 1 and 2: Poets Chiefly before Dante; Dante and his Circle. n.d. 12mo
Royal Irish Academy. *Proceedings for the Year 1907*.
The Rushlight. 1906. crown 8vo
Ruskin, John., *Lectures on Art*. 1904. 12mo
——. *Modern Painters*. 6 vols. 1906. 12mo
——. *St. Mark's Rest*. n.d. 12mo
——. *The Seven Lamps of Architecture*. 1906. 12mo
——. *The Stones of Venice*. 3 vols. 1906. 12mo
S, E. M. *One Thing I Know*. On the power of the unseen. Preface by J. Arthur Hill. 1918. 12mo

Sabin, Arthur K. *Medea and Circe* and other poems. n.d. 18mo

St. Patrick's Day. Verses. 1919?

Saintsbury, G. *Dryden*. English Men of Letters. 1909. 12mo

Sarrar, Benoy Kumar. *Sacred Books of the Hindus*. Vol. 16: *The Positive Background of Hindu Sociology*. 1914. royal 8vo

Sassoon, Siegfried. *Counter-Attack* and other poems. 1919. 12mo

Sastri, K. S. Ramaswami. *The Life, Personality and Genius of Sir Rabindranath Tagore*. n.d. 12mo

Schopenhauer, A. *Counsels and Maxims*. Translated by T. Bailey Saunders. 1892. 12mo

——. *Essays*. n.d. 12mo

——. *Studies in Pessimism*, a series of essays. Translated by T. Bailey Saunders. 1892. 12mo

Scott-Elliott, W. *The Story of Atlantis*. 1896. 8vo

Seal, R. *The Positive Sciences of the Ancient Hindus*. 1915. 8vo

Selden, John. *Table Talk*. Edited by S. W. Singer. n.d. 12mo

Seymour, Sir John D. *St. Patrick's Purgatory*, a mediaeval pilgrimage in Ireland. n.d. 8vo

Shakespear, Olivia. *Uncle Hilary*. 1910. 12mo

Shakespeare, William. *The Works of William Shakespeare*. 1896. 4to

Shanks, Edward. *Poems*. 1916. 12mo

Sharp, William [Fiona Macleod]. *By Sundown Shores*, studies in spiritual history. 1902. 18mo, vellum

——. *The Dominion of Dreams*. 1899. 12mo

——. *Re-issue of the Shorter Stories of Fiona Macleod*, rearranged with additional tales. n.d. 12mo

——. *Where the Forest Murmurs, Nature Essays*. 1906. 12mo

Shelley, P. B. *Poetical Works*. n.d. 12mo

Sigerson, Dora. *A Dull Day in London* and other sketches. Introduction by Thomas Hardy. 1920. 12mo

——. *The Woman Who Went to Hell* and other ballads and lyrics. n.d. 12mo

Sir Gawain and the Green Knight. Retold in modern prose by Jessie L. Weston. 1898. 18mo

Sir Gawain at the Grail Castle. Translated by Jessie L. Weston. 1903. 18 mo

Simonde de Sismondi, Jean. *History of the Italian Republics*. n.d. 12mo

Smedley, Alfred. *Some Reminiscences*, an account of startling spiritual manifestations. 1900. 12mo

Smith, Joseph. *The Book of Mormon*, an account written by the Hand of Mormon. n.d. 12mo

Smith, W. F. *Rabelais*, in his writings. 1918. 8vo

Soldier Poets. Songs of the fighting men. 1916. 12mo

(Ditto) Another printing? 1917. 12mo

Soloviev, E. *Dostoievsky*. His life and literary activity. Translated by C. J. Hogarth. 1916. 12mo

Sophocles. *Oedipus King of Thebes*. Translated by Gilbert Murray. n.d. 8vo

Speeches from the Dock, or protests of Irish patriotism. 1868. 12mo

Spicer, Henry. *Sights and Sounds*, the mystery of the day. 1853. crown 8vo

Spinoza. *Ethics and de Intellectus Emendatione*. 1916. 12mo

Steele, Robert. *The Mirror of Perfection*. Translated from the Cottonian MS. 1903. 12mo

Steeves, G. Walter. *Francis Bacon*, a sketch of his life, works, and literary friends. 1910. 12mo

Steiner, Dr Rudolf. *Initiation and its Results*, a sequel to "The Way of Initiation." 1910. 12mo

Stephen, Leslie. *English Literature and Society in the 18th Century*. 1903. 12mo

Stephens, James. *Green Branches*. 1916. sm 4to Presentation Copy.

——. *The Insurrection in Dublin*. 1916. 12mo

Sterne, Laurence. *Life and Opinions of Tristram Shandy*. 1903. 12mo

Stevenson, Robert Louis. *Kidnapped*. 1914. 12mo

——. *New Arabian Nights*. 1913. 18mo

Stockham, Alice B. *Ethics of Marriage*. 1896. 12mo

Stone, Charles J. *Christianity before Christ* or prototypes of our faith and culture. 1885. crown 8vo

Strindberg, August. *The Inferno*. Translated by Claud Field. 1912. 12mo

——. *Legends, Autobiographical Sketches*. 1912. 12mo

——. *Zones of the spirit*, a book of thoughts. Translated by Claud Field. 1913. 12mo

Swedenborg, Emanuel. *Heaven and its Wonders, and Hell, from Things Heard and Seen.* 1911. 12mo

Swinburne, A. C. *Atalanta in Calydon.* 1897. 12mo

———. *A Channel Passage* and other poems. Title p. missing.

Synge, John M. *Poems and Translations.* 1909. 8vo

Tacitus. *Tacitus.* Vol. 1: *The Annals.* Translated by Arthur Murray. n.d. 12mo

———. Vol. 2: *History.* Translated by Arthur Murray. n.d. 12mo

Tagore, Maharishi Devendranath. *The Auto-Biography of Maharishi Devendranath Tagore.* Translated by S. Tagore. 1909. 8vo

Tagore, Rabindranath. *Glimpses of Bengal Life.* Short stories. Translated by Rajani Ranjan Sen. 1913. 12mo

Talmage, James E. *The Vitality of Mormonism.* 1919. 8vo

Tantra. Hymns to the Goddess. Translated by Arthur and Ellen Avalon. 1913. 8vo

Taylor, Isaac. *The Origin of the Aryans.* 1891. 12mo

Taylor, Rachel Annan. *Rose and Vine.* 1909. 12mo

Templeton, Rosamond. *The Mediators.* n.d. 8vo

Tennant, E. Wyndham. *Worple Flit,* and other poems. 1916. 12mo

Tennyson, Alfred. *Demeter* and other poems. 1889. 12mo

———. *Poems.* With an intro. by Alice Meynell. 1903. 12mo

———. *Poetical Works.* 1899. 12mo

Thackeray, W. M. *Vanity Fair.* n.d. 12mo

Theatre Arts Magazine. 3 numbers. 1917–19.

Theatre-Craft. A book of the new spirit in the theatre. n.d. 8vo

Thomas, H. H. *Little Gardens* and how to make the most of them. 1917. 12mo G[eorge] Y[eats]

Thompson, A. Hamilton. *A History of English Literature.* 1903. crown 8vo

Thompson, Francis. *Selected Poems.* 1908. 12mo

Thomson, C. L. *The Celtic Wonder World.* 1902. 12mo

The Three Men of Gotham, a motion for Marionnettes. Florence. 1919. 12mo

Thucydides. Translated by Richard Crawley. n.d. 12mo

Tietjens, Eunice. *Profiles from China,* sketches in verse, people and things seen in the interior. 1917. 12mo Presentation copy.

Tietkens, Ernest A. *Mediumistic and Psychical Experiences.* n.d. 12mo

Traill, H. D. *S. T. Coleridge.* English Men of Letters. 1909. 12mo Another copy.

Trevelyan, G. M. *Garibaldi and the Making of Italy. June–November 1860.* 1920. 12mo

———. *Garibaldi and the Thousand. May 1860.* 1920. 12mo

———. *Garibaldi's Defence of the Roman Republic. 1848–9.* 1920. 12mo

Tristan and Iseult. n.d. 18mo

Trobridge, G. *Life of Swedenborg* with a popular exposition of his teachings. 1913. 12mo

Trollope, Henry M. *Corneille and Racine.* 1898. 12mo

Twelve Poets. A miscellany of new verse. 1918. 12mo

Tynan, Katharine. *Flower of Youth.* Poems in War Time. 1915. 12mo

———. *Innocencies.* A book of verse., 1905. 12mo Another copy.

———. *Irish Poems.* 1913. 12mo Presentation copy.

———. *An Isle in the Water.* 1895. 12mo

———. *The Middle Years.* 1916. 8vo Presentation copy.

———. *New Poems.* 1911. 12mo Presentation copy.

Van Stone, J. H. *The Pathway of the Soul.* A study in zodiacal symbology. 1912. 12mo

[Veronese]. *Masterpieces of Veronese 1528–1588.* 1910. 12mo

Wade, W. Cecil. *The Symbolism of Heraldry.* 1898. 4to

Wagner, Dr W. and M. W. Macdonall. *Asgard and the Gods:* the tales and traditions of our northern ancestors. 1894. 8vo

Waite, Arthur Edward. *The Hidden Church of the Holy Graal,* its legends and symbolism. 1909. 8vo

Waller, Edmund. *Poems.* Edited by G. T. Drury. Vol. 1. 1893. 12mo

———. *Poems.* Edited by G. Thorn Drury. Vol. 2. n.d. 12mo

Waterhouse, Elizabeth. *A Little Book of Life and Death.* 1902. 18mo

Waters, W. G. *Jerome Cardan.* A biographical study. 1898. 8vo

Welby, Horace. *Predictions Realized in Modern Times*. 1862. 12mo

Wells, H. G. *Russia in the Shadows*. n.d. 12mo

West, Rebecca. *Henry James*. 1916. 12mo G[eorge] Y[eats]

Weston, Jessie L. *The Legend of Sir Gawain*. Studies upon its original scope and significance. 1897. 12mo

———. *The Legend of Sir Perceval*. Studies upon its origin, development and position in the Arthurian cycle. 2 vols. 1906. crown 8vo

———. *Romance Vision Satire*, English poems of the 14th Century, newly rendered in the original metres. 1912. 8vo

———. *The Three Days Tournament*, a study in romance and folk-lore. 1902. 12mo

Weygandt, Cornelius. *Irish Plays and Playwrights*. 1913. 8vo

Whall, C. W. *Stained Glass Work*. A text book for students. 1905. 12mo

Whitney, Orson Ferguson. *Love and Light*, an idyl of the Westland. 1918. 12mo

Whittaker, Thomas. *The Neo-Platonists*, a study in the history of Hellenism. 2nd ed. 1918 8vo

Widtsoe, John A. *Joseph Smith as Scientist*, a contribution to Mormon philosophy.

Wiltonian Hero-Ballads. Translated by Hector Maclean.

Withers, Hartley. *The Cathedral Church of Canterbury*, a description of its fabric, and a brief history of the see. 1911. 12mo

Wordsworth, William. *Poems*. Introduction by Alice Meynell. 1903. 12mo

———. *Poetical Works*. Edited by Matthew Arnold. 1915. 12mo

———. *Poetical Works*. n.d. 12mo

———. *The Recluse*. 1888. 12mo

Wyatt, A. J. and W. H. Low. *Intermediate Text-book of English Literature*. 1909. 12mo

Xenophon. *Anabasis and Memorabilia*. Translated by J. S. Watson. 1915. 12mo

Yonge, Charlotte M. *History of France*. 1909. 18mo

[NOTE: Many books from Yeats family collections, dispersed over the years, turn up in booksellers' catalogues, auction sales, and collections familiar to scholars. *Yeats Annual* will publish lists of such books from time to time, and readers who know of, or possess books from the Yeats family collections might care to write to the editor about them. In some cases a short note might be preferable to a citation, and will be published. In all cases, however, the fuller the provenance the better. *Ed.*]

Location Register of Twentieth-Century English Literary Manuscripts and Letters: a Supplementary Listing of Yeats Holdings

The establishment of the national Location Register of Twentieth-century English Literary Manuscripts and Letters in the University of Reading Library was described in *Yeats Annual* No. 3, pp. 295–303. The work of collecting information has continued through 1984–5, although some repositories with large Yeats collections, most notably the National Library of Ireland, have still to be covered. The Location Register is not yet available for public consultation and the form of the entries which follow is to some extent provisional. Comments would be welcome. These entries are a supplement to those published in *Yeats Annual* No. 3. It is envisaged that a cumulative, re-edited list of all Yeats entries to date will be included in *Yeats Annual* No. 5.

David C. Sutton

YEATS, W. B., 1865–1939
   Cambridge. Churchill College. Archives Centre (Private). In CHAN I 5/21
   4 letters [1 incomplete] from W. B. Yeats to Edith Lyttelton. – [18— and 19—]
   Owned
   Access: by written appointment. – [May 1984]   re00073733

YEATS, W. B., 1865–1939
   Cambridge. Fitzwilliam Museum (Public). In Wilfrid Scawen. Blunt papers
   Photographs of Wilfrid Scawen Blunt, his friends and family – [ca. 1853–1914]. – About 150 items
   Owned. – With other memorabilia of Wilfrid Scawen Blunt, including a piece of oakum from his time in Galway Gaol
   Access: by appointment. – [May 1984]   re00083526

YEATS, W. B., 1865–1939
  Cambridge. Fitzwilliam Museum (Public)
    Letter from W. B. Yeats to Mr Linnell. – 1894
    Autograph. – Owned
    Access: by appointment. – [Mar 1984]   re00088349

YEATS, W. B., 1865–1939
  Cambridge. Trinity College (Cambridge). Library (Private). Myers 22^{87-90};
  25^{14-14}
    Letters from W. B. Yeats to Mrs E. Myers. – 1907–1901
    Owned
    Access: by appointment. – [May 1984]   re0007621x

YEATS, W. B., 1865–1939
  Canterbury. The King's School (Private)
    The isle of statues: an Arcadian fairy-tale in two acts / by W. B. Yeats.–
    49 pages, bound
    Autograph. – Owned. – Published in the "Dublin University Review" in
    1885
    Access: by appointment. – [Feb 1983]   re00002097

YEATS, W. B., 1865–1939
  Dublin. University College Dublin. Library (Public). CUR.L. 5–6
    2 letters from W. B. Yeats to Constantine P. Curran. – [193– and 1936]
    Owned
    Access: by appointment. – [Nov 1983]   re00061352

YEATS, W. B., 1865–1939
  Dublin. University College Dublin. Library (Public). CUR.L. 3
    Letter from W. B. Yeats agreeing to come to Cambridge to speak during the
    summer term. – 1903. – 1 leaf MS (not autograph), signed. – Owned. –
    Recipient unidentified
    Access: by appointment. – [Nov 1983]   re00061336

YEATS, W. B., 1865–1939
  Dublin. University College Dublin. Library (Public). CUR.L.4
    Letter from W. B. Yeats to [W.G.?] Fay about the staging of "The
    hour-glass". – 1903. – 1 leaf
    Signed TS. – Owned
    Access: by appointment. – [Nov 1983]   00061344

YEATS, W. B., 1865–1939
  Edinburgh. National Library of Scotland (Public). In Acc. 7175
    2 letters from W. B. Yeats to John Purves. – [18— or 19—]
    Autograph. – Owned. – [Jul 1983]   re00027952

YEATS, W. B., 1865–1939
Edinburgh. National Library of Scotland (Public). MS. 9331
15 letters from W. B. Yeats to Sir Herbert Grierson. – 1907–1935. – 43 folios
Mostly autograph, some signed TS. – Owned. – [Jul 1983]

YEATS, W. B., 1865–1939
Edinburgh. National Library of Scotland (Public). Acc. 8035
Letter from W. B. Yeats to Mark André Raffalovich. – [18— or 19—]
Owned. – [Jul 1983]   re00034401

YEATS, W. B., 1865–1939
Edinburgh. National Library of Scotland (Public). Dep. 205, Box 1a
Letter from W. B. Yeats to R. B. Cunninghame Graham. – 1914
Signed TS. – On deposit. – [Jul 1983]   re00039632

YEATS, W. B., 1865–1939
Edinburgh. National Library of Scotland (Public). MS. 5914
Letter from W. B. Yeats to Richard Burdon Haldane. – 1918
Owned. – [Jul 1983]   re00040703

YEATS, W. B., 1865–1939
Edinburgh. National Library of Scotland (Public). MS. 4684
Letters from W. B. Yeats to William Blackwood & Sons. – 1898
Owned. – [Jul 1983]   re00038342

YEATS, W. B., 1865–1939
Edinburgh. National Library of Scotland (Public). MS. 9864
Letters to Clement King Shorter and John Malcolm Bulloch, as editors of
various literary magazines. – [18— or 19—]
Owned. – [Jul 1983]   re00026743

YEATS, W. B., 1985–1939
Leeds. Brotherton Library. Brotherton Collection (Public). In Clodd Corre-
spondence
6 letters from W. B. Yeats to Edward Clodd. – [18— and 19—]
Owned
Access: by appointment. – [Jul 1984]   re00089109

YEATS, W. B., 1986–1939
Leeds. Brotherton Library. Brotherton Collection (Public). In Gosse Corre-
spondence
25 letters from W. B. Yeats to Edmund Gosse. – [1903–1917]
Owned
Access: by appointment. – [Mar 1984]   re00062111

YEATS, W. B., 1865–1939
London. British Library. Department of Manuscripts (Public).
Add.Mss. 50553, ff. 142–167
7 letters from W. B. Yeats to Bernard Shaw. – 1901–1932

Autograph & signed TS. – Owned. – With typescript copies of 2 letters by Shaw, and originals of related correspondence by W. G. Fay and others. – [Jul 1984]   re00087726

YEATS, W. B., 1865–1939
London. British Library. Department of Manuscripts (Public). Add.Mss. 57752
Letters in Alida Monro's collected in-mail. – [1914–1969]
Owned
The Arts Council collection of modern literary manuscripts, 1963–1972: a catalogue/by Jenny Stratford (1974), pp. 145–146. – [Jun 1983]   re00023116

YEATS, W. B., 1865–1939
London. University of London. Library (Public). Sturge Moore papers, box 2:76–77
2 letters from W. B. Yeats to T. Sturge Moore, 1 with a draft reply, the other with a draft letter from T. Sturge Moore to Marie Sturge Moore. – [1932–1933?]
On permanent loan. – [Apr 1984]   re00078646

YEATS, W. B., 1865–1939
Oxford. Bodleian Library (Public). MS.Eng.lett. c. 255
2 letters from W. B. Yeats to John Masefield. – 1930–1935
Owned. – [May 1983]   re00017337

YEATS, W. B., 1865–1939
Oxford. Bodleian Library (Public). Dep.Bridges 105; 120, fols. 159–160
Correspondence between Robert Bridges and W. B. Yeats. – [1896–1930]. – Some copies
On deposit. – [Jan 1984]   re00047368

YEATS, W. B., 1865–1939
Oxford. Bodleian Library (Public). MS.Walpole d. 19
Letters and autographs, mostly sent to John Lane, some sent to Hugh Walpole: [various correspondents]. – [19—]
Autograph. – Owned. – Catalogued. – [Jun 1983]   re00017450

YEATS, W. B., 1865–1939
Oxford. Bodleian Library (Public). MS.Don. d. 135
Letters from Robert Bridges to Lascelles Abercrombie and others. – [19—?]
Owned. – Recipients include Lascelles Abercrombie (18 letters) & W. B. Yeats (26 letters, with 2 from Yeats to Bridges). – [Apr 1983]   re00035335

YEATS, W. B., 1865–1939
Oxford. Bodleian Library (Public). In Dep.Bridges 118
Letters of condolence to Mrs Robert Bridges on the death of her husband: [various correspondents]. – 1930
On deposit. – [Jan 1984]   re00047333

YEATS, W. B., 1865–1939
  Reading. University of Reading. Library (Public). MS 293/2/3/2
    Easter 1916: [poem]/ by W. B. Yeats; with corrections by Mrs Yeats. –
    [191–?]. – 4 folios: photocopy
    TS. – Owned. – [Jun 1984]   re00085472

YEATS, W. B., 1965–1939
  Reading. University of Reading. Library (Public). MS 293/2/3/1
    The poems of William Blake: [papers relating to the work (1893)]/ edited by
    W. B. Yeats. – 5 folios
    Autograph. – Owned. – [Jun 1984]   re00085480

YEATS, W. B., 1865–1939
  Reading. University of Reading. Library (Public). MS. 293/2/2
    The works of William Blake . . ./ edited by Edwin J. Ellis and W. B. Yeats.
    – 1893. – 3 volumes
    Autograph & printed book with autograph annotation. – Owned. – In the
    hands of Edwin J. Ellis and W. B. Yeats – With a note on allegory and
    symbol by Edwin J. Ellis. – [Jun 1984]
                                                                   re00085499

YEATS, W. B., 1865–1939
  Reading. University of Reading. Library (Public). MS 293/1/1
    9 letters from W. B. Yeats, 5 to Edwin J. Ellis, 4 to Mrs Ellis. – [ca. 1890–ca.
    1922]
    Owned. – [Jun 1984]   re00085464

YEATS, W. B., 1865–1939
  Stratford-upon-Avon. Shakespeare Birthplace Trust. Records Office.
  ER136/63
    John Sherman; and, Dhoya/ by W. B. Yeats. – [1891?]. – Sheets of the 2nd
    ed., published by T. Fisher Unwin
    Revised proofs. – Owned. – Corrected apparently for a new ed. by the
    Shakespeare Head Press. – Signed "W. B. Yeats, November 1891". – [Feb
    1983]   re00002054

YEATS, W. B., 1986–1939, recipient
  Edinburgh. National Library of Scotland (Public). MS. 8783
    20 letters from William Sharp to various correspondents, including 1 to W.
    B. Yeats. – [1894–1905]
    Owned. – [Jul 1983]   re00029834

YEATS, W. B., 1865–1939, recipient
  London. University College, London. Library (Public). In Plowman Collection, Box 1
    Copybook of letters from Max Plowman on poetry readings. – 1907–1908. –
    Pressed copies
    Autograph. – Owned. – Includes letters to Stopford A. Brooke, E. V. Lucas,

T. Sturge Moore, Sir William Watson & W. B. Yeats
Access: by appointment. – [Nov 1983]   re00058475

YEATS, W. B., 1865–1939, recipient
London. University of London. Library (Public). Sturge Moore papers, boxes
2:112A; 26:179
  2 letters [drafts] from T. Sturge Moore to W. B. Yeats. – [18— or 19—]
  On permanent loan. – [May 1984]   re0007750x

YEATS, W. B., 1865–1939, recipient
London. University of London. Library (Public). A.L. 306
  Letter [draft] from T. Sturge Moore to W. B. Yeats. – 1932
  Autograph. – Owned. – [May 1984]   re00081655

Recent Postgraduate Research

Compiled by K. P. S. Jochum, Olympia Sitwell, and Warwick Gould

As well as catching up upon the reprinting of doctoral abstracts from *Dissertation Abstracts International* (see below p. 301) which were omitted from *YEATS ANNUAL* No. 3 for lack of space, we offer for the first time a wider range of information concerning recently completed postgraduate research. K. P. S. Jochum has kindly provided a list of unpublished European doctoral dissertations on W. B. Yeats, 1969–1980. To this has been added more recent information upon European dissertations including abstracts, when these have proved to be available, though not listed in DAI. Because European M.Phil. and M.Litt. and B.Litt. dissertations are frequently substantial pieces of research, these have been included for the years 1980 to date. They have not been consistently listed for the prior years, yet theses submitted for these degrees, such as that of Peter Kuch: "W. B. Yeats and George Russell: an Inquiry into Their Literary Association" (M.Litt.: Oxford, 1978), or that of A. Armstrong: "The Manuscript of *The Herne's Egg* by W. B. Yeats" (M.Litt., Oxford, 1979), are important pieces of work.

PRELIMINARY CHECKLIST OF UNPUBLISHED EUROPEAN DOCTORAL DISSERTATIONS ON YEATS, 1969–80

K. P. S. Jochum

The following checklist comprises theses not covered in my *W. B. Yeats: an Annotated Bibliography of Criticism* (1978). Theses subsequently published in book form are not included. Many of the items listed below could not be inspected personally. Exceptions are noted by an asterisk.

Agostini, René: "La technique dramatique des auteurs de l'Abbey Theatre 1890–1910", Montpellier III, 1975.
Argoff, N. J. F.: "The Hearth and Road: the Countryman in the Works of W. B. Yeats", University College Dublin, 1980.

Arrell, Douglas Harrison: "The Old Drama and the New: Conceptions of the Nature of Theatrical Experience in the Work of William Archer, G. B. Shaw, W.B. Yeats, E. G. Craig and H. Granville Barker", London, 1976.*

Backès, Jean-Louis: "Aspects du drame poétique dans le symbolisme européen (Blok, Yeats, Claudel, Hofmannsthal)", Paris IV, 1972.*

Beard, William Russell: "Shaw's *John Bull's Other Island*: a Critical, Historical, and Theatrical Study", London, 1974.*

Boué, André: "William Carleton, 1794–1869: Romancier irlandais", Paris III, 1973.*

Bradley, William: "The Poetry of *The Nation*, 1842–1848: a Descriptive and Critical Study with Some Reference to the Influence on the Poetic Development of W. B. Yeats", London, 1977.*

Carlson, Craig Burnham: "The Shock of New Material: the Development of W. B. Yeats's Literary Use of William Blake", Exeter, 1972.*

Cardew, A. L.: "Symbolist Drama and the Problem of Symbolism", Essex, 1980.

Dudek, J. M.: "The Poetics of W. B. Yeats and K. Wierzynski: A Parallel", Oxford, 1980.

Dufour, Michel: "Le symbole de la rose dans l'oeuvre de W. B. Yeats", Caen, 1980.*

Franchi, Florence: "L'influence du no japonais sur les *Four Plays for Dancers* de W. B. Yeats", Montpellier III, 1979.

El-Ghamrawi, Ahmed Abdel-Wahab: "Some Eastern and Esoteric Aspects in the Work of W. B. Yeats", Exeter, 1977.*

Griffiths, E.: "Writing and Speaking: the Work of Eliot, Yeats and Pound", Cambridge, 1980.

Grünwald, Constanze: "Yeats und die Versuchung des Ostens: Die Rolle der indischen transzendentalen Philosophie in Yeats' Dichtung seit seiner Begegnung mit Shri Purohit Swami, 1931", München, 1979.*

Hanna, Nashed G.: "Oriental Influence on the Poetry of W. B. Yeats", University College Galway, 1975.

Khorol'skii, Viktor Vasil'evich: "Poeziia U. B. Ĭetsa 1880-kh–1920-kh godov (Evoliutsiia obraznoĭ sistemy)", Moscow (Mosk. gos. ped. in-t. im. V. I. Lenina), 1978. (Avtoreferat*)

Kornelius, Joachim: "Stilstatistische Untersuchungen zum Drama der 'Irish Renaissance' unter besonderer Berücksichtigung des Dramenwerks J. M. Synges: Ein Beitrag zur mathematisch-stilistischen Analyse der Formalstruktur dramatischer Werke", Giessen, 1974.*

Krivina, Tereza Menakhimovna: "Poeticheskaia drama Vil'iama Batlera Ĭeĭtsa (K probleme interpretatsii natsional'noĭ mifologii i fol'klora)", Leningrad (Leningradskiĭ gos. ped. in-t. im. A. I. Gertsena), 1978. (Avtoreferat*)

Leamon, Warren C.: "Shaw, Yeats and the Modern Theatre", University College Dublin, 1973.

McDonald, Betty Moore: "La influencia de la literatura en el desarollo del nacionalismo irlandés", Valladolid, 1974.

Marshall, Kathleen Engel: "Modern Irish Poets and Dramatists and the Fenian Cycle", Trinity College Dublin, 1973.

Mignot, Alain: "Littérature de l'Insurrection de Paques 1916", Paris III, 1975.*

Moya, Carmela: "L'univers de Sean O'Casey d'après les autobiographies", Paris (Sorbonne), 1970.*

Murphy, Daniel: "Two Mystical Poets: Yeats and AE", University College Dublin, 1969.

Napier, William Michael: "Critical Method in the Early Reviewers of W. B. Yeats: a Bibliographical and Critical Study", Leeds, 1973.*

Nash, J. P.: "Materialist Revolutionary Art and Metaphysical Reactionary Art: Eisenstein and Yeats, Eliot, Pound", Trinity College Dublin, 1977. Cf. *Dissertation Abstracts International*, 38:4 (Summer 1978), 4646 C.

Nimmo, D. C.: "Yeats's Metaphors of the Mind", Newcastle upon Tyne, 1977.

Painter, Susan Gay: " 'Drama within the Limitations of Art': a Study of some Plays of Maeterlinck, Yeats, Beckett, and Pinter", London, 1978.*

Plowright, Poh Sim: "The Influence of Oriental Theatrical Techniques on the Theory and Practice of Western Drama", London, 1976.*

Poliudova, Tat'iana Mikhaĭlovna: "Dramaturgiia U. B. Ĭetsa kontsa XIX–nachala XX vekov (Teoriia poetĭcheskoĭ dramy. Masterstvo dramaturga)", Moscow (Mosk. gos. ped. in-t. im. V. I. Lenina), 1978. (Avtoreferat*)

Qureshi, Zahid Jamil: "The Forming of Yeatsian Drama: a Study of the Manuscripts 1915–1939", Oxford, 1976.*

Ratcliffe, D.: "The Nature of Being as a Preoccupation in Twentieth Century Poetry", Nottingham, 1977.

Rau-Guntermann, Mechthild: "Die Einheit von W. B. Yeats' *The Tower* (1928): Zu einer Poetik des lyrischen Zyklus im Symbolismus", Köln, 1974.*

Stanley, Margaret: "W. B. Yeats et la France", Lille III, 1977.*

Sullivan, Daniel: "The Literary Periodical and the Anglo-Irish Revival 1894–1914", University College Dublin, 1969.

Thilliez, Christiane: "W. B. Yeats – E. G. Craig: Autour d'une correspondance inédite", Lille III, 1977.*

Tishunina, Nataliia Viktorovna: "U. B. Ĭets i stanovlenie teatral'noĭ kul'tury v Irlandii", Leningrad (Leningradskiĭ gos. in-t. teatra, muzyki i kinematografii), 1978. (Avtoreferat*)

Tye, James Reginald: "Literary Periodicals of the Eighteen-Nineties: a Survey of the Monthly and Quarterly Magazines and Reviews", Oxford, 1970.*

RECENT UK DISSERTATIONS

Olympia Sitwell and Warwick Gould

Moran, Gerard: "W. B. Yeats's *Autobiographies* in the context of Irish autobiographical writing", Ph.D., London, 1984. [No abstract available].

Richards, D.: "Literature and Anthropology: the Relationship of Literature to Anthropological Data and Theory, with Special Reference to the Works of Sir Walter Scott, W. B. Yeats and Wole Soyinka", Ph.D., Cambridge, 1982. *ASLIB Index to Theses* 31:2, No. 4370.

ABSTRACT

This thesis surveys the history of anthropological thought from 1750, and demonstrates how anthropological data and theory have assisted three writers in the formation of national and cultural symbols.

In the case of Sir Walter Scott, I examine his background of Rational philosophy, particularly that of the Scottish Enlightenment, and how these thinkers shaped an anthropological conspectus. I trace this influence in the "Scottish" novels of Sir Walter Scott, and examine the divergence of Rationalist and Romantic premises as they are evident in different narrative techniques. To this end I discuss Scott's portrayal of Highland culture and society, and focus on the figure of the Highland "barbarian" and his place in the natural landscape.

The tension evident in the history of anthropology between the rational and the Romantic is sustained in my discussion of the works of W. B. Yeats. I trace the growth of a disillusionment with "scientific" analytical methods and the strengthening of a metaphysical and speculative approach, and I look at the effect this approach has on Yeats's reception of poetic symbols and national politics. I consider, also, the importance of the study of race in forming Yeats's notions of Celtic mythology and culture, and comment upon his presentation of the figure of Cuchulain in this light.

The Romantic and metaphysical strain in anthropological thought is again to the forefront of my discussion of Wole Soyinka. I consider how the ethnography of the Yoruba people of Nigeria, particularly its religious and mythical content, and also the ethno-psychological interpretations of culture, have influenced Soyinka's work. Here, I examine the representation of the deity, Ogun, and Soyinka's assertion of that god's role in the spiritual, cultural, and political life of the Yoruba.

On a more general or theoretical level, the thesis discusses the way in which literary and anthropological writers have recorded or adapted the symbolic forms and relations of a community. At this juncture anthropology intersects with literary concerns, and it is the examination of this nexus which is the motive of this thesis.

Sepida, T.: "Yeats and Women: the Nineteenth Century", Ph.D. Reading, 1981. [No abstract available].

Smith, R. N.: "Romantic Alienation as a Principle of Creativity in the Writings of W. B. Yeats", M.Litt., Aberdeen, 1980. *ASLIB Index to Theses* 31:1, No 364.

ABSTRACT

This study of romantic alienation as a creative principle in Yeats's writings is intended to contribute to a wider understanding of Yeats's views of the artist and the relationship between pain and creativity in Yeats's work. The theme of romantic alienation occurred in various forms in nineteenth century literature and many of the individual aspects of Yeats's own work were anticipated by the romantics notably Blake, Shelley and Keats. Thus Yeats can be connected with his romantic precursors from whom he inherited similar aspects of alienation. However Yeats was able to extend the romantic idea of alienation much further than his predecessors so that his concept incorporated ideas about the necessary consequences of alienation, namely suffering, loss defeat, adversity and the creative possibilities that arise from an awareness of these tragic factors. Yeats's early writings reveal how he readily adapted himself to the romantic notion of isolation, which developed in his middle period to an advanced and more original, but deliberately chosen, awareness of the power of alienation as a positive creative force. In his later years, as exemplified by *The Tower*, Yeats's "embrace" of pain was no longer merely a consciously chosen aesthetic device, but also a brutal reality, whereby his inspiration and creativity were wrought from the sufferings he experienced in old age. Thus, in his complete awareness of the imminence of death, Yeats becomes a kind of tragic hero, as his poetry is made from the defiance of mortality, and his decrepit body and its pain become, paradoxically, a theme for vision and passionate art. Moreover, in the later writings, Yeats projects his ideas of personal suffering outward into a vision of existence, whereby he comes to define life and history as a tragic drama in which the artist plays an important but essentially alienated role.

Southworth, K. H.: " 'The Tradition of Myself' ": Approaches to Personal Experience in the Poetry of W. B. Yeats". M.Phil., London, 1980. [Abstract not available].

Sugiyama, S.: "Yeats and the Ireland of His Time", M.Phil., Leicester, 1980. [Abstract not available to these compilers.] See however *ASLIB Index to Theses* 30:2, No 4529.

DISSERTATION ABSTRACTS, 1982–1983

Note: The dissertation titles and abstracts listed hereunder are published with the kind permission of University Microfilms International, publisher of *Dissertation Abstracts International* (copyright 1982, 1983 by University Microfilms International), and may not be reproduced without their prior permission. Unless otherwise stated, copies of the dissertations are available upon request from University Microfilms International, 300 North Zeeb Road, Ann Arbor, Michigan 48106, USA

IMITATION, FREEDOM, AND THE TRIADIC MODEL IN THE EARLY DRAMATIC
AND NARRATIVE WORKS OF W. B. YEATS
Order No. DA8221057
Bell, Gloria Jean, Ph.D. *University of Colorado at Boulder*, 1982. 258pp.
Director: Associate Professor Edward P. Nolan

Triads and triangles appear everywhere in Yeats – his poetry, prose, drama, and
life. The love triangle, a topic Yeats says "inspired Homer", inspired Yeats as
well, providing him with one of his masks – that of unsuccessful lover. Yeats
collected stories involving love triangles, recording them in *The Celtic Twilight*
and *The Secret Rose* and developing them into numerous lyrics and into dramatic
poems. Sometimes Yeats focused directly on the relationships involved in a
triangle, examining the jealousy and rivalry assumed to be inherent in love
triangles. More often however, his triangle is a structural device for making
comparisons – for example, between the everyday world of reality and a reality
that incorporates a supernatural significance (fairy, occult, or spiritual) or for
exploring susceptibility to the influence of models. In *John Sherman*, overlapping
triangles are used to make comparisons and reveal patterns of mediation. In
Deirdre, a single triangle reveals that selection of a model does not necessarily
mean bondage to a single mediator.

Yeats was also interested in a triangular configuration that is a variety of what
Girard labels *external mediation* – a triangle in which words provide a model for
action. Even in his early works, Yeats reveals his ambivalence toward the power
of the written or spoken word. The ambivalence has two major sources. First, the
model expressed by words is powerful, but the poet cannot be assured of
controlling the power he unleashes. A second cause for anxiety is that any word is
but one model of reality – not the total reality; other words present other pictures.
Hence, choosing between models is inherent in the human condition. In three
early works, Yeats deals with the agony of the human being faced with choice –
Hanrahan, who hesitates; Oisin, who first chooses, then renounces, and finally
reaffirms his choice; and Cathleen, who remains steady in her choice, fully aware
of the opinions she must reject in doing so.

In his later poetic and dramatic works, Yeats continued to deal with these
concepts, as can be seen in a tentative reading of the plays in which Cuchulain is
the central figure. (*DAI* 43:4 [Oct. 1982] 1149-A)

ON THE WAY TO THE RAG-AND-BONE SHOP: A DEVELOPMENTAL STUDY OF W. B.
YEATS'S USE OF EASTERN ICONOLOGIES
Order No. DA8328159
Boyd, Stephen Kent, Ph.D. *The University of Nebraska—Lincoln*, 1983. 198pp.
Advisers: Lee T. Lemon, Paul A. Olson

The dissertation reassesses the role of Eastern thought in Yeats's poetry and
finds it to be lifelong and central to his world view.

Beginning with his earliest poethood (1885) it traces his attractions to both the religious practices of the East and to the conceptual frameworks (iconologies) which complement them. The earliest poetry (1885–90) is marked by a superficial, Romantic exploitation of Eastern materials for their exoticism. At the same time Yeats was adopting a regimen of meditation he called his most important intellectual influence up to his fortieth year. In the 1890s and at the turn of the century he attempted to fulfill his religious impulse (which he singled out as his identifying characteristic) in a pseudo-mystery religion of his own devising.

The early years of the new century witnessed two pivotal realizations in Yeats's life and work: he both came to a profound acceptance of reincarnation and to a deeply felt conviction that meditative practices must be matched by the cultivation of analytical systems ("philosophies") which render intelligible to our ordinary waking consciousness the other realms meditation opens. *Per Amica* and *A Vision* chronicle the pursuit of such knowledge.

In the last two decades of his life, the period of his most profound work, he greatly expanded and particularized his grasp of Eastern thought. The presence of the Tantric schools is especially felt; coming to him both through sacred texts and in intimate friendship with an Tantric adept, he found in them a vision that denied no part of the human totality. Through the Tantra Yeats was able to reconcile the claims of the heart and mind, body and soul. It was as if Yeats's whole life was a preparation for death and, it was in these Eastern systems he at last found the means of self-transformation whereby he might face the "Great Questioner" with a "fitting confidence". (*DAI* 44:8 [Feb. 1984] 2476-A).

THE DANCE OF APOCALYPSE: YEATS AND MICHAEL ROBARTES
Order No. DA8224599
Bronson, Edward Fulton, Ph.D. *University of Maryland*, 1982. 241pp.
Supervisor: Professor Milne Holton

One of the dominant impulses behind the life and work of W. B. Yeats is the drive to unify. Scholars such as Richard Ellmann, Hugh Kenner, John Unterecker, and John Joseph Sullivan have shown in varying ways that Yeats sought to unify his life and reflect it in his writings. What this dissertation lends to their efforts is an appreciation of the role of the fictive character Michael Robartes in Yeats's pursuit of unity. Arising from Yeats's passion for the occult, the character served to point a direction away from Yeats's father. He offered the youthful poet an identity through which he could unify his life and work through an occult conception of symbol. What this meant specifically was that Yeats wanted to integrate his interests through symbol and reflect the unity in his writings. Yeats's interests were Irish nationalism, the occult, and an obsessional sexual passion for the Irish revolutionary Maud Gonne.

In my opening chapters, I will show that Yeats's initial use of Michael Robartes fails to express the unity Yeats sought. The reason has to do, for the most part, with Yeats's confusion over the relation between time and eternal vision, a confusion that expresses itself in the contradictory desire to transcend time while leading a normal sexual life within it. Robartes's early death in the short story "Rosa Alchemica" expresses the impasse.

My middle and concluding chapters will show both the revival of Michael Robartes and Yeats's considerable success in finally being able to integrate his life and work and express the fact through Robartes. Robartes plays an important role in the unity of *The Wild Swans at Coole* and *Michael Robartes and the Dancer*. He is also important to the genesis of *A Vision*, where he makes his last appearance in Yeats's writings. What my study will show, in fact, is that Robartes is an intrinsic part of the personal and historical dialectic that Yeats constructed in order to attain unity, and that he expresses the fact. Yeats made the determination to seek unity early in his life, and he pursued it to the end. (*DAI* 43:5 [Nov. 1982] 1550-1-A).

THE PROSE STYLE OF W. B. YEATS'S *AUTOBIOGRAPHY*
Order No. 8201651
Davies, Joan Mary, Ph.D. *University of Maryland*, 1981. 170pp. Supervisor: Dr John D. Russell

In his *Autobiography* Yeats wrote to fulfill a self-imposed formula: to "write out (our) thoughts in as nearly as possible the language (we) thought them in". Diligent in his commitment, he eschewed the traditional autobiographer's coherence-seeing methods in an attempt to reproduce "as nearly as possible" the workings of the individual mind. By means of close textual analysis of the *Autobiography*, I have isolated certain recurring lexical and syntactical features of Yeats's style which seem to me to contribute to most of the work's obliqueness.

In the introduction I have attempted to validate my method. Reviewing the position of several leading scholars in the field of prose style analysis, I give my sanction to the school of thought which promotes the notion of "epistemic choice" – that is, a writer's basic way of seeing and knowing is discoverable in certain limitations governing the way he says things – and also the notion that style is as much "the essential activity of imaginative prose" as it is of poetry.

The main focus of my study is on the second chapter of the *Autobiography: the Trembling of the Veil* (1922), since *Veil* shows Yeats's style at its most fully developed. It is flanked on the one side by a chapter on *Reveries Over Childhood and Youth* (1916), an account of Yeats's early experiences, and on the other by a chapter dealing with the more fragmentary portions of the *Autobiography, The Bounty of Sweden* (1925), *Estrangement* (1925), *The Death of Synge* (1928), and *Dramatis Personae* (1935). The *Reveries* chapter illustrates the creation of a disjointed, dream-like narrative. The blurred time sequence is the result of the heavy use of passive verbs, unexpected tense shifts and modifying constructions. Further examination reveals frequent ambiguity, series of evasive antithesis and a solidly monosyllabic prose, indicating a narrator less inclined to honest self-revelation than to a marked tendency to posture. The chapter dealing with *The Trembling of the Veil*, shows the same subjective patterning of experience and only the most fragile deference to things as they actually occurred. The authorial voice becomes more patently sophisticated and has more ingratiating devices by way of style markers. For example, there are many more interrogative clauses. The remaining sections of the *Autobiography*, I maintain, are characterized by an altogether different ground style because they are differently motivated. *Dramatis Personae* reflects an intermediary style, still showing the tendency to ellipsis and disjunction but making greater concessions to rhetorical order. *Estrangement* and *The Death of Synge*, as largely verbatim transcripts of diary entries, cause Yeats to appear less interested in the effect of style as far as a future reader is concerned and are shown to be stylistically conventional. *The Bounty of Sweden* (which derives from his experiences in Sweden when he was awarded the Nobel Prize) with its strict chronology and freedom from digression is the furthest removed in style from *Reveries*.

The question of the relationship between Yeats's poetry and his prose is addressed in the last chapter. Analysing several poems, mostly taken from the period around the time of the writing of *Veil*, this chapter establishes a vital similarity – in stylistic terms – between these and Yeats's prose, in effect proving that Yeats's prose in the *Autobiography* (most particularly in *Veil*) is closer to poetry than prose. (*DAI* 42:8 [Feb. 1982] 3609-A)

THE ARCHETYPAL IMAGE: AN INTERPRETATION OF THE POETRY OF THEO-DORE ROETHKE, ARTHUR RIMBAUD, W. B. YEATS, AND ROBERT FROST
Order No. DA8404905
Farrell, Leigh Ann Dawes, Ph.D. *University of Washington*, 1983. 245pp.
Chairperson: Professor Ernst H. Behler

This study of the poetry of Roethke, Rimbaud, Yeats and Frost explores the archetypal images by which these diverse poets attempt to divide and unify experience and resolve the manifold paradoxes of the human condition. Each chapter centres on and elucidates the work of one poet, analysing his uniquely individual themes, symbols, and language in terms of the universal archetypal image informing his poetry. A central assumption of this dissertation is that the common aim of those poets' works is a *symbolon*, a bringing together of heterogeneous natures: child-man, male-female, puer eternus-hero, and positive and negative senex – all polarities of our one human condition.

An examination of the child image of the poetry of Theodore Roethke illustrates that the image reflects not so much the autobiographical child or childhood of Roethke as it reveals the archetypal child at the root of the poet's psyche.

The nostalgic spiritual longing, the *pothos*, at the origin of Arthur Rimbaud's search for an ontological and metaphysical "inconnu", and a central motif in his major poems, "Le Bateau Ivre" and *Une Saison enfer* is examined in the second chapter of this work in relation to the image of the *puer eternus* – the image which lies at the heart of the poet's drive to "se fait voyant", to transcend being, and to reconcile the ambivalent and divergent impulses within his own soul.

A study of the persistent feminine figures in Yeats's poetry as projections of his own psychological opposite, or *anima* – the contrasexual element of his psyche, delineates the basic configuration or inner structure that impels so many of his individual poetic creations and holds the key he seeks in his quest for "Unity of Being".

An analysis of three of Robert Frost's elusive poems, "Mending Wall", "An Old Man's Winter Night", and "Directive", reveals the ambivalent nature of the senex (or old man) archetype, and elucidates the poet's skilful presentation and description of that archetypal ambivalence within human nature. In Frost's depiction of the senex lies the symbolic paradigm of the human situation. (*DAI* 44:11 [May 1984] 377-A)

THE UTOPIAN INVARIANT: INTERIORITY AND EXTERIORITY IN THE TWENTIETH-CENTURY POETIC CONSCIOUSNESS
Order No. 8101929
Finkelstein, Norman Mark, Ph.D. *Emory University*, 1980. 333pp. Adviser: Ronald W. Schuchard

British and American poets of the twentieth century are the inheritors of a complex historical tradition, for their poetry is only the most recent manifestation of the ongoing phenomenologies of poetic consciousness and poetic form. When modern poetry is examined in the light of this tradition, it may be seen as both an outgrowth of and a reaction to certain modes of poetic discourse that come to maturity in the nineteenth century. The phenomenon of Romantic interiority, as identified by Georg Lukács, serves as a philosophical and political foundation for such poets as W. B. Yeats, who inherits from his Romantic precursors a highly rarefied conception of poetic composition that sets the poet at a vast remove from conventional bourgeois society. Yeats's heroic stance, though cloaked by his reactionary ideology, begins a crucial strain of poetic Modernism, particularly when he emerges from his interior world to engage immediate historical circumstances on its own terms.

Yeats's movement towards exteriority is further extended and eventually altered in the work of Ezra Pound, William Carlos Williams, George Oppen, Charles Olson, Robert Duncan and Jack Spicer. While each poet maintains his links to what is here termed the Utopian invariant (the force of Desire manifesting itself against historical necessity to achieve the perfection of Form), he determines his own relationship to the dialectic of interiority and exteriority, which in turn affects his notions of poetic inspiration and composition. To discuss a poet's relation to form is, in effect, to discuss his relation to history, and the complexities of these relationships are herein approached through an examination of the poet's representative works as they evolve over the course of his career.

Thus, in Chapter I, Yeats's early work is placed in the context of his nineteenth-entury Romantic precursors; in Chapter II his later work is placed in juxtaposition to the poetry of his sometime student, Ezra Pound. Chapter III examines William Carlos Williams' poetry of immediacy, a departure from Yeats's and Pound's exteriorized historicism, and concludes with the career of George Oppen, whose political identity in turn modifies what has come to be known as Objectivist poetics. The work of Charles Olson and Robert Duncan is the subject of Chapter IV, for both poets are variously concerned with syntheses of Objectivist and Romantic modes of composition. Chapter V is devoted to Jack Spicer, whose work can be regarded as the complete synthesis of interior and exterior poetic discourse, leading to the dissolution of the dialectic as effective contemporary poetic paradigm.

What emerges from this extended survey is the establishment of a definite strain of poetic influence, as well as the redefinition of Romanticism, Modernism and post-Modernism in terms of certain crucial historico-philosophical constants that poetry continues to embody. Despite the varying ideologies that historical necessity imposes upon individual poets in this century, despite their difficulties in attaining to completed utterance, the poetic consciousness in recent times continues to be an expression of a desire for creative freedom that cannot be stilled. (*DAI* 41:7 [January 1981] 31045–A).

WHAT WILL SUFFICE: CULTURE, HISTORY, AND FORM IN MODERN LITERATURE
Order No. 8126501
Foster, Thomas Carleton, Ph.D. *Michigan State University*, 1981. 208pp.

Through a close examination of four major works: *The Waste Land*, *Ulysses*, *Go Down, Moses* and the lyric poetry of William Butler Yeats, this study discusses Modernist literature as a formal response to historical, political, and cultural forces. It also contains an extensive discussion of previous attempts at defining Modernism and of contemporary critical theories.

Chapter one deals with the existing body of criticism on the Modernists. A great deal of commentary on Modern literature has accepted and promoted the notion that it is an aesthetic, decultured formalism spawned by the Symbolist rebellion against utilitarian art, a suggestion created in part at least by the writers themselves in their various defenses of their writings; or else it has pursued the approach that Modernism grows out of Naturalism carried to its furthest limit. Different though they are in many respects, these two approaches share an understanding of literature as growing out of other literature; that is, to use Eliot's phrase, the works of literature form an ideal order among themselves. In the work of formalist critics from the New Critics through Northrop Frye and Harold Bloom this insular view of literature is carried to its limits: the existing monuments form an order impervious to "extraliterary" forces. Against these views are others, particularly the Marxists', which examine the form of the Modernist work as sociological detritus, as evidence of the breakdown of the bourgeois society. Chapter two considers these conflicting arguments and attempts to map out a course which, rather than privileging either literary history or sociopolitical history, sees literature as an active encounter with its time as well as its own literary antecedents. The chapter moreover suggests that the characteristically Modernist response tends to be formal rather than thematic because changes in society invalidate the previous, specifically Victorian literary practices.

Chapters three through six embody criticism of specific works by Modern writers. Chapter three discusses *The Waste Land*'s formal and mythological elements as Eliot's attempt to come to grips with the effects of World War I as well as his attempt to place his poem among the existing monuments. Chapter four presents a reading of the story, sentence, and novelistic structure of *Go Down, Moses* as exemplary of Faulkner's artistic practice accounting for the constant presence of the remnants of slavery and shattered greatness in the South of his own time. Chapter five attempts to connect Yeats's political concerns with the development of his mythology: finding traditional Irish mythology usurped by nationalistic propaganda, he elaborates a mythology that can account for his personal ambivalence and vacillation regarding the political turmoil of Ireland's struggle for independence. Finally, chapter six adumbrates a reading of *Ulysses* in which the narrative voice of the public episodes, particularly "Aeolus", "Cyclops", and "Sirens", can be explained as the collective experience filtered through collective political, historical, religious, and cultural mythology, as a symbolic as well as linguistic mode of communication. (*DAI* 42:6 [Dec 1981] 2670–A)

THE RHYMERS' CLUB: A SOCIAL AND INTELLECTUAL HISTORY
Order No. DA8309610
Gardiner, Bruce, Ph.D. *Princeton University*, 1983. 256pp.

The Rhymers' Club did more than any other group of poets to resolve the problems that confronted English literary culture in the early 1890s: the problems arising from such issues as the maturing of English imperialism, the crisis in Irish nationalism after Parnell, the rise of Grub Street journalism (and the consequent literary battles between aesthetic and philistine), and late Victorian conflicts over theories of literary inheritance.

The Club was most active between 1891 and 1894; during those years it had fourteen core members, and about thirty associates, composing three successive generations. It was formed in two stages, the first, in mid-1890, joining Dublin literati with London journalists and publishers; and the second, in early 1891, adding Oxbridge aesthetes, thereby pioneering a new kind of semi-professional urban literary community integrating as many of the arts and as many stages of the writing-publishing-reviewing process as possible.

In terms of literary theory, the Rhymers reacted along generational lines to the Victorians' classicist and evolutionary literary theories, and conducted the period's most intelligent and productive debate about Decadence.

In terms of literary politics, while the laureateship remained vacant, the Club contended for the Regency with the imperialistic *National Observer* circle surrounding W. E. Henley. The Rhymers were inspired by Morris's several revolutionary projects, and generally admired the politics of Tennyson and Whitman, despite minority endorsements of Swinburne's and William Watson's. Specifically, the Club played a crucial if de facto role in the Irish renaissance, achieving casually what the soon-disabled Irish Literary Societies had been formed to do. Moreover, the group disintegrated not because of these Celtic projects, but because its publishing alliances faltered and its allies, Wilde and Beardsley, were attacked. (*DAI* 43:12 [June 1983] 3919–A)

MYTH AND POETIC SURVIVAL: A STUDY OF W. B. YEATS AND THE RHYMERS' CLUB OF THE 1890's
Order No. DA8403091
Gardner, Joann Lynn, Ph.D. *The Johns Hopkins University*, 1984. 326pp.

W. B. Yeats was twenty-five years old and relatively new to the London literary scene when the Rhymers' Club was founded in 1890. During this period, his poetry evolved from the Anglo-Romantic verses of *Crossways* to the distinctly aesthetic (and recognizably Irish) concerns of *The Rose* and *The Wind Among the Reeds*. But by 1895 the club he had helped to found had disbanded, and by the end of the century many of its members had met their respective fates. Yeats alone went on to fulfill his professional ambitions, perpetuating in his work the memories of this period and these individuals.

The historical development suggests two basic questions: in what ways did Yeats benefit from his association with the Rhymer's Club, and how had he been able to achieve his ambitions while others of his cenacle had failed. The answers lie at least partially in a consideration of myth: the images that these poets projected for themselves determined the path of their careers, and their willingness to accept a myth of failure turned them into victims of the public's imagination. Yeats shared with these poets a tendency to escapism, a preference for symbolic interpretation, a manipulation of technical skills to produce a "purer", more fluid expression, but he did not view himself as a social victim, and he believed in the power of art to influence and change everyday reality. While others withdrew from a life into preoccupations with death and silence, Yeats fashioned a vision of renewal out of the history and legends of Ireland. His withdrawals into the domain of death were with the intention of returning to the world more knowledgeable and, thus, more powerful than before. (*DAI* 44:11 [May 1984] 3388–A)

POETRY AND MAGIC: A STUDY OF YEATS'S POEMS OF MEDITATION
Order No. DA8304495
Gerety, Jane, Ph.D. *The University of Michigan*, 1982. 250pp. Chairman: George Bornstein

Many scholars have noted the influence of Yeats's occult interests on themes and symbols in his poetry while others have pointed to the convergence of magical philosophy and Romantic aesthetics in his poetic theory. Less attention has been paid, however, to the debt Yeats owes to magic for the structures of his poems, particularly his meditative poems. This study explores the influence of his magical studies on his development as a poet and traces the relationship of certain methods of meditation learned in the practice of magic to his poetry of meditation.

In his early view, Yeats relates poetry to magic by showing the reliance each has on the visionary power of the mind and on symbols. His search for a national tradition on which to found his art leads him to ascribe the beginnings of poetry to magic and to advocate a return to the magical view of the world. Yeats sees Blake and Shelley as visionary artists and follows the example of his Romantic mentors in populating his own early verse with seekers after hidden wisdom.

In Yeats's later writing about the alliance of poetry and magic, he works towards a definition of vision that includes antipathy and confrontation as well as unity and merging. He continues to create visionary personae in his fiction and verse and also to construct poems of meditation in which the speakers, by a complex process of interaction with images, attain vision. The structures of these meditative poems show the influence of the methods of meditation Yeats learned in the Golden Dawn: contemplation of images and symbols; Tarot meditation; and symbolic ritual meditation. By means of these structures, Yeats was able to expand the traditional Romantic form, the greater Romantic lyric, and increase its dramatic potential. In the most fully developed poetry of meditation, that based on recreation of initiation ceremonies, acts of will complement those of imagination in the speaker's quest of a moment of vision. (*DAI* 43:10 [April 1983] 3324–A)

WILLIAM BUTLER YEATS'S *PURGATORY*: TRAGEDY OR ITS MIRROR IMAGE?
Order No. DA 8208452
Gore, Jeanne Guerrero, Ph.D. *George Peabody College for Teachers of Vanderbilt University*, 1981. 96pp. Major Professor: Eva Touster

William Butler Yeats's *Purgatory* may not be a tragedy but a tragedy's mirror-image, a type of play in which the hero's nature, the plot structure, and the magnitude, though directly related to tragedy, are reversed. Failure to distinguish its plot type has led to critical disagreement about the play. Recognizable constants of tragedy (plot, opposition, and perception) are traced from Aristotle's *metaabasis* to derive a working definition and a plot paradigm for tragedy. The definition is then tested on *Oedipus Rex*, *Hamlet*, and *Blood Wedding*.

Poetic tragedy as germane to tragedy's mirror-image is considered as a genre. Eliot's "dualism of planes" and "objective correlative" and Yeats's "emotion of multitude" and "memory of emotion" are compared. Yeats's dramatic mask (the vehicle for poetic tragedy) is the joining of passion with reverie (both motive and understanding) in the hero (such as Oedipus or Hamlet) who undergoes struggle, suffering (as action), release, freedom, and achieves tragic ecstasy.

Yeats's conception of the purgatorial state is examined and its relation to pagan, Greek, and Christian traditions noted briefly. Yeats's scheme includes expiatory and purified phases. It emphasizes the life of the emotions and the imagination as it redeems remorse (often with the help of the living) and moves towards Unity of Being.

Purgatory depicts Yeats's concepts of passion, perception (light), anti-self, the dead past, the living present, the wholeness of the unconscious, and the consubstantiality of the dialectical modes of existence; however, its action (the *pathos* of the Old Man) is committed with full knowledge. No change in the plot (or the purgatorial state) occurs. A conclusion that *Purgatory* is an experiment in poetic drama which has "tragic intensity" is drawn since it does not achieve the magnitude or the *metabasis* of a complex plot tragedy nor is it like other simple plot tragedies or like other Yeatsian tragedies. *Purgatory* is perhaps the antiself of tragedy, its mirror-image. The Old Man's nature seems a farcical reversal of the tragic hero; *Purgatory* is tragedy's daimon and a symbol of the human being's simultaneous inclusion and exclusion from Unity of Being. (*DAI* 42:11 [May 1982] 4832-A)

ESOTERIC COMEDIES: PROTO-MODERN STRATEGIES OF IMAGINATION IN CARLYLE, NEWMAN, AND YEATS
Order No. DA8406375
Helmling, Steven, Ph.D. *Rutgers University The State U. of New Jersey (New Brunswick)*, 1983. 305pp. Director: Professor Thomas R. Edwards

Although it treats Carlyle, Newman, and Yeats at some length, the dissertation is less a study of Victorian or post-Victorian questions than an attempt to clarify the origins of certain aspects of modernism, especially its problematic relation to such issues as genre, convention, tradition, originality, imagination, "belief", and obscurity. I seek to illuminate the varieties of irony and comedy that the collision of Enlightenment rationalism with highly artificial literary conventions affords to certain writers who put themselves self-consciously against the grain of their time. An introductory chapter characterizes "esoteric comedy", suggesting its similarities with and differences from both eighteenth-century precursors (Swift and Sterne) and twentieth-century modernists (Joyce, Pound, Eliot). Separate chapters on Carlyle's *Sartor Resartus*, Newman's *Apologia Pro Vita Sua*, and Yeats's *A Vision* discuss the various ways in which each of these writers – through manipulation of generic conventions, textual play, and ironic self-exposure – contrives to evade, and thus criticize, the constraints which the materialist science and psychology of their era would place upon literary and other kinds of imagination. Carlyle, Newman, and Yeats triumph by courting an appearance of foolishness, superstition, or soft-headedness, and the resulting comedy registers a robust but qualified confidence in the power of the imagination and the possibilities it opens of human freedom. A concluding chapter further considers the "esoteric comedy" of Carlyle, Newman, and Yeats in relation to issues posed by twentieth-century modernism and the New

Criticism. The aim is not only to urge a view of three very different and very instructive modern careers, but to illuminate general problems of modernism and its history. (*DAI* 44:12 [June 1984] 3695-A)

"THE BOOKS OF MY NUMBERLESS DREAMS": A MANUSCRIPT STUDY OF YEATS'S *THE WIND AMONG THE REEDS*
Order No. DA8400800
Holdsworth, Carolyn Anne, Ph.D. *Tulane University*, 1983. 319pp. Major Professor: Richard J. Finneran

In this dissertation I provide transcriptions of manuscripts, many previously unpublished, of the poems from William Butler Yeats's *The Wind Among the Reeds* (1899). The transcriptions are of manuscripts in the collection of Michael B. Yeats in Dalkey, Ireland, from the Berg Collection of the New York Public Library, and elsewhere. After the transcriptions, which present the manuscripts poem by poem, I include three descriptive appendices, which provide additional information on the manuscripts according to their provenance. Three other appendices outline information on Yeats's title changes for the poems; on their order and placement in the published volumes; and on the dates of the earliest extant manuscripts and the printings of the poems prior to *Wind*.

I have prefaced the manuscript materials with four introductory essays. The first, on the reviews of *Wind*, focuses on the critical controversy over Yeats's copious and eccentric notes to the volume; it also discusses, generally, the relation between writer and audience, and, specifically, Yeats's attempt in the notes of *Wind* to annotate the self presented in the poems. The second essay deals with Yeats's manifold difficulties in preparing and publishing *Wind*, a process that extended over at least eight years, and with Yeats's relationships with Maud Gonne and Olivia Shakespear, the women who served as models for the "Beloved" in various *Wind* poems. The third essay details Yeats's habits of composition, revision, and handwriting, as exhibited in the *Wind* manuscripts. The fourth traces the evolution of a representative *Wind* poem, "He tells of the Perfect Beauty." (*DAI* 44:9 [March 1984] 2763-4-A)

A SEARCH FOR AUTHORITY: PROLEGOMENA TO A DEFINITIVE CRITICAL EDITION OF W. B. YEATS'S *A VISION* (1937)
Order No. DA8319325
Hood, Connie Kelly, Ph.D. *The University of Tennessee*, 1983. 289pp. Major Professor: Dr Norman J. Sanders

The groundwork is laid in this project for the text of a definitive critical edition of *A Vision* (1937). Some twenty-one thousand pages of unpublished materials have been examined in order to chart Yeats's process of creating the book, its publishing history, the critical reception, and the interrelationships of the various manuscripts and texts from the automatic writing of 1917 to the 1962 state of the printed text. Instead of a new text of *A Vision*, a list of emendations to the London 1937 copy-text is given. All known marginalia written in copies of the first edition and various states of the second edition in the hands of Yeats, his wife, and Thomas Mark (his editor at Macmillan) are listed. Textual notes explain the sources of the emendations and point out cruces and interesting manuscript variants. A chapter on the "Manuscript" discusses in detail the materials which Yeats sent to the printers. The variants in the printed texts of 1937 (London), 1938 (New York), 1956 (New York), 1961 (London), and 1962 (London) are listed in a chapter of historical collations. A final chapter on word division lists endline hyphenation. The bibliography contains four separate lists: published and unpublished primary and secondary materials which were consulted for this project. (*DAI* 44:4 [October 1983] 1082-A)

GYRES AND SPIRITS: AN EXPLORATION OF SOME PARALLELS BETWEEN W. B. YEATS AND EMANUEL SWEDENBORG
Islam, Syed Manzoorul, Ph.D. *Queen's University at Kingston (Canada)*, 1981.

This study proposes to explore some similarities between the philosophies of W. B. Yeats and Emanuel Swedenborg. Yeats read Swedenborg off and on throughout his long poetic career, as he had most of Swedenborg's important works in his own library, and was influenced by his teachings and doctrines. From Yeats's own admission of the importance of Swedenborg and his thoughts and beliefs, and their closeness to some major themes of his poerty and plays, and from Yeats's borrowing of important elements of Swedenborg's theory of the gyre as given in *The Principia*, it is possible to isolate a number of subjects in Yeats which show both affinities with and the influence of Swedenborg. Five such subjects are treated in this thesis: the re-education of spirits in the afterworld, love and sex on earth and in heaven, the relationship between body and soul, the gyre and the Great Memory – *Anima Mundi*. They are the basis of five separate chapters, while another chapter deals with a number of five separate chapters, while another chapter deals with a number of other minor similarities between some ideas and observations in Swedenborg and Yeats. Yeats's marginalia in a number of copies of Swedenborg's writings are set out in the Appendix.

Yeats's borrowing from Swedenborg was done on two levels: literal and symbolic. While he believed, for instance, that angels do unite in heaven, he was also impressed by the underlying aesthetic harmony and appeal which had strong bearings on his theory of the Unity of Being, highlighting, as it did, the harmonious resolution of contrary aspects of experience. For the marriage bed and the sexual act signified, as Yeats pointed out, the solved antinomies. The thesis deals with the two different levels of interpretation of Swedenborgian ideas whenever possible.

Yeats was attracted to Swedenborg for the strange and compulsive way he wrote down his dreams and visions, his interpretation of the Bible and the spirit world, his view of man-woman relationship, his fascinating experiences with spirits and angels. Yeats found a confirmation of many of his beliefs and thoughts about the afterworld and the state of the soul in Swedenborg. This study analyses Yeats's borrowings from Swedenborg, taking into account his early fascination for, and his study of Swedenborg, and comes to the conclusion that these borrowings, though in many cases barely recognizable, are more extensive than Yeats's critics commonly acknowledge. (*DAI* 42:8 [Feb. 1982] 3610-A)

900852 Order No: Not available from University Microfilms Int'l
YEATS AND DANTE
John, Alan Arthur, (Ph.D. *The University of Chicago*, 1981
In volume X1981
Literature, Comparative
Descriptor Codes: 0295
Institution Code: 0330

A MULTI-DIMENSIONAL EVALUATION OF THERAPEUTIC PROCESS: THE PSYCHOLOGICAL APPLICATION OF W. B. YEATS'S *A Vision*
Order No. DA8201502
Kappler, Kevin Andrew, Ph.D. *California School of Professional Psychology, Berkeley*, 1981. 146pp. Chairperson: Nathan Adler

This dissertation makes W. B. Yeats's *A Vision* more accessible to psychologists through comparing it with the theories of Freud and Jung and the development of psychological testing instruments by the interpersonal psychologists (notably Leary's interpersonal checklist). This study focuses on the ways each system conceptualizes therapeutic process. The recurring structure in Freud, Jung, and the interpersonal theorists is noted, which uses a dialectic set of factors described for psychological process. The delineation of such structure in each theory is examined chronologically and compared with *A Vision*, noting areas for further research in each formulation. (*DAI* 42:10 [April 1982] 4173–B)

KNOWLEDGE AND SWEETER IGNORANCE: THE STRATEGIES OF YEATS'S POETIC STRUCTURES
Order No. DA8308077
Krogfus, Miles Edward, Ph.D. *University of Minnesota*, 1982. 257pp.

The many studies of Yeats's poetry tend to explicate it in relationship to his ideas at the expense of any extended analysis of the poetic structures which embody these ideas. I reverse this familiar pattern, and offer detailed commentaries on some of the important elements of his poetic structures in chapters I through III of my thesis, leading in turn to an examination in chapter IV of heretofore neglected Yeatsian metaphors: lightning and the threshold.

Yeats uses his poetic structures to create magical charms that will have the power to transform reality into what he would desire it to be. The first elements of these structures, which I discuss in chapter I, are Yeats's use of sentence and line in his poetry. Another element of his structures, his use of refrains and repeated phrases, I discuss in chapter II. The next element of Yeats's structures, his use of poetic dialogues, which I discuss in chapter III, is the clearest embodiment of drama in his verse.

The title of my final chapter, as well as that of the entire thesis, comes from Yeats's poem "Shepherd and Goatherd". His vacillation between what his head and heart tell him is forcibly expressed in this phrase. His poetic structures at first seem to allow poet and reader to attain greater knowledge of the world, but the knowledge attained develops more from the heart than the head. The latter is used to skillfully create elaborate structures that seem logical and intellectually comprehensive, but which are more significantly dramatic, and emotionally comprehensive.

Drama is what serves as truth for Yeats. His is a poetry of power, an attempt to so charge diction and syntax that they will embody drama as the central truth of human experience. Through his poetic structures, Yeats attempts to convince himself and the reader that his *dramatis personae* have importance and their words and actions significance. When he accomplishes his intentions, his verse is charged with enough drama so that the merest inflection or slightest change in gesture is rendered dramatic. Drama becomes the final means and end of his verbal magic. (*DAI* 43:11 [May 1983] 3604–A)

BEYOND COLONUS: TRAGIC VISION AND THE TRANSFIGURED IMAGINATION IN THE LATE WORKS OF HENRY JAMES, WILLIAM BUTLER YEATS, AND T. S. ELIOT
Order No. DA8227091
Manning, Dale, Ph.D. *George Peabody College for Teachers of Vanderbilt University*, 1982. 247pp. Major Professor: Eva Touster

This dissertation grew out of an interest in the phenomenon whereby some writers continue to develop as artists into old age, while others follow a more predictable pattern of development through youth and middle age, then a decline or lack of further development. This study's central thesis is that writers who continue such marked development into old age share an ability to transform the confrontation of aging and death into an extraordinary wellspring of inspiration. A commonality of experience and vision among such artists is demonstrated, which may be indicative of an archetypal pattern.

Henry James, William Butler Yeats, T. S. Eliot, and appropriate late works by each are examined as representative of this phenomenon. Separated by generations, influenced by different traditions, these writers worked to some extent in different genres and from different philosophical bases. Such differences indicate the potential universality of the archetype.

Oedipus at Colonus provides the appropriate archetype. The experiences that made Oedipus the man he is at Colonus, his words, insights, the supernatural vision he is granted, and his apotheosis reveal characteristics of the archetype.

The components of this archetypal experience are: arrival at an age beyond mid-life; an emotional or spiritual crisis – even a mental breakdown; a period of struggle through the crisis involving a reworking of earlier experience; breakthrough to a new way of seeing or vision; late renascence of creativity informed by a transfigured imagination.

Characteristics of the archetypal vision are: preoccupation with the supernatural; seeming detachment in such elements as style, personae, point of view an effacement of the artist's personality which is actually an integration of the artist and his art with the universal whole; development of an androgynous mind – part of the process of integration; new awareness of Love as a transforming and redeeming force.

Approximately the first third of this dissertation is devoted to exploring its appropriate context in psychology, philosophy, and literary criticism, and to examination of *Oedipus at Colonus* as an archetype. The remainder of the study is given to applications of the thesis to James, Yeats, Eliot and their late works. (*DAI* 43:6 [Dec. 1982] 1968–A)

YEATS AND NIETZSCHE: MASK AND TRAGEDY, 1902–1910
Order No. DA8406400
Oppel, Frances Nesbitt, Ph.D. *Rutgers University The State U of New Jersey (New Brunswick)*, 1983. 367pp. Director: Professor Carol H. Smith

This dissertation argues that the influence of Nietzsche's thought was crucial to the development of Yeats's concepts of mask and tragedy. The connection between Yeats and Nietzsche began in 1902, when Yeats first read Nietzsche, and continued to the end of his life. The study concentrates on the years between 1902 and 1910, when Nietzsche's thought had its initial impact on Yeats.

In an attempt to reveal the "vitalization" in Yeats after he read Nietzsche, and to assess how the vitalization affected his position as "bearer of a tradition", the study begins with a survey of the Romantic tradition both writers share, react against, and extend into the twentieth century. The body of the study concentrates on the development of Yeats's "mask theory", under the impetus provided by Nietzsche's use of antithesis. It illustrates that the theory grew simultaneously with Yeats's reading, and with his aesthetic practice. It shows the connection between the developing mask theory and Yeats's ideas about tragedy. His play *Where There Is Nothing* shows the first impact of Nietzschean thought on Yeats's conception of tragedy. In revisions of *The Shadowy Waters*, and in *The King's Threshold, On Baile's Strand*, and *Deirdre*, this impact becomes decisive. The study also shows Yeats's unsuccessful struggle to unite "mask" and "tragedy" in early drafts of *The Player Queen*.

The "fruits" of the seed sown by Nietzsche appear in their mature theoretical form in *Per Amica Silentia Lunae* (1916). The dissertation's final chapter, in a conclusion which is also an introduction to Yeats's later work, shows how Nietzsche's affirmation of life, even in its "most difficult" and paradoxical aspects, directs Yeats to his conception and affirmation of life as tragedy. This conception depends on a synthesis of the ideas of mask and tragedy, toward which Yeats had been steadily moving since 1902. The spirit behind Yeats's synthesis – which encompasses aesthetics, ethics, and history – is Nietzsche's. (*DAI* 44:12 [June 1984] 3697–A)

W. B. YEATS AND HIS "SWEET DANCER"
Order No. DA8215356
Salvati, Julianne Mia, Ph.D. *University of Rhode Island*, 1981. 158pp.

Between the years of 1916 and 1939, W. B. Yeats wrote a series of dramas in which the climactic scenes were dramatically expressed through dance. These "dance-plays", he felt, could "suggest" through movement what mere words could not communicate to an audience. From her first careful steps in *At the Hawk's Well*, to her final emotional dance in *The Death of Cuchulain*, Yeats' dancer is an expression of the struggle of man, driven by necessity, to reconcile the constantly combating antinomies of his existence. And since he viewed everything in terms of its opposite – its "mask" – the dancer also became Yeats' dramatic symbol of both natural and supernatural passion, as well as the tragic medium responsible for performing what he considered to be one of the most basic functions of tragedy: "the drowning and breaking of dykes that separate man from man".

The general purpose of this dissertation is to define the nature and the scope of the dancer's dramatic impact in Yeats's dance-plays and to show how each dance sequence suggests a unique and powerful statement concerning Yeats's understanding of the human condition. Part One discusses the various influences which helped to shape Yeats's ideas: the French Symbolist Movement, the designer Gordon Craig, the Noh Theatre of Japan, and the dancer Michio Ito. And Part Two analyzes Yeats's use of dance elements in his tragic dance-plays and discusses the relationship of these works to the playwright's holistic vision. Ultimately, the dance-dramas must be viewed together as one play, since they do not evolve towards a definitive dramatic form. Thus, the essential message of Yeats's dancer seems to be that, in order to realize its own "mask", humanity must struggle both to understand the quarreling impulses of passion and to create a design which explains the meaning of existence. Still, the final irony of the human condition is death itself. Consequently man must realize that "truth" cannot be "known"; it must be "embodied". The truth of Yeats's own "mask" is embodied in the haunting splendour of his "Sweet Dancer". (*DAI* 43:2 [August 1982] 307–8–A)

APOCALYPTIC IMAGERY IN FOUR TWENTIETH-CENTURY POETS: W. B. YEATS,
T. S. ELIOT, ROBERT LOWELL AND ALLEN GINSBERG
Sarwar, Selim, Ph.D. *McGill University (Canada)*, 1983.

In twentieth-century poets such as W. B. Yeats, T. S. Eliot, Robert Lowell and
Allen Ginsberg, the literary apocalyptic – identifiable by its homology with the
major elements of the biblical Apocalypse – undergoes progressively complex
transmutations. While in the early Yeats the apocalyptic is evocative of earnest
Romantic moods, in his later work it is complicated by irony, yoked to the cycles
of Yeatsian history, and counteracted by exaggerated postures of defiance. In
Eliot, a reductive juxtaposition of the apocalyptic and the contemporary
foreshortens the traditional paradigms to a diminutive modern-day scale. In
Lowell, the apocalyptic is manifested variously as a bitter inversion of American
Puritan eschatology, the telescoping of the personal and the cosmic, and a
catastrophe in slow-motion. The climactic point of distortion, however, is
reached in Ginsberg's poetry in which apocalyptic horrors form a bizarre
combination with humour and bathos. While their treatment of the eschatologi-
cal is widely divergent, an element common to all four poets is their ambivalence
towards the paradigms of an apocalyptic new world. (*DAI* 44:5 [Nov. 1983]
1452–A)

YEATSIAN TALK: THE CRITICAL THEORY OF W. B. YEATS AND THE VICTORIAN
BACKGROUND
Order No. DA8228336
Sherman, Debora Anne, Ph.D. *Brown University*, 1982. 432pp.

Yeats's critical and aesthetic theories, often ignored as largely idiosyncratic and
immaterial to the poetry, significantly influence the shape of that work. Such
words as "reverie", "mood", and "emotion of multitude", with their 'ninteyish
cast, reflect deeply-held beliefs about the nature of the poetic vision and poetic
method. Moreover, these beliefs were derived from Yeats's early exposure to a
Victorian aesthetic which revolved around the issues of mood and reverie, an
aesthetic shared in and influenced by Tennyson, Ruskin, Rossetti, Pater,
Swinburne, and the Pre-Raphaelites. This nexus of Victorian theories of reverie
and mood accounts, in fact, for the particularity of Yeats's poetry. Reverie
describes a Victorian adumbration of Romantic theories of poetic perception
which incorporate psychological theories of the mind prevalent in the nineteenth
century to the immanent teleology of Romanticism. Reverie thus represents an
attempt to overcome the problem of Romantic subjectivity through critical
theory. Reverie as a version of the epiphanic moment, became a unique poetic
ethos which Yeats defined as "tragic gaiety." Mood, on the other hand, refers to
the Victorian tendency to regard aesthetic emotion as fundamentally significant
to aesthetic experience because it was both individually observed and universal
in quality. These theories of mood characterize a Victorian aesthetic which
justified the symbol as both universal and self-created, thus suggesting a median

point in critical theory between the transcendent symbols of the Romantics and the self-enclosed poetic worlds of the Symbolists. Yeats developed his theory of "the moods" into a poetic methodology he called "the emotion of multitude" which formed the basis of his later elaborate mythology of the mask. Finally, the symbolic prefiguration and fulfilment which dominates the later poetry suggests the influence of Victorian typological symbolism upon his work. In these several ways, Yeats's aesthetic permutations upon Victorian theory become an important adjunct to the poetry. (*DAI* 43:11 [May 1983] 3606–A)

MODERN VERSE DEFINED BY W. B. YEATS: A COMPARATIVE STUDY OF ROMANCE, TRAGEDY, AND THE LYRIC, WITH AN INTRODUCTION TO TU FU AND HIS ANTITHETICAL TRADITION
Order No. DA8301421
So, Susan Suk-Ning, Ph.D. *Princeton University*, 1982. 493pp.

This is a comparative study of the modern lyric. The theoretical issues raised are those of the lyric and modernity, of cultural and generic differences, of poetic influence and poetic knowledge, of romantic philosophy and tragic vision. The central issue is the modern poet's "calling" in relation to his audience, real and imagined.

Its approach is derived from what Keats calls the "allegorical lives" of poets, what Eliot calls his "perfection of pattern", or what Yeats calls his "perfection of form", the rhythmic body. Its method is derived from a study of Yeats's antithetical theory of poetry and personalities, his "double vision", and his two minds, the critical and the creative, in dialogue.

In terms of craft and technique it is a study of freedom and control. In terms of literary criticism it is a defense of "workshop criticism" and of the "lyrical" approach via Yeats's prose and traditional Chinese criticism. It argues against analytic attitudes and scientific pretensions and calls for the co-operation of the brain and the belly in the comprehension of the poetic process. Ultimately it is a defense of poetry against the separation of art from life, of what Yeats calls "the personal factor" and "the moral element" in literature.

Chapter I sets up the premise of arguments and introduces the "Asiatic" aspect of Yeats's "double vision" via the turn of the century "Cathay", the Chinese antithetical mind, and its sense of tragedy and of romance. Chapters II to V follow Yeats from the years of "Discoveries" through *Per Amica Silentia Lunae* to *A Vision*. These discoveries are then applied to the reading of Yeats's assessment of *Modern Verse: 1892–1935* in Chapter VI, and to Tu Fu's poetry in particular and "Modern Verse" in general in Chapter VII.

Due to the complexities of these poets's enterprise and the "modern" and therefore learned traditions in which they wrote this study of their "allegorical lives" is necessarily complicated by the questions of inheritance and intent. These last will be guided by the description of their journeys to the "Mountain-Top". Yeats's journey is described through his dialogue "of generations for generations" in his "one poem of a lifetime." Tu Fu's journey is described through a selection of his poems (translated by this author) from "Gazing on Mount T'ai" [望嶽] to the 766 song cycles, ending with "From a Height" [登高 (767)]. (*DAI* 43:8 [Feb. 1983] 2660–A)

ONCE OUT OF NATURE: THE USES OF SYSTEM IN WORDSWORTH, ARNOLD, YEATS
Order No. DA8406848
Suleri, Sara, Ph.D. *Indian University*, 1983. 212pp. Chairman: Professor Kenneth R. Johnston

This dissertation focuses on the representation of systematic philosophy in the poetry of Wordsworth, Matthew Arnold, and Yeats. It examines the need to invent a system as a textual prop that far exceeds the weight of any conventional philosophy that such writers may claim to enunciate. Instead, it presents a reading of this need in the context of its rhetorical function, which serves to put the writer "out of nature" by illustrating his desire for a sympathetic readership that can act as a surrogate for a completed philosophy. The idea of system in Romantic and post-Romantic poetry thus functions as architectural drawing that outlines the postures of authority that these poets assume both towards their own writing and towards the readers they hope such writing will engender.

The desire for system indicates an absence of the surety that Romantic philosophy should licence, and causes the writer to invoke the presence of a reader in order to complete a poetic discourse that aims at the authority of philosophy. In focussing on a Romantic, a Victorian, and a Modernist model, this analysis seeks to read the genealogy of modern poetry by rereading the need for system as a surrogate for the relation between writer and reader that the context of philosophy renders a polite formality. (*DAI* 44:12 [June 1984] 3699–A)

SOUL CLAP ITS HANDS AND SING: YEATS'S TO BLAKE
Order No. 8129766
Sutton, Dorothy Moseley, Ph.D. *University of Kentucky*, 1981. 214pp.

There are many parallels between William Blake and William Butler Yeats, and I believe that studying these parallels will lead us to a better understanding of Yeats's poetry and why it evolved the way it did. Some of the parallels are merely coincidental, but I raise the question of whether some may also be a result of Blake's influence on Yeats as the latter worked from 1889 until 1892 on an edition of Blake's poetry. In my dissertation, I point out places of possible influence in this Quaritch edition.

Both Blake and Yeats adhered to an eclectic religion, made up of bits and pieces from many different faiths and philosophies. Both men distrusted materialism and one-sided rationalism. Their interest in the occult stemmed from their strong anti-positivistic beliefs. Both had visionary experiences and spiritual "Instructors". They put their imaginations to work in other ways as well. Each believed in the ability to create new worlds (and to re-order the one we live in) through the power of the imagination. Both created personal myths which embody and explain their personal/universal beliefs.

Neither poet had a formal education in the traditional sense, but both eventually attended art school. Blake became one of the world's most imaginative and capable artists, as well known now in art circles as he is in literary ones. Blake and Yeats were interested in art eventually transcended their interest in politics. The two poets agreed concerning the necessity of opposites in the world. The ultimate theme of both poets is the individual soul struggling against itself to arrive at a workable philosophy.

Yeats did not deliberately set out to imitate Blake, but he recognized his kinship with the earlier poet, and he gained self-confidence and courage from that recognition. The *joie de vivre*, the energy and exuberance that permeates much of Blake's work became one of the most outstanding characteristics of Yeats's work as well. Both poets had their darker side, but ultimately they are poets of affirmation – exhorting soul to "clap its hands and sing". (*DAI* 42:7 [January 1982] 3157–A)

SUBJECTIVITY AND OBJECTIVITY IN THE POETIC MIND: A COMPARATIVE STUDY OF THE POETRY OF WILLIAM BUTLER YEATS AND TU FU
Order No. 8128080
Wang, An-yan Tang, Ph.D. *Indiana University*, 1981. 63pp.

The purpose of this thesis is to examine how a poet's concept of man, the world, and reality determines the degree of subjectivity and objectivity in the process of poetic creation. The discussion centers on a comparison of two poets from two distinctly different cultural traditions: Tu Fu 杜甫 (712–70) from the Chinese classical tradition, and William Butler Yeats (1865–1939) from the Western post-Romantic tradition.

Each poet's idea of man, the world, and reality is considered against the background of his own cultural tradition, whether the poet accepts that tradition *in toto* or devises his own ways of reacting against it. In the Western tradition reality is seen dualistically, with the ideal world of spirit opposed to the actual world of matter. Chinese philosophy, however, recognizes a reality which is an unified whole of spirit and matter existing here and now. Then these concepts are shown to govern the reflection of the external world in the works of each poet: while Yeats emphasizes the supremacy of the poetic mind over the objective world, Tu Fu aims at a harmonious communion between the mind and the objective world. Finally, the thesis explores the temporal and spatial dimensions of the "world" created by each poet, comparing Tu Fu's and Yeats's treatment of history and of landscape.

The conclusion reached is that: when a poet sees intrinsic value in man and in the objective world, and accepts these as realities – as in the case of Tu Fu – his poetry aims at representing life in all its immediacy. His poetic world, therefore, corresponds quite closely to the objective world, indicating a mind more charitably inclined towards objectivity. A harmony develops between his mind and the external world, and the expression of this harmony in poetry is often lyrical and produces a poetry that is naturally metaphysical. Such a harmony between the mind and the world tends to become diminished when a consciousness of separation of the mind and the matter takes places. This loss of harmony is often accompanied by a conviction that the physical world and human life is absurd and insignificant. But a great poet does not turn away in loathing from human life and the world. He insists on finding a way of bridging the gulf between the ideal and the actual, and to justify life's struggles. Thus Yeats's poetry often points toward the redemption of man through conflict. In this attempt, his poetry is often subjective, demonstrating a mind working to overpower and manipulate what the poet sees as shortcomings of the world as well as his own self. The poetic world so constructed reveals the conscious workings of a subjective mind. The poetry is thus frequently characterized by conflict and power, whose effect is dramatic. (*DAI* 42:7 [Jan. 1983] 3152–A)

A Recent Yeats Bibliography, 1983–84

Warwick Gould and Olympia Sitwell

Our second bibliography is a list of recent, published work, including all reviews we have been able to trace. It also includes items recently rediscovered. As it is short enough to be read without too much discomfort, we have abandoned the sectionalisation which we imposed upon " 'Gasping on the Strand': a Yeats Bibliography 1981–83", in *Yeats Annual* No. 3.

Many scholars have kindly helped us. Japanese items in this bibliography have been provided through the kindness of Tetsuro Sano, and French items have been provided by Jacqueline Genet, and Anne and Patrick Rafroidi. Maureen Murphy kindly provided a checklist. Roger Davidge and Angela Carter of The Royal Holloway College library undertook computer searches of several data bases. Others who provided us with valuable listings include James Lovic Allen, Roy J. Booth, Birgit Bramsbäck, Elizabeth Cullingford, Richard Ellmann, John Harwood, K. P. S. Jochum, Colin McDowell, Roger Sharrock, Colin Smythe, Deirdre Toomey.

Next year, bibliographers resident in Eastern Europe will be reporting to us. We should be delighted to continue to receive information from all quarters, including off-prints, review copies and other information.

Ackroyd, Peter, *T. S. Eliot* (London: Hamish Hamilton, 1984).

Adams, Hazard, *Philosophy of the Literary Symbolic* (University Presses of Florida, 1984). Reviewed by Denis Donoghue *TLS* (6 Apr. 1984) 370.

Adams, Joseph, *Yeats and the Masks of Syntax: a Study in Connections* (N.Y.: Columbia University Press, London: Macmillan, 1984).

Allen, James Lovic, "Yeats's Romanticized Reconciliations with the Church of Ireland" in *Reconciliations: Essays in Honour of Richard Harter Fogle*, eds Mary Lynn Johnson and Seraphia D. Leyda (Salzburg Studies in English Literature, etc 96, 1983) 219–34.

Amor, Anne Clark, *Mrs Oscar Wilde: a Woman of Some Importance* (London: Sidgwick & Jackson, 1983).

Anon, "The Wonderful Years of Yeats 1865–1939: the Poet Who 'Could Not Live Without Religion' ", *Feature* (Winter, 1965) no. 79. (with a line drawing). (Reprint distributed by the courtesy of the Swedenborg Foundation, Inc., New York.)

Anon., [Article upon Yeats and Swedenborgianism, referring to Stockholm papers, untitled] *New Church Life* (Lancaster, Penn.), 4 (Apr. 1924) 235–6.

Archibald, Douglas, " 'The Statues' and Yeats's Idea of History", *Gaéliana*, 6 (1984) 165–76.

Archibald Douglas, *Yeats.* Reviewed in *New York Times Book Review* 88 (5 June 1983) 7; *Choice*, 21 (Oct. 1983) 272; *Best Sellers*, 43 (Sept. 1983) 215. *Library Journal*, 108 (15 Apr. 1983) 824.

Armstrong, Alison (ed.), *A Yeats Broadside*, 1:1983 (published as an occasional supplement to the *Irish Literary Supplement*, 2:1 (1983) 19–24. Contains: Richard Kain: "The Yeats Annual" (review of *Yeats Annual* No. 1), 21; Hazard Adams: "Yeats and Folklore" (review of M. H. Thuente: *W. B. Yeats and Irish Folklore*), 21; Maureen Corrigan "Yeats as Critic" (review of Vinod Sena: *W. B. Yeats: the Poet as Critic*) 21; William J. Maraldo: "Echoes of Nietzsche in Yeats" (review of Otto Bohlmann: *Yeats and Nietzsche etc*), 22; Alison Armstrong: "Casting a Cold Eye – Yeats's Epitaph" (review of James Lovic Allen: *Yeats's Epitaph etc.*) 22; James J. Blake "Yeats meets the Twayne" (review of Richard F. Peterson. *William Butler Yeats*), 23; Lucy McDiarmid: "Yeats and Democracy" (review of Gratton Freyer: *W. B. Yeats and the Anti-Democratic Tradition*), 23; Bernard Benstock: "The Soul of Yeats under Fascism" (review of Elizabeth Cullingford: *Yeats, Ireland and Fascism*), 24; Alison Armstrong: "Editorial", 19, 20; Alison Armstrong and Robert G. Lowery "Focus: Stony Brook", 20; Anon: "Focus: Cornell", 20; illustrative collage by John Digby, 19.

——, *A Yeats Broadside*, 2:1983 published as an occasional supplement to the *Irish Literary Supplement* (2:2, 1983, 17–19). Contains: James Lovic Allen: "The Yeats Tapes" 17, 19; George Mills Harper: "Remembering Greece" (review of David R. Clark: *Yeats at Songs and Choruses*), 18; James Lovic Allen: "A Tragic Book" (review of Daniel T. O'Hara: *Tragic Knowledge etc.*), 18; Denis Sampson: "An Old-Fashioned Book" (review of A. E. Dyson: *Yeats, Eliot and R. S. Thomas etc*), 18; Terence Diggory: " 'Casting a Cold "I" ' " (review of Gale C. Schricker: *A New Species of Man etc*), 19; Brian John: "Yeats the Dramatist" (review of Ashley E. Myles: *Theatre of Aristocracy*), 19.

——, "Prosecutors Will Be Violated: Sexuality and Heroism in *The Herne's Egg*",

Canadian Journal of Irish Studies, 9, 2 (Dec.) pp. 43–56.

Bachchan, Harbans Rai, *W. B. Yeats and Occultism: a Study of His Work in Relation to Indian Lore, the Cabbala, Swedenborg, Boehme and Theosophy* (London: Books from India, repr. 1976).

Baker, Carlos, *The Echoing Green: Romanticism Modernism and the Phenomena of Transference in Poetry* (Princeton: University Press, 1984).

Beckett, J. C., "The Irish Writer and His Public in the Nineteenth Century", *Yearbook of English Studies*, 11 (1981) 102–16.

Berridge, Virginia and Edwards, Griffith, *Opium and the People: Opiate Use in Nineteenth-Century England* (London: Allen Lane; N.Y.: St. Martins, 1981) 215 etc.

Birmingham, George A. (i.e. James Owen Hannay) *Hyacinth* (London: Arnold, 1906). A novel with Maud Gonne portrayed as "Augusta Goold", John MacBride as "Captain Quinn", and W. B. Yeats as "Thomas Grealy".

Blackford, Russell, "Witheld Meaning in Yeats's 'Cuchulain Comforted' ", *Journal of the Australasian Universities Language and Literature Association: A Journal of Literary Criticism, Philology and Linguistics*, 57 (May 1982) 24–30.

Bohlmann, Otto, *Yeats and Nietzsche*. Reviewed in: *TLS* (31 Dec., 1982) 1438. *Choice*, 20 (Oct. 1982) 262.

Böker, Uwe, "Die Anfänge der europäischen Blake-Rezeption", *Arcadia*, 16:3 (1981) 266–83.

Bold, Alan (ed.), *The Letters of Hugh MacDiarmid* (London: Hamish Hamilton, 1984).

Bornstein, George, *Transformations of Romanticism in Yeats, Eliot, and Stevens* reviewed in *College Literature*, 9 (Autumn 1982) 190.

Bose, Amalendu, "Bengali: Yeatsian Undertones", *Indian Literature* (New Delhi) 24(6) (Nov.–Dec. 1981) 197–213.

Bramsbäck, Birgit, *Folklore and W. B. Yeats: the Function of Folklore Elements in Three Early Plays* (Uppsala, 1984). Acta Universitatis Upsaliensis Studia Anglistica Upsaliensia 51. Distributed by Almqvist & Wiksell International.

British in Ireland, The: *P.R.O. Class C0904 – Dublin Castle Records, 1880–1921, Parts*

1–3 (Brighton: Harvester Microform, 1984.

Brown, Richard, "Confronting the Anti-Self", *TLS* (2 Oct. 1981) 1125. Review of *Tragic Knowledge*, etc.

Bullock, A. and Stallybrass, O., *The Fontana Dictionary of Modern Thought* (London: Fontana, 1977, etc.). Contains — references to Yeats under headings such as "Abbey Theatre" (Michael Anderson); *"The Criterion"* (Malcolm Bradbury); "Intellectuals" (Daniel Bell); "Mythopoeia" (Martin Seymour-Smith); "Symbolism" (Malcolm Bradbury).

Bullock, Alan and Woodings, R. B. (eds), *The Fontana Biographical Companion to Modern Thought* (London: Collins, Fontana, 1983). Contains "W. B. Yeats" by Eric Homberger. ". . . The sources for his thought are comically eclectic . . . *A Vision* (1925), one of the strangest books of the century", p. 840.

Bunch, Steve, "Yeats, Thoreau, Dr. Williams, Jim Morrison and Mr. Blake" in Bogan, James, and Goss, Fred (eds): *Sparks of Fire: Blake in a New Age* (Richmond, California: North Atlantic, 1982).

Byrne-Sutton, Geoffrey, "To William Butler Yeats", *Journal of Irish Literature*, 10:1 (Jan. 1981) 87. (Poem)

C., M. J., (i.e. Maurice James Craig) "W.B.Y.", *Thoth*, Poetry & Prose. 1. (Jan. 27, 1939), (Cambridge) 4.

Casey, Juanita, "To the Reel 'Homo the Sap': Post-Yeats Songs of Lunacy My Mother Hadn't Time to Teach Me", *Journal of Irish Literature*, 10:2 (May 1981) 27–9. (Poem).

Cave, Richard Allen, Review of *Representative Irish Tales* (1979), *Review of English Studies*, 32:128 (Nov. 1981) 501–2.

——, "Yeats's Late Plays: 'A High Grave Dignity and Strangeness' ", Chatterton Lecture on an English Poet, British Academy 1982 (London: British Academy, 1983). Also published in *Proceedings of the British Academy* vol. LXVIII (1982) 299–327.

Clark, David R., "Yeats's Dragons: the Sources of 'Michael Robartes and the Dancer' and 'Her Triumph' as Shown in the Manuscripts," *Malahat Review*, no. 57 (Jan. 1981), 35–64, 65–88.

Clark, David R., Review of *The Secret Rose, Stories by W. B. Yeats: A Variorum Edition Irish Literary Supplement* 1:1 (1982) 13.

——, *Yeats at Songs and Choruses*. Reviewed in *British Book News* (July 1983) 448.

Coke-Enguidanos, Mervyn, "Juan Ramón en su contexto esteticista, romántico y modernista", *Cuadernos hispanoamericanos*, nos 376–8 (Oct.–Dec. 1981) 532–46.

Clifford, Gay, "Against Yeats", *Encounter*, 56:4 (Apr. 1981) 39. (Poem).

Craig, Cairns, *Yeats, Eliot, Pound and the Politics of Poetry*. Reviewed in *Encounter*, 61 (July 1983) 80; *Criticism*, 24 (Autumn 1982) 398; *TES* (21 Jan. 1983) 31; *New Statesman* 103 (5 Mar. 1982) 23; *British Book News* (July 1982) 422; *Virginia Quarterly Review*, 58 (Summer 1982) 95: *London Review of Books*, 6:19 (8–31 Oct., 1984) 27.

Crandall, David, *Crazy Jane* (a Noh play performed at Tokyo Union Church 29 Sept.–1 Oct. 1983) parallel English// Japanese text published for performances by Clearwater.

Cullingford, Elizabeth (ed): *Yeats: Poems, 1919–1935: a Casebook* (London: Macmillan, 1984). Contains: an introductory essay, extracts from *Essays and Introductions, Autobiographies, Explorations* and Yeats's correspondence. Reprints early critical pieces by Edmund Wilson, F. R. Leavis, R. P. Blackmur, W. H. Auden, Cleanth Brooks, T. S. Eliot, George Orwell and Allen Tate plus later well known essays and extracts by Richard Ellmann, T. R. Henn, Yvor Winters, Thomas Parkinson, Hugh Kenner, Donald Stauffer, C. K. Stead, Daniel A. Harris, Thomas R. Whitaker, G. S. Fraser, Frank Kermode and Harold Bloom, plus a bibliography. Reviewed *London Review of Books*, 6:19 (8–31 Oct. 1984) 27.

——, "How Jacques Molay Got up the Tower: Yeats and the Irish Civil War", *ELH*, 50:4 (Winter, 1983) 763–90.

Davies, Robertson, "Jung, Yeats and the Inner Journey", *Queen's Quarterly* (Canada) 89(3) 1982: 471–7.

Deane, Seamus, "Joyce and Nationalism" in McCabe, Colin (ed.): *James Joyce: New Perspectives* (Brighton: Harvester; Bloomington: Indiana UP, 1982).

Deane, Seamus, "Yeats and the Occult", *London Review of Books* 6:19, (8–31 Oct. 1984) 27. Review Article. Cited under titles reviewed.

Deletic, Mirjana, "Magijsko i okultno u trearijskim radovima i poeziji V. B. Jejtsa", *Knjizevnost* (Beograd), 73 (1–2) (Jan.–Feb. 1982) 210–39.

De Man, Paul, *The Rhetoric of Romanticism* (Guildford: Columbia, 1984).

Diggory, Terence, *Yeats and American Poetry.* Reviewed in *Virginia Quarterly Review* 60 (Winter 1984) 174; *New York Times Book Review*, 88 (5 Jun. 1983) 7; *Choice*, 20 (July 1983) 1595; *Library Journal*, 108 (1 Feb. 1983) 208.

Donoghue, Denis, "Yeats: the Question of Symbolism" in Balakian, Anna (ed. and introd.): *The Symbolist Movement in the Literature of European Languages* (Budapest: Akademiai Kiadd, 1982).

Dorn, Karen: *Players and Painted Stage: the Theatre of W. B. Yeats* (Brighton: Harvester; Totowa, NJ; Barnes & Noble, 1984).

Dunning, Jennifer, "Dances Made from Poems on Two Stages", *New York Times*, 6 March 1981, Cl, Cll. Preview of a performance of a dance cycle based on the Crazy Jane poems and "A Woman Young and Old" by the American Theater Laboratory, New York, directed by Ara Fitzgerald.

Edrich, I. D., *W. B. Yeats: a Catalogue* (I. D. Edrich, 17 Selsdon Rd., London Ell) Sales Catalogue 1983.

Emans, Elaine V., "For William Butler Yeats", *Centennial Reivew*, 25:2 (Spring 1981) 162. Poem.

Empson, William, *Using Biography* (London: Chatto & Windus, 1984).

Finneran, Richard J., "The Composition and Final Text of W. B. Yeats's 'Crazy Jane on the King' ", *ICarbS*, 4:2 (Spring–Summer 1981) 67–74.

——, *Editing Yeats's Poems.* Reviewed in *Irish University Review*, xiv:i (Spring 1984) 153.

——, Review of E. Callan. *Yeats on Yeats: the Last Introductions and the 'Dublin' Edition Irish Literary Supplement*, 1:1 (1982) 13.

——(ed.), *Yeats: an Annual of Critical and Textual Studies* 1, 1983 (Ithaca and London: Cornell University Press). Contains, in addition to items cited in the *Yeats Annual* No. 3 bibliography the fol-

lowing: K. P. S. Jochum: "A Yeats Bibliography for 1981", 155–73; David S. Thatcher: review of Otto Bohlmann's *Yeats and Nietzsche etc*, 188–191, Hugh Witemeyer: review of Cairns Craig's *Yeats, Eliot, Pound and the Politics of Modern Poetry etc*, 191–6, F. S. L. Lyons: review of Grattan Freyer's *W. B. Yeats and the Anti-Democratic Tradition*, 196–8; Ian Fletcher: review of John Porter Houston's *French Symbolism and the Modernist Movement etc.*, 198–202; E. P. Bollier: review of Lawrence Lipking's *The Life of the Poet etc.*, 202–6; George Bornstein: review of Phillip L. Marcus's edition of *The Death of Cuchulain etc.* 206–9; David Krause: review of John Orr's *Tragic Drama and Modern Society*, 209–15; Michael André Bernstein: review of Richard F. Peterson's *William Butler Yeats*, 216–18; Mary FitzGerald: review of Ann Saddlemyer's *Theatre Business etc.*, 218–21; Donald T. Torchiana: review of *Studies in the Literary Imagination*, 14:1 (Spring 1981) 221–6: Mary FitzGerald *"Passim* Brief Notices", 227–231.

FitzGerald, Mary, "How the Abbey Said No: Readers' Reports and the Rejection of 'The Silver Tassie' " in Lowery, Robert G., (ed.) *O'Casey Annual* No. 1 (London: Macmillan; Totowa, NJ: Humanities, 1982).

Flannery, James W., Review of Marcus (ed.): *The Death of Cuchulain Irish Literary Supplement*, 1:2 (1982) 20.

——, "Unsatisfactory History of Drama" (review of Christopher Fitz-Simon: *The Irish Theatre*, 1983) *Irish Literary Supplement*, iii:i, (Spring, 1984) 38.

Foster, John Wilson, "Yeats and the Folklore of the Irish Revival", *Éire-Ireland* 17:2 (Summer 1982) 6–18.

Franchi, Florence, "L'influence des *Four Plays for Dancers* de W. B. Yeats et le theatre européen contemporain". *Gaéliana* (Caen) v (1983) 81–108.

——, "Ulick O'Connor, W. B. Yeats et le Nô japonais", *Cahier du Centre d'Etudes Irlandaises* (Rennes) vii (1982) 43–53. (1982) 43–53.

Freyer, Grattan, *W. B. Yeats and the Anti-Democratic Tradition* reviewed in: *TLS* (6 Aug. 1982) 867; *British Book News* (July 1982) 422; *Choice*, 19 (Apr. 1982) 1008; *New Statesman*, 103 (5 Feb., 1982) 24.

Fujimoto, Reiji, "Meditations in Time of the Civil War: the Anglo-Irishness of W. B. Yeats", *Eigo Eibungaku Kenkyu* (Hiroshima Univ.) (Apr. 1983).

Genet, Jacqueline, "Blake et Yeats: Deux modes d'aproche d'une même tradition", *Etudes Irlandaises*, No. 8, Nouvelle Series (Dec. 1982) 21–39.

——, Review of Allen, *Yeats's Epitaph etc.*; David R. Clark: *Yeats at Songs & Choruses*; Richard J. Finneran: *Editing Yeats's Poems*, (*Etudes Irlandaises*, no. 8, Nouvelle Série) 394–7

——, Review of *The Secret Rose, Stories by W. B. Yeats: a Variorum Edition, Etudes Irlandaises*, no. 7 Nouvelle Série (Dec. 1982) 268–9. Ditto *Etudes Anglaises*, T. xxxvii:1 (1984).

——, "Rituel Païen et Ritual Chrétien dans le drame poetique: Yeats et Eliot", *Gaéliana*, vi (1984) 179–201.

——, "Yeats et les Arts visuels" in *Actes du Colloque: littérature et Arts visuels en Irland*, Societe francaise d'études irlandaises (1983) pp. 27–40. "W. B. Yeats: Purgatory" in *Poetiques*, Domaine anglais SAES (Presses universitaires de Lyon) 1984 pp. 169–84. "W. B. Yeats: Naturel et surnaturel: la recherche de l'Unité par le mythe" in *Volume en hommage à Jean-Pierre Vernier* (Presses Universitaires de Rouen, Mar. 1984).

Gillham, D. G., Review of Vinod Sena, *W. B. Yeats the Poet as Critic*, in *U.C.T. Studies in English*, 13 (Nov. 1983) 72–74.

Goetsch, Paul and Heinz-Joachim, Müllenbrock (eds), *Englische Literatur und Politik im 20. Jahrhundert*. Wiesbaden: Athenaion (1981) vii, 196pp. (Athenaion Literaturwissenschaft, 17.); Lothar Hönnighausen, "Konservative Kulturkritik und Literaturtheorie zwischen den Weltkriegen: Yeats and Eliot", 95–110.

Good, Graham, "The Politics of Yeats and Joyce", *The Canadian Journal of Irish Studies*, ix:1 (June 1983) 81–8.

Gould, Warwick, " 'Sordid' view of Yeats", *The Observer* (5 Feb., 1984) 14. (see Conor Cruise O'Brien "Why Machiavelli and I are 'sordid' ", *The Observer* (29 Jan., 1984) 9).

Hadfield, Alice Mary, *Charles Williams: an Exploration of His Life and Works* (New York: Oxford University Press, 1984).

Hahn, Beverly, "Yeats's 'mysterious wisdom' ", 'Meditations in Time of Civil War' ", *Viewpoints 84* (Melbourne: Longman Sorrett 1983) 243–256.

Harper, George Mills, Review of *Tragic Knowledge etc.*, *W. B. Yeats and the Anti-Democratic Tradition*, *W. B. Yeats and the Emergence of the Irish Free State etc.*, *The Secret Rose, Stories by W. B. Yeats: A Variorum Edition, Modern Philology* (May 1984) pp. 435–40.

Hasegawa, Toshimitsu, "Fenollosa and Pound and Yeats: an Essay on the Translation of Noh", *Lotus* (The Fenollosa Society of Japan) 3 (Mar. 1983).

Hill, John, "Archetypen der irischen Seele", *Analytische Psychologie*, 12:2 (1981) 81–101.

Himber, Alan B., (assisted by George Mills Harper): *The Letters of John Quinn to William Butler Yeats* (Ann Arbor: UMI Research Press, 1983).

Hisgen, Ruud, and Adriaan van der Weel (eds), *Ierse stemmen: Bloemlezing van moderne schrijvers uit het West-Eiland* (The Hague: Nijgh & Van Ditmar, 1981) 208 pp.

Hogan, Robert and Burnham, Richard, *The Art of the Amateur, 1916–1920* (vol. v of *The Modern Irish Drama*) (Mountrath: Dolmen, 1983). Reviewed *TLS*, (29 June, 1984) 733 by Andrew Carpenter.

Hogan, Robert, "Yeats creates a Critic" in Hogan, R.: *"Since O'Casey" and other Essays on Irish Drama* (Gerrards Cross: Smythe, Totowa, NJ: Barnes & Noble, 1983).

Horowitz, Mikhail, Cartoon of W. B. Y., *Irish Literary Supplement*, iii:1, (Spring, 1984) 51.

Hough, Graham, *The Mystery Religion of W. B. Yeats* (Brighton: Harvester, 1984). Reviewed *London Review of Books*, 6:19 (8–31 Oct. 1984) 27.

Hoshino, Toru, "The Visionary Space of W. B. Yeats", in *Space in Literature*, Kasama Shoin (Tokyo), (Mar. 1983).

Hugo, Leon, Review of A. E. Dyson, *Yeats, Eliot and R. S. Thomas: Riding the Echo*, in *UNISA English Studies*, 21, 2 (Sept. 1983) 55–6.

Iri, Matsutoshi, "Yeats's Country House: Coole Park and Thoor Ballylee", *Mulberry* (Aichi Pref. Univ.) 32 (1983).

Jack, Ian, *The Poet and His Audience* (Cambridge University Press, 1984). Reviewed *London Review of Books*, 6:19 (8–31 Oct. 1984) 27.

Jaffe, Grace, M., *Years of Grace* (Sunspot, New Mexico: Iroquois House, 1979) (Autobiography of George Yeats's cousin).

Jakobson, Roman, *Selected Writings, III: Poetry of Grammar and Grammar of Poetry*, edited with a preface by Stephen Rudy (The Hague: Mouton, 1981).

Jakobson, Roman and Rudy, Stephen, "*Yeats's 'Sorrow of Love' through the Years*". Reprinted in *Poetics Today*, 2:1a (Autumn 1980) 97–125. The same issue contains on pp. 87–96 Jakobson's "On Poetic Intentions and Linguistic Devices in Poetry: A Discussion with Professors and Students at the University of Cologne", [originally published in German in *Arbeitspapier* (*Institut für Sprachwissenschaft*, Universität Köln), no. 32 (Dec. 1976) 1–18].

James, Robert, "The Writer's Trilogy I: There Are Joys. A Play in Two Acts", *Journal of Irish Literature*, 10:1 (Jan. 1981) 3–60.

Jeffares, A. Norman, *A New Commentary on the Poems of W. B. Yeats* (London: Macmillan, 1983). Reviewed *London Review of Books* 6:19 (8–31 Oct. 1984) 27. (See also under W. B. Yeats: *The Poems A New Edition*.)

Jeffares, A. Norman, *Yeats, Sligo and Ireland*. Reviewed in *Victorian Studies*, 26, Autumn 1982, 99.

Jefferson, George, *Edward Garnett: a Life in Literature* (London: Jonathan Cape 1982).

Joannon, Pierre, "Sources anglo-irlandaises de l'idéologie nationaliste irlandaise", *Études Irlandaises*, n.s. '6 (Dec. 1981) 137–56.

Johnson, Josephine, "The Music of Speech: Florence Farr and W. B. Yeats", *Literature in Performance: A Journal of Literary and Performing Art* (Chapel Hill), 2(1), (Nov. 1981) 56–65.

Kain, Richard, "No time for uncritical Appreciation" (review of Richard J. Finneran (ed.), *Yeats: an Annual of Critical and Textual Studies* and *Yeats Annual No. 2*.

Irish Literary Supplement, III-I, (Spring 1984) 51.

Keane, Patrick, J., "The Human Entrails and the Starry Heavens: Some Instances of Visual Art as Patterns of Yeats's Mingling of Heaven and Earth", *Bulletin of Research in the Humanities* (Stony Brook) 84:3 Autumn 1981, 366–91.

Kee, Robert, *The World We Left Behind: a Chronicle of the Year 1939* (London: Weidenfeld & Nicholson, 1983).

Kelleher, John V., "Matthew Arnold and the Celtic Revival". Reprinted for ACIS reprints from *Perspectives of Criticism* (Harvard, 1950).

Kenner, Hugh, "The Minims of Language", *TLS* (27 Apr. 1984) 451.

——, " 'The Most Beautiful Book' ", *ELH*, 48:3 (Autumn 1981) 594–605.

Kinahan, Frank, "Armchair Folklore: Yeats and the textual sources of *Fairy and Folk Tales of the Irish Peasants*", *Proceedings of the Royal Irish Academy*, 83, C,: 10, 255–67.

King, S. K., " 'Among School Children' ", in *Crux*. 5, 4 (1971) 20–4, "Six Poems", in *Crux*, 6, 2 (1972) 25–8.

Kline, Gloria C., *The Last Courtly Lover: Yeats and the Idea of Woman* (Ann Arbor, Michigan UMI Research Press) 1983.

Knapp, Bettina, "A Jungian Reading of William Butler Yeats's 'At the Hawk's Well' – an unintegrated anima shapes a hero's destiny", *Etudes Irlandaises*, no. 8 Nouvelle Série (Dec. 1983), 121–38.

Knowland, A. S., *W. B. Yeats, Dramatist of Vision* (preface by Cyril Cusack) (Gerrards Cross: Colin Smythe; Totowa, NJ: Barnes & Noble, 1983). Reviewed by Andrew Carpenter in "At the Abbey", *TLS* (29 June, 1984), 733.

Komesu, Okifumi, *The Double Prespective of Yeats's Aesthetic* (Gerrards Cross: Colin Smythe, 1985).

Kuch, Peter, *Yeats and AE* (Gerrards Cross: Colin Smythe, 1985).

Kunoki, Toshitake: "Arnold Bax and Yeats", *Bulletin* of the Yeats Society of Japan, 13 (Oct. 1982).

Kurdi, Maria, "A kettoseg elemenye Yeats kolteszeteben", *Filologiai Kozlony* (Budapest) 26 (2), (Apr.–June 1980) 194–204.

Larkin, Emmet, "F. S. L. Lyons: an

appreciation", *Irish Literary Supplement*, III:I (Spring 1984) 6–7.

Larkin, Philip, *Required Writing: Miscellaneous Pieces 1955–1982* (London, Boston: Faber & Faber, 1983) see esp. pp. 29, 67.

Lawrence, D. H., *The Letters of D. H. Lawrence* (Cambridge University Press) vol. I edited by James T. Boulton (1979). Several refs to WBY; vol. II edited by J. T. Boulton and George J. Zytaruk, (1981). Only one sig. ref. (Celtic Symbolism).

Laurenson, Ian, "Letters to Australia from Robert Harborough Sherard and Some Wildean Echoes", *Margin* (Monash Australiana Research Group Informal Notes), 5 (Apr. 1980) 1–17. Contains Lord Alfred Douglas's telegram to W. B. Yeats concerning the "absurdly named" *Oxford Book of Modern Verse* "– published here for the first time."

Leamon, Warren, "The Romantic as Playwright", *Western Humanities Review* (Salt Lake City) 36(2) (Summer 1982) 97–108.

Le Brocquy, Louis, *A la Recherche de W. B. Yeats*. Reviewed in *Apollo*, 116 (Sept. 1982) 201.

Lindberg-Seyersted, Brita, (ed.), *Pound/Ford: the Story of a Literary Friendship* (London: Faber, 1983).

Litz, A. Walton, "The Tone of the Nineties", *TLS* (23 Oct. 1981) 1240. Review of *The Secret Rose, Stories by W. B. Yeats: a Variorum Edition*.

——, "Pound and Yeats: the Road to Stone Cottage" in *Ezra Pound among the Poets* ed. G. Bornstein (University of Chicago Press, 1985).

Lowery, Robert G. (ed.), *A Whirlwind in Dublin: "The Plough and the Stars" Riots* (London: Greenwood, 1984).

Lowery, Robert G., *Sean O'Casey's Autobiography: an Annotated Index* (London: Greenwood Press, 1984).

Lynch, David, *Yeats: the Poetics of the Self*. Reviewed in *Journal of English and Germanic Philology*, 82 (July 1983) 457.

Lyons, F. S. L., "Beware the Dark Horse", *TLS* (13 Feb. 1981) 4063:160. Review of George Mills Harper's *W. B. Yeats and W. T. Horton etc.*

——, "The Poet as Politician", *TLS* (15 May 1981) 550. Review of *Yeats, Ireland and Fascism*.

Mac Aodha, Breandan S., "The Big House in Western Ireland The Background to Yeats's Writing", *Gaéliana*, 6 (1984) 217–23.

——, "Place-names in Yeats's Poetry and Plays" *Gaéliana*, 6 (1984) 225–31.

MacDonagh, Thomas, *Thomas Campion and the Art of English Poetry* (Dublin: Hodges Figgis; London: Simpkin Marshall, 1913). Discussion of AE and his chanting of Yeats, and Yeats's "quality of lyric chant" in his "speech-verse".

Mc Cormack, W. J., "Nightmares of History: James Joyce and the Phenomenon of Anglo-Irish Literature" in Stead, Alastair (ed.), *James Joyce and Modern Literature* (London: Routledge, 1982).

McDiarmid, Lucy, *Saving Civilization: Yeats, Eliot and Auden Between the Wars* (Cambridge: University Press, 1984).

McGrath, F. C., "Paterian Aesthetics in Yeats's Drama" in Clifford Davidson, C. J. Gianakaris and John H. Stroupe (eds), *Drama in the Twentieth Century: Comparative and Critical Essays* (NY: AMS Press 1984) (Studies in Modern Literature, No. 11).

MacKenzie, Norman, "The Monk Gibbon Papers", *Canadian Journal of Irish Studies* vols 1 & 2 (Dec. 1983) 5–24. Contains account of Yeats material in the new archive at Queens University, Kingston Ontario.

Mackinnon, Lachlan, "Images of Intensity". Review of M. L. Rosenthal and Sally M. Gall, *The Modern Poetic Sequence: the Genius of Modern Poetry* and M. L. Rosenthal: *Poetry and the Common Life*, *TLS* (30 Dec. 1983) 1455.

Madden-Simpson, Janet, "Tools of the Trade", *Books Ireland*, no. 59 (Dec. 1980) 237–8. Review of E. Callan: *Yeats on Yeats etc.*

Magill, Frank No. ed., *English Literature: Romanticism to 1945*. Pasadena, Calif.: Salem Softbacks (1981). Previously published as *Masterpieces of World Literature in Digest Form* (3rd series, 1960; 4th series, 1969). "William Butler Yeats", 818–32.

Magrini, Giacomo, "La bellezza e la pedagogia in Yeats", *Strumenti critici*, no. 45 (July 1981) 283–307.

Maki, Jacqueline R., "The Dance: Roethke's Legacy from Yeats", *Kentucky*

Philological Association Bulletin (Murray), (1981) 1–23.

Marcus, Phillip L. (ed.), *The Death of Cuchulain etc.* Reviewed in *Choice* 19 (July 1982) 1563.

Martin, Augustine, "Kinesis Stasis, Revolution in Yeatsian Drama", *Gaéliana*, 6 (1984) 155–62.

——, Review of *The Secret Rose. Stories by W. B. Yeats: a Variorum Edition* and *The Celtic Twilight* (1981) in *Irish University Review* (Spring 1982) 113–16.

——, *W. B. Yeats.* Reviewed in *New Statesman*, 107 (6 Jan. 1984) 22.

Martin, Heather, "Yeats as Realist", *Canadian Journal of Irish Studies*, ix:2 (Dec. 1983) 77–86.

Matsumura, Kenichi, "Yeats's Poetry and the Awakening of the Place", *The Rising Generation* (Nov. 1983).

Matsuyama, Akio, *Yeats to Poe no Yugen: Hikaku Bungaku Ronshu* (Tokyo: Hokuseido, 1982).

Maxwell, D. E. S., "A Rhetoric for Politics in the North" in Connolly, Peter (ed.), *Literature and the Changing Ireland* (Gerrards Cross: Colin Smythe, Totowa, NJ: Barnes & Noble, 1982).

Miyake, Tadaaki, "The Purpose and Significance of Yeats's Dramatisation of Deirdre", *Shujitsu Eigaku Ronshu* (Shujitsu Women's College) 1, 1982.

Miyauchi, Hiroshi, "Yeats Bannen no Shiika o megutte", *Eigo Seinen* (Tokyo) 128 (1982) 436–9.

Moriguchi, Saburo, "The Image of Cuchulain in the Works of W. B. Yeats", *Bulletin of the Yeats Society of Japan* 14 (Oct. 1983).

Moriguchi, Saburo, "Yeats's Experience of Morris", *Kenkyu Ronshu* (Saga Univ.) vol. 30, no. 2 (Feb. 1983).

Moynahan, Julian, "The Best Book on Yeats's *Autobiographies*". Review of Shirley Newman: *Some one Myth: Irish Literary Supplement*, III:I (Spring 1984) 51.

Mulryne, Ronnie, "No Fabulous Symbol: Yeats and the Language of Poetry", *Gaéliana* (Caen) v (1983) 67–78.

——, "Yeats and Dowden: Critical Clinamen", *Gaéliana* (Caen) 6 (1984) 137–53.

Murphy, Maureen, Review of Patrick Rafroidi, *Irish Literature in English* and Wayne Hall, *Shadowy Heroes, Irish Literary Supplement*, 1:2 (1982) 12, 19.

Naito, Shiro, *Yeats and Zen: a Study of the Transformation of His Mask* (Tokyo: Yamaguchi, 1983). Contains two new Yeats letters – to Diasetz Suzuki (22 May 1928) and to Kazumi Yano (18 Nov. 1927). Yeats's marginalia, *passim*.

——, "The Conversion of Yeats the Poet", *Seiyo Bungaku Kenkyu* (Otani University), 3 (Dec. 1983).

Nakano, Yoko, "Men Improve with the Years: Old Age in W. B. Yeats's Poems 1891–1918", *Ronshu* (Tsudajuku Women's College) 4 (1983).

——, "Yeats and the Rose", in *Bulletin of the Yeats Society of Japan*, 13 (Oct. 1982).

Nichols, J. G., *The Poetry of Ben Jonson* (London; Routledge, 1969) (61–2, App. B, on Yeats and Jonson).

Noguchi, Shunichi, "On a Certain Poem in Yeats's *Last Poems*", *Eigo Eibungaku Kenkyu* (Hiroshima University) (Apr. 1983).

North, Michael, "The Paradox of the Mausoleum: Public Monuments and the Early Aesthetics of W. B. Yeats", *The Centennial Review* (East Lansing) 26:3 (Spring 1982) 221–38.

——, "The Ambiguity of Repose: Sculpture and the Public Art of W. B. Yeats", *ELH*, 50, 2 (Summer 1983) 379–400.

O'Brien, James H., Review of Mary Helen Thuente, *W. B. Yeats and Irish Folklore*, in *Canadian Journal of Irish Studies*, 9, 2 (Dec. 1983) 100–2.

O'Casey, Sean, *Autobiographies*, 2 vols (London: Macmillan, 1981).

O'Connor, Ulick, *Celtic Dawn: a Portrait of the Irish Literary Renaissance* (London: Hamish Hamilton, 1984).

O'Donnell, William H., *A Guide to the Prose Fiction of W. B. Yeats.* Reviewed in *Choice*, 21 (Dec. 1983) 573.

——, *The Poetry of W. B. Yeats* (NY: Ungar, 1985).

O'h Aodha, Micheál, *Pictures at the Abbey The Collection of the Irish National Theatre* (Portlaoise: Dolmen Press in association with the Irish National Theatre Society 1983).

Okazaki, Toshiichiro, "On Studies of Yeats in Japan", in *Bulletin of the Yeats Society of Japan*, 14 (Oct. 1983).

Oliver, H. J. (ed.), *Timon of Athens* (Arden Shakespeare pb), (London: Methuen, 1950–69), (p. 140 – on Yeats's epitaph and that of Timon).

Olney, James, "Modernism, Yeats, and Eliot". Reviews *inter alia* Otto Bohlmann: *Yeats and Nietzsche*, Cairns Craig: *Yeats, Eliot, Pound and the Politics of Poetry etc.*; Terence Diggory: *Yeats and American Poetry etc*; A. E. Dyson: *Yeats, Eliot and R. S. Thomas etc.*; M. L. Rosenthal and Sally M. Gall: *The Modern Poetic Sequence etc.*; *The Death of Cuchulain etc.*, *The Secret Rose*, *Stories by W. B. Yeats: A Variorum Edition*, *The Sewannee Review* (Summer 1984) 451–66.

Olsen, Lance, "The Ironic Dialectic in Yeats", in *Colby Library Quarterly*, 19, 4 (Dec. 1983) 215–20.

Omond, T. S., *English Metrists: Being a Sketch of English Prosodical Criticism from Elizabethan Times to the Present Day* (Oxford: Clarendon, 1921) W.B.Y.'s methods and recitation discussed, 258, 319).

O'Neill, William, "Yeats on Poetry and Politics", *The Midwest Quarterly: a Journal of Contemporary Thought*, xxv:1 (Autumn, 1983) 64–73.

Orr, John, *Tragic Drama and Modern Society: Studies in the Social and Literary Theory of Drama from 1870 to the Present*, Edinburgh Studies in Sociology (London: Macmillan, 1982).

Osaka, Osamu, "A Reconsideration of 'John Sherman' (2)", *Eigo Eibungaku Ronso* (Kyushu University) 33 (Jan. 1983).

Oura, Yukio, "Women around Yeats (4)", *INSIGHT* (Notre-Dame Women's College), 15 (Mar. 1983).

Palmstierna, Erik, "W. B. Yeats. Ett silhuettlipp", *Dagens Nyheter*, 6 (Feb. 1939).

——, "W. B. Yeats" in *Åtskilliga Egenheter* [*A Number of Eccentricities*] (Stockholm: Tidens Förlag, 1950), 242–4.

Parker, Patricia, A., *Inescapable Romance Studies in the Poetics of a Mode etc* (Princeton University Press, 1979).

Parker, Stewart, "State of Play", *Canadian Journal of Irish Studies*, 7:1 (June 1981) 5–11.

Peterson, Richard F., *William Butler Yeats*. Reviewed in *Book list* 78 (Apr. 1982), 998, *Choice* 19 (June 1982) 1404.

Pfister, Manfred, "Sailing to Innisfree: Stilwandel und ideologische Entwicklung in der Lyrik von W. B. Yeats", in W. Welte (ed.), *Sprachtheorie und angewandte Linguistik Festschrift für Alfred Wollmann zum 60. Geburtstag* (Tübingen, 1982) 113–30.

Piwinski, David, "Yeats's '*Her Courtesy*' ", *Explicator*, 42, 1 (Autumn 1983) 32–4.

Pound, Omar and Litz, A. Walton (eds), *Ezra Pound and Dorothy Shakespear: Their Letters, 1909–1914* (NY: New Directions, 1984).

Prokosch, Frederic, *Voices: a Memoir* (London: Faber & Faber, 1983). Reviewed, *TLS* (23 Dec. 1983) 1420, by Pearl K. Bell.

Rafroidi, Patrick, Review of Richard J. Finneran (ed.), *Yeats Annual* No. 1, *Etudes Irlandaises*, no. 7, Nouvelle Série, (Dec. 1982) 314–15.

——, Review of Richard J. Finneran (ed.), *Yeats Annual* No. 2, *Etudes Irlandaises*, no. 8, Nouvelle Série, (Dec. 1983) 397–8.

Rai, Rama N., *W. B. Yeats: Poetic Theory and Practice* (Salzburg – Poetic Drama Series 1983).

Raine, Kathleen, *Yeats the Initiate: Essays on certain themes in the work of William Butler Yeats*, (Mountrath: Dolmen, USA George Braziller). Includes: "Hades wrapped in Cloud", first published in *Yeats and the Occult*, edited by George Mills Harper (Toronto, 1976); "Fairy and Folk Tales of Ireland", an introduction to Yeats's selection (London: Colin Smythe 1973); "Ben Bulben Sets the Scene", a paper given at the Yeats Summer School, Sligo, 1979. "AE" Beard Memorial Lecture, College of Psychic Studies (London, 1975) published in *Light* (1975); "Yeats's Debt to Blake", a paper given at the Yeats Summer School, Sligo, published in *The Dublin Magazine*, vol. v, no. 2 (Summer 1966); "From Blake to 'A Vision' ", *New Yeats Papers*, xvii (1979); "Yeats, the Tarot and the Golden Dawn", *New Yeats Papers*, iii (1972 2nd edn, rev., 1976); "Death-in-Life and Life-in-Death", *New Yeats Papers*, viii (1974); "Blake, Yeats and Pythagoras", a paper read at the Lindisfarn conference on Pythagoras (Colorado, 1979) published in the *Lindisfarn letter*; "Yeats and Kabir", Inaugural lecture at the Yeats Society of India (Jan. 1983), first published in *Temenos*, 5, (1984); "Purgatory", introduction to

Pierre Leyris's French translation (Paris: Editions Granit); "Yeats's Singing School: a Personal Acknowledgement", given to the Poetry Society (1980), (unpublished).

Reiman, Donald H., "Wordsworth, Shelley and the Romantic Inheritance", *Romanticism Past and Present* (Boston) 5(2), (1981) 1–22.

Rollins, Ronald G., "Enigmatic Ghosts of Swift in Yeats and Johnston", *Eire-Ireland*, XVIII, 2 (Summer 1983) 103–15.

Royal Irish Academy: Committee for the Study of Anglo-Irish Literature, *Handlist of Work in Progress*, no. 10 (Dec. 1980) Dublin: Royal Irish Academy, 1981, 28 pp.; no. 11, Mar. 1983.

Saddlemyer, Ann, *The Collected Letters of John Millington Synge*, vol. 2 (Oxford: Clarendon, 1984).

Salinger, Helmut, *William Butler Yeats, Seine Gedichte und Gedanken*, Francke (Bern-/München, 1983).

Sato, Yoko, "The Structure of *The Player Queen*", *Bulletin of the Yeats Society of Japan*, 14 (Oct. 1983).

Semmler, Clement, "The Ireland of W. B. Yeats". Review of Kenner, Hugh: *A Colder Eye* in *Courier Mail* (Brisbane), (7 July, 1984) p 30.

Schneider, Joseph L., "Yeats and the Common Man", *Studies*, LXXIII:289 (Spring 1984) 37–46.

Schricker, Gale S., *A New Species of Man: the Poetic Persona of W. B. Yeats* (Lewisburg: Bucknell; London: Associated University Presses, 1983).

——, Letter to the editor (with reply by Terence Diggory), *Irish Literary Supplement*, III:I (Spring 1984) 4.

Schuchard, Ronald W., "Synge as Triumvir". Review of Ann Saddlemyer: *Theatre Business: the Correspondence of the First Abbey Theatre Directors: William Butler Yeats Lady Gregory and J. M. Synge*, *Irish Literary Supplement*, III:I (Spring 1984) 39.

Shah, R., *Yeats and Eliot: Perspectives on India* (Atlantic Highlands: Humanities, 1983).

Sharrock, Roger, "Yeats and Death", *Journal of English Language and Literature*, vol. 29, no. 1 (English Language and Literature Association of Korea, Spring 1983) 189–208.

Sinistrari, Ludovica, Maria, (Friar Minor), *Demoniality*. Translated into English from the Latin (with Introduction and Notes) by the Rev. Montague Summers (London: Fortune Press n.d. (1927)) pp. xxix–xxxii – Yeats, *The Celtic Twilight*, Havelock Ellis, and the tradition of Sinistrari.

Smythe, Colin, A Guide to Coole Park, Home of Lady Gregory, (80 illus.; an unpublished quatrain by W. B. Y.) (Gerrards Cross: Colin Smythe, 1983).

Sotheby's (London), *English Literature and English History – Printed Books and Manuscripts* (Sale 16–17 July 1984) Various rare books, letters, etc. of W. B. Y.

Stallworthy, Jon, "The Poet as Archaeologist: W. B. Yeats and Seamus Heaney". *Review of English Studies*, 33–130 (May 1982) 158–74.

Stanford, Donald E. (ed.), *Selected Letters of Robert Bridges*, vol. 1 (London: Associated University Presses, 1984).

Stanley-Vaughan, Margaret, Review of *Le crépuscule celtique in Etudes Irlandaises*, no. 8, Nouvelle Serie (Dec. 1983), 393–4.

Steinman, Michael, *Yeats's Heroic Figures: Wilde, Parnell, Swift, Casement* (London: Macmillan; Albany: State University of NY Press 1983. Reviewed *THES* (24 Feb. 1984) by George J. Watson.

Stevenson, John W., "Poetry as Illusion: the Seeing Imagination", *Humanities in the South*, Spartanburg SC, 48: 5–7 (Autumn 1978).

Stewart, Douglas, "The Last of Yeats", *The Bulletin (Sydney)* (10 July, 1940) Red Page.

Storry, Richard, "The Image of Japan in British Literature" in Chapman, John W. M., Lehmann, Jean-Pierre: *Proceedings of the British Association for Japanese Studies*, 5:1 (1980).

Sugiyama, Sumiko, "On 'The Black Tower' ", *Bulletin of the Yeats Society of Japan*, 14 (Oct. 1983).

Suzuki, Hiroshi, "W. B. Yeats's *Vision* and the Mythological System", in *Genso Bungaku* 2.

——, "W. B. Yeats and Ballads", *Kyoyo Shogaku Kenkyu* (Waseda Univ.) 71.72.73 (Mar. 1983).

——, "W. B. Yeats: Meditation on Death", in *Kyoyo Shogaku Kenkyu* (Waseda University), 67–9 (Mar. 1982).

Symposium on "Byzantium", *Bulletin of the Yeats Society of Japan*, 14 (Oct. 1983). Yasuda, Shoichiro, " 'Byzantium': a

Dogmatic Reading"; Tsuji, Shozo, " 'Byzantium' as a Vision of a New Species"; Kobori, Ryuji, "A Structure of Both Extremities Leading to 'Being': a Note on Byzantium"; Miyauchi, Hiromu, " 'Byzantium' ".

Takahashi, Yasunari, "Yeats and Noh", *Sekai* (June 1983).

Tanaka, Kiyoshi, "W. B. Yeats, *The Tower* (1928): in Pursuit of the Wandering of the Soul", in *Kenku Kiyo* (Koka Women's Junior College) 19.

Tanigawa, Fuyuji, "Life for a Living Man: a Note on 'A Dialogue of Self and Soul' ", in *Bulletin of the Yeats Society of Japan*, 13 (Oct. 1982).

Taylor, Richard, *"A Reader's Guide to the Plays of W. B. Yeats"* (London, Macmillan, NY: St. Martins, 1983). Reviewed by Andrew Carpenter, *TLS* (29 June, 1984) 733 in "At the Abbey".

Thuente, M. H., *W. B. Yeats and Irish Folklore*. Reviewed in: *Clio: a Journal of Literature, History and the Philosophy of History*, 12 (Winter 1983), 202; *Victorian Studies*, 26 (Autumn 1982) 99.

Thwaite, Ann, *Edmund Gosse: a Literary Landscape* (London: Secker & Warburg, 1984).

Thwaite, Anthony, " 'W. B. Yeats" (Letter to Editor) *TLS* (7 Sept. 1984). 995.

Toliver, Harold E., *The Past That Poets Make* (Cambridge, Mass.: Harvard University Press, 1981).

Vlasopolos, Anca, *The Symbolic Method of Coleridge, Baudelaire and Yeats* (Detroit: Wayne State University Press, 1983). Reviewed in *Choice*, 21 (Nov. 1983) 416.

Williams, Edith Whitehurst, "Auden, Yeats, and the Word 'Silly': a Study in Semantic Change", *South Atlantic Review*, 46:4 (Nov. 1981) 17–33.

Watanabe, Hisayoshi, *Yeats* (Tokyo, 1983).

Wicht, Wolfgang: "Die entromantisierte Metapher. Yeats 'Umwertung einer Tradition'," in *Zeitschrift für Anglistik und Amerikanistik*, 31, 3, 211–27.

Wilson, B. M., "Yeats and Eastern Thought", *Comparative Literature*, XXXIV:1, (Winter 1982).

Worth, Katharine, "A Place in the Country". Review of Christopher Murray (ed.), *Selected Plays of Lennox Robinson*)

TLS (2 Sept. 1983) 929. (On "Purgatory" and "The Big House".)

——, "Yeats and Beckett", *Gaéliana*, 6 (1984) 203–13.

Yamaguchi, Kimiho, "The Burning of the Two Lives: an Essay on *At the Hawk's Well*", *Bulletin of Osaka Institute of Technology*, vol. 22, no. 2 (1983).

Yeats, J. B., *Letters to His Son W. B. Yeats and Others 1869–1922* (reprint). Reviewed in: *London Review of Books*, 5 (18 Aug. 1983) 3, *New Statesman* 105 (17 June 1983) 24; *Spectator* 250 (18 June, 1983) 24.

Yeats, W. B., *Byzantium*: paintings by David Finn (Redding Ridge: Black Swan Books) 1983.

——, *The Celtic Twilight*. Reviewed in *British Book News* (July 1982) 422.

——, *Collected Plays*. Reviewed in *New Statesman*, 104, (30 July 1982) 24.

——, *Collected Poems*. Reviewed in *Observer* (21 Nov. 1982) 35.

——, *Fairy and Folk Tales of Ireland* with a foreward by Benedict Kiely (New York: Macmillan, 1983). [The Colin Smythe text of 1973, with a new foreword.]

——, *Les Histoires de la Rose Secrète*. Traduction du Centre de Littérature, Linguistique et Civilisation des Pays de Langue Anglaise de l'Université de Caen, sous la direction de Jacqueline Genet, (Lille: Presses Universitaires de Lille, 1984). [Utilizes copy-text of *VSR*]

——, *The Poems: a New Edition*, ed. Richard J. Finneran (New York: Macmillan, 1983; London: Macmillan, 1984). Reviews as follows: *Library Journal*, 109 (Jan. 1984) 97. *Choice*, 21 (Mar. 1984). Seamus Heaney: "A New and Surprising Yeats', *New York Times Book Review*, 1, 35–6. This review (which also notices Richard J. Finneran's *Editing Yeats's Poems*) includes "A Yeats Sampler", reprinting "Spinning Song", "The Child who chases lizards in the grass", "Should H. G. Wells afflict you" and "I call to the eye of the mind".

Tom Paulin: "Shadow of the Gunmen" *Observer* (19 June 1984) 22. [Also reviews Richard J. Finneran's *Editing Yeats's Poems*, and includes caricature portrait.]

Christopher Ricks: "A Trick of the Voice", *Sunday Times*, (20 May 1984), [includes photo of W.B.Y.]

John Montague: "What to Make of W. B. Yeats", *The Guardian*, (14 June 1984) 21. [Also reviews Richard J. Finneran's *Editing Yeats's Poems* and A. Norman Jeffares' *A New Commentary on The Poems of W. B. Yeats* includes photo of W.B.Y. in 1906].

Denis Donoghue: "Textual Choices", *THES* (8 June 1984) 20. [Also reviews Jeffares' *A New Commentary* etc.]

Augustine Martin "Revision" *Irish Times* (16 June 1984) with photo of W.B.Y. [Also reviews Finneran: *Editing Yeats's Poems*.]

Warwick Gould: "The editor takes possession" *TLS* (29 June 1984) 731–3, [with a caricature portrait of W.B.Y.] Also reviews Finneran's *Editing Yeats's Poems* and A. Norman Jeffares' *A New Commentary etc*. For correspondence arising out of this review article see "Editing Yeats" in *TLS* 30 July 1984) 81. (Denis Donoghue and Mary FitzGerald); *TLS* (3 Aug. 1984) 868–9, (Richard J. Finneran); *TLS* (10 Aug. 1984) 893, (A Norman Jeffares and Warwick Gould); *TLS* (31 Aug. 1984) 969, (Richard J. Finneran); *TLS* (7 Sept 1984) 995, (Anthony Thwaite); *TLS* (21 Sept. 1984) 1055, (Warwick Gould).

For a restatement of his case, see Richard J. Finneran, "The Order of Yeats's Poems", *Irish University Review*, 14:2 (Autumn 1984).

——, *The Poems of W. B. Yeats: a New Selection*. Selected with an Introduction and Notes by A. Norman Jeffares (London: Macmillan 1984). Reviewed in *London Review of Books*, 6:9 (8–31 Oct. 1984) 27.

——, *The Secret Rose. Stories by W. B. Yeats: a Variorum Edition*. Reviewed in *JEGP*, 82 (July 1983) 459; *Victorian Studies*, 26 (Autumn 1982) 99; *Journal of the 1890's Society*: twentieth anniversary special number 14, 1983–4, 28. [By Derek Stanford].

——, *La taille d'une Agate et autres essais*, Présentation par Pierre Chabert, traduction etc. sous la direction de Jacqueline Genet (Paris: Klincksieck, 1984).

Yoshino, Masaaki, "An evidence of the Poet: an Essay on 'Easter 1916' ", Eigo *Eibungaku Ronso* (Kyushu University) 32 (1982).

——, "Yeats and Maud Gonne: or the Revision of *The Wild Swans at Coole*", *Eigo Eibungaku Ronso* (Kyushu University), 33 (Jan. 1983).

Forthcoming Titles

Bridges, Robert, *The Selected Letters of Robert Bridges*, ed. Donald E. Stanford, Vol. 2 (Newark: University of Delaware Press; London: Associated University Presses, 1984).

Bushrui, Suheil, and Prentki, Tim, *An International Companion to the Poetry of W. B. Yeats* (Gerrards Cross: Colin Smythe, 1985).

Clark, David Ridgely, *Visible Array* (Mountrath: Dolmen, 1984).

Kinahan, Frank, *Early Yeats in Context* (London: Allen & Unwin, Spring 1985).

Kohfeldt, Mary Lou, *Lady Gregory: the Woman Behind the Irish Renaissance* (New York: Atheneum, 1985).

Moore, George, *Collected Letters*, vol. I, ed Robert Becker, (Gerrards Cross, Colin Smythe, 1985).

——, *George Moore on Parnassus: Letters (1900–1933) to Secretaries, Publishers, Prin-*

ters, Agents, Literati, Friends, and Acquaintances, ed. with notes and a critical biographical commentary by Helmut Gerber. 3 vols (Newark: University of Delaware Press; London: Associated University Presses, 1985).

O'Shea, Edward, *A Descriptive Catalog of W. B. Yeats's Library* (New York & London: Garland, 1985).

Pyle, Hilary, *A Catalogue Raisonnée of the Paintings of Jack B. Yeats* 2 vols (Gerrards Cross: Colin Smythe, forthcoming).

Russell, George W. (Æ), *The Descent of the Gods – the Mystical Writings* (Gerrards Cross: Colin Smythe, 1985).

Saddlemyer, Ann and Smythe, Colin (ed.), *Lady Gregory Fifty Years After* (Gerrards Cross: Colin Smythe, 1985).

Yeats, W. B., *The Collected Edition*, gen. eds, Richard J. Finneran and George Mills Harper. Forthcoming titles include *Auto-*

biographies, eds, Douglas Archibald and J. Fraser Cocks III; *The Celtic Twilight & The Secret Rose*, eds, Warwick Gould, Phillip L. Marcus and Michael J. Sidnell; *Early Essays*, ed., Warwick Gould; *Later Essays* ed. George Bornstein & Hugh Witemeyer: *The Irish Dramatic Movement*, ed., Mary FitzGerald; *The Plays*, ed., David R. Clark; *Prefaces and Introductions*, ed., William H. O'Donnell; *A Vision* (1937), eds, M. C. K. Hood and Walter K. Hood.

——, *The Collected Letters*, vol. 1, eds, Eric Domville and John S. Kelly (Oxford University Press, 1985).